ROBERT H. DOKTOR
The International Institute of Management—Berlin
School of Management, SUNY-Binghamton

MICHAEL A. MOSES
Wharton School
University of Pennsylvania

MANAGERIAL INSIGHTS

Analysis, Decisions, and Implementation

PRENTICE-HALL, INC., Englewood Cliffs, New Jersey

Library of Congress Cataloging in Publication Data

Doktor, Robert H   comp.
    Managerial insights.

    Includes bibliographical references.
    1. Industrial management—Addresses, essays,
lectures. I. Moses, Michael A., joint comp.
II. Title.
HD31.D564   658   72-5228
ISBN   0-13-550103-2

© 1973 by Prentice-Hall, Inc., Englewood Cliffs, N. J.

Printed in the United States of America

10   9   8   7   6   5   4   3   2   1

Prentice-Hall International, Inc., *London*
Prentice-Hall of Australia, Pty. Ltd., *Sydney*
Prentice-Hall of Canada, Ltd., *Toronto*
Prentice-Hall of India Private Limited, *New Delhi*
Prentice-Hall of Japan, Inc., *Tokyo*

To
Judy and Kristie
and
Liza and Andrew

Contents

IV

MANAGERIAL SOLUTION IMPLEMENTATION   *279*

V

MANAGERIAL ALTERNATIVE FUTURES   *369*

Preface

Management is quite a bit more difficult than is commonly believed. In order to help simplify the understanding of this field, we have selected these readings, which we have used time and again in our own elementary courses in management, by a process of trial and error, in conjunction with our own initial intuitive judgments. These articles are the set of materials we feel will be most essential to a manager in the last quarter of the twentieth century. This book, then, is meant not to be read once and then cast aside, but to remain as a permanent part of the library of a practicing manager—to be referred to in the years ahead as problems are defined, analyzed, and solved, resulting in the implementation of action decisions.

We believe that two words—*adaptive integrator*—summarize the manager of the future. For this reason we stress some of the basic foundations that the future manager will have to bring to bear on any problem. In the overview chapter we give him a method for attacking the problem that he wishes to solve. His success in part will depend on how well he integrates the problem-solving method with the tools available to him from various other fields and in part on his capacity for adaptive response.

We would like to take this opportunity to thank those who have been helpful in the completion of this text: John Gross and John deVoogd, instructors in the course for which this book was designed; Vaughan James, our tireless secretary who made sure that we sent the right materials to the right people; and our wives, whose enthusiasm and ideas appear throughout the book.

Robert H. Doktor
Michael A. Moses

1

A CONCEPTUAL FRAMEWORK

Concepts of Management

The Definition of Management

Management may be defined as *the application of the interdisciplinary systems science that studies problem-analysis, decision-making, and solution implementation within an organization.* Let's take a closer look at the meanings of the key words in this definition.

Management is an *applied* field. People in management are action-oriented. The research of management scholars is primarily what Kurt Lewin termed action research; that is, the research has two goals: to develop and refine theory and, concomitantly, to solve a specific problem, make a decision, and implement a solution. This does not mean that scholars who research only to develop and refine theory do not make contributions to management. They do. They develop theory and fact within their own disciplines, and their disciplines are part of the science that management applies. Often the contributions of these scholars have profound individual effects upon management. Men in management are thankful for these contributions. This gratitude is shown by endeavoring to apply as effectively as possible the theories and tools of the sciences that are the foundation of management.

Given an understanding of the word application in the definition of management, let us move on to the phrase *interdisciplinary systems science.* Management is not the application of any one discipline. It is the application of the integration and interaction of theories and tools from many disciplines. It is not sufficient to view the theories and tools of one science, such as economics, as relevant to one aspect of a management problem, and the theories and tools of another science, such as psychology, as relevant to a second aspect of the problem. Rather, the manager must understand how the theories of one scientific discipline integrate with and are supplementary to the theories and tools of other disciplines as he applies his knowledge to a management problem. Thus, *interdisciplinary* is chosen for the definition rather than the word multidisciplinary or some other term that might fail to capture the integrative nature inherent in the concept of management. The term *systems science* is at the crux of the definition of management in that it highlights the *interactive nature* so very necessary among the disciplines applied to a management problem. It is this dynamic interaction that occurs as diverse disciplines are interfused which is at the heart of management; for the whole that emerges is greater than the sum of the parts. This interaction results in a new interdisciplinary systems science that is more than the application of psychology plus the application of economics plus the application of mathematics, and so on. And this whole, not the sum of the parts, is the science behind management.

Now that we have dissected the first part of the definition of management, let us examine the middle part of the definition. Specifically, let us investigate the terms problem-analysis, decision-making, and solution implementation. *Problem-analysis* is the definition of the situation, the processing of the information, and the generation of alternative solutions to a problem. *Decision-making* is the development and specification of an objective function or other decision criteria followed by an analysis and evaluation of the consequences of alternative solutions generated during problem-analysis. This evaluation is made with reference to the decision criteria such that a specific solution may be selected as "optimal." *Solution implementation* consists of applying the chosen solution to the problem situation and observing the outcome with the possibility of modifying the situation contingent upon the analysis of the new information thus obtained.

The last term in the definition to be examined is *organization.* An organization is a group of people bound together by a formal and/or informal structure in pursuit of a common goal or goals through the implementation of technology. Thus, our definition of management concerns the case where we have more than one person in an interactive situation so that a common goal is sought by the use of certain techniques or technologies.

This, then, is what we mean by *management:* the application of the interdisciplinary systems science that studies problem analysis, decision-making, and solution implementation within an organization.

Everyone Is a Manager

In some ways, everyone analyzes problems, makes decisions and implements solutions as he goes about his life's activities. In a very real sense, we all are managers. Some of us are better life-managers than others. Indeed, much of what we have to say in this book can be applied to our everyday-life situations. It is because we are all managers to some small degree that people felt there was no formal science of management. Only recently has management overcome the burden of ubiquitousness to emerge as an intellectual domain of study relevant to man. Strangely enough, this emergence brought with it a formal ubiquitousness which far surpasses the informal ubiquitousness, which had previously existed. Thus, phrases like *managerial ecology, urban management, learning contingency management, value management,* and *alternative management* abound about us.

Few People Are Professional Managers

In other ways, very few people really manage well enough to be worthy of the title *professional manager.* At the heart of the performance of management is the concept of *linking together* systems of diverse disciplines and bringing this linkage to bear upon a specific problem. It is not enough to be multidisciplinary; one must be interdisciplinary. It is not enough to be scientific; one must be systemic. It is not enough to be theoretical, one must be applied.

This crucial role of the manager has been termed by Rensis Likert the *linking pin role* which points directly to the necessary quality of a professional manager. It is the ability to synthesize from among several disciplines and to bring this synthesis to bear upon the specific problem. This is what separates the professional manager from the everybody-manager.

Paul Lawrence and Jay Lorsch have used the term *organizational integration* to help describe the process of the linking pin role. But in order to understand the concept of organizational integration, one must first understand the concept of *organizational differentiation.*

The concept of differentiation in organizational studies has received renewed interest with the publication of the landmark research effort by Lawrence and Lorsch entitled *Organization and Environment.* In this work, as meaningful to practicing managers as to organizational scholars, differentiation is defined as "the difference in cognitive and emotional orientation among managers in different functional departments." (p. 11). Following a lead established by March and Simon in their book *Organizations,* Lawrence and Lorsch state that differentiation among managers develops in part as a function of both education and experience. Specifically, on page 9 of *Organization and*

Environment the following statement appears: "Both because of their prior education and experience and because of the nature of their task, they would develop specialized working styles and mental processes. . . ."

In order to measure differentiation among managers, Lawrence and Lorsch consider three parameters: (1) goal orientation, (2) time orientation, and (3) interpersonal orientation. For example, goal orientation differences may be manifest by the extent to which managers in sales units may be concerned with different objectives than their counterparts in production. An illustration of time orientation differences could be the contrast between the concern of production executives with more immediate problems than those that may be of primary concern to design engineers. Last, differences in interpersonal orientation are suggested by the preoccupation of some managers with getting the job done while other managers may pay more attention to maintaining relationships with their peers.

On one side of the coin is the concept of organizational differentiation; on the other side is the concept of *organizational integration*. Lawrence and Lorsch define integration as "the quality of the state of collaboration that exists among departments that are required to achieve unity of effort by the demands of the environment" (p. 11). Integration, of course, is the key to successful performance in organizational management. However, the manager who wishes to achieve successful integration is behooved to understand the quantity and quality of differentiation existent within his organization. Here, then, is the crux of the issue and the focal point at which the heuristic power of knowledge of the concept of organizational differentiation becomes evident. Long-run successful performance is keyed on successful integration within the organization. Achievement of this high quality of integration may be significantly facilitated by knowledge and sensitivity toward the nature of differentiation existent within an organization. The *professional manager* is the manager who strives to achieve organizational integration through the linking pin role.

The Foundations of Management

In general, management has three foundations: the classical school, the behavioral sciences, and the quantitative sciences.

The classical school was the child prodigy of management. Today it is still considered to be extremely influential in the practice of management. The classical school consists in both the works of such men as Frederick W. Taylor in his development of *scientific management* and the works of men like Gulick and Curwick in their development of what March and Simon[1] have termed *administrative management theory*.

---

[1] The authors are indebted for the logical format of this section to Chapter 2 of *Organizations* by James G. March and Herbert A. Simon.

Scientific management endeavored to study how best to couple men to machines in the performance of the organization's tasks. A primary methodology of scientific management is called *time and motion study*. Specifically, scientific management studies the physiological characteristics of the worker in relation to his job. Then a set of methods are prescribed that allow the worker to effectively perform his task in the minimum amount of time. In addition to Taylor, other notable contributors to scientific management have been the Gilbreths (Frank and Lillian), Henry Laurence Gantt, and Charles Babbage. Scientific management made its greatest contributions just after the turn of the twentieth century.

Administrative management theory is associated with men like Luther Gulick, Harrington Emerson, Henri Fayol, Henry Metcalfe, L. Urwick, J. D. Mooney, and A. C. Reiley. The major contributions of these writers were well known by the 1930's. The administrative management theorists were interested in getting things done. Their contemporary counterparts are sometimes referred to as the *management process school*. Through analysis, planning, direction, and control, people are organized and tasks are accomplished. While in its formative years, administrative management theory concentrated on the development of a set of management principles that would aid in the management of an organization irrespective of the task, the contemporary contingent (management process school) emphasizes the development of *organizational techniques* to get the job done. For example, the principles of division of labor, scalar and functional processes, and span of control were more the concern of the early administrative management theorist. Today their counterparts are concerned with the organizational techniques of hierarchical structure, departmentalization, line-staff differentiation and integration, centralization and decentralization, committee organization, and top management committees.

The classical school regards management as a universal process responsive to the nature of the organization and its environment. However, we would be the first to point out that their intellectual weakness lies in this foundation of management. Although we trained in the behavioral sciences and the quantitative sciences, nonetheless, we hold sincere admiration for the accomplishments of the classical school.

The behavioral sciences emerged to stand beside the classical school. The pioneers in behavioral science applied to management were Mary Parker Follett, Elton Mayo, and Chester Barnard. Since their time the list has grown beyond mentionable proportions.

What are the behavioral sciences? They are those disciplines interested in the study of activities performed by organisms that can be observed by another person or an experimenter's instruments. To fully qualify as a behavioral science, the discipline must also be committed to the methods of science. Psychology is generally considered to be a behavioral science, as are sociology and anthropology. Each of these disciplines have subdisciplines. Examples are experimental psychology, clinical psychology, social psychology, experimental social psychology, and many more. Different subdivisions contribute differentially to management.

The behavioral sciences have not as yet fulfilled the potential they hold as a contributor to management. Expectations are high and in all probability our lifetime will see that behavioral contributions profoundly influence management. Nonetheless, significant contributions have been made. The major problem of our time for the managerial behavioral scientist is to implement the theoretic contributions that have been propounded.

The quantitative sciences have only been utilized extensively, in a management context, since the start of World War II. They have been prolific in the supply of tools that, when appropriately employed, improve the efficiency and effectiveness of management. The names associated with the major initial contributions of the quantitative sciences to management are R. Bellman, G. B. Dantzig, R. L. Ackoff, and C. W. Churchman.

Operations research, decision theory, information theory and computer sciences are some of the major areas that apply the quantitative sciences to management. In its own way each attempts to establish analytical representation amenable to computer solution of management decision and control problems. Optimization, simulation, cost effectiveness, risk analysis, critical path, and information control are words that have become commonplace in the vocabulary of the modern manager because of the growing importance and acceptance of these areas.

The initial successes of operations research, for example, have usually been where a single part or task of an organization was being modeled. Quantitative solutions to production, inventory, scheduling, and distribution problems for both industry and government are now commonplace. The goal of the future is the modeling of the entire organization. To do this effectively, of course, an interdisciplinary systems science approach will be necessary. Thus, the behavioral sciences and the classical school must be incorporated into a complete quantified model.

In summary, then, there are three foundations of management: the classical school, the behavioral sciences and the quantitative sciences. The interactions of the foundations are indicated in Figure 1. It is the application of the interaction of these interdisciplinary foundations that is the subject of the study of management.

The Fields of Management

There are many fields of management, some of which are finance, accounting, marketing, public administration, international business, transportation, industrial relations, and health care administration.

FIGURE 1

The Foundations of Management

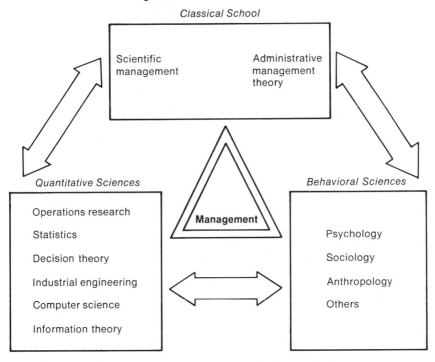

A *field of management* applies the foundations of management, in conjunction with one or more of the social sciences, to problems within a specific content area. For example, finance applies the foundations of management with the social science of economics to the problems of the sources and uses of funds. But economics is not the only social science applied in conjunction with the foundations of management. For example, the public administration field draws heavily upon the discipline of political science; international business draws heavily upon the social science of international relations. Yet economics stands out as being the single most important social science relevant to the fields of management.

The Functions of Management

The functions of management have been enumerated in the definition of management. They are *problem-analysis, decision-making,* and *solution implementation.*

As depicted in Figure 2, problem-analysis is the definition of the situation, the processing of the information, and the generation of alternative solutions. Decision-making is the development and specification of an objective function or other decision criteria, followed by an analysis and evaluation of the consequences of alternative solutions generated during problem-analysis. The evaluation is made with reference to the decision criteria so that a specific

FIGURE 2

Pictorial Definition of the Functions of Management

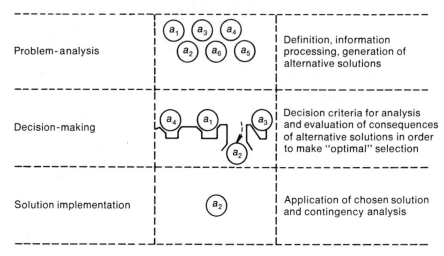

solution may be selected as "optimal." Solution implementation consists of applying the chosen solution to the problem situation and observing the outcome, with the possibility of modifying the situation contingent upon the new information thus obtained.

Figure 3 illustrates how each of the foundations of management highlights the functions of management. Note how the beams of each of the flashlights of the foundations intersect over parts of the functions' circle, and how other parts of the functions' circle are covered by the light of but one foundation flashlight. That is, the functions of management are represented by the dark-lined circle and consist of problem-analysis, decision-making and solution implementation. These functions draw upon and are illuminated by the three foundations of management: classical, quantitative, and behavioral. Figure 3 attempts to illustrate the interactive nature of the functions by the foundations of management.

In each of the fields of management, one will find the functions of management performed. Thus, in finance, the financial manager analyzes problems, makes decisions, and implements solutions as he combines the social

FIGURE 3

Foundations Highlight Functions

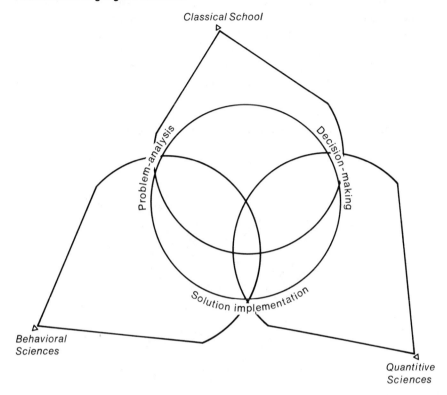

Classical School

Problem-analysis

Decision-making

Solution implementation

Behavioral
Sciences

Quantitive
Sciences

science of economics with the foundations of management in order to determine the sources and uses of funds.

The Plan of This Book

This book concerns itself with the general application of the foundations of management toward the performance of the functions of management. Examination of the specific fields of management are beyond the scope of this text. Thus, in Part II of this book we will investigate the contributions and interaction of each of the foundations with respect to the function of problem-analysis. In Part III we will turn our attention to the relationship between the foundations and the function of decision-making. Part IV will investigate the contribution and interaction of each of the foundations with respect to the function of solution implementation. The last section of the book, Part V, will investigate the future of management, both in terms of contemporary problems and alternative futures.

Figure 4 gives relative indices of weight to the contribution of the three foundations of management to the functions of management. These weights are the subjective judgments of your authors. It is the authors' opinion that each of the foundations has contributed a total of six index weights to the functions. It is the relative distribution, not the absolute magnitude of the contribution, that differentiates the three foundations along functional lines.

FIGURE 4

The Interaction of Foundations and Functions of Management

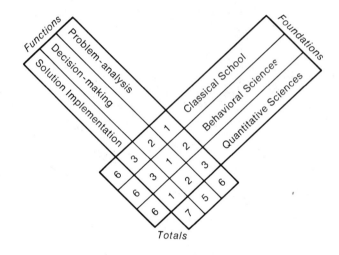

Totals

Functions and Foundations of Management

In the previous discussion management was defined as the application of the interdisciplinary systems science that studies problem-analysis, decision-making, and solution implementation in an organization. This chapter describes in greater depth these functions of the manager. The classical, behavioral, and quantitative approaches to each of the functions is also discussed. This section presents an overview of what will be forthcoming in the remainder of the text.

The Functions of Management

PROBLEM-ANALYSIS

The first function of management, problem-analysis, can be divided into the following subtasks: definition of the situation, processing of the information, and generation of alternative solutions. Definition of the situation begins with the specification of a list of problems that require solution. Since it is often easier to work on only one or two problems at a time, the list can be arranged either by order of importance or by association. Often there is a problem of paramount importance that should be solved first; at other times there is no dominant critical problem. In the latter case it might be best to work on that set of problems with the closest interrelationships. Other ways of ranking the problems are to first attack those with the most stringent time limitations or those with the likelihood of becoming more difficult with the passage of time. Static problems can be handled later. Once a problem has been chosen from the list, it must be defined. Definition includes determination of the problem's broad objectives and restraints; examination of the environment in which we are operating; familiarity with the language, the people, and other things associated with the problem; and isolation of those factors that may or may not be controllable. The result of the process of definition should be a short, clear statement of the quantitative and qualitative characteristics of the situation.

After completing the definition of the problem situation, the second task of problem-analysis is processing the information. The first step in the information processing task is building a model of the problem. The model translates the verbal definition of the problem into a framework that relates the variables of the model to actual problem restrictions and measures of effectiveness. Iconic models resemble what they are supposed to represent, such as architectural models, *Playboy* foldouts, children's toys, and so on. Analogue models relate the properties of what is being modeled with other properties that are both descriptive and meaningful, such as thermometers, seismographs, speedometers, and the like. Symbolic models represent a notational description of the process or problem under investigation. Often symbolic models are mathematical models that represent a translation of the problem into quantitative terms. Thus, the model $TR = [P \cdot Q]$ states that the total revenue from sales equals the unit price multiplied by the number of units sold. This equation from economic theory is an example of a convergent problem, that is, one that has one optimal solution. Another class of problems are those that are considered to be divergent. For this class of problems there exists a number of acceptable solutions but no optimal solution. Speculating on the number of consequences to the problem of how man would behave if he had six fingers on each hand is an example of a divergent problem. Historic models[1] are based on the principle that prior experience is often the best estimate of the short-term future. The assumption that this month's sales will equal last month's; that air passenger demand will be 3 percent greater than last month; that production from a specific department has always been substandard, so it must be substandard today are but a few examples of the widely used managerial model. Extraorganizational models are based on information, available through trade journals, on what an organization's competitors are doing. In their simplest form these models state that if company X can produce our product at a cost of 50¢ , then so can we; or, if division Y can produce so much output, then we can also. All these model types are useful to the modern manager.

Once a model has been developed, a period of validation and experimentation is necessary to insure that the model coincides with the reality of the problem. This is the time to attempt to quantify or estimate the relationships

---

[1]For more information on nonanalytic models, see William Pounds, "The Process of Problem Finding," *Industrial Management Review*, Fall 1969, Vol. 11, No. 1, pp. 1-19.

among the controllable variables of the problem. For example, one might determine how demand is correlated with price changes or how output is affected by an increase in inputs. During this stage, feedback, one of the essential features of any managerial task, comes into play. Feedback is the use of an observed occurrence to alter assumptions or decisions made previous to the observation. One's model may assume that demand is negatively related to price (that is, as price increases, the quantity demanded of that item is expected to decrease). But in the validation and experimentation stage, a market survey determined that demand for the product was positively related to its price (that is, as price increases, quantity demanded increases). Therefore, for the model to be valid, the assumption about demand in our original model must be changed. This is an example of feedback. Feedback during the validation and experimentation stage usually leads to changes in problem definition and model formulation.

Once the model is accurate, the third and most important phase of problem-analysis is entered: the generation of alternative solutions. The goal of the problem-analysis function is to delineate in a clear and concise manner as many feasible alternatives as possible. Alternatives are feasible if they satisfy the basic restrictions imposed by the model formulation. Since most model restrictions are based on assumptions of future environments, an evaluation of some nonfeasible solutions that might have been feasible under a different set of assumptions is called for. This procedure will be discussed in the decision-making function. In order to generate alternative solutions, a solution methodology must be developed. This methodology may be as simple as throwing darts at the *Wall Street Journal* to determine alternative stocks to buy, or as sophisticated as using intricate mathematical procedures (such as mathematical programming) to determine alternative depot locations for a transcontinental trucking firm. One of the major tasks of the solution methodology is to select from among all possible solutions only those alternatives that are feasible. Careful analysis of the alternatives commonly yields feedback to the model formulation stage, which can be useful in achieving better specification of the model. If we determine that there are no feasible alternatives, a change in the model might be desirable.

DECISION-MAKING

The decision-making function follows the problem-analysis function. The function of decision-making can be divided into the following subtasks: statement of goals; development and specification of a measure of performance; analysis and evaluation of the consequences of alternative solutions; choice of a preferred solution. The first task of decision-making is the statement of the general goals toward which the organization is attempting to move. The next task in decision-making, and often the most difficult of any management task, is the development and specification of a suitable measure of performance or criteria by which feasible alternatives may be evaluated and an individual one chosen. These measures represent observable aspects of the general goals of the organization. A performance measure will also be called an objective function or criterion function. Performance measures for firms are often clear and easily quantified; maximization of profit, maintaining a specific market share, and maximization of sales are only a few. In contrast, performance measures for other entities in the public and private sectors of the economy such as governmental departments, universities, and foundations are often unclear and difficult to quantify. What should be the goal of a fire or police department, HUD, HEW, or your university? The development and specification of the performance measure often involves definition, model formulation, and test/experimentation stages, that result in a more precise statement and better understanding of the performance measure.

The third task in the decision-making function is the analysis and evaluation of the consequences of alternative solutions. Often this step may comprise merely the application of the performance measure to each of the consequences of the feasible alternative solutions and the simple ranking of these solutions according to their performance measure values. But the model of the problem is only an approximation of the true environment, often based on assumptions and estimates concerning the state of a set of uncertain environmental conditions. This makes it desirable to utilize a more complex procedure: to vary the assumptions and approximations of the model and to record the resulting fluctuations in the value of the performance measure for the alternative solutions. This is called postoptimal analysis. The object of postoptimal analysis is to determine the robustness, or insensitivity to basic changes, of the consequences of alternative solutions of the model. This type of analysis is usually performed only on a subset of the feasible alternative solutions, those with the highest values of the performance measure. Often the solution that yields the highest performance measure value is quite sensitive to changes in the environment, whereas near optimal solutions can be less sensitive to environmental changes. For instance, the production of the Edsel may have been an alternative yielding the highest profit if successful. It may also have been an alternative yielding the largest loss if it were a failure. The introduction of a smaller car or simply a new model of an old line would probably have produced less potential profit but also a far smaller loss if it were not a success.

The choice of one preferred solution is the last task of decision-making performed by the manager. It is his choice of the one preferred solution. It is usually not the five best but simply *the* best. The choice can be the solution with the highest value of a performance measure; the solution that is the most insensitive to changes in the environment; the solution resulting from the toss of a coin or other chance device—a best guess solution; or the traditional managerial "seat of the pants" solution. No matter how it is determined, an alternative solution must be picked—a decision made.

SOLUTION IMPLEMENTATION

The solution implementation function follows the decision-making function. The function of solution implementation can be divided into the following subtasks: applying the chosen solution to the problem situation; observing the outcome; and modifying the solution or situation contingent upon new information. In general, after development and specification of an objective function, the most difficult managerial task is applying the chosen alternative solution to the problem situation. This is the heart of the solution implementation function. It is not sufficient for a manager to say, "This is my decision—now you go out and implement it." This will almost always lead to inefficiency, if not total disaster. The task of applying the chosen solution to the problem situation must be as carefully planned and thought out as the model-building and evaluation of alternative solution tasks of problem-analysis and decision-making. The manager must insure that the manpower, material, and capital available to him are so organized as to facilitate the application of the chosen solution. The manager must insure that he has the proper people to carry out his orders and that these people fully comprehend what his orders entail. He must have communication channels available so that misunderstandings can be avoided and general questions arising from the application of the order can be answered. The predictable problems caused by the application of the solution should be determined, considered, and methods of handling them devised before the actual implementation begins. Thus, a "game plan" for applying the chosen solution to the problem situation should be a major goal of this managerial task.

The second task of the solution implementation function is observing the outcome of applying the chosen solution to the problem situation. The manager must set up information and control systems that allow him to monitor the results of his chosen solution to the problem. In practice it is at this stage that the manager can first determine whether or not he chose the proper solution to his problem. Some managers require frequent, detailed reports on the results of their decision, whereas others require reports only concerning exceptional occurrences; but every manager must have some type of reporting system to allow him to monitor the repercussions of his decisions.

The major reason for monitoring the outcome of decisions is to enable the manager to complete the last phase of solution implementation: the task of modifying the solution or situation contingent upon new information. This is simply a formal feedback task that will usually affect most of the other subtasks we have discussed. The processes of problem definition, performance-measure determination, and application of the chosen solution will certainly be affected by this task. The manager must constantly change or modify what he does as he gathers additional information, because the right decision today may be the wrong decision tomorrow, especially since tomorrow will probably be different from today. If the manager is aware of the necessity for flexibility at this stage,

FIGURE 1

The Functions of Management

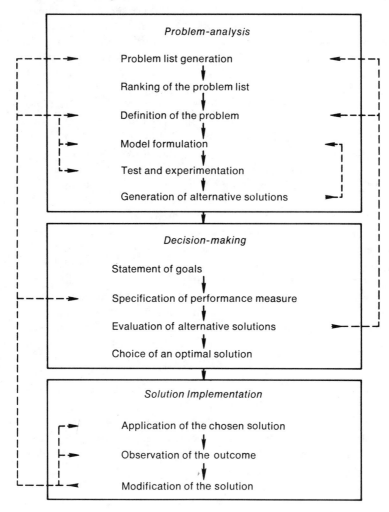

he will facilitate the inclusion of the changes resulting from the new information.

The functions of management are summarized in Figure 1 in which the broken lines indicate feedback.

The Functions of Management: An Example

Here is a hypothetical illustration of a quantitative approach that many firms take in analyzing corporate strategic planning (C. S. P.) alternatives. These alternatives usually include acquisitions, divestments, internal developments, and alternative financing schemes. In the discussion of this general example, the author will draw on his experience in developing a C. S. P. model for a large multinational firm. In this section we will formulate and organize this task along the functional lines discussed in the preceding section.

PROBLEM-ANALYSIS

Once the top management of a firm has decided to formalize its corporate strategic planning process, some of the following problems, in order of importance, are usually encountered:

1. Should the study be done internally by the corporate staff, or externally by a management consulting firm?
2. At what level in the corporation should S. P. be done?
3. How often should the S. P. process be done and how long should the planning horizon be?
4. Should the procedure be qualitative or quantitative?

For the firm under consideration it was decided that the study should be done by the corporate staff (the Comptroller's Department) with the technical assistance of outside consultants; that the plans should be done at the subsidiary level (individual companies which are owned by the corporation), once a year and for a five-year planning horizon; and that the process should be quantitative, involving simulation and as much optimization as possible. For this example we will only describe the optimization part of the process. To simplify the model we will assume that the corporation owned three subsidiaries all of which could be divested, was considering two acquisitions, and had available only two forms of financing; preferred stock and long term debt; and that the planning horizon was only one year. The initial problem definition was select a set of S. P. alternatives which maximized the corporate performance measure but which did not conflict with the set of financial, legal and operating limitations imposed by the corporate executive and the financial community. Some of the restrictions were as follows:

1. Corporate income must grow at a rate of 15 percent higher than the previous year.
2. Corporate return on assets must be 13 percent.
3. Total corporate debt must be less than half of corporate equity.
4. Funds on hand at start of each planning year must be greater than thirty million dollars.
5. A subsidiary company momentum strategy must either be accepted or that company must be divested.
6. Funds utilized from any financing issue must be less than the total amount of funds available from that source.

The corporation assumed that it could not influence or control the state of the economy over the planning horizon but did assume that all subsidiary and staff performance parameters were based on the same assumption about the course of the economy. Thus the only variables under the firm's control were: which companies to acquire or divest, which internal development to undertake, and how all these activities would be financed.

Given the above restrictions and controllable variables the following symbolic model can be formulated. Let each subsidiary momentum strategy be represented by the symbol X_i and its divestment strategy by D_i. Each acquisition candidate is represented by the symbol A_i, each long-term debt issue by the symbol Y_i and each preferred stock issue by the symbol P_i. (i) is a subscript which means a single variable for a class for variables (since there are three subsidiary companies their momentum strategies are indicated by X_1, X_2, X_3, and X_i would be the second if i were equal to 2). The X_i's, D_i's, A_i's, P_i's and Y_i's are the decision variables of our model. In order to write a symbolic representation of the restrictions of our model we need a representation of the contributions of each of our decision variables to each of the restrictions that they are involved in, as follows (each decision variable has a unique coefficient but for simplification we illustrate only the ith where $i = 1 \ldots 12$; $3X$'s, $3D$'s, 2 A's, 2 Y's, $2P$'s):

I_i = the contribution of the ith strategy to income
B_i = the contribution of the ith strategy to corporate assets
C_i = the contribution of the ith strategy to corporate debt
F_i = the net cash generation or demand of the ith strategy
J_i = the contribution of the ith strategy to corporate equity
R_i = maximum number of preferred shares that can be sold in issue i
I_t = total corporate income in the previous year
Q_i = maximum amount of long term debt available from source i

The decision variable X_i, D_i, and A_i cannot have a value greater than one (i.e., we cannot acquire or divest more than 100 percent of any company but we can acquire less than 100 percent of a company).

Using these symbols the restrictions listed above can be represented by the following equations:

$$I_1X_1 + I_2X_2 + I_3X_3 + I_4D_1 + I_5D_2 + I_6D_3 + I_7A_1 + I_8A_2 \quad (1)$$
$$- I_9Y_1 - I_{10}Y_2 - I_{11}P_1 - I_{12}P_2 \geq (1.15)I_T$$

$$[I_1X_1 + I_2X_2 + I_3X_3 + I_4D_1 + I_5D_2 + I_6D_3 + I_7A_1 + I_8A_2 \quad (2)$$
$$- I_9Y_1 - I_{10}Y_2 - I_{11}P_1 - I_{12}P_2] - .13[B_1X_1 + B_2X_2$$
$$+ B_3X_3 + B_4D_1 + B_5D_2 + B_6D_3 + B_7A_1 + B_8A_2$$
$$+ B_9Y_1 + B_{10}Y_{10} + B_{11}P_1 + B_{12}P_2] \geq 0$$

$$[C_1X_1 + C_2X_2 + C_3X_3 - C_4P_1 - C_5D_2 - C_6D_3 + C_7A_1 \tag{3}$$
$$+ C_8A_2 + C_9Y_1 + C_{10}Y_2] - .5[J_1X_1 + J_2X_2 + J_3X_3$$
$$+ J_4D_1 + J_5D_2 + J_6D_3 + J_7A_1 + J_8A_2 + J_{11}P_1$$
$$+ J_{12}P_2] \leq 0$$

$$F_1X_1 + F_2X_2 + F_3X_3 + F_4D_1 + F_5D_2 + F_6D_3 - F_7A_1 \tag{4}$$
$$- F_8A_2 + F_9Y_1 + F_{10}Y_2 + F_{11}P_1 + F_{12}P_2 \geq 30,000,000$$

$$X_1 \quad + D_1 \qquad\qquad = 1 \tag{5}$$
$$X_2 \quad\quad + D_2 \qquad\quad = 1 \tag{6}$$
$$X_3 \quad\quad + D_3 \qquad = 1 \tag{7}$$
$$Y_1 \qquad \leq Q_1 \tag{8}$$
$$Y_2 \qquad \leq Q_2 \tag{9}$$
$$P_1 \quad \leq R_1 \tag{10}$$
$$P_2 \leq R_2 \tag{11}$$

Equation (1) states that the contribution of all accepted strategies to income must be 15 percent (1.15) greater than last year's total income (I_t). The coefficient of long-term debt and preferred stock are negative since they usually detract from income while the coefficients of the other decision variables are positive since they normally have a positive effect on income. Equation (2) states that the total contribution to income from all accepted strategies be 13 percent (.13) greater than the total assets of all accepted strategies. Equation (3) states that the difference between the total debt of all accepted strategies and 50 percent (.5) of the total equity of all accepted strategies be less than zero. Equation (4) states that the net cash generated from all accepted strategies must be greater than thirty million dollars. Restriction (5) is represented by the equations (5), (6), and (7). They state that the proportion of a momentum strategy and the proportion of the divest strategy for a subsidiary company must equal one. Thus we cannot accept both a momentum and its related divestment $(1 + 1 > 1)$ and we cannot reject both a momentum and its related divestment $(0 + 0 < 1)$ but we can accept ½ of a momentum and ½ of its related divestment (½ + ½). Restriction (6) is represented by equations (8) through (12). They state that the total amount of debt issues one and two and the total number of shares issued in preferred offers one and two must be less than the one and two respectively. Sets of momentum, divestment, acquisition and financing alternatives which satisfy equations (1) through (11) are feasible solutions to the strategic planning problem. It should be emphasized at this point that the preceding model, even this naive one, was based on many assumptions that were too complex to be included in the statement of the model. Thus, the model must be subject to a thorough analysis to determine the effects of changes in these assumptions before a valid decision could or should be reached.

The test and experimentation task involved obtaining the values of I_i,

B_i, C_i, F_i, and J_i for each strategic alternative. The contribution of momentum strategies to income, assets, debt, cash generation and equity where derived from annual strategic planning data submitted by the subsidiaries. These plans were based on a set of assumptions about the U.S. economy and other planning data external to the subsidiaries over the planning horizon derived by the corporate staff and passed on to the subsidiaries at the start of the planning cycle. The contributions of acquisition, divestment, and financing alternatives to income, debt, etc. were generated by different parts of the corporate staff. At this time management's desires for the levels of constraint compliance stated earlier, rate of income growth, return on assets desired, minimum funds balance, etc., were obtained. Since the actual time from model design to data gathering was approximately three months a data and model validation task was undertaken and the model was adjusted accordingly. Once this task was completed it was possible to move to the decision-making function since the generation of alternative solutions could be accomplished by an existing solution technology, mathematical programming (to be discussed in Part II).

DECISION-MAKING

Since the corporation was publicly held its chief executive felt that its overriding goal should be to maximize the wealth of its individual shareholders. This goal usually involves some trade-off between capital gains and dividend income. To better understand the desires of the stockholders in this procedure the chief executive commissioned a consulting firm to undertake a stockholder opinion survey. The result of the survey was that most stockholders (of this company) were mainly interested in capital gains income as long as some minimal dividend payout was maintained. Thus the corporate goal became the maximization of the capital gain potential of its stock. It was determined that the best way of achieving continued increases in stock price was to demonstrate consistent compound growth in earnings per share. But since no solution methodology was available that could handle this goal it was decided that the next best quantifiable performance measure was the maximization of income over time subject to a constraint of a minimum of 15 percent compound growth in income over time. This led to the use of equation (12) as the objective function and equation (1) as an important restriction.

$$\text{Max } Z = I_1X_1 + I_2X_2 + I_3X_3 + I_4D_1 + I_5D_2 + I_6D_3 + I_7A_1 \qquad (12)$$
$$+ I_8A_2 - I_9Y_1 - I_{10}Y_2 - I_{11}P_1 - I_{12}P_3$$

Equation (12) states that our objective is to pick that set of strategic alternatives that maximizes corporate income. The application of our performance measure (12) to the set of feasible alternative solutions to restriction (1-11) determines that set of strategic alternatives which yields the highest value of the performance measure. This step was accomplished quite easily utilizing the quantitative technique of linear programming (to be discussed in depth in Part II). Since our model was based on many assumptions and since the performance measure was not the true goal of the firm a postoptimal analysis was performed. In determining the sensitivity of our proposed solution to possible changes in the assumption or environment of our original model definition it was discovered that the set of strategic alternatives that yielded the highest value of the performance measure was quite sensitive to the ratio between debt and equity (Restriction 3). In fact, corporate income could be increased by 12 percent if corporate debt was allowed to increase by 3 percent. This possibility was discussed with the chief financial officer of the company who said his original figure was an estimate and that an increase of 3 percent would not have a deleterious effect on the company's image in the financial community. Other changes in restrictions occurred due to the postoptimal analysis and the final result was a set of strategic alternatives that was quite insensitive to changes in the environment and yielded a near optimal value of the performance measure. The result of the analysis was the chief executive's decision to acquire one new company, sell a subsidiary company, and finance all strategies by debt rather than equity financing. (These were also the results of the model after postoptimal analysis.)

SOLUTION IMPLEMENTATION

In applying the chosen solution to the problem situation, the chief executive communicated his decisions as to which strategic alternatives he had chosen to the responsible group vice-presidents. Along with this information he instructed the responsible group vice-presidents to determine whether the data gathered for the initial plans, of the chosen alternatives, was still valid and to report back to him in two weeks. This allowed for one last update as to the validity of the data and assumptions on which the model was based. It turned out that the only major change was that the contribution to income of the subsidiary to be divested was 10 percent less than had been expected. This did not change the decision since it had been determined in the postoptimal analysis stage that a range of 20 percent variation about the assumed divestment proceeds would not change the divestment decision. Once this stage was completed the only control devices set up by the corporate executive, other than the normal monthly operating planning control reporting system that was already in operation, were semi-monthly reports on the progress of the one divestment and the one acquisition being undertaken. This was caused by the possible wide swings in divestment and acquisition prices as negotiations were underway and the usual ease of reversing this type of decision if new information on the contributions of the strategies showed changes outside the bounds of those determined by the postoptimal analysis. After the entire strategic plan was consummated, the only major modification that was undertaken previously for the new planning cycle (occurs yearly) was a change in performance measure. The new performance measure was the maximization of earning per share subject to a growth in earning per share constraint. The new performance measure was instituted due to an advance in solution methodology that occurred during the original planning cycle. It was also felt that this performance measure was more highly correlated with the firm's real goal, maximization of the capital gains potential of the firm's stock, than the one used in the previous planning cycle.

The Foundations of Management

AN OVERVIEW OF THE CLASSICAL SCHOOL

For purposes of this text we will consider the contribution of the classical school of management to comprise the following schools: scientific management, management principles, and management process. A way to view the subject of management is to focus on it as a process. Usually this process involves certain steps often called functions, that managers perform; these functions, if isolated, studied, defined, and reduced to basic principles or maxims, can enhance one's understanding of the process. The functional approach and the search for generalizable principles or maxims unifies the writers and researchers of the classical school. This school had its major impact on management in the first half of this century. Today its contribution to management is still significant. The major flaw of the classical school compared to the other two foundations is that it tells the manager what to do but rarely tells him why or how to do it. As an example, the classical school only tells the manager *to plan*, whereas the quantitative and behavioral schools, exemplified in the book *A Concept of Corporate Planning* by Russ Ackoff, tell him *how to plan*. The other foundations address themselves to all three questions in great detail with the behavioral sciences stressing the "why" in theoretical research and the "how" in applied research. The quantitative sciences stress the development of techniques that tend to tell the manager "how." It should be noted that there are numerous exceptions to the above classification and that the above should be treated cautiously as a broad generalization. The classical school usually considers that managers perform the following five functions:

Planning—the procedure by which a manager inspects alternative future states of nature and, based on this inspection, tries to determine alternative courses of action available to him. Planning usually includes a model-building and data-analysis stage called analyzing.

Organization—the determination of an organizational structure that will facilitate the allocation and coordination of tasks so that the organization's goals can be readily attained.

Staffing—the determination of which individuals to allocate to which tasks so that the organization's goals can be readily attained. This function includes the attraction, selection, and retention of individuals by and to the organization.

Directing—the manner or way the manager puts into effect the decisions that have been made previously for attaining the goals of the organization. Directing usually includes the managerial task of transmitting ideas or information from one individual to another.

Controlling—the process that determines means for measuring a current activity, comparing it to a performance measure, and correcting the current activity to achieve an improvement in performance.

In Part II the contributions of the classical school to problem-analysis, the analyzing portion of the classical function of planning, is discussed. The contributions of scientific management and the juxtaposition of line and staff and the process of departmentation (dividing operating work into units) are also discussed. Historically, the generation of alternative solutions has been a staff rather than a managerial task and has thus received little attention from the classical school. In Part III the contributions of the classical school to decision-making, the decision-making part of the classical planning function, is discussed. Since the "how" of decisions was left to entrepreneurial wisdom rather than quantitative analysis by the classical school, the role of committees and boards of directors is also discussed. The other major topics of this part are the ideas of decentralization (dividing managerial work into units) and the concept of bureaucracy. In Part IV the contributions of the classical school to solution implementation, the staffing, directing, and controlling functions, are discussed. It is in the function of solution implementation that the classical school has made the greatest contribution to management. It is the goal of Part IV to give the student an appreciation for the breadth and character of the classical school's achievements in this most important management function.

AN OVERVIEW OF THE BEHAVIORAL SCHOOL

The behavioral school deals with the disciplines of psychology, social psychology, sociology, and cultural anthropology. Each of these disciplines contributes differentially to the three functions of management outlined in this text. Indeed, there exists a new field on the horizon of management thought called *organizational behavior*. This field is an interdisciplinary combination of the major disciplines mentioned above. Organizational behavior is a new interdisciplinary field dedicated to the study of organizations, their internal workings, and their relationships with one another and with the environment.

For a recent view of the status of this new field, see the reading by H. J. Leavitt, a founding father of the field.

The behavioral science chapters which seek to examine problem-analysis (Part II), decision-making (Part III), and solution implementation (Part IV) from the behavioral perspective are really chapters in organizational behavior. But these chapters do not cover the whole field of organizational behavior. Instead they limit themselves to an analysis of one component element in the organization—the manager. We seek in these sections to understand the behavior of a manager in an organizational context.

Problem-analysis for the behavioral scientist has to do with the way individuals define a problem and come up with alternative solutions to that defined problem. Decision-making, in the behavioral viewpoint, considers the relationship of individual needs to the goals of groups and organizations. These goals, or desired end-states, are derived from collectivities of needs. So too, do these needs give us a criterion of choice, with which we can decide which alternative solution best suits our needs. Solution implementation is, to the behavioral scientist, the manner in which the manager secures the participation and commitment of members of an organization to the goals of that organization, be those goals stable or changing.

AN OVERVIEW OF THE QUANTITATIVE SCHOOL

The quantitative sciences comprise the following fields: applied mathematics, statistics, probability theory, mathematical economics, econometrics, information systems, and the like. It was only after the Second World War that most of the quantitative sciences were applied to business problems. As the nature and scope of these applications grew, a discipline grew with them. This discipline or field is often called operations research or management science. The procedures, techniques, or model solution methodologies that are the contributions of the quantitative sciences applied to the functions of management would be classified as part of the discipline of management science. The field of management science has been the most active in developing mathematical techniques that allow computer solutions to problems faced by managers in any type of organization. That is, the techniques developed are not designed for specific problems but are general analytical procedures that can be applied to any problem that meets the requirements of the mathematical structure of that procedure. For example, the technique of linear programming can be used to solve any problem with a linear performance measure and linear problem restrictions or constraints as illustrated by the "one-potato, two-potato" problem in the Wagner readings and the "strategic planning problem" discussed earlier in this chapter. These two problems have nothing in common except their mathematical structure, but both are solved by the technique called linear programming. The techniques of management science are used to solve managerial problems. But in this context the word "solve" has the expanded definition that includes part of the problem-analysis and decision-making functions. In the management science vocabulary "to solve" means to formulate a symbolic model of the problem restrictions and performance measure, to determine model coefficients via test and experimentation, to generate alternative solutions, and to evaluate alternative solutions. Once the symbolic model has been specified and its coefficients determined, a computer may be utilized to generate and evaluate the alternative solutions. When a management scientist discusses a management problem, he not only solicits from the manager the definition of the problem restrictions but also the desired performance measure. Given this information, it is incumbent upon the management scientist to report to the manager not only the optimal solution but a set of feasible solutions and the sensitivity of each to changes in the problem environment. That set of techniques that management science utilizes to do those parts of the problem-analysis and decision-making functions are classified as quantitative science approaches to problem-analysis. It is for this function as just defined, that management scientists have developed the largest number of techniques, made the greatest advances, and received the most acceptance in the application of quantitative analyses to management. The quantitative techniques most often utilized in the problem-analysis function usually address themselves to the following types of problems:

1. commodity flow;
2. resource allocation;
3. inventory;
4. waiting lines;
5. scheduling.

These problems may be solved by either analytical or enumerative techniques. An analytical solution is usually based on a mathematical theorem or algorithm (a set of instructions that when properly followed always leads to the desired end—a recipe for Mom's apple pie), which guarantees a solution requiring fewer steps than an exhaustive search (testing each feasible solution) and cannot be improved upon even by total enumeration (application of the performance measure to every feasible alternative). Enumerative techniques, often called simulations, reach an answer after a great number of trials or experiments have been made with the solution often being the one that occurs most frequently. Mechanics tell us that a fairly weighted coin will come up heads 50 percent of the time. An enumerative technique for determining the probability of a head for a coin could be to flip it, say, one thousand times and use the percentage of times the coin comes up heads as the probability of a head. Simulation is often helpful when the problem is too complex to be amenable to an analytical solution; thus, managers often must employ both approaches in the quest for problem solutions.

Part II will discuss in some depth the problems of resource allocation, distribution, and the art of simulation. The techniques developed by the quantitative sciences for the problem-analysis function presume the specification of a performance measure by the manager. To assist management in this task, the quantitative sciences have developed techniques which provide a systematic method for determining the appropriate performance measure or objective in various circumstances. This is one contribution of the quantitative sciences to the decision-making function. Another method discussed in Part II is the utilization of the techniques of problem-analysis to evaluate alternative solutions.

The approach most often taken in the derivation of the appropriate performance measure for an individual or a group can be called "axiomatic." An axiom is defined as an established principle in some art or science that although not a necessary truth, is universally accepted, or is a self-consistent statement about an undefinable object that forms the basis for discourse. The basic approach is as follows: a set of axioms is postulated, each one being acceptable to a "rational" individual or group. All the axioms are then used as the basis for a mathematical problem, which states that if an individual who agrees to adhere to or his behavior follows these axioms, then to be "rational" or "consistent" he must use the derived performance measure in specific situations covered by the axioms. In Part III we will illustrate that if an individual adheres to five axioms postulated by Von Neuman and Morgenstern, then in situations involving risk he must pick the alternative that maximizes his expected utility. We will also discuss performance measures, such as Laplace and Minimax Regret, and others, for which it cannot be shown unequivocally that one is better than another, from which the decision-maker may choose the performance measure that appeals to him the most.

The quantitative sciences have made their smallest contributions in relation to the solution implementation function. There has been no single technique developed that will tell the manager how to totally implement his chosen solution. What has been developed are specific utilizations of the techniques of problem-analysis to aid the manager in doing some of the classical functions of solution implementation such as staffing, organizing, controlling, etc. These contributions of the quantitative sciences to the managerial function of solution implementation are covered in Part IV. Discussion includes which parts of a system need close control and which parts can be left to run themselves, what information is necessary to run different organizational forms, and how best that information can be manipulated.

HARVEY M. WAGNER

The Art and Science
of Executive Decisions

1.1 Before Getting Started . . .

You may well be curious to know how a subject with so abstruse a name as *operations research* could beget a several hundred page introductory text purportedly dealing only with principles. The ambiguous term *operations research* was coined during World War II. At that time, it was an apt description of the subject matter. Unfortunately, the name stuck, even though present-day applications of operations research are considerably more diverse than they used to be.

Now there is a worldwide confederation of professional societies named Operations Research. The staffs of many industrial organizations bear the title. So do departments in leading universities, which have gone on to sanctify the term by granting advanced degrees bearing its name. These vested interests are so well entrenched that the name *operations research* is unlikely to be supplanted in our lifetime.

Source: Harvey M. Wagner, *Principles of Operations Research, with Applications to Management Decisions*. Englewood Cliffs, N.J.: Prentice-Hall, Inc., (1969), pp. 3-31. Reprinted with permission.

Disgruntled though we may be, saddled as we are with a title that is undescriptive if not downright misleading, we nevertheless must show our respect. After all, the scientists who originated the term were on the winning side of the war. (Who knows what might have happened if the other side had invented the approach first?)

1.2 By Any Other Name

Numerous synonyms for operations research are in common use. The British like *operational research*. A frequent American substitute is *management science*. (The popularity of this name is fostered by yet another international professional society called the Institute of Management Science. The Operations Research Society and the Institute of Management Science regularly hold joint meetings, and their membership overlaps to a large extent.) As a beginning student, fortunately, you can afford to assume a lofty indifference to the whole matter, leaving this semantic bone of contention for your seniors to wrangle over.

For convenience, and with reasonable accuracy, you can simply define operations research as a scientific approach to problem-solving for executive management. An application of operations research involves:

—Constructing mathematical, economic, and statistical descriptions or models of decision and control problems to treat situations of complexity and uncertainty.

—Analyzing the relationships that determine the probable future consequences of decision choices, and devising appropriate measures of effectiveness in order to evaluate the relative merit of alternative actions.

It is sometimes believed that operations research refers to the constant monitoring of an organization's ongoing activities—and, in fact, decision and control problems often do concern certain daily "operations" of the organization. Examples of this sort include production scheduling and inventory control, facility maintenance and repair, and staffing of service facilities, to name a few applications.

But many operations research studies treat other kinds of decisions that bear on daily operations only indirectly. These studies usually have a planning orientation. Illustrations include determining the breadth of a firm's product line, developing a long-term program for plant expansion, designing a network of warehouses for a wholesale distribution system, and entering a new business by merger or acquisition.

It is bad enough that the word "operations" inadequately describes the diversity of present-day applications. To make matters worse, the word "research" creates the false impression that the method is a "blue-sky approach."

A Conceptual Framework

On the contrary, in the past decade operations research has proved time and again to be a powerful and effective approach for solving critically real management problems. You will learn most of the reasons in this chapter, and you will know the full story after reading the main chapters of this book.

Of course, fundamental research in the *methods* of operations research continues, mainly at universities and at governmental and industrial research laboratories. Unlike the situation with basic research in other sciences, however, relatively little time elapses between an important discovery in operations research and its implementation by experienced practitioners in industrial groups.

BETTER DECISIONS IN A COMPLEX
AND UNCERTAIN ENVIRONMENT

A preferable term to describe the subject of this book is *decision analysis*. An emphasis on making decisions or taking actions is central to all operations research applications.

Decision analysis separates a large-scale problem into its subparts, each of which is simpler to manipulate and diagnose. After the separate elements are carefully examined, the results are synthesized to give insights into the original problem. You may wonder why such complex decision-making problems arise in the first place.

One reason is that in today's economy, technological, environmental, and competitive factors typically interact in a complicated fashion. For example, a factory production schedule has to take account of customer demand (tempered by the likelihood of a price-cut by competitors), requirements for raw materials and intermediate inventories, the capacities of equipment, the possibility of equipment failures, and manufacturing process restrictions. It is not easy to make up a schedule that is both realistic and economical.

Other reasons for complexity in real decision-making situations are that the organization (perhaps only half-knowingly) may be pursuing inconsistent goals, the responsibility and authority for making the required decisions may be greatly diffused within the organization, and the economic environment in which the company operates may be uncertain.

To be successful, an operations research approach must improve the managerial decision-making process—the improvement being measured by the net cost of obtaining it. You should keep in mind the distinction between improved decision making and improved performance, or more succinctly, between a good decision and a good outcome. For example, by all prior analysis, your betting on the Irish Sweepstakes may not appear to be a good decision (economically or morally); but *after* betting, the outcome will be good if you win. Improving decision analysis is important because the only thing *you* control is your decision prior to the uncertain outcome.

DISTINGUISHING CHARACTERISTICS

There are many ways to approach management problems, and most of these ways are related. Certainly there is no clear boundary line isolating the solutions derived by professional operations researchers from those derived by such people as industrial engineers, or economists specializing in economic planning, or accountants or financial analysts oriented toward management information systems. But most operations research applications possess certain distinguishing characteristics. Specifically, a suggested approach to a particular problem must contain all the following qualities before we would call it an operations research approach:

i. A primary focus on decision-making. The principal results of the analysis must have direct and unambiguous implications for executive action.

ii. An appraisal resting on economic effectiveness criteria. A comparison of the various feasible actions must be based on measurable values that unequivocally reflect the future well-being of the organization. In a commercial firm, these measured quantities typically include variable costs, revenues, cash flow, and rate of return on incremental investment. A recommended solution must have evaluated the tradeoffs and have struck an optimum balance among these sometimes conflicting factors.

iii. Reliance on a formal mathematical model. The procedures for manipulating the data should be so explicit that they can be described to another analyst, who in turn would derive the same results from the same data.

iv. Dependence on an electronic computer. This characteristic is not really a desideratum but rather a requirement necessitated by either the complexity of the mathematical model, the volume of data to be manipulated, or the magnitude of computations needed to implement the associated management operating and control systems.

IN SCIENCE WE TRUST

To embrace operations research, a company must believe that applying the scientific method is relevant to the analysis of managerial decisions. This statement is not the platitude it may seem to be at first reading. The adoption of operations research calls for an act of faith in the benefits of a systematic approach to decision-making, and not all corporation executives are ready to make that act as yet.

It may sound strange, at this late date, to hear a plea for faith in science—and operations research is a science. After all, the legitimacy of the scientific method in the study of other subjects, such as physical phenomena, is hardly open to question. After hundreds of years of experience, chemists and physicists have developed efficacious laboratory techniques. But the virtue of applying scientific procedures to decision-making problems of significance is not so well-established; its recognition still calls for what the poet Coleridge described, in another context, as "the willing suspension of disbelief." Here is why.

Rarely, if ever, can a company perform what most people would regard as a bona fide "scientific" experiment to test the merit of an operations research solution. Consider a company that is contemplating using a mathematical model to arrive at its annual operating plan. Since the company's economic environment differs from year to year, it can never exactly repeat history, and therefore can never prove indisputably that the model solution will produce a realized improvement over the company's current planning approach.

Consider a second illustration. Suppose that an operations research model has been suggested for controlling a company's inventories. Again, testing whether the new system will definitely yield an improvement over the present approach is inherently limited. Although you could use historical data to compare how the suggested rule would have operated in the past, the comparison does not represent a truly scientific experiment with controlled variables. For one thing, you can only *assume* that historical data are indicative of what will happen in the future. For another, if the suggested rules improve service and customers recognize the improvement, then there may be an increase in customer demand. In other words, the very operation of the suggested policy can alter the environment.

Thus, the historical data may not be typical of the future. And because the decision system itself influences the environment, it is not really possible to operate both the present and new systems "in parallel." (Occasionally, you can run part of the system under the new set of rules and the other part under the old set of rules. Explain why this test, also, is not a truly controlled experiment.)

Of course, before a manager accepts a specific operations research solution, he should perform various tests of reasonableness, including historical comparisons. But at some point after making such tests, even in an ideal situation, the manager will have to accept as axiomatic that a scientific approach has intrinsic merit. We make three amplifying observations before leaving this conclusion.

First, even though a company may be convinced about the worthiness of the scientific method to aid decision-making, it need not accept the results of a particular operations research study as being valid. After all, the specific project may have been ill-conceived or poorly executed.

Second, a trust in science does not imply the abandonment of hunch and intuition. On the contrary, the history of science itself is studded with cases of important discoveries made through chance, hunch, serendipity—even dreams. Behavioral scientists have not yet developed ways to induce such flashes of brilliance consistently. But most executives who use their hunches well also seem to possess a high level of knowledge and understanding about their activities. So the question is not when to apply science and when to rely on intuition, but rather how to combine the two effectively.

Third, the inherent difficulty of demonstrating that a suggested solution is a sure-fire improvement is not unique to operations research. Because of the inability to duplicate history, an act of faith is also required to accept any other proposed solution—including maintaining the status quo.

PAST, PRESENT, AND FUTURE

Although the term "operations research" was coined during World War II, the scientific origins of the subject date much further back. Primitive mathematical programming models were advanced by economists Quesnay in 1759 and Walras in 1874; more sophisticated economic models of a similar genre were proposed by Von Neumann in 1937 and Kantorovich in 1939. The *mathematical* underpinnings of linear models were established near the turn of the 19th century by Jordan in 1873, Minkowski in 1896, and Farkas in 1903. Another example of early development is the seminal work on dynamic models accomplished by Markov, who lived from 1856 to 1922. Two further illustrations are the innovative suggestions for economical inventory control, published in business and industrial engineering journals during the 1920's, and the pioneering studies of waiting-line phenomena completed by Erlang, who lived from 1878 to 1929.

Even though these early starts received recognition and acclaim, only recently have mathematical models for decision analysis taken hold in business. Why? At least two factors are important. First, the competitive pressures of doing business have increased tremendously since World War II. Executives of large corporations now find it essential in maintaining profits to improve on the traditional ways of collecting and analyzing data. Second, the fantastic development and widespread adoption of high-speed electronic computers have fostered the growth of more sophisticated means for assessing decision alternatives.

There are many reasons to believe that the process of implementing operations-research-oriented systems will quicken. For example, new technological developments in what is called *time-shared computing* bring the power of an electronic computer literally into an executive's office. It is a pipedream to suppose that, in the next few years, most corporation presidents will have computer consoles on their desk tops for querying at a moment's notice. But already, financial vice presidents in several industrial companies do have such consoles to evaluate major investment alternatives. The future is getting closer all the time.

1.3 Boundaries of Quantitative Analysis

As should be obvious, quantitative analysis can never provide the entire basis for *all* strategic decisions. It is inconceivable that the selection of a corporation president by a company's board of directors, for example, could (and should) ever rest solely on the manipulation of quantitative data, although some numerical information may be relevant.

It is probably less apparent that even when quantitative analysis is of central importance for a managerial decision process, an operations-research-oriented system never supplies all the information required for action, no matter how sophisticated the system's design. Furthermore, a truly successful implementation of an operations research system must apply behavioral as well as mathematical science, because the resultant system must interact with human beings. And finally, the very process of constructing an operations research system involves the exercise of judgment in addition to the logical manipulation of symbols and data. We discuss below each of these boundaries on quantitative analysis.

PROBLEMS SOLVED AND UNSOLVED

As you read the chapters of this book, you will learn the ways an executive can be aided by the different operations research models that are treated. We therefore limit our comments in this section to more generally applicable remarks.

We have already mentioned that at the inception of implementing an operations research system it is necessary for experienced executives to discern the relevance of the model. This alone is not enough, of course. Since the corporate owners hold these men responsible for wisely managing the firm, executives must continue to exercise their judgmental duty well beyond initial acceptance of the model. In one way or another, they must monitor the system to ensure that the underlying model remains valid, and in particular that it continues to be used properly to provide insights into the real decision-making problems of the company. (Managers must guard against thinking of the model as being reality, and hence of the accompanying answers as being sacrosanct.)

A newly implemented operations research system may well bring about a restructuring or an amplification of information. As a result, executives may act differently from how they might have acted without such information. There is no getting away from the fact, however, that an executive, not the model, takes the action.

In short, an operations research model is never sufficient unto itself; it cannot become entirely independent of judgment supplied by knowledgeable managers. This boundary on quantitative analysis is always manifest, because the number of questions that managers can pose is boundless, whereas the kinds of answers that a single model can provide are inherently limited.

SYSTEMS ARE FOR PEOPLE

The above discussion also suggests that there is more to a successful implementation of an operations research system than the mere design of a mathematically correct model. Clearly, the system must operate in the larger context of managerial activity. The model must take account of the data sources, with respect both to quality of the data and to the goals and expertise of the people responsible for collecting the data. The system must also reflect the information requirements of the managers who review the analytic results, expecially the needs for descriptive and interpretive commentary.

Most experienced practitioners of operations research know how to solve these so-called problems of communication. But there is a more fundamental limitation on quantitative analysis: rarely, if ever, is a suggested operations research system in perfect harmony with previously existing managerial attitudes and predilections. To ignore this fact is to invite internal conflict, subterfuge, and sometimes downright sabotage of a new system.

For example, a corporate planning model may call for the development of *realistic sales forecasts.* You would expect that marketing executives should ordinarily be entrusted to provide these figures; but the traditional orientation of the marketing department may make it impossible for these personnel to articulate anything other than *sales goals.* If the motivational drive of the sales organization is to set up targets and then try to meet them, and if it is then called upon to enunciate both targets *and* realistic forecasts, severe organizational conflicts may break out.

What can be done about this kind of limitation on quantitative analysis? Presently, considerable research is under way by behavioral scientists to discover successful means of instituting effective organizational change. Such developments in administrative science will certainly have a fundamental effect on the actual degree of success and speed of implementation of operations research systems.

THE ART OF MANAGEMENT SCIENCE

The problem-solving ingenuity of professional operations researchers is still a limiting factor in the spread of quantitative analysis. Despite the enormous growth in the acceptance of management science models, there are preciously few "standard" applications. Even in areas of decision-making where the relevance of mathematical models has become well established, designing particular applications in specific companies requires significant skill on the part of the management scientist. Model formulations remain tailor-made to a large degree.

Conceivably, in the next decade some of the well-developed applications of operations research will have become so widely adopted that procedures for building these models can be codified, as many of the techniques in industrial engineering and managerial accounting have been. The unabated expansion of quantitative analysis into previously untouched areas of decision-making is so enormous, however, that the need for imaginative and talented problem-solving will remain undiminished for some time.

In other words, a considerable amount of "art" is still required for the successful practice of management science. This in turn means that whether you are a managerial user or a practitioner of operations research, you must have some facility with both the artistic and the scientific ingredients of the subject. A textbook, such as this one, can teach you many of the scientific aspects, and give you a modicum of practice in the art through the study of toy examples and the formulation and solution of small-scale problems. Unfortunately, however, it can do no more than make you aware of the artistic elements.

To help you understand this interplay between the art and the science of applying operations research, we offer an analogy with the fine arts. A knowledge of scientific principles, such as the chemistry of paint, the physiology of the eye, the physics of light, the psychology of color, and the laws of perspective, helps the artist master fully the craft of painting. Likewise, such knowledge also distinguishes the true connoisseur from the casual, albeit appreciative, Sunday museum-goer. By the same token, an understanding of the fundamentals of operations research is essential not only for the practitioner, but for the manager who wants to make truly effective use of the approach. If today's business world continues to become more complex, an executive will not be able to compete successfully in the role of a casual onlooker, or he himself may end up as a museum exhibit.

1.4 Importance of Model-Building

If you study this text diligently, you will learn a considerable amount of mathematical technique. But a benefit that far transcends the mastering of specific algorithms is the facility you will gain in formulating, manipulating, and analyzing mathematical models. *Model-building is the essence of the operations research approach.* It is the counterpart to laboratory experimentation in the physical sciences.

Constructing a model helps you put the complexities and possible uncertainties attending a decision-making problem into a logical framework amenable to comprehensive analysis. Such a model clarifies the decision alternatives and their anticipated effects, indicates the data that are relevant for analyzing the alternatives, and leads to informative conclusions. In short, the model is a vehicle for arriving at a well-structured view of reality.

A MIXED BAG

The word "model" has several shades of meaning, all of which are relevant to operations research. First, a "model" may be a substitute representation of reality, such as a small-scale model airplane or locomotive. Second, "model" may imply some sort of idealization, often embodying a simplification of details, such as a model plan for urban redevelopment. Finally, "model" may be used as a verb, meaning to exhibit the consequential characteristics of the idealized representation. This notion conjures up in the mind those television commercials dramatizing how love and happiness will result after a single application of the sponsor's product.

In operations research, a model is almost always a mathematical, and necessarily an approximate, representation of reality. It must be formulated to capture the crux of the decision-making problem. At the same time, it must be sufficiently free of burdensome minor detail to lend itself to finding an improved solution that is capable of implementation. Striking a proper balance between reality and manageability is no mean trick in most applications, and for this reason model-building can be arduous.

You will find three pervasive and interrelated themes in operations research model-building. The first is an emphasis on optimization. Concentrating on decisions that are optimal according to one or more specified criteria has been the forcing wedge for attaining *improved* decision-making. Typically, the optimization is constrained, in that the values of the decision variables maximizing the stated objective function are restricted so as to satisfy certain technological restraints. Often, the model includes restrictions that mirror the impact of dynamic phenomena.

The second theme is derivation of the analytic properties of a mathematical model, including the sensitivity of an optimal solution to the model's parameters, the structural form of an optimal solution, and the operating characteristics of the solution. To illustrate, if you have a mathematical model leading to an inventory replenishment policy, you will want to know how the rule depends on forecasts of customer demand, the specification of the rule (such as, "when down to n, order again"), and the long-run frequency of stockouts and the average inventory level.

The third theme is explicit recognition of system interactions. One of the difficult tasks in writing an elementary text is to convey how, in real applications, the model-building effort is oriented toward management system considerations. The results of an operations research analysis must be integrated into the management information, decision-making, and control systems fabric of the organization. Operations research applications cannot be undertaken in isolation from the surrounding managerial environment. For these reasons, an operations research project should be regarded, at least in part, as a systems effort.

IN ONE EASY LESSON

Many of the scientists who pioneered present-day applications of operations research are still alive and carry forward their individual banners of progress. One cannot help but be struck by the way each of these men treats nearly all of the significant decision-making problems he encounters by using his own specialty, such as linear programming, dynamic programming, inventory theory, or simulation, etc. This ability to apply a single solution technique or mathematical construct to a diverse range of problems—and to do so effectively—attests not only to the sheer genius of these innovators but to the flexibility of their approaches.

The experience of these scientists not withstanding, most operations research analysts, when faced with a difficult managerial decision problem, usually do not find it *self-evident* that a single solution technique or model is patently most appropriate. For example, an analysis of what markets a company should serve, what products it should manufacture, what investments it should undertake, or where it should locate its plants and warehouses rarely leads to an immediate selection of a linear programming, or a dynamic programming, or a simulation approach. This being the case, you may well wonder how you will go about building or selecting a model when faced with a particular decision problem.

We know that the notion of model-building, as described in a textbook, carries with it an aura of mystery. Regrettably, it is virtually impossible to provide you with a checklist for infallibly selecting and developing a model. But rest assured, there is considerable evidence that most students who have been trained in either the sciences, engineering, mathematics, business administration, or economics have little trouble building models in practice, provided they are inclined to do so. And nowadays, rarely, if ever, will you be faced with applying operations research unaided by an experienced practitioner. Therefore, you can count on being tutored at least the first time you use operations research.

1.5 Process of Quantitative Analysis

We outline below the stages that are standard in applying quantitative analysis. An experienced practitioner takes these steps almost instinctively, and frequently does not attach formal labels to them. Actually, and components are not entirely distinct, and at any point in time, several of the phases proceed in concert. As a beginner, however, you will find it helpful to look over the entire process seriatim, so that you can plan ahead accordingly.

A prelude to a quantitative analysis of a decision problem should be a thorough qualitative analysis. This initial diagnostic phase aims at identifying what seem to be the critical factors—of course, subsequent analysis may demonstrate that some of these factors are not actually so significant as they first appear. In particular, it is important to attain a preliminary notion of what the principal decisions are, what the measures of effectiveness are among these choices, and what sorts of tradeoffs among these measures are likely to ensue in a comparison of the alternatives. There will be trouble ahead unless you get a good "feel" for the way the problem is viewed by the responsible decision-makers. Without this appreciation, you may encounter considerable difficulty in gaining acceptance and implementing your findings. What is worse, your results could very well be erroneous or beside the point.

FORMULATING THE PROBLEM

The preceding diagnostic should yield a statement of the problem's elements. These include the controllable or decision variables, the uncontrollable variables, the restrictions or constraints on the variables, and the objectives for defining a good or improved solution.

In the formulation process, you must establish the confines of the analysis. Managerial decision-making problems typically have multifold impacts, some of them immediate and others remote (although perhaps equally significant). Determining the limits of a particular analysis is mostly a matter of judgment.

BUILDING THE MODEL

Here is where you get down to the fine detail. You must decide on the proper data inputs and design the appropriate information outputs. You have to identify both the static and dynamic structural elements, and devise mathematical formulas to represent the interrelationships among these elements. Some of these interdependencies may be posed in terms of constraints or restrictions on the variables. Some may take the form of a probabilistic evolutionary system.

You also must choose a time horizon (possibly the "never-ending future") to evaluate the selected measures of effectiveness for the various decisions. The choice of this horizon in turn influences the nature of the constraints imposed, since, with a long enough horizon, it is usually possible to remove any short-run restrictions by an expenditure of resources.

PERFORMING THE ANALYSES

Given the initial model, along with its parameters as specified by historical, technological, and judgmental data, you next calculate a mathematical solution. Frequently, a solution means values for the decision variables that optimize one of the objectives and give permissible levels of performance on any other of the objectives. The various mathematical techniques for arriving at solutions comprise much of the contents of this text.

As pointed out previously, if the formulation of the model is too complex and too detailed, then the computational task may surpass the capabilities of present-day computers. If the formulation is too simple, the solution may be patently unrealistic. Therefore, you can expect to redo some of the steps in the formulation, model-building, and analysis phases, until you obtain satisfactory results.

A major part of the analysis consists of determining the sensitivity of the solution to the model specifications, and in particular to the accuracy of the input data and structural assumptions. Because sensitivity testing is so essential a part of the validation process, you must be careful to build your model in such a way as to make this process computationally tractable.

IMPLEMENTING THE FINDINGS AND UPDATING THE MODEL

Unfortunately, most tyro management scientists fail to realize that implementation begins on the very first day of an operations research project. There is no "moment of truth" when the analyst states, "Here are my results," and the manager replies, "Aha! Now I fully understand. Thanks for giving me complete assurance about the correct decision."

We consider the entire process of implementation in Chap. 22. But we mention here the importance of having those executives who must act on the findings participate on the team that analyzes the problem. Otherwise, the odds are heavy that the project will be judged only as a provocative, but inconclusive, exercise.

It is common for an operations research model to be used repeatedly in the analysis of decision problems. Each time, the model must be revised to take account of both the specifics of the problem and current data. A good practitioner of operations research realizes that his model may have a long life, and so documents its details as well as plans for its updating.

WHAT'S IT ALL ABOUT?

Having learned the basic components of the quantitative analysis process, you should step back to see what the entire approach accomplishes.

The major effort is constructing a mathematical representation of a complicated situation, along with gathering the required data. The model is essentially approximate—elaborate enough to capture the essentials, yet gross enough to yield computable solutions. The balance between detail and tractability is found by a trial and error process, involving considerable examination of preliminary findings and extensive sensitivity analysis.

When operations research is applied in a planning context, the solution usually consists of a most favorable set of values for the decision variables, with some information as to the cost of deviating from these values. When management science is used for developing an operating system, such as a means for controlling inventories, then the solution consists of a set of decision rules.

Often, these rules are embodied in a computer program. For an inventory system, the computer routines analyze historical demand data, permit judgmental adjustments if specified, signal when replenishment is to take place and calculate the reorder amount.

Only rarely does an operations research solution represent a precise forecast of what will happen in the future. Such an accurate prediction would be of interest; but the crux of the decision problem is to select among alternatives, not to forecast. A well-built model makes a valid comparison among the alternatives. In case this distinction between accurately predicting an outcome and legitimately comparing alternatives is puzzling, consider the following illustration.

A company is about to decide whether or not to open a new plant in Europe. An operations research model is constructed that contains forecasts of sales, costs, and revenues; the resultant solution probably indicates anticipated production levels. If the economic advantage of opening this new plant is relatively insensitive to a range of reasonable values for the forecasted figures, then the company can make the correct expansion decision. It does *not* need to commit itself, at the same time, to production levels; they would be determined subsequently when more accurate demand forecasts are available.

1.6 Operations Research, Lilliputian Style

Before explaining how and why quantitative analyses have been valuable in aiding executive decision-making, we will examine a few highly simplified illustrations of operations research models. Since our only purpose is to show what mathematical decision models look like, we make no pretense abou the realism of these formulations; you will find more practical versions in the subsequent chapters.

ONE-POTATO, TWO-POTATO PROBLEM

A frozen-food company processes potatoes into packages of French fries, hash browns, and flakes (for mashed potatoes). At the beginning of the manufacturing process, the raw potatoes are sorted by length and quality, and then allocated to the separate product lines.

The company can purchase its potatoes from two sources, which differ in their yields of various sizes and quality. These yield characteristics are displayed in Fig. 1. Observe that from Source 1, there is a 20 percent yield of French fries, a 20 percent yield of hash browns, and a 30 percent yield of flakes; the remaining 30 percent is unrecoverable waste. The figures for flakes and waste are also 30 percent for potatoes from Source 2, but the yield of French fries is relatively higher.

A Conceptual Framework

FIGURE 1

Potato Yields for a Unit of Weight

Product	Source 1	Source 2	Purchase Limitations
French fries	0.2	0.3	1.8
Hash browns	0.2	0.1	1.2
Flakes	0.3	0.3	2.4
Relative Profit	5	6	

How many pounds of potatoes should the company purchase from each source? The answer depends, in part, on the relative profit contributions of the sources. These relative figures are calculated by adding the sales revenues associated with the yields for the separate products, and subtracting the costs of purchasing the potatoes, which may differ between the two sources. (We have used the term *relative profit contribution* because we are ignoring other variable expenses, such as sales and distribution costs. These depend only on the products and not the sources of the raw potatoes, and so do not affect the purchase allocation decision.) Suppose the relative profit contribution is 5 for Source 1 and 6 for Source 2. Even though Source 2 is more profitable, it does not follow that the company should purchase all of its potatoes from Source 2.

At least two other factors are relevant to the purchase decision: the maximum amount of each product that the company can sell, and the maximum amount that the company can manufacture—given its production facilities. To keep the exposition simple, suppose that the two factors, in concert, imply that the total production cannot exceed 1.8 for French fries, 1.2 for hash browns, and 2.4 for flakes, where these constants are measured in terms of an appropriate unit of weight (such as millions of pounds). These restrictions can be expressed mathematically as follows.

Let P_1 denote the amount (in weight of potatoes that will be purchased from Source 1, and P_2 the amount from Source 2. Then the values for P_1 and P_2 are constrained by the linear inequalities.

$$.2P_1 + .3P_2 \leq 1.8 \quad \text{for French fries}$$
$$.2P_1 + .1P_2 \leq 1.2 \quad \text{for hash browns}$$
$$.3P_1 + .3P_2 \leq 2.4 \quad \text{for flakes}$$
$$P_1 \geq 0 \quad \text{and} \quad P_2 \geq 0. \tag{1}$$

The nonnegativity restrictions $P_1 \geq 0$ and $P_2 \geq 0$ are imposed because a value such as $P_1 = -4$ would have no physical significance.

FIGURE 2

Feasible Purchasing Policies

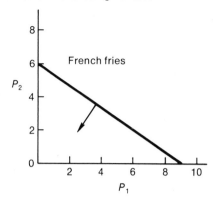

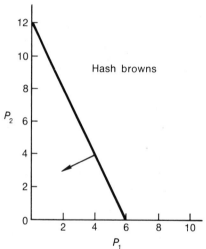

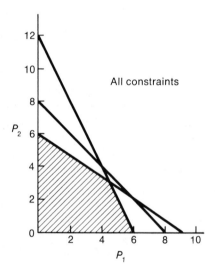

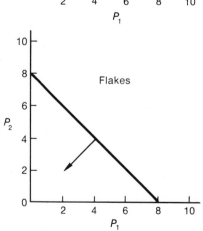

All the values for P_1 and P_2 satisfying (1) are shown in the shaded region in Fig. 2. Notice that each line in the diagram is represented by a restriction in (1) expressed as an equality. The arrow associated with each line shows the direction indicated by the inequality signs in (1). Explain why a pair of values for P_1 and P_2 that satisfies *both* the French fries and hash brown constraints will also satisfy the flakes constraint.

Optimal values for P_1 and P_2 are found by making the relative profit contribution as large as possible, consistent with the constraints. Therefore, the optimization problem is to

$$\text{maximize } (5P_1 + 6P_2) \qquad (2)$$

subject to (1). In this simple problem, the solution can be exhibited graphically, as in Fig. 3.

Each of the parallel straight-line segments represents different combinations of P_1 and P_2 that give the same value for the linear objective function $5P_1 + 6P_2$. The highest segment still having a point in the feasible constraint region is

FIGURE 3

Relative Profit

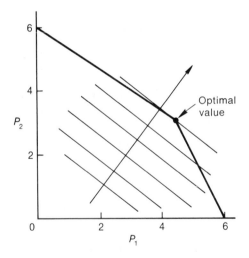

the optimal value of the objective function, and such a point is an optimal solution. You can see in Fig. 3 that there is only one optimal solution in this example; it occurs at the intersection of the French fries and hash brown constraints. Consequently, you can calculate the optimal values by solving the associated simultaneous linear equations

$$.2P_1 + .3P_2 = 1.8 \quad \text{for French fries}$$

$$.2P_1 + .1P_2 = 1.2 \quad \text{for hash browns.} \qquad (3)$$

Verify that the optimal answers are P_1 = 4.5 and P_2 = 3, as shown in Fig. 3, giving an objective-function value of 40.5.

This problem illustrates what is termed a *linear programming model.* Real applications of linear programming usually involve hundreds of constraints and thousands of variables. You will learn how to formulate and solve such models in Chaps. 2 through 7.

SECRETARY PROBLEM

An executive wishes to hire a new secretary, and is about to ask a placement service to send qualified girls for him to interview. He has found from past experience that he can determine from an interview whether a girl, if hired, will turn out to be terrific, good, or just fair. He assigns a relative value of 3 to a terrific secretary, 2 to a good one, and 1 to a fair one. His previous experience also leads him to believe that there is a .2 chance of interviewing a girl who will be a terrific secretary, a .5 chance that she will be a good one, and a .3 chance that she will be a fair one.

He wishes to see only three girls at most. Unfortunately, if he does not hire a girl immediately after an interview, she will take another job; hence, he has to decide right away.

If the first girl he sees is terrific, he will hire her immediately, of course. And if she is fair, he has nothing to lose by interviewing a second girl. But if the first girl looks good, then he is not sure what to do. If he passes her by, he may end up with only a fair secretary. Yet if he hires her, he surrenders the chance of finding a terrific girl. Similarly, if he chooses to see a second girl, he will again face a difficult decision in the event that she turns out to be good.

The selection problem can be displayed conveniently by a so-called *decision tree,* shown in Fig. 4. The circled nodes represent the interviewed girls, and the

FIGURE 4

Decision Tree for Secretary Problem

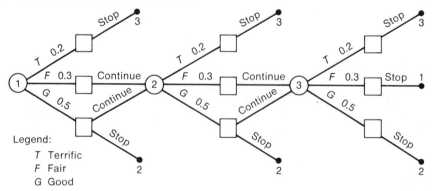

Legend:
T Terrific
F Fair
G Good

branches from these nodes show the chance events and their probabilities. The boxes indicate where a decision must be made, and the number at the end of a branch gives the relative value of stopping the decision process at that point.

The problem of finding an optimal decision strategy can be solved by what is termed *dynamic programming,* and in particular, by a process known as *backward induction.* You will study dynamic programming models and solution techniques in Chaps. 8 through 12, and Chaps. 17 and 18. The solution process is so simple in this example that you can compute the optimal hiring strategy very easily, as we have done below.

Suppose that the executive does end up interviewing, and hence hiring, a third girl. Then the expected value associated with the uncertain event is

$$3(.2) + 2(.5) + 1(.3) = 1.9. \tag{4}$$

In other words, the average value of a girl selected at random for an interview is 1.9. Assume that this expectation legitimately represents the executive's evaluation of the chancey event. Mark the number 1.9 above the circled Node 3 in Fig. 4.

Next consider what happens if the executive does interview a second girl, and she turns out to be good. If he decides to stop, then he obtains a value 2. But if he continues, then he can expect to receive only the value 1.9. So he should stop when the second girl looks good. Put an X on the branch indicating "Continue" when the second secretary is good; this signifies not to take that action.

Now you are ready to determine the correct decision if the first girl looks good. By stopping, the executive would obtain the value 2. But if he continues, then the expected value associated with the chancey outcome of the second interview, and possibly the third, is

$$3(.2) + 2(.5) + 1.9(.3) = 2.17. \tag{5}$$

The first term in (5) is for the event of seeing a terrific secretary, whom he hires; the second term is for the event of seeing a good secretary, whom he hires, as you already determined in the preceding paragraph; and the third term is for the event of seeing a fair secretary, and consequently continuing to the third chancey event that has a value of 1.9, given in (4). Since 2.17 is larger than 2, the executive should pass up the first girl if she turns out to be good. Mark 2.17 above the circled Node 2 in Fig. 4, and put an X on the branch indicating "Stop" when the first secretary is good.

To summarize, the optimal policy is to stop after the first interview only if the girl is terrific, and to continue after the second interview only if the girl is fair. The overall expected value of the interviewing process, given that the executive acts optimally, is

$$3(.2) + 2.17(.5) + 2.17(.3) = 2.336. \tag{6}$$

Explain why. Mark this number above the circled Node 1 in Fig. 4. Since the quantity 1.9 calculated in (4), also represents the expected value if the executive interviews only a single secretary and hires her, the difference (2.336−1.9=.436) is the incremental value from interviewing as many as two more girls.

WHERE-OR-WHEN PRODUCTION PROBLEM

The name of this problem arises from the observation that the associated mathematical model has several interpretations. One is in terms of deciding optimal production levels at each of several plants in a single time period; another is in terms of choosing optimal production levels at a single plant in each of several time periods. (The model also can be interpreted as a combination of the two problems, that is, as a where-and-when problem.)

Starting with the multiplant version, suppose a company has N plants, and must manufacture a total of D units of a single item during a stated time period. Hence, letting x_t denote the amount of production at Plant t, the levels x_1, $x_2, \ldots, x_n$ must satisfy the constraints

$$x_1 + x_2 + \cdots + x_N = D \quad \text{and all} \quad x_t \geq 0. \tag{7}$$

Assume that the cost of producing x_t at Plant t is given by $(1/c_t)\,x_t$, where $c_t > 0$ is known from historical accounting information. Consequently, optimal values for the x_t are those that

$$\text{minimize} \left(\frac{x_1^2}{c_1} + \frac{x_2^2}{c_2} + \cdots + \frac{x_N^2}{c_N} \right) \tag{8}$$

subject to (7).

This optimization problem can be solved by dynamic programming methods as well as by some simple nonlinear programming techniques, which are discussed in Chaps. 14 and 15. The numerical answers can be easily computed from the insightful formula

$$\text{optimal } x_1 = \frac{c_t \cdot D}{c_1 + c_2 + \cdots + c_N} \quad \text{for } t = 1, 2, \ldots, N, \tag{9}$$

which yields the associated minimum cost

$$\frac{D^2}{c_1 + c_2 + \cdots + c_N} \quad \text{(optimal policy).} \tag{10}$$

Turning to the multiperiod version, suppose you interpret x_t as being the level of production in a single plant during Period t. Notice that in this version, all the costs are due to production, and no storage costs are incurred while the units are inventoried from Period 1 to the end of Period N, when the demand requirement D must be met. Given this view, you can state what would be the optimal value for x_t if the preceding levels $x_1, x_2, \ldots, x_{t-1}$ were already determined [not necessarily by (9)], namely,

$$\text{optimal conditional } x_t = \frac{c_t \cdot (D - x_1 - x_2 - \cdots - x_{t-1})}{c_t + c_{t+1} + \cdots + c_N}$$

$$(x_1, x_2, \cdots, x_{t-1} \text{ are specified}). \qquad (11)$$

As you can verify, calculating $x_1, x_2 \ldots, x_n$ recursively (that is, successively, one by one starting with x_1 from (11) yields the same values as computing each of them from (9).

ECONOMIC ORDER QUANTITY PROBLEM

In Chaps. 9 and 19, and Appendix II you will study a variety of inventory replenishment models that have proved successful in practice. The formulation below is perhaps the simplest such model. Its precise assumptions are only rarely satisfied in real life. Nevertheless, the resultant solution turns out to be sufficiently close to optimal for many practical situations as to make it a very useful approximation.

Consider a company that consumes (or sells) an item at the rate of, say, M units per week. For simplicity, suppose there is no uncertainty about this consumption. Hence, if the inventory level is kM units, then this stock is depleted in exactly k weeks. Further, suppose the rate M is unchanging over time, so that the company must regularly place a replenishment order. The decision problem is to determine the most economical order quantity. (Assuming that the delivery time for an order is also known exactly, each replenishment action is initiated early enough so that the order arrives just when the inventory level falls to zero.)

Let the order quantity be denoted by Q. Then the level of inventory can be pictured by the sawtooth pattern shown in Fig. 5. Observe that each time a replenishment arrives, the inventory level shoots up by the order quantity Q. Then the level diminishes, as shown by the downward slope of the sawtooth, which equals $-M$.

An optimal order quantity strikes a balance between the costs associated with replenishing and withholding inventory. Specifically, assume that a fixed setup cost K is incurred each time an order is placed, that a purchase cost c is paid for each item ordered, and that a holding cost h is assessed for each unit of inventory held per week. The setup cost is related to the effort expended in placing and receiving the order. The holding cost is associated with storage, insurance, and the capital tied up in inventory.

Let the economic criterion of effectiveness be measured as average cost per

FIGURE 5

Pattern of Inventory Levels

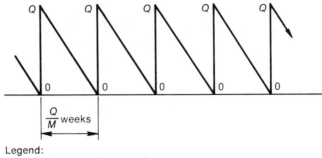

$\frac{Q}{M}$ weeks

Legend:

M demand per week

Q order quantity

week. Then the contribution due to setup costs is $K(M/Q)$, since there are M/Q setups per week. The contribution due to purchase costs is cM, since M items are consumed per week. And the contribution due to holding costs is $h(Q/2)$, since $Q/2$ is the average level of inventory, as you can see in Fig. 5. Adding the components you have

$$\text{average cost per week} \equiv AC = \frac{KM}{Q} + cM + \frac{hQ}{2}. \tag{12}$$

The economic order quantity that minimizes AC is

$$\text{optimal } Q = \sqrt{\frac{2KM}{h}}, \tag{13}$$

which can be found by setting the derivative of AC with respect to Q equal to 0, and solving for Q. It follows from (13) that the optimal order quantity only doubles when the demand rate quadruples. Also note that the optimal quantity is determined by the *ratio* of setup to holding costs.

O-R AIRLINE PROBLEM

The One-Ride Airline Company is opening a reservation service to be located in a suburban shopping center. A passenger making reservations will be able to telephone the office and state his request. The O-R Airline Company wants to decide how many telephone lines to install for answering reservation calls. It can easily compute the telephone and personnel expenses that vary with the number of lines. But it also wishes to compare the level of service for several different numbers of lines. In particular, suppose the company seeks to

9 2 3 1 3

determine the percentage of time all the lines will be busy and the average length of such busy periods.

This sort of analysis is classified as *queuing* or *waiting-line theory*, and is explained in Chaps. 20, 21, and Appendix III. We could construct an explicit model and subject it to rigorous mathematical analysis, but instead, we explain here how the method of simulation can be used to determine the service figures. To keep the explanation easy, we present only a rudimentary technique, and suggest that you read Chap. 21 for a more detailed exposition of the simulation approach.

Suppose the company obtains data showing the statistical frequencies of minutes between successive incoming telephone calls. As a first approximation, assume that these successive interval times are completely independent (such independence does not hold precisely if, for example, a passenger calls up, finds the lines busy, and immediately redials the number). A convenient way to summarize this distribution is to use a pie diagram, such as the one in Fig. 6, where we assume for simplicity that the time between incoming calls never exceeds 5 minutes.

Imagine a pointer, or spinner, affixed to the center of the pie diagram—the mechanism would look something like a wheel-of-chance at carnivals, or a device that is often included in a child's game to determine how many advances a player's piece may take at each turn. You can simulate the traffic of incoming calls by giving the pointer a succession of sharp spins, and jotting down the resultant sequence of interarrival times.

In addition, suppose the company has a frequency distribution of the number of minutes that incoming calls require. Assume that these service times are independent of each other and of the interarrival times. Then another pie

`FIGURE 6`

The Distribution of Telephone Interarrival Times.

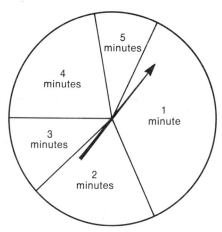

diagram and spinner mechanism can be constructed for generating the service times.

You are now ready to simulate the system. To begin, suppose there is only a single telephone line. Then a simulated history may look like that in Fig. 7. The instants of incoming calls are recorded with X's on the time axis, and are determined by successive spins of the pointer mechanism for interarrival times. The telephone line becomes busy as soon as the first call arrives. The length of the busy period is determined by a spin of the pointer mechanism for service times. Notice that the calls arriving at the instants circled in Fig. 7 are not answered because the single telephone line is busy. You can obtain a good estimate of the percentage of time the line will be busy and the average length of a busy period by calculating the corresponding statistics for a fairly long simulated run.

Suppose next that there are two telephone lines. Then the same sequence of incoming calls can lead to a service history like that in Fig. 8. Observe that more incoming calls are answered. Here a busy period is defined to be a length of time

FIGURE 7

Simulated History for One Telephone Line

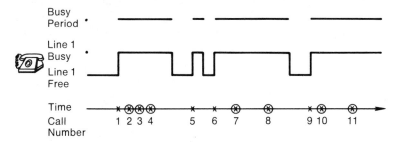

FIGURE 8

Simulated History for Two Telephone Lines

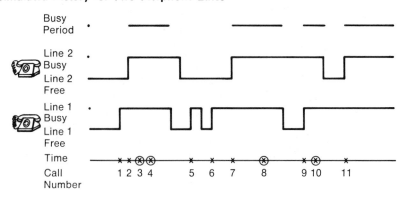

A Conceptual Framework

during which both telephone lines are tied up. Note how these periods are shorter in Fig. 8 than in Fig. 7 for the particular history. As you can see, the same approach can be used to estimate service for any number of lines.

COMMENTARY

As we stated at the beginning of this section, the above examples illustrate how mathematical models are constructed to analyze decision problems. We have made no attempt to be "realistic" in these examples. But as you continue reading this book, you will discover how to build practical models, and learn way to solve problems with them.

1.7 At the End of the Rainbow

Today, virtually every major corporation employs personnel who are responsible for applying operations research. Usually, these people constitute a staff group at headquarters level. The group often reports to the controller, the chief financial officer, or the head of corporate planning; but with growing frequency, companies are also assigning operations researchers to report directly to line managers. In a parallel fashion, operations research activity has enjoyed a widespread growth within federal and local governments, as well as in other nonprofit organizations. This section tells why management science has succeeded so well.

MERITS OF A RATIONAL PROCESS

Obviously, executives must and do make decisions all the time. For a particular situation, an operations research model *may* yield the very same conclusion that an experienced manager would arrive at solely on intuitive grounds. Therefore, the benefits of using operations research have to be evaluated in terms of its long-run impact on the entire managerial process.

The proper comparison is well represented by the question, "If a company does not use operations research to guide the decision process, then what will it use, and will the answers be consistently as good?" Corporations that apply operations research—even when the approach does not meet all of the company's initial expectations—find that analyzing complicated managerial problems this way is a sounder method than traditional means. This assertion is amply borne out by the steadily increasing support given to operations research in both the private and public sectors.

Qualities inherent in this particular rational approach make it a valuable method, regardless of whether a company's operations research personnel attain the highest level of accomplishment for a specific project. These benefits include:

—Emphasis on assessing the system-wide interactions and ramifications of decision alternatives. Intrinsic in an operations research approach is the construction of a model that synthesizes the segments of an enterprise that are affected by a decision choice. Each individual part is constructed by personnel who are the most knowledgeable about the relevant data.

—Impetus to developing a full range of decision alternatives. The number of action possibilities that can be analyzed increases tremendously by the application of mathematics and computers.

—Focus on resolving the critical issues. The approach proceeds in the fashion of establishing implications of the form, "if Hypothesis H is true and Action A is taken, then Result R will occur." The method fosters interdepartmental communication. As a consequence, clashes of opinion within an organization can be sorted into disagreements over the probable truth of different hypotheses, and over the assumptions used in deriving the implications of different actions.

Important ancillary benefits emerge from the direction provided by the model for gathering data, quantifying the value of additional information, and documenting factual knowledge that may be required in subsequent decision analyses.

Having listed several of the important merits stemming from the rational analytic process of operations research, we hasten to point out that the advantages will occur to a greater or lesser degree, depending on the skill used in carrying out the study.

MANAGERIAL CUTTING EDGE

The preceding paragraphs dealt with *why* operations research is helpful in analyzing decision problems. Now we discuss *how* the approach is beneficial. We have classified the ways into four somewhat arbitrary and partially overlapping categories:

i. Better decisions. Frequently, operations research models yield actions that do improve on intuitive decision-making. A situation may be so complex (because of intricate interrelationships among decisions, voluminous data pertinent to operations, and uncertainties of market activity) that the human mind can never hope to assimilate all the significant factors without the aid of operations-research-guided computer analysis.

Of course, in the past, managers have made decisions in these situations without the aid of operations research. They had to. But the depth of their understanding and the quality of their decisions improve with the application of such models, as considerable experience has shown. Particular decisions may ultimately turn out to be wrong, but the improved decision-making process reduces the risk of making such erroneous decisions.

ii. Better coordination. Sometimes operations research has been instrumental in bringing order out of chaos. The following example, drawn from an actual application, illustrates what can happen.

During special campaigns, a food manufacturer runs advertising that significantly increases sales volume. But manufacturing production facilities are limited, the supply of the foodstuff is limited, and the sales response is often erratic. In the past, consequently, the marketing and manufacturing divisions have been at opposite poles in terms of cooperative actions. An operations-research-oriented planning model becomes a vehicle for coordinating marketing decisions within the limitations imposed on manufacturing capabilities.

iii. Better control. The managements of large organizations recognize that it is extremely costly to require continuous executive supervision over routine decisions. Operations research approaches combining historical experience with the scientific method have resulted in standardized and reliable procedures for handling everyday activities and for signaling dangerous trends. Executives have thereby gained new freedom to devote their attention to more pressing matters, except for those unusual circumstances which, when they arise, necessitate reviewing the course of everyday action. The most frequently adopted applications in this category deal with production scheduling and inventory replenishment.

iv. Better systems. Often, an operations research study is initiated to analyze a particular decision problem, such as whether to open a new warehouse. Afterwards, the approach is further developed into a system to be employed repeatedly. Thus the cost of undertaking the first application may produce benefits that are longer lasting than originally envisioned.

WHERE THE ACTION IS

By this time, applications of operations research are so common in industry and government, and so diverse in the functional areas of decision-making, that we cannot hope to provide a complete survey. To give you some idea, however, we mention that there are numerous applications in industries such as aircraft, apparel, chemicals, cement, glass, computers, electronics, farm and industrial machinery, food, metal manufacturing and products, mining, motor vehicles, paper and wood products, petroleum refining, and pharmaceuticals, as well as in commercial banks, insurance companies, merchandising firms, public utilities, and transportation companies.

Depending on the industry, the applications pertain to extraction of natural resources, manufacturing, transportation and warehousing, plant size and location, inventory management, scheduling of men and machines, forecasting, new product development, marketing, advertising, cash management and finance, portfolio management, mergers, and both short- and long-range corporate planning.

Most companies' early operations research projects deal with monthly or quarterly scheduling, annual planning, inventory control, and other fairly well-defined areas of decision-making. After the operations research group demonstrates its capability in these areas, a company then applies its operations research talents to the study of high-level strategic problems, such as selecting new plant sites, entering new markets, acquiring overseas affiliates, and so forth.

Operations research has provided a significant advance in the techniques of long-range strategic planning. Even senior executives have difficulty piecing together all the important considerations involved in a well-designed long-range plan. What is more, the operations research approach lends itself to the formulation of contingency plans, that is, a complete strategy indicating which courses of action are appropriate for various future events. In addition, the findings may include directions for obtaining and then utilizing critical information about such future events. In this way, the operations research model suggests the actions to be taken immediately and the ones to be postponed, and when to undertake a reassessment. For these reasons, more and more frequently, boards of directors of large corporations find strategic proposals being justified on the basis of extensive operations research studies.

PROFITABLE APPLICATIONS IN NONPROFIT ORGANIZATIONS

The growth of operations research in government and nonprofit corporations has been phenomenal. A long succession of military applications began during World War II. Now governmental applications involve health, education, and welfare; air and highway traffic control; air and water pollution; police and fire protection; voter and school redistricting; and annual planning and budgeting by program, to name only a few.

Certainly, much of the credit for the great impetus in the adoption of operations research in the public sector goes to the RAND Corporation (located in Santa Monica). Many fundamental concepts and techniques in operations research can be traced to the innovative ideas of RAND scientists. At present, there are several other research organizations similar to RAND serving the Federal Government; a number of these (RAND among them) work on state and city management problems as well as on military projects.

How different is operations research applied in the public sector from that used in the private sector? The answer depends on the aspects of operations research you are considering. Specifically, the problem-solving characteristics, the ensuing benefits, the emphasis on model-building, the limitations of the scientific method, and the analytic process discussed above, all hold with equal validity in applications to governmental and nonprofit organizations.

There does seem to be a noticeable difference, however, in the sorts of solution techniques used. For example, linear programming has gained widespread acceptance in industry, but is employed only occasionally in governmental planning. The opposite has been true of simulation models.

Sometimes it is claimed that the lack of clear-cut objective functions to be optimized in nonprofit organizations raises a significant difference between applications in the private and public sectors. Industry most often measures improvement in terms of contribution to profit, but this criterion is by no means the only relevant one for decision-making. Businesses are always compromising among different objectives. Therefore, we feel that the absence of a profit measure is less important than it might seem at first glance.

Probably the most important difference between the public and private sectors concerns the exercise of decision-making responsibilities. The organizational structures of big corporations are complex, and the authority for taking actions may not always be precisely defined. But these structures are simple indeed in comparison with most governmental structures. The difference can be stated this way. In a commercial company, there is no one left to pass the buck to, once the necessity for making a decision reaches top management (or the board of directors). In an organization such as the Federal Government, even the President's decisions are subject to the review of—and thus become partly the responsibility of—Congressmen, who, along with the President, are publicly elected. Understand that diffuse responsibilities and authority only make it *difficult* to apply operations research outside of industry. As the record shows, plenty of applications are being made in governmental and nonprofit organizations.

1.8 In the Beginning . . .

Studying linear optimization models is an excellent way to begin learning about operations research. Hence, this subject is taken up in the next chapter and several to follow. As you read about linear and other models throughout the text, try to keep in mind the boundaries and the process of quantitative analysis (which we discussed in Secs. 1.3 and 1.4). By so doing, you will maintain a perspective on the strengths and limitations of operations research.

HAROLD J. LEAVITT

Organizational Behavior, 1969

Mason asked for an overview of the field, and an overview he shall have; a highly personal and subjective one, which will probably cost me my entire idiosyncrasy credit account.

This overview, to mix my first metaphor, shall have four movements. The first two are sort of Russian; nostalgic, romantic, tragic, and too long. The last two are American; challenging, gauche, short.

Part I, I shall call Childhood and Adolescence: The Stunted Growth of Organizational Behavior.

Part II bears a Churchillian title: Ideology and Protagonism, the fighting years.

Part III: the Years of Relativism, OB's tolerant, moderate, understanding middle age.

Part IV: Out of the Black Box, OB as a menopausal astronaut.

The authors wish to extend special thanks to H. J. Leavitt for permission to reprint this paper, which was presented as an invited lecture at the February, 1969, M.I.T. Seminar in the Behavioral Sciences in Management, chaired by Mason Haire. Because this is, to our knowledge, the first major distribution of this lecture, the authors reserve full responsibility for all typographical and other editorial errors herein.

Part I: The Stunted Growth of OB

Now seems to be a plateau time, indeed a down time in our field. It is not a down time insofar as the problems before us are concerned. There are plenty of those; richer, tougher ones than were ever around before; racial problems, campus problems, international problems; problems of adaptation to change and creation of change. But it is not a time in which we are rich in *ideas*. It is not, in my opinion, a creative time.

The late forties, after the war, were a creative time, especially right here at M.I.T. There was lots of excitement, lots of ideas. McGregor, Knickerbocker, Bavelas and Haire had something good going. And across the campus Kurt Lewin and Company had good things going, too.

One idea that came out of all that was the idea of the *group* as a rich and viable unit for study and manipulation. A related one was the idea of *participation*. And with some outside inputs, Bethel was one of the applied children of those ideas.

There must have been a period like that around the Harvard Business School two decades earlier when Mayo and Roethlisberger were rediscovering the psyches of blue-collar workers.

I was lucky enough to hit the same kind of excitement in quite a different realm, ten years later at Carnegie Tech; when March and Simon, with strong assists from Cooper and Modigliani, began to look at organizations psychologically, but also systematically and analytically. Each of those exciting groups seemed to last for one or two graduate student generations. Then their original leadership either dissipated or was institutionalized into the establishment. They continue to live, but as suburbians, not bohemians. That phenomenon should not surprise us. Dissident subgroups on large institutions almost always have to hit and run before the institutional tide imbibes them.

I smelled the M.I.T. excitement in those early days—even from an isolated spot in the Navy a thousand miles away. Then I smelled out Carnegie Tech in time to climb onto that bandwagon. So I have come to the immodest conclusion that my nose for exciting ideas may be pretty sensitive. Right now I can't smell any very exciting ideas. It isn't the excitement that's missing. Just the ideas. There are several places where people are excited. There's excitement at Irvine, at Vanderbilt, at S.M.U., at Texas. There was some at Case a few years ago; there's a lot at U.C.L.A. But so far it's not clear that major pregnant new ideas have been bubbling up in the '60's at any of those. As one of our graduate students touring the job market put it: "This year there seem to be only two kinds of schools, exciting ones and good ones."

Once, before the Leavitts built a house in Pittsburgh, we borrowed a collection of old architectural annals showing prize-winning houses of the thirties, forties, and fifties. An astonishingly high proportion of those prizewinners looked absolutely grotesque by the sixties. There were only a very few creative designs that appeared retrospectively to have been the seed of good contemporary architecture. Most of the others had apparently led down culs de sac.

Correspondingly, it seemed appropriate for this seminar to look back over the relevant organizational annuals in search of those seminal ideas that seem really to have borne fruit in our field. And that thought led immediately to the question of criteria; criteria of fruitfulness.

Arbitrarily, I established three: First, has the idea generated research activity? Has it sent graduate students scurrying off to try new experiments or field studies? Some of you may no longer value that criterion very highly. I do. Because ideas that influence graduate students have a high probability of influencing the world. And because journal articles are still an important means for communicating ideas.

The second criterion: Has the idea influenced practice? Do managers, workers, administrators behave differently as a consequence of this idea? Are organizations operated differently? Are they designed differently? Are there new roles in organizations, new specialists as a consequence of these ideas?

And the third is a much more personal criterion. Have these ideas influenced *me*? Do I think about them when I encounter problems? When I consult with organizations? Or when I try simply to understand the nature of organizational and social problems that I encounter in my own life?

When, very unsystematically, I apply these criteria retroactively to Human Relations, or Industrial Social Psychology, or Organizational Behavior, a short list of ideas passes through all three screens. Maybe some of you will want to challenge the items included on the list, or point out significant oversights. But these are the ones that occurred to me:

1. The idea of participation. This big idea came out of the Roethlisberger, McGregor, Lewin complex. It's one of the two big ideas that were generating excitement at M.I.T. in the late forties.

2. The second was a related idea that soon led to a technology. It was the idea of the group as a viable unit. Conceptually this idea was coupled almost from the start with the idea of participation. The group idea was mostly not really about the group, but about the individual-in-the-group. Technically it led to tools for manipulating groups to modify that man-group relationship, and to tools by which the group could be placed in the service of the individual. The T-group mechanism was one of its major engineering fruits.

Since 1946 or so, we've been refining and elaborating those two ideas. They have been elaborated differently in different places. More puristic social psychologists have tried to describe, measure, predict individual behavior in groups. Ren Likert's most recent book is one good example of a more applied, more engineer-like refinement and elaboration. So is the organizational development

A Conceptual Framework

movement with Dick Beckhard and TRW and a growing collection of other organizations and individuals.

These two ideas fit all three criteria quite satisfactorily for me. They have strongly influenced research directions in psychology and administration. They have influenced managerial practice, significantly changing the ways that many managers view their jobs, and some new specialists are at work within organizations to do precisely this kind of intraorganizational work.

My guess is that the organizational effects of these activities have been massive. Of course, it would still be nice to see a clever graduate student try to measure, comparatively, the quantity of participation at U.S. Steel in 1938 as compared with 1968, with appropriate corrections for size and technology. I think the difference between then and now would be very great, but I'm not perfectly sure.

As for the third criterion, it is clear that the group-participation ideas have influenced me. I talk about them, teach students about them, talk to managers about them, think about them in my family and in day-to-day relations with my fellows. They have also now become a kind of thorough-bass accompaniment to my thinking about complicated social research problems.

Those two ideas got their big start in the late forties. What have we had since then? Probably nothing of equivalent size and scope. But we have had several smaller fish that pass through all three nets.

3. Alex Bavelas, here, came up with the communication networks notion in the very late forties. Certainly that stimulated research, more than a hundred papers. The effect of that work on practice has been limited. But by indirection it has been influential, especially since the ideas are partially consonant with some of the ideas of participation. For me personally, networks-generated ideas have been very important. They have led me more and more to a position of relativism about what is organizationally right. They have made me less a protagonist, more an analyst, for they carried some new seeds, different from the slightly earlier group-participation seeds. They were structural experiments, indicating that formal structure could significantly affect both task behavior and relationships, and that structure was susceptible to systematic analysis and manipulation. But the network idea has *not* led to an applied technology in any way comparable to the T-group.

4. Then Abe Maslow came along in the early fifties with the almost too simplistic notion of the need hierarchy. That small modification of Freud and Murray carried an inordinate impact on the thinking and practice of people working in our field. It did not, did it, stimulate much research? It has not had very significant impact on the way I think about motivation, although it did not pass me unnoticed. Yet here my third criterion wavers, for I know it has much influenced my colleagues and students, and the self-actualization part of the idea, more even than the hierarchy, seems really to have taken hold.

A whole series of other ideas about work satisfaction and motivation should perhaps be mentioned at about this point; but since I profess neither objectivity nor thoroughness in this analysis, and since my third personal criterion is really the first on my information processing list, I shall ignore them.

5. The next highly significant idea emerged in the later fifties, relatively unheralded within our field: Sherif's Robbers' Cave experiments. Bob Blake was the person who introduced me to those ideas with his imaginative variations on them in laboratory training programs. That work was extremely stimulating and thought-provoking, perhaps because conflict between groups was becoming pressingly apparent in our society. But even more important than its social salience, was its emphasis on the group as a unit, rather than on the group as a collection of individuals. What the intergroup competition studies have burned into me more deeply even than the networks experiments is the potential predictability of *group* behavior, in this case because of the presence of other groups, almost regardless of the individual composition of the groups. Studies of intergroup relations generated a different level of thinking, a different set of units. One could now think operationally about communities of groups. Those studies began to get me out of my individual-in-the-group hang-up. And that has been a major hang-up in our field. Now we could begin to think of complex organizations, not as awesomely complex networks of individuals, almost impossible to analyze, but as communities of interacting groups. Not only are the numbers of units thus reduced, but we can get past problems of personality variance. Even more important, we can begin to see the organization as a political system, as a set of interacting power groups, rather than as a massive collection of individuals albeit packaged in work groups.

6. Somewhere in those late fifties, Leon Festinger extrapolated from balance theory and came up with his cognitive dissonance ideas. Whether cognitive dissonance theory is really a theory or not isn't the big issue. It is important and creative, whatever it is. It has *really* generated Ph.D dissertations, in hordes. It has been a stimulant to practice-related research on reward systems and other organizational problems. And on the third criterion, I find myself "explaining" social problems to my children (and myself) by calling upon cognitive dissonance. And again, speaking personally, cognitive dissonance theory, like the intergroup work, like the networks work, supported my accelerating movement away from the notion that participation is *it*, toward a more relativistic position.

7. Off on the periphery of OB, at about the same time, Dave McClelland made a connection between his not very exciting need achievement ideas and the issue of economic development. And that connection proved to be a rich one. It wasn't the world's neatest research, but it was bubbling with ideas and implications. McClelland took us back to the individual again, but started people in several countries worrying about how to increase achievement motivation. And I

find myself calling upon McClelland's ideas in an attempt to understand national differences in organizational styles, in attitudes toward entrepreneurship, and in administrative behavior generally.

It's been difficult to reconcile McClelland with the values we associate with participation and laboratory training. McClelland's entrepreneurial go-gettem flavor doesn't match well with the more diffident let's-hold-hands-and-respect-one-another orientation of the participative literature of the past. Most social scientists just don't seem to like people with very high achievement needs. But it looks real to me, and sooner or later we're going to have to connect McClelland's finding into the system. When we do I think it will emphasize further the relativistic notion that many roads can lead to heaven.

8. Herb Simon and Jim March and later Cyert and March, began to kick up their heels in the late fifties, too. Theirs was a different base altogether. They had come out of political science; they were strongly committed scholars and researchers; and they were unquestionably more analysts than protagonists. Their cold, analytic effort to propositionalize descriptions of organizational systems must rate high on any list of pregnant ideas, close in its long-run influence to the idea of participation. But it was really a methodology and an orientation they offered, more than a substantive set of ideas about organizations. The methodology included simulation. The orientation—as I view it—had two parts. First, the decision-making process of the individual could be behaviorally analyzed. Second, the organization could be viewed as a complex, large, self-regulating dynamic set of interrelated subsystems, almost as an organism whose behavior could be studied in its totality via its exchanges with its environment. For me, theirs was an enriching, multisided view.

The March and Simon orientation stirred up research. Dissertations, damn good ones, came pouring out of Carnegie Tech, and several other schools. But if they have influenced administrative practice, the influence has been much more subtle, via a much more devious route. McGregor carried the word directly to the manager and caused the manager to change his behavior. Most managers have never heard of March or Simon. Executive programs seldom teach their stuff. If there is impact, it comes through changes in the approach of staff specialists, of technicians, or researchers, and via the new generation of more analytic MBA's. Its influence has also shown up much more via its connections with the social movement of Management Science than with the social movement of Participative Management, via the development of simulation techniques and heuristic programming, on the shoulders of computer technology. It has influenced the technology of management much more than the art, the staff much more than the line.

I seldom even remember a proposition from March and Simon. Yet I look over my shoulder at their approach very often, at their treatment of the organization as a complex, functioning system, susceptible to analysis, description, and prediction. And they have led me even more firmly toward organizational polytheism. There are many good gods; many paths to many organizational nirvanas.

Now all the ideas we have just talked about showed up in 1958 or earlier. Yet that's the end of the major American list. Am I just getting old, or have organizational behaviorists really not turned out anything comparable since '58?

I've got a short B list:

How about Fiedler's contingency model of leadership? But Fiedler really started that one in the fifties. It has stimulated research alright. It's beginning now to have significant effect on practice. And it pleases me because of its relativistic emphasis, even though I think it's probably overly simple and perhaps wrong. Fiedler not only argues for several routes to leadership heaven, but indeed, that the routes aren't free alternatives. They are constrained by the local environment.

Maybe the human resources accounting program at Michigan, stimulated by Ren Likert, will turn out to be a great new idea. I think the probabilities are moderate. But certainly the broader work on social indicators looks very rich.

Then there's a new kind of work in the March and Simon, or at least the analytic tradition, that won't bust the field wide open but may move us way beyond our present boundaries, the kind of simulations that Haire and Miller are doing in manpower models. But those kinds of computer-assisted analytic approaches seem, for the moment at least, almost orthogonal to problems of organization as we have viewed them in the past: They are bypassing the old field rather than changing it.

What else? Where are the ideas? Maybe they are across the sea?

Part II: Ideology and Protagonism

So Kurt Lewin and others taught us about groups and about participation. And we have elaborated and applied those ideas through laboratory training and organizational development. And we also developed an ideology. Partially our enemies forced us to develop it by pooh-poohing us; partially we were self-selected from a population of do-gooders; partially we simply supported what we had helped to create, just as participative theory predicted we would. The ideology values individuals and individual autonomy and creativity and growth. It values change in individuals and groups. It views organized organizations as constrainers of the individual and therefore as basically bad. It prefers disorganized organizations. We found a series of temporary and phony solutions to the individual freedom vs. organizational productivity dilemma, first by arguing that morale generates productivity, then that the dilemma only holds for authoritarian organizations. Participative organizations really maximize individual autonomy rather than constrain it. In a *good* group, group standards aren't constraints on freedom, they *are* freedom. Antichrist is Christ, so we can sin without guilt.

At first we began to say productivity isn't as important as we thought. What's it all for? Let's go the people route. That set of thoughts in some sense set us free of our ancillary status as organizational procurers and manipulators in the service of traditional robber-baron organizational goals. We were helped, too, by technological evolution and economic expansion that caused even robber barons to worry more—at higher organizational levels—about people.

Then some of us pushed our values much further, and essentially chose one side of the dilemma. Academia is overorganized and constraining and counter-creative with its ideas about publications and scientific standards, and examinations, so screw all that. We'll call upon existentialism for any minimal intellectual support we need to escape from intellectual rules. The T-group gives way to the encounter group; the encounter group goes public; let everybody do his thing, so who needs special skills? At this point we don't even need intellectual support. We have social support from an itchy youth. And the new Mid-peninsula Free University offers 46 courses in encounter. Only the names of the course leaders are listed, not their credentials; credentials are too straight to communicate, even though many of the encounter groups are about how to get rid of hang-ups in communication.

But that's an ideological side road; a diversion. The main organizational thrust is to make organizations participative, no longer just for productivity, but for humanity. We oscillate between changing ideology in the face of reality and changing reality. Yugoslav professors Mason and I met last summer spent a lot of their time showing how a market economy is really Marxist, and less of their time changing the economy to something more like the Marxism that existed before the Marxism was changed to make it consonant with the economy. We move from an ideology of happiness for productivity to happiness for humanity's sake, to a more socially realistic ideology of authenticity, and some of us move on to an ideology of Joy for the hell of it.

Indeed, many of us have become so preoccupied with ideological issues, supported by our society's instability, that we have become less and less concerned with understanding the nature of organizations, or with possible alternative ways of building them. Instead we want to make over organizations in the image of ourselves.

But that brings us to another important subpoint about ideology. We value individual freedom; we value democracy. But I, at least, still don't know exactly what we mean. We used to define our ideology by defining our enemies. Authority was an enemy. So we wanted to rid the world of autocracy. To the extent that we could make organizations less authoritarian we felt we had moved in the direction we wanted to go. We have never yet very satisfactorily specified how far down that road we want to go.

But perhaps we have begun to learn and grow here, too. I know some notes of optimism are dissonant right here, but they add color and counterpoint. Maslow is positive. He isn't just against autocracy. He's for self-actualization. Organizational development is positive. Efforts at intergroup conflict resolution are positive, searching for new behaviors instead of urging only the abandonment of old. Perhaps we have begun to grow.

The behavioral science of organizations has, I think, carried a third value, a value for emotionality and against intellectual*ization* (which we have occasionally argued is not the same as intellectual*lism*). At first we argued, for example, that unexpressed emotions in groups interfered with the reasoning process. Hence, one should release emotional expression, clear the emotional air, to permit reasonable problem-solving to occur. This sensible hypothesis was derived in part from earlier Freudian discoveries about the effects of catharsis, in part from developments like nondirective counseling, and in part from direct rediscovery in T-groups.

But since then I think some of us have generalized that idea into an unwarranted and overly simple dichotomy, an intellectual versus emotional dichotomy. And we know which side we are on, the emotional side. Current education is too intellectual; it is emotionally impoverishing. Let's not be intelligent, let's be meaningful. Let's not be right, let's be beautiful. Somehow, some of that position appears to argue, if the affective is good, the cognitive must be bad. I don't know whether the extensions of that line are as frequent here as they are along the San Andreas fault. There they continue into the idea that the natural state of man is infancy—all affect and impulse. All other states of man, especially intellectual adulthood, are unnatural and wicked states, sort of like smog.

Part III: Relativism

This is the first happy movement. But it's quiet, it doesn't swing. I have just said we are behaving badly. But we are growing up. We are coming into an era of quiet relativism. It's happened before to other fields. Return with me now to Hugo Munsterberg describing industrial psychology and its possibilities at Harvard in 1913. He had fire in his eye; visions of sugar plums; but it was all generated by, of all things, selection tests. "Still more important," he wrote, "than the valued commercial profit on both sides is the cultural gain that will come to the total economic life of the nation, as soon as everyone can be brought to the place where his best energies may be unfolded and his greatest personal satisfaction secured. The economic experimental psychology offers no more inspiring ideas than this adjustment of work and psyche by which mental dissatisfactions with the work, mental depression and discouragement, may be replaced in our social community with overflowing joy and perfect inner harmony."

A Conceptual Framework

And did we envision less for participative management? Didn't we project the whole man, what Drucker called "the industrial citizen," emerging from the energetic application of our participative notions to organizations? But the partisans of other new ideas thought they had the world by the tail, too, and they too increased their followings thereby. Jesus Christ almost did it! Frederick W. Taylor was sure scientific management would save the world. How about your old neighbor, Tim Leary?

But let me not denigrate the man with fire in his eye. He may not save the world, but he sure changes it. And we have changed it, too.

But as it must to all innovations, the end comes to protagonism and the end is hastened by the abrasiveness of reality tests. The process of integrating our ideas with other ideas then begins; a time to find our place in a world in which other ideas have places, too; and a time to put the several together in new ways.

It's been a slow process, perhaps because it has been so easy in our case to find enemies against whom to take our strong normative position. Right here at M.I.T. over in building 1, we carried on the battle in the old days. On the third floor Truth was ensconced, embodied in McGregor, and Knickerbocker, and Bavelas and Haire. And way down at the lower levels, where it belonged, lay the traditional, the classical department of Business and Engineering Administration. Accountants and industrial engineers and methods men lurked down there. Verily the children of Satan. We fought them in the corridors and in the stair wells; and as we fought, the justness, indeed the greatness of our cause became ever more obvious.

But in a period that will live in infamy, the computer nuts and the quantitative types launched a surprise attack, and from the rear, yet. As these new insensitive, imperceptive, emotionally impoverished but intellectually and materially well-equipped hordes set upon us, they, of course, drove us more deeply into our beliefs.

But even our own "colleagues" soon turned upon us. Old-fashioned industrial psychologists attacked us, and experimental rats fled to their laboratories, shunning us, and even worse, refusing to hire our graduate students.

We even bifurcated amongst ourselves. The first time I had ever gone to Bethel, I came back through Boston to chat with Doug McGregor and Alex Bavelas in Doug's office. They interrogated me about my experience at Bethel. And an interrogation it was. It was not an inquiry. A few years later Doug joined the cause, but Alex hasn't yet—and believe me, he isn't about to.

As our ingroup was forcibly formed, so was our protagonism. The protagonism led us to experimentation and exploration. And that was good, except that much of our search was for support as much as for truth. And that was bad. Indeed, we were led, consciously or unconsciously, to train our students more and more narrowly. As an external observer of this Sloan School, for example, it seemed to me for a while that young men were almost being kept away from the other large and clearly relevant resources available here. But the rest of us are not blameless. Recently at Stanford, a couple of our graduate students shocked me when they raised the same point. They felt their training was far too limited, that it permitted too little opportunity for them to explore the rest of our great university. They are right. And we had better change.

But take heart. This old man is relativistic. He thinks the field is growing old with him. He thinks we are shifting from a strongly protagonistic position to a position of relativism; to a gradual recognition that we are not alone in wisdom; and even to the heresy that there may be some secondary negative consequences to some of the seed we have thus far sown.

What are the signs of this relativism?

First, we have rediscovered Great Britain. Joan Woodward will talk with you later. She has been quietly suggesting for a long time that task has something to do with the way we organize. And Burns and Stalker offered some relativistic ideas too. Indeed, the British have a long history of broad field research that forces the researcher into contact with task and technology and other organizational variables, that we have oversimplified in our laboratory experiments and actively ruled out in our counseling and laboratory training traditions. They have been using a wide angle lens for a long time. The organizational Church of England is catholic.

Then Fred Fiedler offered a model of leadership not only more complicated but more sensible than the old trait view, and also more complicated and sensible than our popular functional view that there ain't no leaders, just functions; and that those ought to be spread out to minimize the possibility that a powerful leader-person might arise.

Bob Blake has gone relativistic too, but in a highly protagonistic way. By setting up a two-dimensional scheme, he wants executives to attend to people, but also to task, and thinks that the two are in no way mutually exclusive.

Lawrence and Lorsch also published a very relativistic book recently, again asserting that organizational form varies with task and environmental conditions. And some of us have even been striving to understand and integrate our ideas with systems peoples' ideas, and with management scientists' ideas. We have moved toward relativism, too, when we added an intergroup focus. Perhaps we can now even begin to talk about the use of power in organizations without revulsion.

My nose says we are becoming relativistic, that even the practitioners amongst us are beginning to consider alternative ways of effecting change in organizational system. But I only smell relativism in a few places, and faintly at that.

Part IV: Out of the Black Box

Having attacked protagonists, herewith some protagonism. There's no pizazz in relativism. It's middle-aged, tolerant, old-fashioned, liberal. It says that hard-working people in diverse fields tend to develop useful ideas. They usually end up being less useful than each builder's projections, but useful nevertheless. The ideas sooner or later meet and are cut and fitted to one another. Together they provide net additions to both understanding and skill. The people you will be meeting in this series have done a good deal of such net adding.

Now where do we go from here? Where shall we prospect if we want to go on past consolidation and refinement to newer ideas. I think we should climb out of the black box into organizational outer space. I think we should, I think we have to. We have to because that's where the next generation of organizational problems lies. We should because that's also where some key new ideas must surely lie.

We have to because it is becoming so patently obvious that new pressures are arising at the interface between the organization and its environment; between organizations and government, organizations and social groups, organizations and organizations. Because some problems are extremely pressing, it is obvious too that we must use existing tools and ideas where we can; that we cannot act like academic dilettantes—at least not entirely.

But here let me support what may appear to be one sort of dilettantism. Let's not devote all our resources directly to the crises of our times. Let's not push all the panic buttons; not yet. We ought to hold out a few reserves. There will be other crises ahead.

Many of the problems are ecological. We don't know much about organizational ecology, and maybe we have time to learn. Maybe, that is, we should work on the organization's relationship with its environment in a middle-range as well as a short-range way. Maybe not all of us should leap to the seductive barricades of the immediately here and now pressing social problems. Let's some of us try to work at the conceptual interface between organizations and their environments. Maybe conceptualizing the organization in its environment will add new ideas and new tools to our repertoire; ideas and tools better fitted than those we must now adapt from intraorganizational work to extraorganizational. I think there is great promise here. By studying groups we learned about their individual members. By studying interaction among groups we learned a great deal about groups. By looking at organizations in interaction with other organizations and other institutions I think we can learn about organizations as *social* organizations, in ways we have never learned about them before.

Indeed, retrospectively it seems inconceivable to me that we have looked so little at the organization in its social setting; that we have thus far taken such an exclusively micro view of organizations. Can you think of a major piece of research on interorganizational behavior? I think the predominately psychological roots of most of us is the big reason for our position. Our great leaders, after all, were Lewin and McGregor and Rogers and Maslow. Psychologists all; starting from a concern with nature of man—in the singular. We have built from the individual outward, painfully, to dyads, to groups, to organizations; in contrast to our colleagues in sociology and economics who started elsewhere, looking at societies and institutions first.

Indeed, the study of the economics of the firm is almost a mirror image of the study of the psychology of the firm. Economists treated the firm as an entity quite early, and considered the behavior of hypothetical firms in interaction with other hypothetical firms in the market place. In the development of oligopoly theory they dealt only with the firm's decisions in the market, assuming that the firm behaves like a single rational organism, not asking even hypothetically about the insides, about the microprocesses through which market decisions would develop. But then Simon and Cyert and March pushed economics *into* the organizational black box; demonstrating relationships between internal organizational processes and outside decisions, opening a more micro examination of the firm. I propose it is time for us to do the converse; to climb out, conceptually, asking what psychological forces on the outside contribute to the workings of the inside.

It is time, I think, for us to join hands with sociologists or to develop our own organizational sociology, to consider the organization in situ; to ask how organizations affect one another; how they communicate with one another; how changes in environment affect processes like specialization and integration; to treat the organization as a dependent variable.

Perhaps I am overstating the case. It is clear that lots of us are working outside the organization—with collections of community groups, with union-management relations, with cross-cultural studies. That's great. Let's do more of it, especially conceptually. Let's study communities of organizations, networks of interactions among organizations, the interorganizational use of power; the effect of the local environment on organizational behavior.

I am also overstating in another sense. I don't think organizational ecology is the only place to prospect. The computer-plowed pathway is still just opening up. Way back at the level of the individual there seem to be rich possibilities for connecting up with new ideas emerging from current developmental psychology.

But organizational ecology looks very pregnant indeed. The organizational isolation of the past is giving way to more and more interaction among different sorts of organizations; universities, governments, community groups, industry. Technological developments are changing the ease and speed of organizational interactions. The resolution of large social problems appears unquestionably to require the pooling of organizational resources of many kinds. We'd better look at the social life of organizations.

We should remember, too, that we have again and again achieved new insight into the smaller unit by studying the larger unit. We began to understand much more about the individual man when we looked at him in social interaction; much more about the group when we began to observe its behavior in the presence of other groups. And we will surely learn much more about the organization when we look, as my mother used to say, at the company it keeps.

To do this means, I think, to be sloppy for awhile; to do a good deal of field research on communities of organizations. That's what Trist and Company may be trying to do, and what some engineering systems people at Stanford are pushing toward too. If we put our minds to it, we may be able to invent or at least modify methodologies that will help us tighten up. We've started a couple of such projects at Stanford, modestly. One is about the networks of relationships between parent organizations, their foreign offshoots, among the offshoots and between the offshoots of their host environments. It's slow going. But I think we are beginning to germinate some ideas. The area is surely rich, and surely we will learn much about organizational insides from observing responses to forces on its outside. And we had better. Because in this society it's beginning to hurt just there, where the inside meets the outside.

II

MANAGERIAL PROBLEM-ANALYSIS

Primer:
The Notion of a Model

"... The poet's eye, in a fine frenzy rolling, doth glance from Heaven to earth, from earth to Heaven; and as imagination bodies forth the forms of things unknown, the poet's pen turns them to shape and gives to airy nothing a local habitation and a name; such tricks hath strong imagination ..."—Shakespeare

We believe that the development of cognitive models is the most important intellectual activity undertaken by man.

Often such models are not formal or explicit, but quite implicit to the individual. Babies build models of their universe. They learn the boundaries of their behavior and form hypotheses of cause-and-effect relationships operative within that universe. All this is done informally and sometimes even unconsciously. But as it is done; it is the first act of management in their life. For such models give shape to airy nothingness, and, like the poet's pen, hath strong imagination.

Managers have always built models in their organizational lives. Recently, management scientists have attempted to make these models explicit. And so, the entire field of mathematical modeling has become a leading edge in the study of management problem analysis.

The readings in this part of our text aim at understanding the notion of modeling in its most elemental form. The notion of the *image* is the primary message of this part. Each reading has been carefully selected, not so much to coordinate with its counterparts, but rather to complement them in an effort to apply a broad brush across the underlying issues of model-building as viewed by each of the foundations of management.

The classical school is represented by an excerpt from Frederick Taylor's classic book, *Scientific Management.* Taylor's analyses into the correct way to do a job must be considered the foundation from which most analytical modeling has grown. The quantitative sciences are represented by articles on mathematical programming and simulation. These articles are on an introductory level and should give the reader a basic understanding of the what and how of these two most important analytical tools used in managerial problem analysis. So pervasive is their use that a young manager without some rudimentary understanding of them must consider himself at a disadvantage. The behavioral sciences are represented by articles dealing with different aspects of problem analysis. These articles try to help us understand the nonanalytical, highly subjective and qualitative aspects of individual and group problem analysis. The totality of these articles yields insights into human plans, images, motivation, needs, learning, etc. and how these factors influence problem analysis.

ROBERT H. DOKTOR

Problem-Analysis:
A Behavioral Viewpoint

Introduction

Managerial behavior, like all behavior, can be looked upon as consisting of a series of observable task activities which are carried out by subjects in response to the stimulation of the subjects' environment.

Further, these task activities can be analyzed and classified into a number of elementary categories. In this text, the task categories have been defined as being

1. problem-analysis
2. decision-making, and
3. solution implementation.

Overview of the Functions of Management
from the Viewpoint of Behavioral Science

From the viewpoint of this text, problem analysis has to do with the manner in which individuals define and come up with alternative solutions to a problem. Decision-making, to the behaviorist, concerns itself with the values and norms generated through interaction of a number of individuals in a group such that a decision criterion is created and applied. And the behavioral scientist views implementation as the manner in which the participation and the commitment of members of an organization is rallied toward the goals of the organization, be these goals stable or changing.

Analysis of Problem Analysis

Problem analysis behavior can be broken down into a number of categories of response activities. Let us consider two of these:

1. problem definition
2. idea generation

Each of the above subcategories is a response activity on the part of a manager, or a group of managers, to a stimulus input. That is, the manager when confronted by his environment with a stimulus situation, absorbs the stimulus, operates upon it, and responds with behavior. When the response behavioral activity falls into one of the categories enumerated above, then we say the manager is engaged in problem analysis.

It will be the task of this chapter to begin to understand what transpires between the stimulus and the response during managerial problem analysis. That is, we want to learn more about the *throughput*. We want to learn how a manager defines a problem, and how he generates alternative solutions to the problems he defines.

Definition of a Problem

By problem we mean something quite specific. A problem exists when a desired future state is not a sure thing. That is, when we want the future to be thus and so, and yet it is not absolutely certain (i.e., probability = 1.00) that the future state will be thus and so, then we have a problem. The problem is: What can we do to increase the chances that the future state will be more like that which we wish it to be?

For example, we might want our ROI (Return on Investment) to be 15% or more during the next fiscal year. We have a problem! How can we increase our chance of a 15% or more ROI for the next year This problem may be analyzed into a number of subproblems, the solution of each contributing to the solution of the whole.

All those situations that we usually think of as problems can be thought of in terms of the above definition.

Just keeping things at the status quo can be a problem. There exist forces in all of our environments which are continually operative toward change. Over a few of these forces we have great control. Over many of these forces we have moderate or little control, and over all too many forces we have no control. These forces, be they partially controllable, or noncontrollable, may be operating toward change and so just desiring to keep the status quo can surely be a problem.

Not everyone agrees on which forces are partially controllable, and indeed on what is the extent of the adjective "partial." That is, we all have different *models* of the universe. By model, we mean theory, that is, a model is our theory of what the future will bring. We consider a number of causal variables, the trends in these variables and their interaction, and then we predict the future. If the future is not the one we desire, then we have a *problem* and so we go to our model and pick out the causal variables over which we have some control. We plan to manipulate these partially controllable variables in such a way as to increase the probability that the future will conform to our desires (i.e., change the prediction of our model such that the outcome is more like our desired state of nature).

So far, the definition of a problem can thus be broken down into:

1. Having a model,
2. Having a desired future state of nature,
3. Having the model predict the future state of nature,
4. Being aware of a difference.

COMMENT: Problem-Finding

The work of William Pounds has contributed significantly to much of that which has proceeded (see, for example, "Industrial Management Review," Vol. 11, No. 1, pp. 1-20).

In addition to ideas similar to those presented above, Dean Pounds points to the necessity of rank ordering the problems a manager "finds" according to some priority system, and allocating resources to these according to this priority rating.

Further, organizationally, a manager is free to problem-find as long as he meets the budget expectations and profit expectations set for him. If the manager fails to meet these expectations, then he can expect a good deal of "help" from above. This help will be in terms of how he should or should not problem-find. In other words, the freedom to problem-find belongs to the manager only as long as he lives up to the expectations of his superiors.

Once we are aware of a difference between our desired state of nature and the predicted state of nature, then we have identified our problem. But more must be accomplished before we can say the problem has been fully defined.

We are aware of differences between the predicted and desired future state, but we do not as yet know which variables of our model can be manipulated to minimize this difference. Thus we must diagnosis[1] our model so that we can isolate the variables which are partially controllable, and effective in changing our model's prediction to be more like our desired end-state. That is, we must find the controllable and causal variables.

For example, to increase ROI so that it exceeds 15%, our model may suggest one of the reasons our ROI is not in excess of 15% is that our sales are too low, that our fixed costs are, on the average, too high for each item sold.

Thus, the last stage of problem definition concerns itself with the necessity of diagnosis. That is, with identifying within our model those variables which may be the cause of our problem.

COMMENT: Cause vs. Symptom

It is important to note the difference between the concept of a cause and a symptom. Cause is a subset of symptom. A runny nose and fever are symptoms of a cold which may be caused by a virus. However, the fever may result in a chill to the body, thus worsening the condition and becoming a cause of the continued cold.

Generation of Ideas—Alternative Solutions

The last stage in defining a problem—diagnosis—hints at what some of the solutions to the problem may be. That is, diagnosis gives us clues to the way ideas are generated as alternative solutions to the defined problem.

As the problem is diagnosed, we look to our model in order to isolate the causal variables—the variables which result in discrepancies between the desired and predicted end-state. We further isolate those causal variables over which we have some control.

Once we have isolated the controllable, causal variables, we must *plan* the operations necessary in order to create a predicted end-state more like our desired end-state. That is, we must generate a sequence of activities, which, if carried out, would change the prediction of our model.

In the 15 percent ROI example, we have diagnosed that sales and high fixed

---

[1]This conception, "diagnosis," is drawn from the work of H. Igor Ansoff. See, for example, Chapter 6 of J. Blood (ed.), *Management Science in Planning and Control,* 1969.

Managerial Problem-Analysis

FIGURE 1

The Iterative Nature of Problem Solving

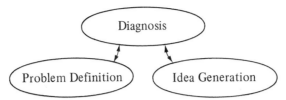

costs are the causal agents of the problem. These elements of our model may hint that increased advertising (a planned operation) will tend to increase sales with only minor increase to fixed costs, such that ROI can be increased.

This generation of operations—that is, the formation of a plan—is the first stage of idea generation.

But idea generation is more than the formation of a plan.

We continually receive feedback from our environment with regard to the consequences of the plan we make with reference to our models. That is, when our plans don't result in the consequences that our models have predicted, then we begin to question and modify and adapt our models. In other words, when our plans do not solve our problems, we begin to question the validity of our models.

The process of model modification and adaption in response to feedback from the environment is called *learning.* That is to say, our models are products of the interaction of the experiences impinged upon us by our environment and our genetic capacities:

$$\text{Model} = f \, (\text{experience} \times \text{genes})$$

In other words, in order to understand how alternative solutions are generated, we must understand how our models are formed and modified. And, in order to understand the formation and modification of models, we must investigate the phenomena called learning.

COMMENT: We Learn Our Models

And the kinds of alternative solutions we generate are consequences of the kinds of models we have learned.

In our 15 percent ROI example, the manager's model had built into it (learned) that increased advertising tended to increase sales. In addition, the manager's model had learned from past experience that the fixed costs of advertising in his business contributed relatively little to the total fixed costs of his product. These learned elements of his model lead directly to the association of inferences that increased sales could be obtained by increasing advertising and the ROI could thus be increased.

Problem-Analysis: A Behavioral Viewpoint

Learning and Motivation

Motivation is best viewed as *needs* which seek satisfaction. All humans have needs. Abraham Maslow has classified these needs into a hierarchy.

FIGURE 2

The Hierarchy of Needs

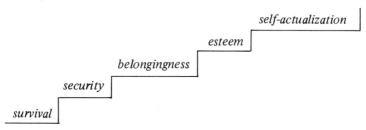

When a lower need, such as security, and a higher need, such as esteem, are both present, then we will attend to the lower (more dominant) need. For example, when given the choice of risking our life in order to gain the esteem of others, most of us would choose not to risk our lives. Here, the lower, more dominant, need is said to be prepotent.

However, not everyone agrees with Maslow's theory of a hierarchy. It is certainly true that many people have been known to risk their lives. The question of the existence of a hierarchy remains largely indeterminate because of the difficulty of measuring the *intensity* of needs.

Nonetheless, even if a hierarchy does not exist, Maslow's five classifications of needs is a convenient vocabulary to use when one discusses human motivation. On this note, the last need category—self actualization—deserves clarification. An individual is said to self-actualize when he strives to attain his full native potential. That is, when I seek to live up to all I can be, be that a creative musician or an effective plumber, then I am said to be self actualizing.

Motivation has both direction and intensity. That is, motivated behavior is a response directed toward the reduction of a need, and its intensity is determined by the perceived intensity of the need, relative to other concomitantly perceived needs.

Human satisfaction is the automatic experience resulting from the information feedback that the need has been perceived to be successfully reduced. That is, human satisfaction is an involuntary response which accompanies the perception of successful need reduction. The perception of unsuccessful need reduction through motivated behavior results in the involuntary response of the experience of dissatisfaction.

Therefore, human satisfaction and motivation are two sides of the needs coin. Needs which have been reduced are said to be gratified (the automatic experience of satisfaction has resulted from the feedback that the need is perceived to have been successfully reduced), and gratified needs are not motivators. However, as Maslow indicates, when one set of needs is gratified, a new set of needs emerges. Therefore, man is always in a motivated state. The intensity and direction of the motivation, however, depends upon the individual's perception of his needs.

A psychological cue, which increases our perceptual awareness of a need, is called an incentive. An employer can motivate you by making you aware of a need through the use of an incentive. For example, the offering of wages is an incentive to cue an individual to his own perceptual awareness of a host of needs which can be gratified through the acquisition of wages.

Now, motivation is responsible for our interaction with the environment, and the learning which results from this interaction can be said to be a by-product of motivation.

But learning is not a simple function of motivation. That is, it is *not* necessarily true that learning is directly tied to motivation. Performance and learning are not one and the same. Learning can be viewed as the upper limit of expected performance.

Therefore, our motivation sends us out into the world, where we learn our models, but rarely is it the case that we are motivated to learn a particular model (except in totalitarian states). And even when this is the case, very rarely is it so that we only learn what we are motivated to learn.

Learning and Perception

We are continuously bombarded with stimuli. Of these, we perceive only a small fraction. And the small fraction of stimuli is not passively imputed. The concept of perception is an active one. Our model of the world dictates a cognitive set which operates upon the transformation of stimuli we encounter. Two men may look at the same scene, and each may perceive different components of that scene. In part, these differences in perception are caused by the difference in the current models that each man possesses.

But models are not the only factor influencing perception. Human needs, which may arise apart from the model, often influence perception. A hungry man will be more apt to notice a picture of food in an art gallery than will a nonhungry man.

Our perceptions and our motivation influence, in a complex way, the nature of the model we learn. And, since man is a system, it is logical to expect and find that our models influence, in a complex way, the nature of our motivations and perceptions.

In Review

The manager learns models of his world. He tries out plans, and the feedback he receives from the environment, modified by his needs and perceptions, cause him to validate or alter his models. His plans are his alternative solutions, and these are a direct consequence of the nature of his model.

Probably no two managers have the same model. Therefore, when managers work together in groups, we expect and find that many different alternative solutions arise.

Our models guide the way we think. Some of us have learned that the world rewards hard-nosed analytic and logical reasoning. This is part of our model and we tend to try to reason *analytically and logically*, no matter what the nature of our problem.

Others of us have been rewarded for more *intuitive* thought processes. These people have found the formation of associations and associations of inference has more often given them workable and rewarding solutions to problems.

Most of us have the capacity to think in both cognitive processes, but tend to have a predilection for one or the other.

These cognitive styles are part of our models.

Creativity and Idea Generation

Many psychologists believe that the capacity to be creative is linked to the capacity to think associatively. In our terms, these scientists hold that those of us with models which encourage intuitive thought (i.e., associative) thinking are apt to be more creative than those who have models which tend to prefer and encourage logical analytic thinking.

With this contention, we disagree. Different problems demand different modes and processes of thought. Indeed, different subparts of a single problem demand different thought styles. The individual who can shift gears, using diverse styles of thought, appropriately matched to the requirements of the problem is the creative individual. Creativity in idea generation comes with a model which encourages many modes and processes of thought and flexible mobility from one mode or process to another, as required by the problems at hand.

Model-Building—Conscious or Unconscious

It remains to be pointed out that most of us are not aware, most of the time, of the models we are learning.

Most managers do not set out to learn how to think about the world. Their models are by-products of their activities as they go about their jobs and their lives. But the manager is a system, and soon it becomes clear that his model, a by-product of his activities, does shape and guide the nature of these activities.

We all have models. Becoming aware of them helps us understand how we analyze problems. By understanding how we analyze problems, perhaps we can learn how to do a better job of it in the future.

FREDERICK WINSLOW TAYLOR

The Principles of Scientific Management

The writer has found that there are three questions uppermost in the minds of men when they become interested in scientific management.

First. Wherein do the principles of scientific management differ essentially from those of ordinary management?

Second. Why are better results attained under scientific management than under the other types?

Third. Is not the most important problem that of getting the right man at the head of the company? And if you have the right man cannot the choice of the type of management be safely left to him?

One of the principal objects of the following pages will be to give a satisfactory answer to these questions.

Source: Frederick Winslow Taylor, "The Principles of Scientific Management," *Scientific Management,* pp. 30-77. Copyright 1911 by Frederick W. Taylor; renewed 1939 by Louise M. S. Taylor. Reprinted with permission of Harper & Row, Publishers, Inc.

The Finest Type of Ordinary Management

Before starting to illustrate the principles of scientific management, or "task management" as it is briefly called, it seems desirable to outline what the writer believes will be recognized as the best type of management which is in common use. This is done so that the great difference between the best of the ordinary management and scientific management may be fully appreciated.

In an industrial establishment which employs say from 500 to 1000 workmen, there will be found in many cases at least twenty to thirty different trades. The workmen in each of these trades have had their knowledge handed down to them by word of mouth, through the many years in which their trade has been developed from the primitive condition, in which our far-distant ancestors each one practiced the rudiments of many different trades, to the present state of great and growing subdivision of labor, in which each man specializes upon some comparatively small class of work.

The ingenuity of each generation has developed quicker and better methods for doing every element of the work in every trade. Thus the methods which are now in use may in a broad sense be said to be an evolution representing the survival of the fittest and best of the ideas which have been developed since the starting of each trade. However, while this is true in a broad sense, only those who are intimately acquainted with each of these trades are fully aware of the fact that in hardly any element of any trade is there uniformity in the methods which are used. Instead of having only one way which is generally accepted as a standard, there are in daily use, say, fifty or a hundred different ways of doing each element of the work. And a little thought will make it clear that this must inevitably be the case, since our methods have been handed down from man to man by word of mouth, or have, in most cases, been almost unconsciously learned through personal observation. Practically in no instances have they been codified or systematically analyzed or described. The ingenuity and experience of each generation—of each decade, even, have without doubt handed over better methods to the next. This mass rule-of-thumb or traditional knowledge may be said to be the principal asset or possession of every tradesman. Now, in the best of the ordinary types of management, the managers recognize frankly the fact that the 500 or 1000 workmen, included in the twenty to thirty trades, who are under them, possess this mass of traditional knowledge, a large part of which is not in the possession of the management. The management, of course, includes foremen and superintendents, who themselves have been in most cases first-class workers at their trades. And yet these foremen and superintendents know, better than any one else, that their own knowledge and personal skill falls far short of the combined knowledge and dexterity of all the workmen under them. The most experienced managers therefore frankly place before their workmen the problem of doing the work in the best and most economical way. They recognize the task before them as that of inducing each workman to use his best endeavors, his hardest work, all his traditional knowledge, his skill, his ingenuity, and his good-will—in a word, his "initiative," so as to yield the largest possible return to his employer. The problem before the management, then, may be briefly said to be that of obtaining the best initiative of every workman. And the writer uses the word "initiative" in its broadest sense, to cover all the good qualities sought for from the men.

On the other hand, no intelligent manager would hope to obtain in any full measure the initiative of his workmen unless he felt that he was giving them something more than they usually receive from their employers. Only those among the readers of this paper who have been managers or who have worked themselves at a trade realize how far the average workman falls short of giving his employer his full initiative. It is well within the mark to state that in nineteen out of twenty industrial establishments the workmen believe it to be directly against their interests to give their employers their best initiative, and that instead of working hard to do the largest possible amount of work and the best quality of work for their employers, they deliberately work as slowly as they dare while they at the same time try to make those over them believe that they are working fast.[1]

The writer repeats, therefore, that in order to have any hope of obtaining the initiative of his workmen the manager must give some *special incentive* to his men beyond that which is given to the average of the trade. This incentive can be given in several different ways, as, for example, the hope of rapid promotion or advancement; higher wages, either in the form of generous piecework prices or of a premium or bonus of some kind for good and rapid work; shorter hours of labor; better surroundings and working conditions than are ordinarily given, etc., and, above all, this special incentive should be accompanied by that personal consideration for, and friendly contact with, his workmen which comes only from a genuine and kindly interest in the welfare of those under him. It is only by giving a special inducement or "incentive" of this kind that the employer can hope even approximately to get the "initiative" of his workmen. Under the ordinary type of management the necessity for offering the workman a special inducement has come to be so generally recognized that a large proportion of those most interested in the subject look upon the adoption of some one of the modern schemes for paying men (such as piece work, the premium plan, or the bonus plan, for instance) as practically the whole system of management. Under scientific management, however, the particular pay system which is adopted is merely one of the subordinate elements.

Broadly speaking, then, the best type of management in ordinary use may be defined as management in which the workmen give their best *initiative* and in return receive some *special incentive* from their employers. This type of management will be referred to as the management of "*initiative and incentive*"

---

[1]The writer has tried to make the reason for this unfortunate state of things clear in a paper entitled "Shop Management," read before the American Society of Mechanical Engineers.

in contradistinction to scientific management, or task management, with which it is to be compared.

The writer hopes that the management of "initiative and incentive" will be recognized as representing the best type in ordinary use, and in fact he believes that it will be hard to persuade the average manager that anything better exists in the whole field than this type. The task which the writer has before him, then, is the difficult one of trying to prove in a thoroughly convincing way that there is another type of management which is not only better but overwhelmingly better than the management of "initiative and incentive."

The universal prejudice in favor of the management of "initiative and incentive" is so strong that no mere theoretical advantages which can be pointed out will be likely to convince the average manager that any other system is better. It will be upon a series of practical illustrations of the actual working of the two systems that the writer will depend in his efforts to prove that scientific management is so greatly superior to other types. Certain elementary principles, a certain philosophy, will however be recognized as the essence of that which is being illustrated in all of the practical examples which will be given. And the broad principles in which the scientific system differs from the ordinary or "rule-of-thumb" system are so simple in their nature that it seems desirable to describe them before starting with the illustrations.

Under the old type of management success depends almost entirely upon getting the "initiative" of the workmen, and it is indeed a rare case in which this initiative is really attained. Under scientific management the "initiative" of the workmen (that is, their hard work, their good will, and their ingenuity) is obtained with absolute uniformity and to a greater extent than is possible under the old system; and in addition to this improvement on the part of the men, the managers assume, for instance, the burden of gathering together all of the traditional knowledge which in the past has been possessed by the workmen and then of classifying, tabulating, and reducing this knowledge to rules, laws, and formulas which are immensely helpful to the workmen in doing their daily work. In addition to developing a *science* in this way, the management takes on three other types of duties which involve new and heavy burdens for themselves.

These new duties are grouped under four heads:

First. They develop a science for each element of a man's work, which replaces the old rule-of-thumb method.

Second. They scientifically select and then train, teach, and develop the workman, whereas in the past he chose his own work and trained himself as best he could.

Third. They heartily cooperate with the men so as to insure all of the work being done in accordance with the principles of the science which has been developed.

Fourth. There is an almost equal division of the work and the responsibility between the management and the workmen. The management take over all work for which they are better fitted than the workmen, while in the past almost all of the work and the greater part of the responsibility were thrown upon the men.

It is this combination of the initiative of the workmen, coupled with the new types of work done by the management, that makes scientific management so much more efficient than the old plan.

Three of these elements exist in many cases, under the management of "initiative and incentive," in a small and rudimentary way, but they are, under this management, of minor importance, whereas under scientific management they form the very essence of the whole system.

The fourth of these elements, "an almost equal division of the responsibility between the management and the workmen," requires further explanation. The philosophy of the management of "initiative and incentive" makes it necessary for each workman to bear almost the entire responsibility for the general plan as well as for each detail of his work, and in many cases for his implements as well. In addition to this he must do all of the actual physical labor. The development of a science, on the other hand, involves the establishment of many rules, laws, and formulas which replace the judgment of the individual workman and which can be effectively used only after having been systematically recorded, indexed, etc. The practical use of scientific data also calls for a room in which to keep the books, records,[2] etc., and a desk for the planner to work at. Thus all of the planning which under the old system was done by the workman, as a result of his personal experience, must of necessity under the new system be done by the management in accordance with the laws of the science; because even if the workman was well suited to the development and use of scientific data, it would be physically impossible for him to work at his machine and at a desk at the same time. It is also clear that in most cases one type of man is needed to plan ahead and an entirely different type to execute the work.

The man in the planning room, whose specialty under scientific management is planning ahead, invariably finds that the work can be done better and more economically by a subdivision of the labor; each act of each mechanic, for example, should be preceded by various preparatory acts done by other men. And all of this involves, as we have said, "an almost equal division of the responsibility and the work between the management and the workman."

To summarize: Under the management of "initiative and incentive" practically the whole problem is "up to the workman," while under scientific management fully one-half of the problem is "up to the management."

Perhaps the most prominent single element in modern scientific manage-

---

[2]For example, the records containing the data used under scientific management in an ordinary machine shop fill thousands of pages.

ment is the task idea. The work of every workman is fully planned out by the management at least one day in advance, and each man receives in most cases complete written instructions, describing in detail the task which he is to accomplish, as well as the means to be used in doing the work. And the work planned in advance in this way constitutes a task which is to be solved, as explained above, not by the workman alone, but in almost all cases by the joint effort of the workman and the management. This task specifies not only what is to be done but how it is to be done and the exact time allowed for doing it. And whenever the workman succeeds in doing his task right, and within the time limit specified, he receives an addition of from 30 percent to 100 percent to his ordinary wages. These tasks are carefully planned, so that both good and careful work are called for in their performance, but it should be distinctly understood that in no case is the workman called upon to work at a pace which would be injurious to his health. The task is always so regulated that the man who is well suited to his job will thrive while working at this rate during a long term of years and grow happier and more prosperous, instead of being overworked. Scientific management consists very largely in preparing for and carrying out these tasks.

The writer is fully aware that to perhaps most of the readers of this paper the four elements which differentiate the new management from the old will at first appear to be merely high-sounding phrases; and he would again repeat that he has no idea of convincing the reader of their value merely through announcing their existence. His hope of carrying conviction rests upon demonstrating the tremendous force and effect of these four elements through a series of practical illustrations. It will be shown, first, that they can be applied absolutely to all classes of work, from the most elementary to the most intricate; and second, that when they are applied, the results must of necessity be overwhelmingly greater than those which it is possible to attain under the management of initiative and incentive.

The first illustration is that of handling pig iron, and this work is chosen because it is typical of perhaps the crudest and most elementary form of labor which is performed by man. This work is done by men with no other implements than their hands. The pig-iron handler stoops down, picks up a pig weighing about 92 pounds, walks for a few feet or yards and then drops it on the ground or upon a pile. This work is so crude and elementary in its nature that the writer firmly believes that it would be possible to train an intelligent gorilla so as to become a more efficient pig-iron handler than any man can be. Yet it will be shown that the science of handling pig-iron is so great and amounts to so much that it is impossible for the man who is best suited to this type of work to understand the principles of this science, or even to work in accordance with these principles without the aid of a man better educated than he is. And the further illustrations to be given will make it clear that in almost all of the mechanic arts the science which underlies each workman's act is so great and amounts to so much that the workman who is best suited actually to do the work is incapable (either through lack of education or through insufficient mental capacity) of understanding this science. This is announced as a general principle, the truth of which will become apparent as one illustration after another is given. After showing these four elements in the handling of pig iron, several illustrations will be given of their application to different kinds of work in the field of the mechanic arts, at intervals in a rising scale, beginning with the simplest and ending with the more intricate forms of labor.

One of the first pieces of work undertaken by us, when the writer started to introduce scientific management into the Bethlehem Steel Company, was to handle pig iron on task work. The opening of the Spanish War found some 80,000 tons of pig iron placed in small piles in an open field adjoining the works. Prices for pig rion had been so low that it could not be sold at a profit, and it therefore had been stored. With the opening of the Spanish War the price of pig iron rose, and this large accumulation of iron was sold. This gave us a good opportunity to show the workmen, as well as the owners and managers of the works, on a fairly large scale the advantages of task work over the old-fashioned day work and piece work, in doing a very elementary class of work.

The Bethelem Steel Company had five blast furnaces, the product of which had been handled by a pig-iron gang for many years. This gang, at this time, consisted of about 75 men. They were good, average pig-iron handlers, were under an excellent foreman who himself had been a pig-iron handler, and the work was done, on the whole, about as fast and as cheaply as it was anywhere else at that time.

A railroad switch was run out into the field, right along the edge of the piles of pig iron. An inclined plank was placed against the side of a car, and each man picked up from his pile a pig of iron weighing about 92 pounds, walked up the inclined plank and dropped it on the end of the car.

We found that this gang were loading on the average about 12½ long tons per man per day. We were surprised to find, after studying the matter, that a first-class pig-iron handler ought to handle between 47[3] and 48 long tons per day, instead of 12½ tons. This task seemed to us so very large that we were obliged to go over our work several times before we were absolutely sure that we were right. Once we were sure, however, that 47 tons was a proper day's work for a first-class pig-iron handler, the task which faced us as managers under the modern scientific plan was clearly before us. It was our duty to see that the 80,000 tons of pig iron was loaded on to the cars at the rate of 47 tons per man per day, in place of 12½ tons, at which rate the work was then being done. And it was further our duty to see that this work was done without bringing on a strike among the men, without any quarrel with the men, and to see that the men were happier and better contented when loading at the new rate of 47 tons than they were when loading at the old rate of 12½ tons.

Our first step was the scientific selection of the workman. In dealing with

[3]See footnote 4 on page 100.

workmen under this type of management, it is an inflexible rule to talk to and deal with only one man at a time, since each workman has his own special abilities and limitations, and since we are not dealing with men in masses, but are trying to develop each individual man to his highest state of efficiency and prosperity. Our first step was to find the proper workman to begin with. We therefore carefully watched and studied these 75 men for three or four days, at the end of which time we had picked out four men who appeared to be physically able to handle pig iron at the rate of 47 tons per day. A careful study was then made of each of these men. We looked up their history as far back as practicable and thorough inquiries were made as to the character, habits, and the ambition of each of them. Finally we selected one from among the four as the most likely man to start with. He was a little Pennsylvania Dutchman who had been observed to trot back home for a mile or so after his work in the evening, about as fresh as he was when he came trotting down to work in the morning. We found that upon wages of $1.15 a day he had succeeded in buying a small plot of ground, and that he was engaged in putting up the walls of a little house for himself in the morning before starting to work and at night after leaving. He also had the reputation of being exceedingly "close," that is, of placing a very high value on a dollar. As one man whom we talked to about him said, "A penny looks about the size of a cart wheel to him." This man we will call Schmidt.

The task before us, then, narrowed itself down to getting Schmidt to handle 47 tons of pig iron per day and making him glad to do it. This was done as follows. Schmidt was called out from among the gang of pig-iron handlers and talked to somewhat in this way:

"Schmidt, are you a high-priced man?"

"Vell, I don't know vat you mean."

"Oh yes, you do. What I want to know is whether you are a high-priced man or not."

"Vell, I don't know vat you mean."

"Oh, come now, you answer my questions. What I want to find out is whether you are a high-priced man or one of these cheap fellows here. What I want to find out is whether you want to earn $1.85 a day or whether you are satisfied with $1.15, just the same as all those cheap fellows are getting."

"Did I vant $1.85 a day? Vas dot a high-priced man? Vell, yes, I vas a high-priced man."

"Oh, you're aggravating me. Of course you want $1.85 a day—everyone wants it! You know perfectly well that that has very little to do with your being a high-priced man. For goodness' sake answer my questions, and don't waste any more of my time. Now come over here. You see that pile of pig iron?"

"Yes."

"You see that car?"

"Yes."

"Well, if you are a high-priced man, you will load that pig iron on that car tomorrow for $1.85. Now do wake up and answer my question. Tell me whether you are a high-priced man or not."

"Vell—did I got $1.85 for loading dot pig iron on dot car tomorrow?"

"Yes, of course you do, and you get $1.85 for loading a pile like that every day right through the year. That is what a high-priced man does, and you know it just as well as I do."

"Vell, dot's all right. I could load dot pig iron on the car to-morrow for $1.85, and I get it every day, don't I?"

"Certainly you do—certainly you do."

"Vell, den, I vas a high-priced man."

"Now, hold on, hold on. You know just as well as I do that a high-priced man has to do exactly as he's told from morning till night. You have seen this man here before, haven't you?"

"No, I never saw him."

"Well, if you are a high-priced man, you will do exactly as this man tells you tomorrow, from morning till night. When he tells you to pick up a pig and walk, you pick it up and you walk, and when he tells you to sit down and rest, you sit down. You do that right straight through the day. And what's more, no back talk. Now a high-priced man does just what he's told to do, and no back talk. Do you understand that? When this man tells you to walk, you walk; when he tells you to sit down, you sit down, and you don't talk back at him. Now you come on to work here tomorrow morning and I'll know before night whether you are really a high-priced man or not."

This seems to be rather rough talk. And indeed it would be if applied to an educated mechanic, or even an intelligent laborer. With a man of the mentally sluggish type of Schmidt it is appropriate and not unkind, since it is effective in fixing his attention on the high wages which he wants and away from what, if it were called to his attention, he probably would consider impossibly hard work.

What would Schmidt's answer be if he were talked to in a manner which is usual under the management of "initiative and incentive"? say, as follows:

"Now, Schmidt, you are a first-class pig-iron handler and know your business well. You have been handling at the rate of 12½ tons per day. I have given considerable study to handling pig iron, and feel sure that you could do a much larger day's work than you have been doing. Now don't you think that if you really tried you could handle 47 tons of pig iron per day, instead of 12½ tons?"

What do you think Schmidt's answer would be to this?

Schmidt started to work, and all day long, and at regular intervals, was told by the man who stood over him with a watch, "Now pick up a pig and walk. Now sit down and rest. Now walk—now rest," etc. He worked when he was told to work, and rested when he was told to rest, and at half-past five in the afternoon had his 47½ tons loaded on the car. And he practically never failed to work at this pace and do the task that was set him during the three years that the writer was at Bethlehem. And throughout this time he averaged a little more than $1.85 per day, whereas before he had never received over $1.15 per day, which was the ruling rate of wages at that time in Bethlehem. That is, he received 60 percent higher wages than were paid to other men who were not working on task work. One man after another was picked out and trained to handle pig iron at the rate of 47½ tons per day until all of the pig iron was handled at this rate, and the men were receiving 60 percent more wages than other workmen around them.

The writer has given above a brief description of three of the four elements which constitute the essence of scientific management: first, the careful selection of the workman, and, second and third, the method of first inducing and then training and helping the workman to work according to the scientific method. Nothing has as yet been said about the science of handling pig iron. The writer trusts, however, that before leaving this illustration the reader will be thoroughly convinced that there is a science of handling pig iron, and further that this science amounts to so much that the man who is suited to handle pig iron cannot possibly understand it, nor even work in accordance with the laws of this science, without the help of those who are over him.

The writer came into the machine shop of the Midvale Steel Company in 1878, after having served an apprenticeship as a pattern-maker and as a machinist. This was close to the end of the long period of depression following the panic of 1873, and business was so poor that it was impossible for many mechanics to get work at their trades. For this reason he was obliged to start as a day laborer instead of working as a mechanic. Fortunately for him, soon after he came into the shop the clerk of the shop was found stealing. There was no one else available, and so, having more education than the other laborers (since he had been prepared for college) he was given the position of clerk. Shortly after this he was given work as a machinist in running one of the lathes, and, as he turned out rather more work than other machinists were doing on similar lathes, after several months was made gang-boss over the lathes.

Almost all of the work of this shop had been done on piecework for several years. As was usual then, and in fact as is still usual in most of the shops in this country, the shop was really run by the workmen, and not by the bosses. The workmen together had carefully planned just how fast each job should be done, and they had set a pace for each machine throughout the shop, which was limited to about one-third of a good day's work. Every new workman who came into the shop was told at once by the other men exactly how much of each kind of work he was to do, and unless he obeyed these instructions he was sure before long to be driven out of the place by the men.

As soon as the writer was made gang-boss, one after another of the men came to him and talked somewhat as follows:

"Now, Fred, we're very glad to see that you've been made gang-boss. You know the game all right, and we're sure that you're not likely to be a piecework hog. You come along with us, and everything will be all right, but if you try breaking any of these rates you can be mighty sure that we'll throw you over the fence."

The writer told them plainly that he was now working on the side of the management, and that he proposed to do whatever he could to get a fair day's work out of the lathes. This immediately started a war; in most cases a friendly war, because the men who were under him were his personal friends, but none the less a war, which as time went on grew more and more bitter. The writer used every expedient to make them do a fair day's work, such as discharging or lowering the wages of the more stubborn men who refused to make any improvement, and such as lowering the piecework price, hiring green men, and personally teaching them how to do the work, with the promise from them that when they had learned how, they would then do a fair day's work. While the men constantly brought such pressure to bear (both inside and outside the works) upon all those who started to increase their output that they were finally compelled to do about as the rest did, or else quit. No one who has not had this experience can have an idea of the bitterness which is gradually developed in such a struggle. In a war of this kind the workmen have one expedient which is usually effective. They use their ingenuity to contrive various ways in which the machines which they are running are broken or damaged—apparently by accident, or in the regular course of work—and this they always lay at the door of the foreman, who has forced them to drive the machine so hard that it is overstrained and is being ruined. And there are few foremen indeed who are able to stand up against the combined pressure of all of the men in the shop. In this case the problem was complicated by the fact that the shop ran both day and night.

The writer had two advantages, however, which are not possessed by the ordinary foreman, and these came, curiously enough, from the fact that he was not the son of a workingman.

First. Owing to the fact that he happened not to be of working parents, the owners of the company believed that he had the interest of the works more at heart than the other workmen, and they therefore had more confidence in his word than they did in that of the machinists who were under him. So that, when the machinists reported to the superintendent that the machines were being smashed up because an incompetent foreman was overstraining them, the superintendent accepted the word of the writer when he said that these men were deliberately breaking their machines as a part of the piecework war which was going on, and he also allowed the writer to make the only effective answer to this vandalism on the part of the men, namely: "There will be no more accidents to the machines in this shop. If any part of a machine is broken the man in charge of it must pay at least a part of the cost of its repair, and the fines collected in this way will all be handed over to the mutual beneficial association to help care for sick workmen." This soon stopped the willful breaking of machines.

Second. If the writer had been one of the workmen, and had lived where they lived, they would have brought such social pressure to bear upon him that it would have been impossible to have stood out against them. He would have been called "scab" and other foul names every time he appeared on the street, his wife would have been abused, and his children would have been stoned. Once or twice he was begged by some of his friends among the workmen not to walk home, about two and a half miles along the lonely path by the side of the railway. He was told that if he continued to do this it would be at the risk of his life. In all such cases, however, a display of timidity is apt to increase rather than diminish the risk, so the writer told these men to say to the other men in the shop that he proposed to walk home every night right up that railway track; that he never had carried and never would carry any weapon of any kind, and that they could shoot and be d———.

After about three years of this kind of struggling, the output of the machines had been materially increased, in many cases doubled, and as a result the writer had been promoted from one gang-boss-ship to another until he became foreman of the shop. For any right-minded man, however, this success is in no sense a recompense for the bitter relations which he is forced to maintain with all of those around him. Life which is one continuous struggle with other men is hardly worth living. His workman friends came to him continually and asked him, in a personal, friendly way, whether he would advise them, for their own best interest, to turn out more work. And, as a truthful man, he had to tell them that if he were in their place he would fight against turning out any more work, just as they were doing, because under the piecework system they would be allowed to earn no more wages than they had been earning, and yet they would be made to work harder.

Soon after being made foreman, therefore, he decided to make a determined effort to in some way change the system of management, so that the interests of the workmen and the management should become the same, instead of antagonistic. This resulted, some three years later, in the starting of the type of management which is described in papers presented to the American Society of Mechanical Engineers entitled "A Piece-Rate System" and "Shop Management."

In preparation for this system the writer realized that the greatest obstacle to harmonious cooperation between the workmen and the management lay in the ignorance of the management as to what really constitutes a proper day's work for a workman. He fully realized that, although he was foreman of the shop, the combined knowledge and skill of the workmen who were under him was certainly ten times as great as his own. He therefore obtained the permission of Mr. William Sellers, who was at that time the president of the Midvale Steel Company, to spend some money in a careful, scientific study of the time required to do various kinds of work.

Mr. Sellers allowed this more as a reward for having, to a certain extent, "made good" as foreman of the shop in getting more work out of the men, than for any other reason. He stated, however, that he did not believe that any scientific study of this sort would give results of much value.

Among several investigations which were undertaken at this time, one was an attempt to find some rule, or law, which would enable a foreman to know in advance how much of any kind of heavy laboring work a man who was well suited to his job ought to do in a day; that is, to study the tiring effect of heavy labor upon a first-class man. Our first step was to employ a young college graduate to look up all that had been written on the subject in English, German, and French. Two classes of experiments had been made: one by physiologists who were studying the endurance of the human animal, and the other by engineers who wished to determine what fraction of a horsepower a manpower was. These experiments had been made largely upon men who were lifting loads by means of turning the crank of a winch from which weights were suspended, and others who were engaged in walking, running, and lifting weights in various ways. However, the records of these investigations were so meager that no law of any value could be deduced from them. We therefore started a series of experiments of our own.

Two first-class laborers were selected, men who had proved themselves to be physically powerful and who were also good steady workers. These men were paid double wages during the experiments, and were told that they must work to the best of their ability at all times, and that we should make certain tests with them from time to time to find whether they were "soldiering" or not, and that the moment either one of them started to try to deceive us he would be discharged. They worked to the best of their ability throughout the time that they were being observed.

Now it must be clearly understood that in these experiments we were not trying to find the maximum work that a man could do on a short spurt or for a few days, but that our endeavor was to learn what really constituted a full day's work for a first-class man; the best day's work that a man could properly do, year in and year out, and still thrive under. These men were given all kinds of tasks, which were carried out each day under the close observation of the young college man who was conducting the experiments, and who at the same time noted with a stopwatch the proper time for all of the motions that were made by the men. Every element in any way connected with the work which we believed could have a bearing on the result was carefully studied and recorded. What we hoped ultimately to determine was what fraction of a horsepower a man was able to exert, that is, how many foot-pounds of work a man could do in a day.

After completing this series of experiments, therefore, each man's work for each day was translated into foot-pounds of energy which the man exerted during a day and the tiring effect of his work. On some kinds of work the man would be tired out when doing perhaps not more than one-eighth of a horsepower, while in others he would be tired to no greater extent by doing half a horsepower of work. We failed, therefore, to find any law which was an accurate guide to the maximum day's work for a first-class workman.

A large amount of very valuable data had been obtained, which enabled us to know, for many kinds of labor, what was a proper day's work. It did not seem wise, however, at this time to spend any more money in trying to find the exact law which we were after. Some years later, when more money was available for this purpose, a second series of experiments was made, similar to the first, but somewhat more thorough. This, however, resulted as the first experiments, in obtaining valuable information but not in the development of a law. Again, some years later, a third series of experiments was made, and this time no trouble was spared in our endeavor to make the work thorough. Every minute element which could in any way affect the problem was carefully noted and studied, and two college men devoted about three months to the experiments. After this data was again translated into foot-pounds of energy exerted for each man each day, it became perfectly clear that there is no direct relation between the horsepower which a man exerts (that is, his foot-pounds of energy per day) and the tiring effect of the work on the man. The writer, however, was quite as firmly convinced as ever that some definite, clear-cut law existed as to what constitutes a full day's work for a first-class laborer, and our data had been so carefully collected and recorded that he felt sure that the necessary information was included somewhere in the records. The problem of developing this law from the accumulated facts was therefore handed over to Mr. Carl G. Barth, who is a better mathematician than any of the rest of us, and we decided to investigate the problem in a new way, by graphically representing each element of the work through plotting curves, which should give us, as it were, a bird's-eye view of every element. In a comparatively short time Mr. Barth had discovered the law governing the tiring effect of heavy labor on a first-class man. And it is so simple in its nature that it is truly remarkable that it should not have been discovered and clearly understood years before. The law which was developed is as follows:

The law is confined to that class of work in which the limit of a man's capacity is reached because he is tired out. It is the law of heavy laboring, corresponding to the work of the cart horse, rather than that of the trotter. Practically all such work consists of a heavy pull or a push on the man's arms, that is, the man's strength is exerted by either lifting or pushing something which he grasps in his hands. And the law is that for each given pull or push on the man's arms it is possible for the workman to be under load for only a definite percentage of the day. For example, when pig iron is being handled (each pig weighing 92 pounds), a first-class workman can only be under load 43 percent of the day. He must be entirely free from load during 57 percent of the day. And as the load becomes lighter, the percentage of the day under which the man can remain under load increases. So that, if the workman is handling a half-pig, weighing 46 pounds, he can then be under load 58 percent of the day, and only has to rest during 42 percent. As the weight grows lighter the man can remain under load during a larger and larger percentage of the day, until finally a load is reached which he can carry in his hands all day long without being tired out. When that point has been arrived at this law ceases to be useful as a guide to a laborer's endurance, and some other law must be found which indicates the man's capacity for work.

When a laborer is carrying a piece of pig iron weighing 92 pounds in his hands, it tires him about as much to stand still under the load as it does to walk with it, since his arm muscles are under the same severe tension whether he is moving or not. A man, however, who stands still under a load is exerting no horsepower whatever, and this accounts for the fact that no constant relation could be traced in various kinds of heavy laboring work between the foot-pounds of energy exerted and the tiring effect of the work on the man. It will also be clear that in all work of this kind it is necessary for the arms of the workman to be completely free from load (that is, for the workman to rest) at frequent intervals. Throughout the time that the man is under a heavy load the tissues of his arm muscles are in process of degeneration, and frequent periods of rest are required in order that the blood may have a chance to restore these tissues to their normal condition.

To return now to our pig-iron handlers at the Bethlehem Steel Company. If Schmidt had been allowed to attack the pile of 47 tons of pig iron without the guidance or direction of a man who understood the art, or science, of handling pig iron, in his desire to earn his high wages he would probably have tired himself out by 11 or 12 o'clock in the day. He would have kept so steadily at work that his muscles would not have had the proper periods of rest absolutely needed for recuperation, and he would have been completely exhausted early in the day. By having a man, however, who understood this law, stand over him and direct his work, day after day, until he acquired the habit of resting at proper intervals, he was able to work at an even gait all day long without unduly tiring himself.

Now one of the very first requirements for a man who is fit to handle pig iron as a regular occupation is that he shall be so stupid and so phlegmatic that he more nearly resembles in his mental make-up the ox than any other type. The man who is mentally alert and intelligent is for this very reason entirely unsuited to what would, for him, be the grinding monotony of work of this character. Therefore the workman who is best suited to handling pig iron is unable to understand the real science of doing this class of work. He is so stupid that the word "percentage" has no meaning to him, and he must consequently be trained by a man more intelligent than himself into the habit of working in accordance with the laws of this science before he can be successful.

The writer trusts that it is now clear that even in the case of the most elementary form of labor that is known, there is a science, and that when the man best suited to this class of work has been carefully selected, when the science of doing the work has been developed, and when the carefully selected man has been trained to work in accordance with this science, the results obtained must of necessity be overwhelmingly greater than those which are possible under the plan of "initiative and incentive."

Let us, however, again turn to the case of these pig-iron handlers, and see whether, under the ordinary type of management, it would not have been possible to obtain practically the same results.

The writer has put the problem before many good managers, and asked them whether, under premium work, piecework, or any of the ordinary plans of management, they would be likely even to approximate 47 tons[4] per man per day, and not a man has suggested that an output of over 18 to 25 tons could be attained by any of the ordinary expedients. It will be remembered that the Bethlehem men were loading only 12½ tons per man.

To go into the matter in more detail, however: As to the scientific selection of the men, it is a fact that in this gang of 75 pig-iron handlers only about one man in eight was physically capable of handling 47½ tons per day. With the very best of intentions, the other seven out of eight men were physically unable to work at this pace. Now the one man in eight who was able to do this work was

[4]Many people have questioned the accuracy of the statement that first-class workmen can load 47½ tons of pig iron from the ground on to a car in a day. For those who are skeptical, therefore, the following data relating to this work are given:

First. That our experiments indicated the existence of the following law: that a first-class laborer, suited to such work as handling pig iron, could be under load only 42 percent of the day and must be free from load 58 percent of the day.

Second. That a man in loading pig iron from piles placed on the ground in an open field onto a car which stood on a track adoining these piles, ought to handle (and that they did handle regularly) 47½ long tons (2240 pounds per ton) per day.

That the price paid for loading this pig iron was 3.9 cents per ton, and that the men working at it averaged $1.85 per day, whereas, in the past, they had been paid only $1.15 per day.

In addition to these facts, the following are given:

47½ long tons equal 106,400 pounds of pig iron per day.

At 92 pounds per pig, equals 1156 pigs per day.

42 percent of a day under load equals 600 minutes; multiplied by 0.42 equals 252 minutes under load.

252 minutes divided by 1156 pigs equals 0.22 minutes per pig under load.

A pig-iron handler walks on the level at the rate of one foot in 0.006 minutes. The average distance of the piles of pig iron from the car was 36 feet. It is a fact, however, that many of the pig-iron handlers ran with their pig as soon as they reached the inclined plank. Many of them also would run down the plank after loading the car. So that when the actual loading went on, many of them moved at a faster rate than is indicated by the above figures. Practically the men were made to take a rest, generally by sitting down, after loading ten to twenty pigs. This rest was in addition to the time which it took them to walk back from the car to the pile. It is likely that many of those who are skeptical about the possibility of loading this amount of pig iron do not realize that while these men were walking back they were entirely free from load, and that therefore their muscles had, during that time, the opportunity for recuperation. It will be noted that with an average distance of 36 feet of the pig iron from the car, these men walked about eight miles under load each day and eight miles free from load.

If any one who is interested in these figures will multiply them and divide them, one into the other, in various ways, he will find that all of the facts stated check up exactly.

in no sense superior to the other men who were working on the gang. He merely happened to be a man of the type of the ox,—no rare specimen of humanity, difficult to find and therefore very highly prized. On the contrary, he was a man so stupid that he was unfitted to do most kinds of laboring work, even. The selection of the man, then, does not involve finding some extraordinary individual, but merely picking out from among very ordinary men the few who are especially suited to this type of work. Although in this particular gang only one man in eight was suited to doing the work, we had not the slightest difficulty in getting all the men who were needed—some of them from inside the works and others from the neighboring country—who were exactly suited to the job.

Under the management of "initiative and incentive" the attitude of the management is that of "putting the work up to the workmen." What likelihood would there be, then, under the old type of management, of these men properly selecting themselves for pig-iron handling? Would they be likely to get rid of seven men out of eight from their own gang and retain only the eighth man? No! And no expedient could be devised which would make these men properly select themselves. Even if they fully realized the necessity of doing so in order to obtain high wages (and they are not sufficiently intelligent properly to grasp this necessity), the fact that their friends or their brothers who were working right alongside of them would temporarily be thrown out of a job because they were not suited to this kind of work would entirely prevent them from properly selecting themselves, that is, from removing the seven out of eight men on the gang who were unsuited to pig-iron handling.

As to the possibility, under the old type of management, of inducing these pig-iron handlers (after they had been properly selected) to work in accordance with the science of doing heavy laboring, namely, having proper scientifically determined periods of rest in close sequence to periods of work. As has been indicated before, the essential idea of the ordinary types of management is that each workman has become more skilled in his own trade than it is possible for any one in the management to be, and that, therefore, the details of how the work shall best be done must be left to him. The idea, then, of taking one man after another and training him under a competent teacher into new working habits until he continually and habitually works in accordance with scientific laws, which have been developed by some one else, is directly antagonistic to the old idea that each workman can best regulate his own way of doing the work. And besides this, the man suited to handling pig iron is too stupid properly to train himself. Thus it will be seen that with the ordinary types of management the development of scientific knowledge to replace rule of thumb, the scientific selection of the men, and inducing the men to work in accordance with these scientific principles are entirely out of the question. And this because the philosophy of the old management puts the entire responsibility upon the workmen, while the philosophy of the new places a great part of it upon the management.

With most readers great sympathy will be aroused because seven out of eight of these pig-iron handlers were thrown out of a job. This sympathy is entirely wasted, because almost all of them were immediately given other jobs with the Bethlehem Steel Company. And indeed it should be understood that the removal of these men from pig-iron handling, for which they were unfit, was really a kindness to themselves, because it was the first step toward finding them work for which they were peculiarily fitted, and at which, after receiving proper training, they could permanently and legitimately earn higher wages.

Although the reader may be convinced that there is a certain science back of the handling of pig iron, still it is more than likely that he is still skeptical as to the existence of a science for doing other kinds of laboring. One of the important objects of this paper is to convince its readers that every single act of every workman can be reduced to a science. With the hope of fully convincing the reader of this fact, therefore, the writer proposes to give several more illustrations from among the thousands which are at hand.

For example, the average man would question whether there is much of any science in the work of shoveling. Yet there is but little doubt, if any intelligent reader of this paper were deliberately to set out to find what may be called the foundation of the science of shoveling, that with perhaps 15 to 20 hours of thought and analysis he would be almost sure to have arrived at the essence of this science. On the other hand, so completely are the rule-of-thumb ideas still dominant that the writer has never met a single shovel contractor to whom it had ever even occurred that there was such a thing as the science of shoveling. This science is so elementary as to be almost self-evident.

For a first-class shoveler there is a given shovel load at which he will do his biggest day's work. What is this shovel load? Will a first-class man do more work per day with a shovel load of 5 pounds, 10 pounds, 15 pounds, 20, 25, 30, or 40 pounds? Now this is a question which can be answered only through carefully made experiments. By first selecting two or three first-class shovelers, and paying them extra wages for doing trustworthy work, and then gradually varying the shovel load and having all the conditions accompanying the work carefully observed for several weeks by men who were used to experimenting, it was found that a first-class man would do his biggest day's work with a shovel load of about 21 pounds. For instance, that this man would shovel a larger tonnage per day with a 21-pound load than with a 24-pound load or than with an 18-pound load on his shovel. It is, of course, evident that no shoveler can always take a load of exactly 21 pounds on his shovel, but nevertheless, although his load may vary 3 or 4 pounds one way or the other, either below or above the 21 pounds, he will do his biggest day's work when his average for the day is about 21 pounds.

The writer does not wish it to be understood that this is the whole of the art or science of shoveling. There are many other elements, which together go to make up this science. But he wishes to indicate the important effect which this one piece of scientific knowledge has upon the work of shoveling.

At the works of the Bethlehem Steel Company, for example, as a result of this law, instead of allowing each shoveler to select and own his own shovel, it became necessary to provide some 8 to 10 different kinds of shovels, etc., each one appropriate to handling a given type of material; not only so as to enable the men to handle an average load of 21 pounds, but also to adapt the shovel to several other requirements which become perfectly evident when this work is studied as a science. A large shovel tool room was built, in which were stored not only shovels but carefully designed and standardized labor implements of all kinds, such as picks, crowbars, etc. This made it possible to issue to each workman a shovel which would hold a load of 21 pounds of whatever class of material they were to handle: a small shovel for ore, say, or a large one for ashes. Iron ore is one of the heavy materials which are handled in a works of this kind, and rice coal, owing to the fact that it is so slippery on the shovel, is one of the lightest materials. And it was found on studying the rule-of-thumb plan at the Bethlehem Steel Company, where each shoveler owned his own shovel, that he would frequently go from shoveling ore, with a load of about 30 pounds per shovel, to handling rice coal, with a load on the same shovel of less than 4 pounds. In the one case, he was so overloaded that it was impossible for him to do a full day's work, and in the other case he was so ridiculously underloaded that it was manifestly impossible to even approximate a day's work.

Briefly to illustrate some of the other elements which go to make up the science of shoveling, thousands of stop-watch observations were made to study just how quickly a laborer, provided in each case with the proper type of shovel, can push his shovel into the pile of materials and then draw it out properly loaded. These observations were made first when pushing the shovel into the body of the pile. Next when shoveling on a dirt bottom, that is, at the outside edge of the pile, and next with a wooden bottom, and finally with an iron bottom. Again a similar accurate time study was made of the time required to swing the shovel backward and then throw the load for a given horizontal distance, accompanied by a given height. This time study was made for various combinations of distance and height. With data of this sort before him, coupled with the law of endurance described in the case of the pig-iron handlers, it is evident that the man who is directing shovelers can first teach them the exact methods which should be employed to use their strength to the very best advantage, and can then assign them daily tasks which are so just that the workman can each day be sure of earning the large bonus which is paid whenever he successfully performs this task.

There were about 600 shovelers and laborers of this general class in the yard of the Bethlehem Steel Company at this time. These men were scattered in their work over a yard which was, roughly, about two miles long and half a mile wide. In order that each workman should be given his proper implement and his proper instructions for doing each new job, it was necessary to establish a detailed system for directing men in their work, in place of the old plan of handling them in large groups, or gangs, under a few yard foremen. As each workman came into the works in the morning, he took out of his own special pigeonhole, with his number on the outside, two pieces of paper, one of which stated just what implements he was to get from the tool room and where he was to start to work, and the second of which gave the history of his previous day's work; that is, a statement of the work which he had done, how much he had earned the day before, etc. Many of these men were foreigners and unable to read and write, but they all knew at a glance the essence of this report, because yellow paper showed the man that he had failed to do his full task the day before, and informed him that he had not earned as much as $1.85 a day, and that none but high-priced men would be allowed to stay permanently with this gang. The hope was further expressed that he would earn his full wages on the following day. So that whenever the men received white slips they knew that everything was all right, and whenever they received yellow slips they realized that they must do better or they would be shifted to some other class of work.

Dealing with every workman as a separate individual in this way involved the building of a labor office for the superintendent and clerks who were in charge of this section of the work. In this office every laborer's work was planned out well in advance, and the workmen were all moved from place to place by the clerks with elaborate diagrams or maps of the yard before them, very much as chessmen are moved on a chess-board, a telephone and messenger system having been installed for this purpose. In this way a large amount of the time lost through having too many men in one place and too few in another, and through waiting between jobs, was entirely eliminated. Under the old system the workmen were kept day after day in comparatively large gangs, each under a single foreman, and the gang was apt to remain of pretty nearly the same size whether there was much or little of the particular kind of work on hand which this foreman had under his charge, since each gang had to be kept large enough to handle whatever work in its special line was likely to come along.

When one ceases to deal with men in large gangs or groups, and proceeds to study each workman as an individual, if the workman fails to do his task, some competent teacher should be sent to show him exactly how his work can best be done, to guide, help, and encourage him, and, at the same time, to study his possibilities as a workman. So that, under the plan which individualizes each workman, instead of brutally discharging the man or lowering his wages for failing to make good at once, he is given the time and the help required to make him proficient at his present job, or he is shifted to another class of work for which he is either mentally or physically better suited.

All of this requires the kindly cooperation of the management, and involves a much more elaborate organization and system than the old-fashioned herding of men in large gangs. This organization consisted, in this case, of one set of men, who were engaged in the development of the science of laboring through time study, such as has been described above; another set of men, mostly skilled laborers themselves, who were teachers, and who helped and guided the men in their work; another set of tool-room men who provided them with the proper implements and kept them in perfect order, and another set of clerks who planned the work well in advance, moved the men with the least loss of time from one place to another, and properly recorded each man's earnings, etc. And this furnishes an elementary illustration of what has been referred to as cooperation between the management and the workmen.

The question which naturally presents itself is whether an elaborate organization of this sort can be made to pay for itself; whether such an organization is not top-heavy. This question will best be answered by a statement of the results of the third year of working under this plan.

	Old plan	New plan task work
The number of yard laborers was reduced from between	400 & 600 down to about	140
Average number of tons per man per day	16	59
Average earnings per man per day	$1.15	$1.88
Average cost of handling a ton of 2240 lb	$0.072	$0.033

And in computing the low cost of $0.033 per ton, the office and tool-room expenses, and the wages of all labor superintendents, foremen, clerks, time-study men, etc., are included.

During this year the total saving of the new plan over the old amounted to $36,417.69, and during the six months following, when all of the work of the yard was on task work, the saving was at the rate of between $75,000 and $80,000 per year.

Perhaps the most important of all the results attained was the effect on the workmen themselves. A careful inquiry into the condition of these men developed the fact that out of the 140 workmen only two were said to be drinking men. This does not, of course, imply that many of them did not take an occasional drink. The fact is that a steady drinker would find it almost impossible to keep up with the pace which was set, so that they were practically all sober. Many, if not most of them, were saving money, and they all lived better than they had before. These men constituted the finest body of picked laborers that the writer has ever seen together, and they looked upon the men who were over them, their bosses and their teachers, as their very best friends; not as nigger drivers, forcing them to work extra hard for ordinary wages, but as friends who were teaching them and helping them to earn much higher wages than they had ever earned before. It would have been absolutely impossible for any one to have stirred up strife between these men and their employers. And this presents a very simple though effective illustration of what is meant by the words "prosperity for the employee, coupled with prosperity for the employer," the two principal objects of management. It is evident also that this result has been brought about by the application of the four fundamental principles of scientific management.

As another illustration of the value of a scientific study of the motives which influence workmen in their daily work, the loss of ambition and initiative will be cited, which takes place in workmen when they are herded into gangs instead of being treated as separate individuals. A careful analysis had demonstrated the fact that when workmen are herded together in gangs, each man in the gang becomes far less efficient than when his personal ambition is stimulated; that when men work in gangs, their individual efficiency falls almost invariably down to or below the level of the worst man in the gang; and that they are all pulled down instead of being elevated by being herded together. For this reason a general order had been issued in the Bethlehem Steel Works that not more than four men were to be allowed to work in a labor gang without a special permit, signed by the General Superintendent of the works, this special permit to extend for one week only. It was arranged that as far as possible each laborer should be given a separate individual task. As there were about 5000 men at work in the establishment, the General Superintendent had so much to do that there was but little time left for signing these special permits.

After gang work had been by this means broken up, an unusually fine set of ore shovelers had been developed, through careful selection and individual, scientific training. Each of these men was given a separate car to unload each day, and his wages depended upon his own personal work. The man who unloaded the largest amount of ore was paid the highest wages, and an unusual opportunity came for demonstrating the importance of individualizing each workman. Much of this ore came from the Lake Superior region, and the same ore was delivered both in Pittsburgh and in Bethlehem in exactly similar cars. There was a shortage of ore handlers in Pittsburgh, and hearing of the fine gang of laborers that had been developed at Bethlehem, one of the Pittsburgh steel works sent an agent to hire the Bethlehem men. The Pittsburgh men offered 4-9/10 cents a ton for unloading exactly the same ore, with the same shovels, from the same cars, that were unloaded in Bethlehem for 3 and 2/10 cents a ton. After carefully considering this situation, it was decided that it would be unwise to pay more than 3-2/10 cents per ton for unloading the Bethlehem cars, because at this rate, the Bethlehem laborers were earning a little over $1.85 per man per day, and this price was 60 percent more than the ruling rate of wages around Bethlehem.

A long series of experiments, coupled with close observation, had demonstrated the fact that when workmen of this caliber are given a carefully measured task, which calls for a big day's work on their part, and that when in return for this extra effort they are paid wages up to 60 percent beyond the wages usually paid, that this increase in wages tends to make them not only more thrifty but better men in every way; that they live rather better, begin to save money, become more sober, and work more steadily. When, on the other hand, they receive much more than a 60 percent increase in wages, many of them will work irregularly and tend to become more or less shiftless, extravagant, and dissipated.

Our experiments showed, in other words, that it does not do for most men to get rich too fast.

After deciding, for this reason, not to raise the wages of our ore handlers, these men were brought into the office one at a time, and talked to somewhat as follows:

"Now, Patrick, you have proved to us that you are a high-priced man. You have been earning every day a little more than $1.85, and you are just the sort of man that we want to have in our ore-shoveling gang. A man has come here from Pittsburgh, who is offering 4-9/10 cents per ton for handling ore while we can pay only 3-2/10 cents per ton. I think, therefore, that you had better apply to this man for a job. Of course, you know we are very sorry to have you leave us, but you have proved yourself a high-priced man, and we are very glad to see you get this chance of earning more money. Just remember, however, that at any time in the future, when you get out of a job, you can always come right back to us. There will always be a job for a high-priced man like you in our gang here."

Almost all of the ore handlers took this advice, and went to Pittsburgh, but in about six weeks most of them were again back in Bethlehem unloading ore at the old rate of 3-2/10 a ton. The writer had the following talk with one of these men after he had returned:

"Patrick, what are you doing back here? I thought we had gotten rid of you."

"Well, sir, I'll tell you how it was. When we got out there Jimmy and I were put on to a car with eight other men. We started to shovel the ore out just the same as we do here. After about half an hour I saw a little devil alongside of me doing pretty near nothing, so I said to him, 'Why don't you go to work? Unless we get the ore out of this car we won't get any money on pay-day.' He turned to me and said, 'Who in————are you?' 'Well,' I said, 'that's none of your business'; and the little devil stood up to me and said, 'You'll be minding your own business, or I'll throw you off this car!' 'Well, I could have spit on him and drowned him, but the rest of the men put down their shovels and looked as if they were going to back him up; so I went round to Jimmy and said (so that the whole gang could hear it), 'Now, Jimmy, you and I will throw a shovelful whenever this little devil throws one, and not another shovelful.' So we watched him, and only shoveled when he shoveled.——When pay-day came around, though, we had less money than we got here at Bethlehem. After that Jimmy and I went in to the boss, and asked him for a car to ourselves, the same as we got at Bethlehem, but he told us to mind our own business. And when another pay-day came around we had less money than we got here at Bethlehem, so Jimmy and I got the gang together and brought them all back here to work again.

When working each man for himself, these men were able to earn higher wages at 3-2/10 cents a ton than they could earn when they were paid 4-9/10 a ton on gang work; and this again shows the great gain which results from working according to even the most elementary of scientific principles. But it also shows that in the application of the most elementary principles it is necessary for the management to do their share of the work in cooperating with the workmen. The Pittsburgh managers knew just how the results had been attained at Bethlehem, but they were unwilling to go to the small trouble and expense required to plan ahead and assign a separate car to each shoveler, and then keep an individual record of each man's work, and pay him just what he had earned.

Bricklaying is one of the oldest of our trades. For hundreds of years there has been little or no improvement made in the implements and materials used in this trade, nor in fact in the method of laying bricks. In spite of the millions of men who have practiced this trade, no great improvement has been evolved for many generations. Here, then, at least, one would expect to find but little gain possible through scientific analysis and study. Mr. Frank B. Gilbreth, a member of our Society, who had himself studied bricklaying in his youth, became interested in the principles of scientific management, and decided to apply them to the art of bricklaying. He made an intensely interesting analysis and study of each movement of the bricklayer, and one after another eliminated all unnecessary movements and substituted fast for slow motions. He experimented with every minute element which in any way affects the speed and the tiring of the bricklayer.

H. CLIFFORD SPRINGER
ROBERT E. HERLIHY
ROBERT I. BEGGS

Mathematical Programming

1. Introduction

Although its origins go back in mathematical antiquity to the theories of linear equations and inequalities, the subject of linear programming, with a name and a domain of interest, was created in 1947. That there exist linear programming problems in mathematics, economic theory, and business had been known prior to that time, but there had been no codification of the subject matter. Interestingly enough, the most profound recognition of the relevance to business and the most significant theoretical discussions prior to 1947 had been made by mathematicians in the Soviet Union, but their work had gone unnoticed abroad.

The father of linear programming is George B. Dantzig, who was at that time a mathematician employed by the United States Air Force in Washington, and working on logistics planning problems. He noticed that many logistic problems naturally took the form which we now recognize as a linear program, and he suspected that he had uncovered a significant mathematical structure. He was encouraged in this belief by the mathematician J. von Neumann, and the

Source: H. C. Springer, R. E. Herlihy, and R. I. Beggs, *Advanced Methods and Models* (Homewood, Ill.: Richard D. Irwin, Inc., 1965), pp. 202-34. Reprinted with permission.

economists L. Hurwicz and T. C. Koopmans, whose work on the theory of games and other models of economic behavior involved similar mathematical concepts. A name for the subject was given, "programming of interdependent activities in a linear structure," which was later blessedly shortened to "linear programming."

At the same time, finding no known formal procedure or algorithm for solving a linear program, Dantzig invented one. For reasons which were not very good then, and have become even less persuasive with time, he called his algorithm the *simplex method*. Although alternative methods have since been suggested (and a resurrection of nineteenth-century mathematical literature has turned up some other candidates), it is the simplex method (albeit slightly modified) which is used in almost all linear programming calculations today.

From 1948 on, a variety of scholars from various fields have joined Dantzig in contributing to the growth in understanding of linear programming. The number of such contributors has been enormous, but it seems proper to cite the team of A. Charnes and W. W. Cooper as having played a key role in developing applications in industry, publishing excellent expository articles in various magazines, and writing the first textbook.

It seems also important to note the simultaneous growth of both the management sciences and the electronic computing machine industry. Linear programming participated reciprocally in both. And, as the years have passed, one can also note an ever-increasing amount of literature on the subject of linear programming, or LP as it is often called. Most of this linear programming literature is devoted either to pure questions of mathematical theory, or to methods of calculating answers once the equations and conditions have been numerically formulated. Such discussions are generally of little use to the research worker in a business, who is unconcerned with mathematical esoterica and is interested in methods of calculation only to the extent of knowing if a machine can handle his problem and at what cost in time and money. There is, however, a growing number of articles on *applications* of linear programming, and this is worth examining. It is very unlikely that the particular problem being discussed in such an article transliterates into a different business situation, but one can get a general feeling about the way a model gets formulated in various situations.

Just to give some idea as to what these applications articles are like, three sample selections from two of these articles will be quoted here. The first selection is from a pioneering article by Henderson and Schlaifer which appeared in the May-June, 1954, issue of the *Harvard Business Review*. Its title was "Mathematical Programming—Better Information for Better Decision Making." The first two paragraphs of the article went as follows:

> In recent years mathematicians have worked out a number of new procedures which make it possible for management to solve a wide variety of important company problems much faster, more easily, and more accurately

than ever before. These procedures have sometimes been called "linear programming." Actually, linear programming describes only one group of them: "mathematical programming" is a more suitable title.

Mathematical programming is not just an improved way of getting certain jobs done. It is in every sense a *new* way. It is new in the sense that double-entry bookkeeping was new in the Middle Ages, or that mechanization in the office was new earlier in this century, or that automation in the plant is new today. Because mathematical programming is so new, the gap between the scientist and the businessman—between the researcher and the user—has not yet been bridged. Mathematical programming has made the news, but few businessmen really understand how it can be of use in their own companies.[1]

The claims for LP in this article, as you can see, are far from modest. Perhaps even more interesting is the fact that these words are nearly as appropriate today, ten years later, as they were then. That gap between the scientist and the businessman still exists, although it is narrowing little by little. No doubt a few *more* businessmen really understand how mathematical programming can be used in their companies, but there are certainly many who are still puzzled by the questions "what is it?" and "how can I use it?"

The second quotation is much more recent, and indicates the extent to which the LP method is beginning to be seriously considered for direct application to problems of financial management and accounting activities. The following two paragraphs lead off an article by Ijiri, Levy, and Lyon in the Autumn, 1963, issue of the *Journal of Accounting Research*. Their paper is accurately titled "A Linear Programming Model for Budgeting and Financial Planning."

This paper reports on an experiment in applying modern mathematical methods to management problems in budgeting and financial planning. In this experiment the techniques of linear programming and double-entry accounting are joined by means of suitable models and interpretations in order to see what might be gained in the way of a unified approach to total enterprise planning.

Two very general aspects of this study may be identified. Starting from an initial statement of the balance sheet accounts, the first aspect of this study was concerned with devising ways of planning (and identifying) the transaction flows that would, in terms of some relevant objective: (*a*) bring the corporation into the best possible end-of-the-period balance sheet and, (*b*) make due allowance for other aspects of management policy, technological limitations, etc. The second aspect of this study was concerned with synthesizing information that could be utilized by management to evaluate all aspects of the problem. That is, it was desired to erect a model which could be used to supply information by means of which a company's management might readily determine the dollar consequences that could be

---

[1]*Harvard Business Review*, Vol. 32, No. 3, p. 73.

expected to flow from altering the firm's policies or the environment in which it operated, and so on.[2]

Now this short quotation is enough to suggest that the authors are seriously contemplating the addition to the existing double-entry accounting model of this relatively new mathematical technique, as an integral part of it, in order to enhance the quality of information supplied to business-decision-makers. It's still in the experimental stages, of course, but who can say how long it will be before such extensions will be commonplace.

But these authors don't even stop there. Consider the two concluding paragraphs of their article:

> Other applications of linear programming to accounting have shown the relationships between programming to goals and break-even budgeting. This could be combined with our application to form a unified approach to planning when multiple (and sometimes conflicting) objectives exist among the various divisions of a firm. Such an approach might be in order, for example, to determine a system of transfer prices for guiding decentralized operations in a way that will produce the best *over-all* results from each department's operations. These applications are available as a result of previous research in the theory and applications of linear programming. Additional research might produce further advantages if it were devoted to, say, investigating accounting models and applications as such. As Charnes et al. have shown, the network features of accounting models offer promising avenues of exploitation. With suitably arranged objective functions, linear programming and simulation approaches can be joined together with further increases in the scope and power of each.
>
> Finally, all of these topics are closely associated with the rapidly evolving developments and uses of electronic computers for business purposes. Further research in this direction is also warranted if the full value of these devices for managerial accounting applications is to be achieved.[3]

What they are suggesting is nothing short of a revolution in the design of accounting information systems. Are they overoptimistic? Probably so—scientists often are. Are they, and the others like them who are writing about the impact of mathematics on financial management, correct in their estimates of the directions such progress will take, or in the amount of time which will elapse before such changes are widespread? Maybe yes, maybe no. But one thing is becoming clear: if business managers of the sixties are to be ready to meet the "winds of change" which are blowing toward the seventies, they should understand the mathematical and technical principles upon which these changes may be based, before they cope with the far more difficult questions of profitably applying these new methods. In this chapter, we will consider, then, the mathematical ideas underlying linear programming.

[2] *Journal of Accounting Research,* Vol. 1, No. 2.
[3] *Ibid.*

2. Linear Programming

2.1 WHAT IS A LINEAR PROGRAM?

A clear distinction should be made between a *linear program,* which is a mathematical model having a very definite structure, and *linear programming,* which is the name given to the process of matching a business problem with a corresponding linear program. In programming, one attempts to model a real business situation in mathematical terms suitable for subsequent analysis; in a wide assortment of situations encountered in business, the mathematical model so produced can be stated in an LP form, for which solution techniques like the simplex method are available. Formulating a problem in this way, however, requires a clear notion regarding the *form* of the mathematical model known as a linear program.

A *mathematical program* has three main ingredients: a set of *choice variables,* a set of *constants,* and an *objective function.*

> *Choice variables* are those variables in the problem whose values are arbitrarily chosen and changed by the analyst in his search for a "best" set of values. The choice variables are related to each other and to other variables whose values are assumed to be specified by the circumstances of the situation. The choice variables in the mathematical program are a reflection of the decision choices business managers may make.
>
> *Constraints* are relationships among variables, usually in the form of inequalities, which restrict in some way the values that may be assigned to the choice variables.
>
> An *objective function* is a mathematical expression, involving some choice variables (and sometimes other quantities), whose value may be computed when the values of all variables are specified.

A *linear program* is a mathematical program in which the constraints and the objective function involve the choice variables in a mathematically linear way. In other words, the choice variables enter into the statements of the program only with exponents of unity; no squares, cubes, square roots, exponentials, etc., are involved.

A *solution* of a linear program is a particular *set of values* for the choice variables, for which the constraints are all satisfied. More than one solution may exist, if any exist at all. The *optimum solution* is a solution for which the computed value of the objective function is as large (or as small[4]) as possible. As a simple example, try right now to find values for two choice variables x and y, subject to the constraints that x is no bigger than twice y, and y is no larger than

---

[4]It makes little difference whether the objective function is to be maximized or minimized. If one desires the objective function to be a minimum, he could simply change the algebraic sign of all its terms, and strive to maximize the new expression. In both cases, the solution to the linear program would be the same.

12, in such a way that the objective function x plus y has the largest possible value.

In the language of ordinary algebra, this problem is written as a linear program as follows:

Choice-variables: x and y

Constraints: $\quad x \leqslant 2y$

Constraints: $\quad y \leqslant 12$

Objective function: $x + y$.

Required: Maximize the value of $x + y$.

If you have never before personally solved a linear program, you would have just done so for the first time if you chose x equal to 24 and y equal to 12 as the optimum solution. (Check these values—are they "best"?)

1. Solve the following linear program, by trial and error if necessary:

Choice variables: p and q

Constraints: $p-q \leqslant 2$

Constraints: $\quad q \leqslant 5$

Constraints: $\quad p \geqslant 4$

Objective function: $p + q + 6$

Problem: Choose numerical values for variables p and q so that all constraints are satisfied and the objective function is maximized.

Solution: $p =$ _____ $q =$ _____

2. In the previous exercise, replace the objective function with the following one:

$$p + q - 3.$$

What is the solution to this new linear program?

$p =$ _____ $q =$ _____

Suppose the objective function to be maximized in Exercise 1 had been $p^2 + 2q$.

Is this new problem a linear program? _____ Why? _____

Does this problem have a solution?

If so, state it: $p =$ _____ $q =$ _____

2.2 USING GRAPHS TO SOLVE AN LP

When there are only two choice variables in a linear program, and regardless of how many constraints there are on those variables, it is possible to find the solution by graphical means. Once this graphical method is understood, it serves to illustrate several of the other characteristics of a linear program. We will now solve the problem of Exercise 1 this way, as soon as we refresh our memories on drawing graphs of linear relationships.

What is the graph of the linear equation $y = x + 2$, for example? To plot it we need only select two values for x and y that correspond, plot them on a set of coordinate axes, and draw the straight line through the points. This straight line will be the *graph* of the algebraic equation, as follows:

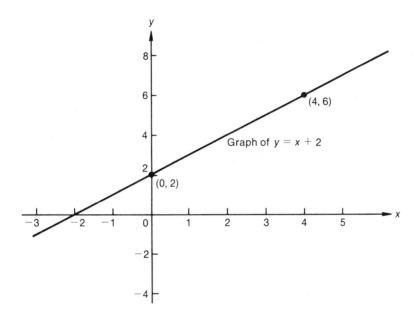

The line shown is the graph of the equation, because every point on the graph "satisfies" the equation. This is familiar territory for most people, but the next step may be new: what does the graph of the linear *in*equality, $y \leqslant x + 2$, look like?

The algebraic statement whose graph we seek is an inequality, which says that the values of x and y that satisfy (i.e., make a true statement of) the inequation are such that the y-value is always less than or equal to 2 plus the corresponding x-value. (It does not say how much less, but only that it is less by some amount.) Therefore, the graph we are looking for is the set of *all* points which possess this property. This graph turns out to be what is technically known as a *half-plane*. It looks like this:

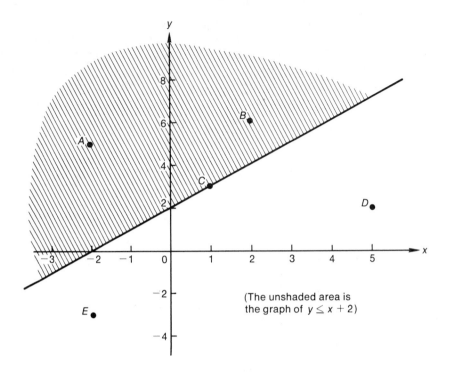

(The unshaded area is
the graph of $y \leq x + 2$)

Every point in the area which is *not* crosshatched satisfies the inequality. For example, the diagram shows five points, *A, B, C, D,* and *E*. The coordinates of the points can be tested as follows:

Point	Coordinates	Test	Part of the Graph?
A	$(-2, +5)$	is $+5 \leqslant -2 + 2$?	No
B	$(+2, +6)$	is $+6 \leqslant +2 + 2$?	No
C	$(+1, +3)$	is $+3 \leqslant +1 + 2$?	Yes
D	$(+5, +2)$	is $+2 \leqslant +5 + 2$?	Yes
E	$(-2, -3)$	is $-3 \leqslant -2 + 2$	Yes

So points *C, D,* and *E* are part of the graph, and in like way others could be verified.

Did you notice anything different about the test of point C? In that case, the value of *y* was exactly equal to $x + 2$; point *C* is part of the graph of the inequality, however, because the equation had a " $\leqslant$ " sign, so the "equal" cases qualify as satisfiers of the inequation. In a similar way, all the points along the border of the unshaded area satisfy the condition $y = x + 2$. But the condition $y = x + 2$ is just the equation of the straight line forming the edge of the half-plane. In other words, the graph of the *inequation* is the entire area which lies *on* or *to one side* (in this case the "lower-right" side) of the *equation* which corresponds.

3. On the sets of coordinate axes shown below, sketch in the graphs of the following inequalities. (Use crosshatching to indicate which portion of the half-plane is *not* included in the graph.)

a) $y \geqslant 4$
b) $y \geqslant 2x$
c) $x \leqslant 5$

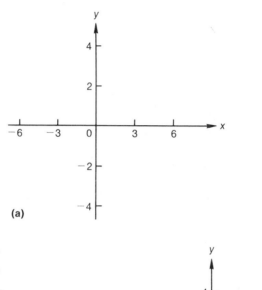

(a)

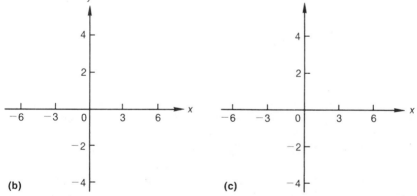

(b) (c)

We are now ready to use our knowledge of half-plane graphs to solve a linear programming problem. Let's take the one in Exercise 1, and plot on *one* set of axes *all* the constraints on the choice variables p and q. The constraints were:

a) $p - q \leqslant 2$ (or equivalently: $p \leqslant q + 2$)
b) $q \leqslant 5$
c) $p \geqslant 4$

The resulting figure is as shown.

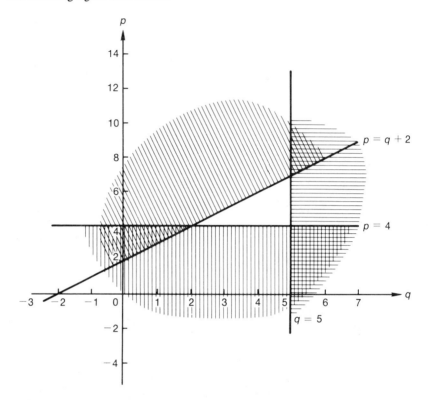

So now comes the key question: what points satisfy all *three* constraints? We want to know this because we set out to find values of the choice variables p and q which first, satisfy all constraints, and then second, maximize the objective function. Putting this second part aside for a moment let's try to take the first step: to identify *all* points that satisfy *all* constraints. If those points are known, then we have reduced the linear programming problem to choosing a "best" one from among only those that satisfy all constraints. This two-step approach not only cuts down the number of trials which lead to errors, but as we see in a moment, simplifies finding the optimum as well.

In the figure with the three half-planes, one for each constraint, the small triangular "window" area, with its straight-line borders, constitutes the set of points which satisfy all three constraints simultaneously.

Managerial Problem-Analysis

4. Select any point which is inside the triangle shown in the figure. Substitute its p and q values in the three inequalities (constraints) to verify that they are all satisfied. Repeat with a point on the *border* of the triangle (but not a vertex, where two sides of the triangle meet). How many of the constraints are satisfied with the = sign instead of the $\leqslant$ sign? _____

If you were to choose a vertex of the triangle, how many constraints would be satisfied with the = sign? _____

The name of the set of points which satisfy *all* constraints in a linear programming problem is the *feasible set.* It is called that because all members of the set are feasible solutions to the program. Points outside the feasible set can never be solutions, because they fail to satisfy one or more of the constraints on the choice variables. In case you had already asked yourself the question "what if there isn't any window—what if the half-planes overlap and don't leave any opening?" you might have already guessed the answer, too. In such cases, the feasible set is *empty;* it just has no members. Hence the linear program *has no solution.* Of course, that's another good reason for examining the problem for a feasible set—if it turns out to be empty, you can stop right there.

But suppose the feasible set has points in it. We are left with the problem of choosing from the set the point (or points) which maximize the objective function. For this purpose, it is handy to have a theorem that mathematicians have proved: *the optimum solution is always a vertex of the feasible set!* So with only three vertices in this problem, we only have to try all three. But that's not the end of the story. If we are going to understand how *big* LP's are solved, we need to do more than reduce the number of trials to just the numbers of vertices. In our example, with two choice variables, we can represent the feasible set as a two-dimensional figure on flat paper. With three variables we would have to build a three- dimensional model or else represent the problem by a perspective drawing on two-dimensional paper. With four or more choice variables, we leave behind the idea of graphic or pictorial representation completely. But with a linear program having, say, forty variables and a hundred constraints, the feasible set is a lump in *forty*-dimensional space whose borders are as many as a hundred thirty-nine dimensional surfaces, and this frightening lump might have a tremendous number of vertices. Far worse than that, one would have to solve forty simultaneous equations with up to forty variables in each one just to locate one vertex. Since the number of vertices is finite, one could imagine solving such sets of equations repeatedly until solutions corresponding to each of the vertices had been obtained. It is then conceivable to compare all solutions to determine which produces the greatest value of the objective function, hence the optimum. While it is possible to conceive of such a trial-and-error approach, it is incredible to imagine actually attempting it.

That's just why the simplex method was developed. The result is a method that eliminates the need to find solutions corresponding to each vertex. Instead, this method points the way from one solution to a better solution using rather simple mechanical rules and a convenient tabular scheme for keeping track of progress. The method moves efficiently from one solution to the next as long as a better one exists. When the objective function cannot be improved by finding other solutions, the process ends; for this, then, is the optimum solution.

Rather than go through the mechanics of the simplex method there's an easier way to illustrate the underlying notion. Take the objective function from our sample problem, and plot the linear equations which correspond to various values of the objective function:

Objective function: $p + q + 6$

Some possible values of it: 9, 12, 15, 18, 21

The five equations which correspond to these five values:

$p + q + 6 = 9$
$p + q + 6 = 12$
$p + q + 6 = 15$
$p + q + 6 = 18$
$p + q + 6 = 21$

Now plot these five linear equations on a set of coordinate axes' on which the triangular feasible set has been also plotted:

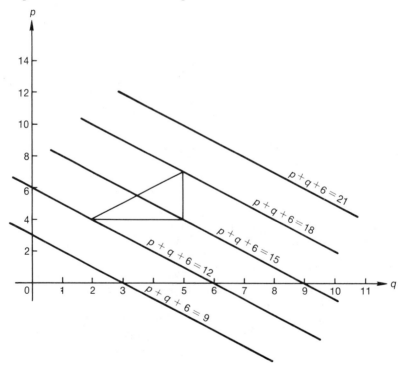

Managerial Problem-Analysis

Notice that every point which is on the line $p + q + 6 = 18$ has values of p and q such that the value of the objective function $(p + q + 6)$ is equal to 18 (because that's the way we made up the equations we plotted). Notice also, that as one moves his eyes from lower left to upper right, looking in turn at the lines which correspond to values of the objective function, these values steadily increase, from 9 to 12 to 15 and so on. If you can now imagine taking hold of the ends of such a line at the lower left, holding it at a constant angle and moving it upward to the right, you have conceived of the problem of maximizing the objective function as a problem of finding the furthest position of the line for which it still just touches the feasible set. That limiting position of the line is shown on the figure as $p + q + 6 = 18$, and it passes through the vertex $p = 7, q = 5$, of the feasible set triangle. If you move the line further "up," it will no longer pass through a feasible point. In other words, a higher value of the objective function cannot be attained under the given constraints. In short, this line-sweeping operation has found for us, graphically, the solution to the linear program, $p = 7$, $q = 5$, for which the objective function $p + q + 6$ attains its maximum value of 18. (Does this check with your own solution in Exercise 1?) In the next section you can try your hand at using this graphical method in solving a small linear program for the proprietors of the Onwego Company.

2.3 THE ONWEGO CASE

The Onwego Company manufactures and sells two products, tips and flaps. It is a small firm, run entirely by the three owners who have divided the responsibilities among them. Tom, an engineer, handles sales and engineering, Dick runs the shop and personnel matters, while Harry is in charge of accounting and financial matters. As Dick often says, "Tom tells me what to make, I make it, then Harry tells us we didn't make any money *that* way!"

Lately, the partners have been increasingly concerned about the effects of product mix on their business. They instinctively felt that there must be a "best" mix. While each had his own pet ideas as to how the present mix could be improved, none of them knew quite how to go about figuring out what the "best" mix was. Harry suggested one day that they talk it over with Van Orman, a mathematician friend of his, who was willing to take a crack at finding the answer. The following Tuesday, the four of them met at Harry's house and discussed the problem with suitable liquid accompaniment.

(Van made notes on the significant statements and also his translation of them into mathematical form. On the next pages are the important statements that came out in the meeting, interspersed with Van's mathematics. There is also space provided for *you* to *draw the graphs* which correspond to the various constraints on product mix which Tom, Dick, and Harry imposed.)

Harry: We make only two products, Van, tips and flaps.

Van: Let T = annual unit sales of tips
F = annual unit sales of flaps.

(Van only talks like this when he's working!)

Tom: We've got to sell at least a thousand each of these products if we want people to know we're in this business. I won't settle for anything less than that.

Van: $T \geqslant 1,000; F \geqslant 1,000.$

5. Minimum Allowable Sales

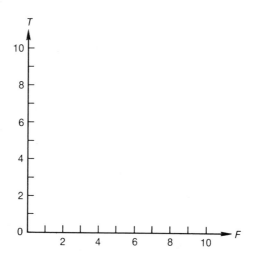

(The scales on this and the following graphs are in thousands of units.)

Tom: The way things look in the market, Van, there's no hope of selling more than 6,000 of either product in the next year.

Van: $T \leqslant 6,000; F \leqslant 6,000.$

6. Maximum Allowable Sales

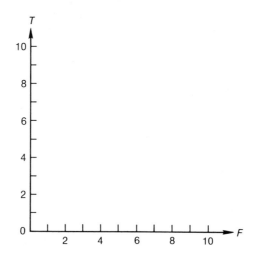

Dick: You guys can talk about *sales* limits all day, but I've got to get the stuff through the shop. Under present circumstances, we won't be able to produce more than 4,000 flaps; our machines just won't handle rates higher than that. Besides that, for every three flaps, I've got to make at least one tip, or our process won't work at all.

Van: $F \leqslant 4,000; 3T \geqslant F.$

7. Maximum Flap Capacity and Ratio Restriction

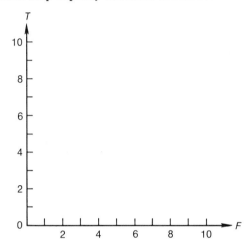

Dick: I'll say we've got restrictions on the amount of labor! With our old equipment, I've got to have at least five men to run that shop, no matter what we make. And even with a little rearrangement, the most men I can keep fully productive is twelve.

Harry: The amount of labor per unit? Oh, it's about 2.5 direct hours for a tip, and 2.0 for a flap. Those figures are O.K. for your estimates, Van.

Van: Assume 2,000 hours/man/year.

$$2.5\,T + 2.0\,F \geqslant 10,000$$
$$2.5\,T + 2.0\,F \leqslant 24,000.$$

8. Minimum and Maximum Labor Available

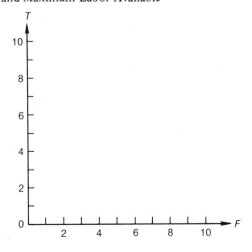

Harry: We're all right on working capital. I'd say we've covered about all the restrictions, Van.

Van: Values of (T,F) must satisfy all the following conditions:

1. $T \geqslant 1,000$
2. $F \geqslant 1,000$
3. $T \leqslant 6,000$
4. $F \leqslant 6,000$
5. $F \leqslant 4,000$
6. $3T \geqslant F$
7. $2.5T + 2.0F \geqslant 10,000$
8. $2.5T + 2.0F \leqslant 24,000$

9. Van took time out to put all the graphs of the constraints together, but all his final sketch showed clearly was the feasible set of solutions. On his diagram reproduced below, sketch in and label all the constraint half-planes, referring to the separate diagrams you made before. (Do you agree with Van on the shape of the feasible set?)

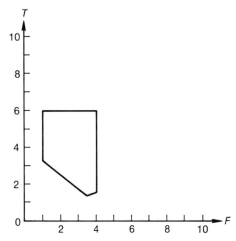

Van: Well, just what do you feel are your objectives in this business, fellows?

Tom: Good question. As I see it, our margin is greatest on flaps, so we should be aiming to sell as many of those as we can.

Dick: You know, Tom, I hate to disagree with you, but I'm becoming more and more convinced that our best bet is to keep the shop loaded with as much work as we can, that is, really go out after total dollar volume.

Harry: Don't pay any attention to these fellows, Van. All of us are really trying to operate at the greatest possible profit; they just talk in terms of their pet scheme for accomplishing that.

Van: To get at profit, Harry, I'll need some cost and price data.

Harry: Well, for your purposes, you can take our annual fixed costs to be $150,000. In the volume ranges we've been running, our variable costs are about $40 on a tip and $45 on a flap. And Tom is expecting prices to be a little softer this year. You should probably figure on the basis of a $70 price on the tips, and, let's see, about $90 on the flaps. But those figures are strictly ballpark, Van. Do you think you can work with them?

Van: Oh, sure, they ought to be close enough for what I'm doing now. I don't expect the math to do more than put us on the right track—we can always detail it out or put more accurate numbers in later. In fact, we ought to do that, just to make sure. But in most cases like this one, a first cut at the answer goes a lot faster when you don't go into all the gory details that slow you up but don't really affect the big picture very much. In fact, with what I've got now, I can give you fellows a reading on the optimum solution to these three linear programs in just a few minutes. Then we can talk about whether or not the solution of the math problem has any chance of being a solution to the real business problem that I've tried to translate into mathematics. All I'm trying to do now is just write down *your* problem in *my* language. Most of the time it works fine, but you've always got to make sure. So I'll need a look at that cost data of yours later, Harry. But let me see, now, since you've thrown three different objectives at me, I've got to solve all three problems. I'll try to get it all on this one sheet of paper, so you three can fight about your objectives on the same battlefield!

Van (continues): Tom's objective: to maximize F

Dick's objective: to maximize $70T + 90F$

Harry's objective: to maximize $30T + 45F - 150,000$.

10. Check these expressions with the verbal statements of the objectives given earlier. Did Van translate correctly?

If this were a real case, instead of a "toy" for illustrative purposes, Van would now be ready to apply one of the standard ways of solving his linear program. Most likely he would be going to a data processing installation to get the constraints and objective functions punched in the proper formats, and get the results out of the computer. Or he might apply the simplex method by hand. Because he (and we) chose the graphical method, which works well when there are only two choice variables, Van now has to plot his objective functions on the same diagram as the feasible set "window" appears. If he's been through this before, he will simply take each of the three objective functions in turn, find the slope of the straight line each of them represents, set his ruler at that angle on the page, and holding that angle constant, move it across the page until he reaches the furthermost vertex of the window. For example, the graph corresponding to a value for Tom's objective function, whose equation is $F = a$ constant, is a vertical straight line. So by holding his ruler vertically, and moving it to the right as far as he can while still touching the feasible set, Van would find the vertex (or vertices, in this case) at which the maximum value of F occurs.

11. On the graph below, which shows the feasible set of solutions, plot the following equations, representing three positions of Van's ruler for each of the three objective functions:

a) For flap production:
$$F = 3,000$$
$$F = 4,000$$
$$F = 5,000$$

b) For sales volume:
$$70T + 90F = 510,000$$
$$70T + 90F = 780,000$$
$$70T + 90F = 1,050,000$$

c) For profit dollars:
$$30T + 45F - 150,000 = 150,000$$
$$30T + 45F - 150,000 = 210,000$$
$$30T + 45F - 150,000 = 270,000$$

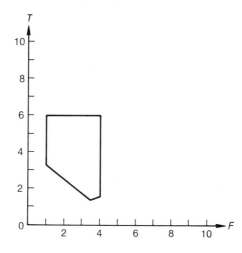

12. What is the maximum number of flaps that can be sold, and still satisfy all the constraints? _____

What is the maximum sales volume which it is feasible to attain?
_____

What is the maximum feasible profit? _____

Can Tom, Dick, and Harry agree on how many tips and flaps to make?

Van: Well for cryin' out loud! All the objectives are maximized at the same product mix, 6,000 tips and 4,000 flaps. So you're all in complete agreement, whether you knew it or not. Now that we're all done, the answer seems kind of obvious, doesn't it? Just make and sell as many of each as you can. But I don't know, lots of times you can't see what's obvious until you've gone through an analysis like this. It sure forces you to get explicit about the constraints and objectives and so on—sometimes I think the mathematics pays for itself just for doing that, even if you don't carry it all down until the last dog is hung. In fact, that's what I've been saying for a long . . . .

Tom: Yeah, Van, yeah, you're beginning to sound just like me when I'm on the road selling. Your analysis looks good to me, not because I understand all the ins and outs of your equations and so on, but because the answer seems to look darned reasonable, now that we've thought the whole thing through so carefully. As a matter of fact, about half the things we three sit around arguing about don't seem to make any difference at all, as far as shop load and sales goals are concerned, anyway. All those corners down at the bottom of your diagram don't get in the way at all, do they? Say, Dick, are you *sure* you can't turn out more than 4,000 flaps next year? How much would it cost to get those machine capacities up? I can sell 'em if you can crank them out. Why not . . . .

Harry: Now, Tom, there you go again. It takes dough to modify those old machines, and . . . .

Dick: We've been through that a million times, and a million times I've told you . . . .

Van: Hey fellows, wait . . . .

The story doesn't end here, but Van's day did. Next thing you know, though, they'll invite him back, and this time there'll be a whole new set of signals, maybe a new linear program. Probably just as well they built a simple model with approximate data, after all, eh?

2.4 WHEN IS A SOLUTION A SOLUTION?

If we assume for the moment that we understand the method by which we get solutions to mathematical models of the linear program type, there are still some questions which we need to look at before thinking seriously about applying such models in a business setting.

1. Is there a solution? This is a reasonable question to ask, for it is not at all unusual to discover in a linear programming application that the choice variables are subjected to such stringent constraints that not even *one* set of values can be found for which all constraints are satisfied. That is, the feasible set is empty, so that no solution of any kind is possible.

In the example we used, a solution did exist; in fact, there were infinitely many choices[5] of T and F which will satisfy all the constraints specified by Tom, Dick, and Harry. Suppose, though, there had been no solution to the program; what could be done? There would be several alternatives open to the Onwego managers. Some values of the choice variables must be chosen eventually (they won't go out of business entirely, we hope). The objective function has nothing to do with the *existence* of a solution, of course, so these alternatives all involve some modification to one or more of the constraints. Changing the constraints, one way or another, is the only way to get feasible solutions. Sometimes managers want to have their cake and eat it, too—they put on a lot of constraints they think are necessary, but which taken together rule out any chance of satisfying all of them with one solution. Manipulation of the linear program itself can sometimes measure the merit of various alternatives that may be suggested.

2. Is there a "best" solution? A hasty answer to this question would be that the "best" solution is an optimum solution, one which produces, say, the largest value for an objective function. There are at least three reasons why one should pause before jumping to this conclusion, though.

First, it can be proved that if any solutions exist, then an optimum solution exists for a linear program. There is still the possibility, however, that the optimum value for the objective function is an *unsatisfactory* value, according to standards of judgment *outside* the confines of the mathematical program. In a sense, this optimum value is the best that can be done under the constraints, but if this best is not yet good enough from the business point of view, perhaps the constraints must suffer a critical reexamination. The optimum solution to the linear program, as formulated, may be a far cry from the best solution to the business problem which is confronting the managers. In our example, for instance, when Tom saw the best that could be done, he attacked the capacity constraint that Dick had set.

Secondly, there is no guarantee that the optimum solution will be unique; there could be many solutions for which the maximum or minimum value of an objective function were attained. In such circumstances, a choice among the many optimum solutions must still be made, but the basis for the choice must come from outside the linear program itself. By and large, these alternate selections of choice variables will not be equally desirable, when subjected to criteria and judgments which were never explicitly included in the mathematical formulation. Thus, a best solution may exist, but the linear program, by itself, will be unable to yield it. As far as Tom was concerned (remember he wanted to maximize the number of flaps) any number of tips between 1,333 and 6,000

---

[5]This is strictly correct only if it were possible to produce fractional parts of tips or flaps. If the solution were restricted to integer values, i.e., whole numbers of units, the number of feasible solutions in our example would no longer be infinite.

would have been equally "optimum" since the line for his objective function came to rest along the right-hand border of the feasible set. After he saw this solution to his LP, he could then choose among the many possibilities according to other criteria.

In the third place, when a so-called "optimum" solution is found from a linear program, there is a high probability that this solution will not *actually* produce an extreme value of the objective function at all! For a practical man, it is too much to expect of a relatively clean-cut and highly idealized mathematical model that it produce the very best possible solution. Even if the objective function used were the sole criterion for judging the commendability of a particular solution, the very uncertainties in the estimated values of the data going into the program would already make the optimum solution suspect. Even worse, the mathematical equations which are used to approximate relationships in the real world can only lead to "approximately best" solutions.

There will usually be a best solution to the business problem, of course. After sufficient time has passed, a backward look would reveal what would have been the best values of the choice variables to use. That linear programming cannot perform as well as hindsight is not surprising. When intelligently applied, however, this technique does have the capability of producing solutions to incredibly complex operational decision problems far beyond the capability of the unaided mind.

3. How much "better" is the best solution? Subject to all the qualifications of the preceding paragraphs, we still should consider the extent to which an optimum solution is better than some other nonoptimum solution to a linear program. The admission that business criteria will exist, other than the objective function itself, that may influence the desirability of various solutions implies the possibility that some solution which is near-optimum may be "better" than the optimum. In most cases the existence of an optimum solution to a linear program implies also the existence of many "neighboring" solutions, for which the value of the objective function is about the same as for the optimum choice. In such cases, the problem is not sensitive to small deviations from the optimal solution. This low level of sensitivity, when it exists, is often useful in practical applications of linear programming. Thus the Onwego Company would do nearly as well making 3,900 flaps and 5,800 tips—that's close to the optimum, and nearly as good.

2.5 A MORE COMPLICATED EXAMPLE

Unfortunately, it is common for the technical man who gets his first glimpse of linear programming to get overenthusiastic and plunge headlong into a full-scale application without sizing up the consequences. One factor that will catch him up quickly is the amount of numerical input data that a really big program can chew up. Because the basic concepts of LP become so transparent (to the technical man) he makes insufficient allowance for the learning problem of the people for whom he is working, or for the demands for information about the situation being modeled. It must be understood that the development of an elaborate linear program is a *long process*. One rarely finds all the data handed on a silver platter. Getting constraints established is like pulling teeth—the model forces the builder to ask questions of the businessman which he has given little thought to in such explicit terms. Even working with guesstimates, sloppy constraints, and first-stab objective functions, the formulation of the linear program to the point of going to the computer for the first time may occupy several *months* of a man's time. It is not uncommon for a really important program, involving an entire chemical plant for example, to be literally years in construction. In cases like these, of course, the LP is being built to use repeatedly, as a model for operating the plant optimally over long periods of time. You don't start on such applications lightly or without a thorough period of study ahead of time.

To give you some idea of how such a large linear program might be put together, we are reproducing below a letter from a team of management consultants to their client in a fictitious picture tube business. In this letter, the consultants describe one possible approach for assisting in planning a manufacturing-distribution system and marketing policies to go along with it. (As you read through the letter, *ignore* any technical details which bore or confuse you. Instead just try to get an overall impression of what a medium-sized linear program is like. In other words, be a spectator only.)

Kansas City
October 1, 1964

Mr. John K. Bakerman
Acme Tube Company
West Haven, Ohio

Dear John,

Since our meeting last Tuesday we have been giving some thought to the picture tube problem and would like to try out a few ideas. The outline below is an approach to the situation which seems feasible from a business as well as a technical sense.

We assume that at each city i there is a yearly demand for new and/or rebuilt tubes—call it d_i —and a yearly volume of old tube trade-ins—call it e_i.

We assume that a lot-size policy for transporting bulbs or tubes from any point to any other point has been established. Then, we can calculate transportation costs for either bulbs or tubes between any two cities.

Managerial Problem-Analysis

Let

a_{ij} be cost of transporting a tube from city i to city j (a_{ij} may not be
the same as a_{ji} due to lot-size policy)

b_{ij} be cost of transporting a bulb (old tube) from city i to city j.

We assume that in any city i, a demand for yearly manufacturing production can be related to

yearly operating and reserve cost, without transportation expenses—say $f_i(x_i)$ where x_i is the yearly production, and $f_i(x_i)$ the yearly cost

net investment required—say $g_i(x_i)$ (these figures to include the existence of present facilities, of course).

Finally, let h_i be the capacity of the supplier of new bulbs at city i (if no supplier is located there, $h_i = 0$), and c_i be the unit cost of a new bulb at city i (no transportation charges included).

We take now for quantities requiring decision, i.e., *choice variables*:

x_i yearly number of new bulbs and/or old tubes to be converted into new tubes and/or rebuilt tubes

s_{ij} yearly number of new tubes and/or rebuilt tubes to be shipped from city i to city j

t_{ij} yearly number of new bulbs and/or old tubes to be shipped from city i to city j

p_i yearly number of new bulbs to be purchased in city i

A sensible solution in this situation will probably preclude, for any pair i, j, that both s_{ij} and t_{ij} be positive. Similarly, if x_i is zero, the meaning is that no manufacturing is to be done at city i. If p_i is zero, no new bulbs are purchased at city i.

The assumptions and information discussed above can be summarized as follows:

Assumptions
1. Points of distribution (including distributors, manufacturing facilities, and bulb suppliers) are assumed to be fixed by prior decision.
2. Demand of tubes, and rate of trade-in of old tubes are assumed to be fixed by prior decision (market policies) and estimated by managers (market research).
3. A lot-size policy in transportation of bulbs or tubes is assumed to be fixed by prior decision.
4. New and rebuilt tubes are not differentiated, nor are old tubes and new bulbs, insofar as their common possible uses and transportation characteristics are concerned (this done for simplicity of the example).

Information
Quantities given by the situation are labeled by letters at the top of the alphabet—$a, b, \ldots, h$; quantities requiring decision are from the bottom half—p, s, t, x. Subscripts $i, j, \ldots$, refer to cities which contain distribution points. Tube means new and/or rebuilt tube; bulb means new bulb and/or old tube.

a_{ij} cost of transporting a tube from city i to city j
b_{ij} cost of transporting a bulb from city i to city j
c_i cost of new bulb at city i
d_i yearly demand for tubes at city i
e_i yearly volume of old tube trade-ins at city i
$f_i(x_i)$ yearly operating cost at city i at yearly production x_i
$g_i(x_i)$ net investment required at city i at yearly production x_i
h_i capacity of new bulb supplier at city i
p_i yearly number of new bulbs purchased at city i
s_i yearly number of tubes shipped from city i to city j
t_{ij} yearly number of bulbs shipped from city i to city j
x_i yearly number of tubes manufactured at city i .

The quantities above have many interrelationships and also determine the cost of operating the system. Our next step is simply to minimize the cost of operating the system by selection of particular quantities p_i, s_{ij}, t_{ij}, x_i (for all i, j) which satisfy the consistency requirement of the interrelationships.

We describe the cost of the system, and the consistency requirements, then summarize them.

The essential costs of the system are those of manufacturing, transportation, and purchase of new bulbs (costs of trade-ins are part of the buying and selling–pricing–situation; by prior decision they belong to the system). We can calculate them separately, and add them. For the purposes of the example, we take the applicable cost to be

$$C + kI$$

where C is the total yearly cost of the system, I is the net investment in the system, and k is an appropriate percentage to be derived from the objectives of the manager.

Manufacturing Cost. If x_i tubes are produced at city i, the yearly cost will be

$$f_i(x_i).$$

To get the total manufacturing cost of the system, we sum this over all cities, i.e.,

Total Manufacturing Cost: $\Sigma_i f_i(x_i)$.

Transportation Cost. If s_{ij} tubes are sent from city i to city j, the cost of sending tubes from city i to city j is $a_{ij}s_{ij}$ Similarly, the cost of sending t_{ij} bulbs from city i to city j is $b_{ij}t_{ij}$. Hence, the transportation cost in shipments from city i to city j is

$$a_{ij}s_{ij} + b_{ij}t_{ij}.$$

To get the total transportation cost, we sum this over all pairs of cities:

Total Transportation Cost: $\Sigma_{ij}(a_{ij}s_{ij} + b_{ij}t_{ij})$.

Bulb Purchase Cost. If p_i bulbs are purchased in city i, the cost of purchase there will be $c_i p_i$, and by summing:

Total Purchasing Cost: $\Sigma_i c_i p_i$.

Investment Cost. The investment at city i will be $g_i(x_i)$ and as assumed above:

Total Investment Cost: $k\Sigma_i g_i(x_i)$.

Adding these up, we get

Total Cost: $\Sigma_i f_i(x_i) + \Sigma_{ij}(a_{ij}s_{ij} + b_{ij}t_{ij}) +$
$\Sigma_i c_i p_i + k\Sigma_i g_i(x_i) = \Sigma_i [f_i(x_i) + kg_i(x_i) + c_i p_i] +$
$\Sigma_{ij}(a_{ij}s_{ij} + b_{ij}t_{ij})$.

This is the *objective function*, i.e., the expression we wish to minimize, subject to the requirements of consistency (or *constraints*) given below.

To begin with, p_i, s_{ij}, t_{ij}, x_i are physical quantities which cannot be negative, i.e.,

$$p_i \geqq 0, \quad s_{ij} \geqq 0, \quad t_{ij} \geqq 0, \quad x_i \geqq 0, \text{ all } i, j.$$

Next, consider the situation at city i. In order to meet its demand, the total number of tubes shipped into it must be at least as great as the demand. Since s_{ji} is the number of tubes shipped from city j to city i (s_{ij} is the number i "ships" to itself), then

$$\Sigma_j s_{ji}$$

is the total number of tubes city i gets from all sources. Recalling d_i is the demand at city i, we can replace "tubes shipped into any city i must be at least as great as the demand at city i" by

$$\Sigma_j s_{ji} \geqq d_i, \text{ all } i.$$

Similarly, "tubes shipped out by any city i cannot be greater than the production at city i" can be replaced by

$$\Sigma_j s_{ij} \leqq x, \text{ all } i.$$

Also regarding bulb flow, "bulbs shipped into any city i must be at least as great as the tube production at i" can be replaced by

$$\Sigma_j t_{ji} \geqq x_i, \text{ all } i$$

and "bulbs (old tubes and new bulbs) shipped out of any city i cannot be greater than the old tubes traded in plus the new bulbs purchased at city i" by

$$\Sigma_j t_{ij} \leqq (e_i + p_i), \text{ all } i.$$

We also recall that the capacity of the supplier of new bulbs at i is h_i. Hence,

$$p_i \leqq h_i.$$

To summarize the problem of total cost and requirements of consistency we have the objective:

$$\text{minimize } \{\Sigma_i [f_i(x_i) + kg_i(x_i) + c_i p_i] + \Sigma_{ij}(a_{ij}s_{ij} + b_{ij}t_{ij})\}$$

subject to the constraints (holding for all i, j).

$$h_i \geqq p_i, s_{ij} \geqq 0, t_{ij} \geqq 0, x_i \geqq 0,$$
$$\Sigma_j a_{ji} \geqq d_i, \Sigma_j s_{ij} \leqq x_i,$$
$$\Sigma_j t_{ji} \geqq x_i, \Sigma_j t_{ij} \leqq (e_i + p_i).$$

Depending on the form of the functions $f_i(x_i)$ and $g_i(x_i)$, this problem is called a linear or nonlinear program. In either case it is solvable, and we can find the p_i, s_{ij}, t_{ij}, x_i which minimize the desired expression and satisfy the requirements of consistency. When they are found, they specify the cities in which manufacturing should take place, i.e., x_i will be positive, and the correct amount of manufacturing in each city will be specified. The quantities s_{ij}, t_{ij} specify where and how much each city should ship to every other city, while the p_i specifies the amounts of new bulbs to be purchased from each supplier.

The approach is essentially open-minded—any solution from a centralized manufacturing system to a completely decentralized manufacturing system is possible; this will depend on the actual data which is put in, of course.

We can introduce many refinements into the assumptions and information. For instance, we can:

1. Introduce more points into the distribution system, e.g., a major OEM
2. Distinguish between demand for new and rebuilt tubes by cities
3. Distinguish between manufacturing costs of producing tubes from new bulbs, and rebuilding old tubes
4. Introduce probability distribution for the demand rates—accounting also for seasonal trends
5. Introduce inventory considerations into the system
6. Distinguish between lot-size policies in transporting, and include finding an optimal policy as part of the problem
7. Introduce time lags in setup of manufacturing facilities, and in-transit inventories
8. Introduce time dimension in managers' objectives.

With these refinements, the form of the problem could call for finding optimal quantities requiring decision corresponding to:

1. Manufacturing capacities at each city (an extension of the idea of x_i above)
2. Distribution policies (extension of s_{ij}, t_{ij}) including
   a) Rate of flow of new bulbs, old tubes, new tubes, and/or rebuilt tubes between cities
   b) Lot sizes of shipments in any situation
3. Purchasing policies (extension of p_i).

In addition, the analysis will point up critical properties of the demand probability distributions insofar as the costs are concerned, as well as the dependence of all information on the values of the quantities of decision found to be optimal.

We sincerely hope this gives you a good start towards your goal, John. We wish you the best of luck, and don't hesitate to call us again if we can be of further assistance.

Very truly yours,

Lew

Lew Millis and Associates
Management Consultants

3. Application of LP and Related Methods

3.1 INDUSTRIAL APPLICATION OF
LINEAR PROGRAMMING

The industrial applications of linear programming have been of two general sorts, which may be classified as exploratory and routine.

A routine application is a regularly scheduled use of a linear programming model to make specific business decisions about the numerical values of certain variables. Generally, the form of the model and a great *many* of the constants remain the same from one use to another; at each use, only *some* of the constants are changed. There is generally some kind of "check for reasonability" of the answers by human beings, but this check tends to become perfunctory as confidence grows that the model truly represents reality.

Routine applications have been most frequently made to problems in production scheduling, purchasing, and distribution. They are only possible in those instances where there is very little doubt that the linearity assumptions are satisfied and that the objective function is clear and unambiguous. To attempt the routine use of a linear program in other circumstances is not only poor business in principle, but also administratively impossible. On the other hand, when the circumstances are appropriate, and when experience shows that, even considering the costs of calculation, the linear programming answers are a substantial improvement over what has been previously achieved by less formal methods, then it would be as absurd *not* to use linear programming as it would be to throw away one's adding machine.

One further remark about routine applications. They are generally found in areas of the business where people with assigned responsibility are already making decisions, and making them with careful consideration of the factors involved. Linear programming can only contribute a little formal mathematics to such decision-making, nothing more, and it is unreasonable to expect that the mathematics can contribute more than a small percentage improvement. It *may* do better, but one is not justified in assuming, before he begins, that it *will* do better. (Indeed, perhaps the largest contribution in these instances is in the formal statement of relations—i.e., the how and why.) It follows, therefore, that if the objective function is measured in dollars, the dollars should be very substantial before one mounts an effort that seems to tend in the direction of a routine application of linear programming. For to try to save a small percent of a small number of dollars hardly seems a judicious allocation of research and computing effort.

The *exploratory* applications of linear programming are generally applications where the hypothesis of linearity may not be so obviously true, and where the objective functions may not be clear and unambiguous. Most important of all, if the system being studied is very complex, the mathematician knows full well that, conscientious as he may be in explicitly listing his restrictions, there are a host of other restrictions that do not become part of the formal model. He may know their nature, but be unable to fit them into a linear description. He may even know they are linear, but be unable to obtain any data. Or he may not even know their nature, although he is vaguely aware of their existence.

In such circumstances the linear programming model represents a faith that, despite the lack of confidence in some of its constituents, the model nevertheless represents a picture of some portion of reality sufficiently important that answers obtained from the model should play a role in a manager's decision.

By contrast with routine applications, in which the linear programming answers generally dominate the decision, the answers from exploratory applications do not and should not. They are one piece of information, namely that certain assumptions imply certain conclusions, but the assumptions may be fairly shaky. Accordingly, there is no justification in common sense for endowing the linear programming answers in exploratory work with more meaning than that they show consequences of certain assumptions.

On the other hand, assuming the calculations are correct, the answers are unimpeachable consequences of the assumptions, and such instances of logical development are sufficiently unusual to be worthy of serious consideration in a manager's decision-making.

As to the areas where linear programming has been applied, either as routine or exploratory applications, the literature is full of illustrations. Most of the management science technical literature contains articles in nearly every issue. Applications range from investment policy formulation to executive compensation studies to marketing strategy determination; from cattle feed mixing to gasoline blending; from plant layout to truck scheduling to production-inventory balancing. Hardly any area of business activity has not been looked at as a potential ground for LP payoff. Some of these applications are classic cases by now, some as great successes, and some of the other kind, too. And the best way to learn more about these applications is to read about them in the original text. Since that's easily available, we will not take the space here to describe specific applications.

3.2 RELATED MATHEMATICAL METHODS

Since the term linear programming was coined nearly twenty years ago, many other methods which are more or less related to LP have received the attention of mathematicians. Because practical applications of these are only beginning to appear, we will do little more than mention their names:

1. *Parametric programming*—a way of introducing into the linear formulation the capability of treating several different objectives having priorities

attached, and determining the effects on these objectives of changing various conditions of the problem.

2. *Duality Theorem*—an important result from the *theory* of linear programming which establishes a relationship between two different formulations of the same problem, which leads to important advantages in setting up a program, computing a solution, or interpreting the results. As a side issue, the fundamental theorem of Game Theory can be exhibited as a consequence of the Duality Theorem.

3. *Integer Programming*—a variant of LP in which the solutions are restricted to being whole numbers.

4. *Stochastic Programming*—a very technical extension of linear programming in which elements of uncertainty and risk are introduced into either the data or the model formulation itself.

5. *Quadratic Programming*—a name given to a problem which looks much like a linear program, except the objective function is of second degree, i.e., contains squared terms in it.

6. *Convex Programming*—a more general form than quadratic programming, in which the objective function is what mathematicians call a "convex function." Computational methods exist for convex programs. Quadratic and linear programs are both special cases of convex programming, which in turn is a special case of nonlinear programming.

7. *Nonlinear Programming*—in which the constraints and objective functions can have just about any mathematical form. There are almost no general theoretical approaches available for solving nonlinear programs, although a few special types can be solved.

8. *Dynamic Programming*—a name for a mathematical optimization technique which is often mentioned in references on LP, even though the two methods have practically nothing to do with one another. It is a very difficult mathematical subject, not yet widely applied or even understood.

3.3 SOME CONSIDERATIONS IN CLOSING

Our discussion in this chapter has centered on three aspects of linear programming: what it is, how one formulates an LP, and some of the practical considerations in its application. We have not elaborated on the mathematical, as opposed to graphical, methods of solving the LP. The reason is that any of the mathematical methods are onerous to apply manually. They involve only simple arithmetic operations applied according to a set of rules (algorithms), but the process is iterative in nature so the number of simple operations quickly becomes astronomical. This, of course, is the reason LP is a natural for electronic computers.

In regard to the computational aspects of linear programming some comments are appropriate. The first point is that LP computer programs are readily available; in all but the simplest of problems their use is essential. An example of one of the better general-purpose LP programs is a new GE 225 program identified as CD225D7.005. This particular program can handle problems having as many as 300 constraint equations; the number of choice variables is limited only by tape capacity. Included in this program are many useful features. For example, before attempting to solve the problem, the computer first checks the feasible set. If the feasible set is found to be empty or if the constraints fail to bound a feasible set, the word INFEASIBLE is printed out and the computer stops before much time is wasted. And, especially useful for exploratory applications, is a feature that allows the program to be stopped and restarted after insertion of intermediate data changes, e.g., changing coefficients in the objective function.

In regard to computation, a word of caution! An LP can consume literally fabulous amounts of computer time compared to most of the previous scientific computer applications described in prior units. A problem with 65 constraint equations and 100 variables, requiring 120 iterations to arrive at the optimum set of values, was solved in 40 minutes on a large-scale computer. This can be misleading, however. To illustrate, let us assume that this example was an exploratory application in which, as a result of the first run, the linearity of the relationships became suspect. In such a situation it is not uncommon to divide the problem into smaller pieces so that the assumption of linearity applies within smaller ranges of variation. (The idea here is not unlike establishing a step budget.) Suppose that in the case mentioned above the problem was divided into three portions. The result would be an approximate tripling of the number of variables and constraints and the number of iterations would exceed 200. To solve this new problem now would require approximately 10 hours of running time on current large-scale computers. Maybe it would be worth it, maybe not! At any rate the economics of the situation are an important consideration when the potential benefits are this heavily mortgaged.

And now a word of encouragement! The nonmathematician can take comfort from the fact that the majority of successful applications of linear programming made to date in industry—and there have been many—were conceived by businessmen who knew enough of the basic concepts of LP to suspect its relevance to their work, and who then trained themselves to formulate their own LP models.

R. McMILLAN
D. GONZALEZ

Simulation

DEFINITION

In its most general sense, simulation means the representation of reality. Hence, verbal description and schematic or diagrammatic representation of some part of the real world constitutes simulation. Holstein and Soukup observe, however, that these forms of simulation are not new. On the other hand,

> If . . . simulation necessarily involves the use of mathematical expressions and equations which closely approximate random fluctuations in the simulated system, and which are so complex as to be impossible of solution without the aid of massive electronic computers, then simulation is a very recent development.[1]

Another writer defines simulation as *dynamic representation achieved by*

Source: R. McMillan and D. Gonzalez, *Systems Analysis: A Computer Approach to Decision Models* (Homewood, Ill.: Richard D. Irwin, Inc., 1965), pp. 13-28. Reprinted with permission.

[1]W. K. Holstein and William R. Soukup, *Monte Carlo Simulation,* Institute Paper No. 23, Institute for Quantitative Research and Economics and Management. Graduate School of Industrial Administration, Purdue University, Lafayette, Ind., 1962, p. 1.

building a model and moving it through time.[2] The model—a mathematical model—is an abstraction of a system which has its counterpart in the real world.

In these definitions we note the references to mathematical models and the computer. Since the system models are processed by the computer, they are *computer models* as the term was defined in the previous chapter.

> We use the term "computer model" to denote a special kind of formal mathematical model, namely a model which is not intended to be solved analytically but rather to be simulated on an electronic computer. Simulating a computer model consists in using a digital or analogue computer to trace numerically or graphically the time paths of all endogenous variables [for example, profit, inventory, price, output] generated by the model.[3]

Before we pursue the definition of computer simulation it is useful to note briefly what has been done using this technique to analyze business systems. The Eastman Kodak Company simulated a system for roll-film spooling, in which product mix and length of production runs varied, to solve problems of equipment design, utilization of operators, and maintenance.

General Electric Company used simulation to test alternative production scheduling procedures. A model of a production system was processed to learn the effect of different machine-loading, scheduling, and dispatching procedures. The company thus avoided the cost of trying out new scheduling procedures in the real system.

Imperial Oil modeled its physical distribution system, including hundreds of field warehouses and product flows throughout the system. Results of the simulation were used to determine the feasibility of central warehousing operations.

United Airlines modeled the operations of a large airport; and several months of activity were simulated in a matter of minutes. The model treated weather conditions, maintenance, aircraft, and manpower. The simulation proved useful for planning changes in the requirements for spare aircraft and standby personnel, and for testing the profitability of alternative operating plans.

Other simulations reported in 1959[4] included one by the Humble Oil Company to simulate oil-tanker scheduling. The Port of New York Authority simulated traffic patterns and demands for service prior to designing a central bus terminal. Thompson Products was one of several firms to simulate inventory systems under conditions of uncertainty.

[2]William Arthur, "To Simulate or Not to Simulate: That is the Question," *Educational Data Processing Newsletter*, Vol. 2, No. 4, p. 9.

[3]Kalman J. Cohen, "Simulation of the Firm," *The American Economic Review*, May, 1960, p. 534.

[4]*Report of the Second System Simulation Symposium*, American Institute of Industrial Engineers, Evanston, Ill., 1959.

At the same time that system-design and operating problems were being resolved with simulation techniques, nonbusiness systems also were being modeled. Economists employed simulation to predict the rate of economic growth in underdeveloped countries. Sociologists modeled populations so as to better understand and predict voting behavior. In 1960 simulation was used to predict the influence of religion on voting behavior. And psychologists are modeling the learning process and making use of simulation to test the reasonableness of their explanations of this phenomenon. What we have indicated about the widespread use of systems simulation in business, economics, and the social sciences is only a modest start if it is compared with the use of simulation in the physical sciences. There, as in the social sciences, the computer has increased the power of the technique.

From the preceding we may conclude—as one author has—that there has been a veritable explosion of simulation in recent years. However, it is not simply the popularity of a technique nor the ease with which it may be employed that recommends it to students of management. We need to understand *why* the technique is applied and *what distinguishes* it from more formal analytical problem-solving methods.

WHY SYSTEMS SIMULATION?

[Systems] simulation is useful in the study of a class of problems wherein the operating rules, policies, procedures, and other elements that control production, inventory, etc., are under question . . . [and in which the] number of variables involved, the uncertain nature of inputs, among other things, makes these problems, which are referred to generally as a system, difficult to analyze.[5]

Or, stated somewhat differently:

Mathematical analysis is not powerful enough to yield general analytical solutions to situations as complex as are encountered in business. The alternative is the experimental approach.

The mathematical model of the industrial system is constructed. Such a mathematical model is a detailed description that tells how conditions at one point in time lead to subsequent conditions at later points in time. The behavior of the model is observed and experiments are conducted to answer specific questions about the system that is represented by the model.

"Simulation" is a name often applied to this process of conducting experiments on a model instead of attempting the experiments with their real system. . . .

In business, simulation means setting up in a digital computer the conditions

[5]D. G. Malcolm, "The Use of Simulation in Management Analysis: A Survey," *Report of the Second System Simulation Symposium* (Evanston, Ill.: American Institute of Industrial Engineers, 1959), p. 18.

that describe company operations. On the basis of the descriptions and assumptions about the company, the computer then generates the resulting time charts [time paths or series] of information concerning finance, manpower, product movement, etc. Different management policies and market assumptions can be tested to determine their effects on company success.

Instead of going from the general analytical solution to the particular special case we have come to appreciate the great utility, if not the mathematical elegance, of the empirical approach. In this we study a number of particular situations, and from these we generalize as far as we dare.[6]

In summary then:

1. Simulation is a problem-solving technique.
2. It is an experimental method.
3. Application of simulation is indicated in the solution of problems of (*a*) systems design and (*b*) systems analysis.
4. Simulation is resorted to when the systems under consideration cannot be analyzed using direct or formal analytical methods.

Now let us consider several of these points in greater detail.

Properties of simulated systems. The definitions of simulation described systems (for which simulation methods are appropriate) as complex, subject to random fluctuations, and having relationships which are difficult if not impossible to analyze mathematically. By *complexity* we mean that the system is large in terms of the number of variables, parameters, relationships, and events to which the system is responsive.

The existence of *random variables* was implied in the definition which referred to 'the uncertain nature of inputs" of a system. Much of the discussion which follows in this text treats the manner in which random variables, or rather the processes (sequences of events) which assign successive values to the variable, are modeled.

The third property of systems for which simulation is an appropriate method of investigation concerns the relationships among system entities and attributes which are not well-behaved, or, as the mathematicians would say, are *not mathematically tractable.*[7] We do not expect that this property, so briefly described, will be immediately meaningful to the student. However, in subsequent expositions of various models the student should develop an awareness that simulation does indeed facilitate the analysis and evaluation of complex,

---

[6]Jay W. Forrester, *Industrial Dynamics* (Cambridge, Mass., and New York: The M.I.T. Press and John Wiley & Sons, 1961), pp. 17-18.

[7]For example, a relationship which determines values conditional on existing information. (See the discussion of "decision rules," which follows.)

dynamic relationships which, in many instances, cannot be expressed mathematically except with advanced concepts and difficult evaluation procedures.

SYSTEM DESIGN

The two applications of simulation listed are the *design* of systems and the *analysis* of system behavior. Design or the design problem simply means that typically the analyst has alternative ways of putting system components together. Given the specification of the desired output of the proposed system, he seeks a design that optimizes some measure of system behavior, such as profit, cost, time, resource utilization, stability, etc. A model of the system is processed incorporating successive changes which correspond to alternative designs. The influence of design on the measure of effectiveness is traced, and the analyst then has a basis for selecting the design which most effectively achieves the desired result or system output. This application, the comparison of alternative designs, is comparable with those experiments that use physical models of aircraft in wind tunnels or ship models in laboratory basins. When we referred to simulation as a kind of management laboratory, we had this application in mind.

To illustrate, consider the problem of designing a retail inventory system in Figure 1.

FIGURE 1

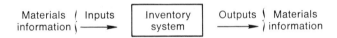

The inputs to the system are receipts of new stocks from suppliers and customer orders, which are designated "information inputs." The outputs are orders shipped and some form of customer billing. (These sets of inputs and outputs are actually incomplete, but they are sufficient for our discussion.) Average time to process or fill an order is arbitrarily selected as the measure of system effectiveness. (Obviously, the other measures of effectiveness could have been selected.) The box labeled Inventory System represents the set of entities, stock items, clerks, documents, etc., which the designer may arrange in any order to minimize the average order processing time.

When he specifies the contents of the box (entities, attributes of entities, and relationships; for example, the way in which attributes take on values) the designer is proposing a design alternative. Assume in this case that the analyst wishes to consider and compare design alternatives A, B, and C (and assume that Design A is the standard or reference configuration, and that B and C represent changes or alterations from design A). When Design A is modified we have indeed specified a different system, but it is convenient to simply speak of changes in a model rather than different models.

Alternative designs may differ in the number of clerks, amount of documentation, order in which customers are serviced, rules for reordering stock, etc. Now suppose that a system model of Design A is provided with information about a sequence of customer orders and that the model is processed or "run" so that it traces the activity of processing orders and replenishing stocks of the inventory items. Assume also that the model can be made to report periodic values of various attributes: inventory level, stock on order, back orders, etc. From this information the analyst can obtain the measure of effectiveness dependent on Design A.

Next, Design A is modified so that the alterations or changes we summarized as Design B are introduced. The procedure is repeated. Then changes corresponding to design alternative C are made and the model is processed. Using the three values of the measure of effectiveness, the analyst has a comparative

FIGURE 2

Simulation for System Design

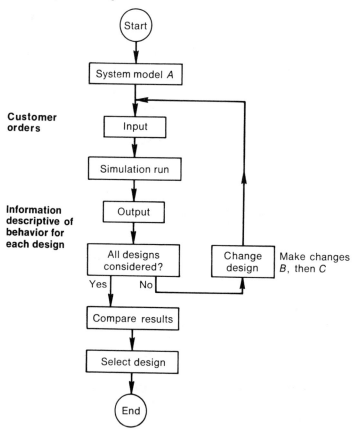

basis for settling on one of the designs for implementation; i.e., construction in the real world. This procedure is shown schematically in Figure 2. It should also be noted that our principal use of simulation in this text will be for the purpose of deciding what the design of particular systems should be.

SYSTEMS ANALYSIS

The second general application of simulation is to analyze the behavior of systems. The analyst observes systems inputs and outputs and seeks to explain how the transformation is achieved. He postulates a configuration of the system in terms of entities and their relationships, composes a computer model of his theoretical system, provides the model with inputs like those in the real system, and attempts to produce outputs from the model that correspond to those of the real world. The degree to which he succeeds is taken as a measure of the validity of the model; i.e., verification that the analyst can explain what took place in the real system.

The two applications appear to be similar, but in fact they are not. In the first case, simulation is used to obtain information about a system(s) which the analyst has created and about which he knows a great deal. In the second case, the analyst uses simulation to test hypotheses about a system which he does not know well, and whose behavior he can explain only by presuming the existence of particular entities and relationships. The procedure for systems analysis via simulation is diagrammatically shown in Figure 3.

FIGURE 3

Simulation-Systems Analysis

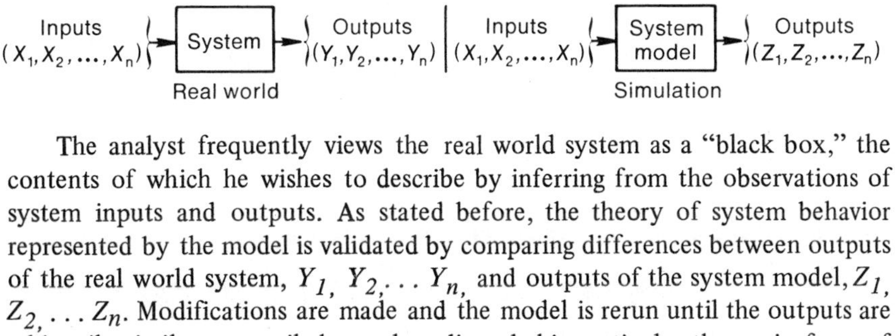

The analyst frequently views the real world system as a "black box," the contents of which he wishes to describe by inferring from the observations of system inputs and outputs. As stated before, the theory of system behavior represented by the model is validated by comparing differences between outputs of the real world system, Y_1, Y_2, ... Y_n, and outputs of the system model, Z_1, Z_2, ... Z_n. Modifications are made and the model is rerun until the outputs are arbitrarily similar—or until the analyst discards his particular theory in favor of another.

Methodology

In the following we present the general methodology of computer simulation (regardless of the application), but it is of course the purpose of the text to

FIGURE 4

Simulation Procedure

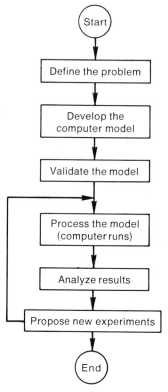

Identify systems components and their properties. State what variables are of interest, their interrelationships and how their values are determined.

Flow charting and coding (programming) the model.

Check for program errors. Does the model represent reality as planned?

Provide values for systems parameters, initial values for system variables. Provide input to the model; arrange for the reporting of specific measures of systems performance.

Adapted from Daniel Teichroew and John F. Lubin, "Computer Simulation: Discussion of the Techniques and Comparison of Languages," Working Paper No. 20, (Graduate School of Business, Stanford University, Stanford, Calif., 1964), pp. 27-29.

illustrate in detail how the methodology is implemented. The flow chart, Figure 4, outlines the procedure.

Computational concepts in simulation.[8] Reference has been made to a number of concepts which should now be defined. Attributes of system entities may change through time, in which case we call them *system variables* or, alternatively, *state variables.* The latter term is often used since the set of attribute values at any point in time defines the "state of the system." The state of our inventory system at any time would be obtained by noting the values of such attributes as Inventory on Hand, Inventory on Order, etc., which are attributes

---

[8]Adapted from Daniel Teichroew and John F. Lubin, "Computer Simulation: Discussion of the Techniques and Comparison of Languages," *Working Paper No. 20* (Graduate School of Business, Stanford University, Stanford, California, 1964), pp. 32-33.

of the entity, Stock Item. Attributes of other system entities would also be noted.

Parameters are considered to be those attribute values which do not change during the simulation. For example, a stock item might have the attribute Cost per Unit. For certain cases this attribute would be fixed during a simulated time, and it is necessary to state only initially what the parameter value is. System or state variables, on the other hand, must be given an initial value, but relationships in the system are periodically evaluated so that the system model is said to generate values for these variables. And (not to add to the confusion) we might point out that because these values are generated within the model, and depend on what happened earlier in the simulation, these values—or rather the variables to which the values are assigned—are called *endogenous variables*. Thus we will use the three terms interchangeably: *system, state,* and *endogenous* variables.

To process a model it is necessary not only to state parameter values and initial values for system variables, but some provision must be made for "moving the model through time." We are interested in the dynamic behavior of the system. Typically, the simulation begins at time zero, at which time the parameters and system variables have the initial values provided by the analyst.

Next, various events are generated or input to the model which cause changes to take place and which result in new values for the system or state variables. For example, in the inventory system the receipt of the first customer order (an event) results in changes in inventory and in the value of customer billings (or accounts receivable). The reduction in inventory might occasion an order to the supplier for new stock. In the computer all this activity takes place in a fraction of a minute but it corresponds, let us say, to the firm's activity during a full day.

Now provision for advancing the clock or the calendar is required; that is, we move to the next day or we input the next exogenous event and the model processes the information, describing the event, and, according to the relationships contained in the model, a second set of values of the state variables is computed. The process continues until all events have been input or until the simulation has run for the desired length of time.

Finally, two additional computational requirements exist in order to conduct simulations. We shall not detail them here since we have already alluded to them—and since their exploration must be deferred to those chapters which review some elements of probability and descriptive statistics. The requirements, however, are the provision for generating values of random variables, which are treated as the outcomes of exogenous events, and the summarization and analysis of the results of the simulation.

Simulation and Decision-Making

Relationships among entities and attributes take several forms. One kind of relationship may be illustrated with reference to an inventory system by considering the attributes, BEGINNING INVENTORY, ENDING INVENTORY, CUSTOMER ORDERS. These attributes (variables) may be related in the fashion:

$$\text{ENDING INVENTORY} = \text{BEGINNING INVENTORY} - \text{CUSTOMER ORDERS.}$$

We imply that the values have meaning at certain times; that is, at the beginning and end of the day or at some other points in time, and that the magnitudes are expressed in common units, dollars or physical units. When modeling a system it is necessary that we express many such relationships in order to obtain sequential values of state variables.

Another and more interesting relationship might be illustrated by the following expression:

$$\text{When INVENTORY ON HAND} \leqslant 50 \text{ units; order 200 units.}$$

This relationship is known as a *decision rule.* Whether or not an order is placed is conditional on the value of INVENTORY ON HAND. However, the relationship serves to compute the value of an attribute which we might call INVENTORY ON ORDER. At the start of the simulation the value of this state variable might be zero and would remain so until INVENTORY ON HAND $\leqslant$ 50. At that time the model would employ the decision rule to order 200 units and the value of INVENTORY ON ORDER would be 200. Thinking ahead we can see that this variable would be decreased whenever an order from a supplier was received. A second relationship, describing INVENTORY ON HAND, INVENTORY ON ORDER, and INVENTORY RECEIVED, would have to be specified.

Simulation is especially powerful for testing and comparing the way decision rules affect system behavior. Many design changes are changes of the parameters of decision rules (50 and 200 in our example) as well as changes of the form of the rule. For example, we might wish to substitute as a reorder rule the following:

$$\text{Order 100 units every day.}$$

Not all decision-making is so unambiguous. Neither are certain decisions made regularly. Yet, as we have implied, decision-making can be interpreted literally as modifying the state of a system.

DECISION-MAKING

The decision-maker is assumed to act periodically to influence the design of the system in order to transform a set of inputs into a set of outputs which have economic value. We assume further that the system has been designed to achieve transformation or conversion of inputs in a reasonably effective fashion.

However, we may observe that in the best designed systems conversion does not always measure up to the designer's plans. Things go wrong—availability of inputs of required quantity or quality are not completely controllable. Faulty production occurs, orders are delayed in processing, machines break down, the market places changing values on the product or service output of the systems, and so on.

The effects of such events change the system state in a way that prompts the decision-maker to modify something about the system. Perhaps he rearranges the set of inputs, or changes its composition. These changes, modifications, or redesign of the system constitute decision-making of a particular kind. The decision-maker elects to modify the system in order to better achieve the purpose(s) or ideal set of outputs for which the system was created, given information that outputs are not being achieved according to the measure of effectiveness. Decisions of this type may also be made on the basis of anticipated environmental changes which could lead to unsatisfactory system behavior.

There is a second type of decision, unlike that described above, which is imposed irregularly on the decision-maker. Some decisions are routinely required simply because the system is not automatic. Here we might imagine that activity takes place within the system and that the conversion of inputs proceeds to a particular state, the description of which is available to the decision-maker. He then initiates one of several regular courses of action. He is constrained by existing policy or he uses the information in conjunction with a decision rule of the form described above.

Courses of action usually involve commitments either to purchase or to hire resources: for example, the decision rule that when the inventory of stock item $Z \leqslant x$ units, order A number of units from the supplier; or, if the number of jobs scheduled today $> H$ number of machine hours, start up the standby machine; or, if plant utilization $< P$ percent this week, lay off workers, etc.

In both cases, decision making is a response by the manager who tries to control the behavior of the system. Conditions, or rather events exogenous to the system, can compel the manager to make decisions; or decisions may in part be planned and periodic responses required to sustain activity in the system. Simulation is used to improve the quality of other kinds of decision-making.

An Illustrative Example

To summarize many of the concepts and the simulation methodology, let us consider a small exercise in simulation which is intended merely to demonstrate certain features of the procedure. The student should not hazard an evaluation of simulation on the basis of the example in which simplifying assumptions are made and methodological short cuts used.

We fall back on the classical problem of the newsboy who seeks to fashion an inventory ordering rule so that the amount of his profit is maximized. Uncertainty exists in this situation because the number of papers purchased daily by his customers cannot be predicted. In such an inventory system we have the entities Newspapers, Customers, Newsboy, and Profit. The entity Newspapers has attributes: NUMBER ORDERED, NUMBER SOLD, COST, and PRICE. Profit has a single attribute of interest, AMOUNT. Attributes of Newspapers are recorded in units; the attribute of Profit, AMOUNT, in dollars.

A relationship can be written to express the way in which AMOUNT takes daily values:

$$\text{AMOUNT} = (\text{NUMBER SOLD})\,(\text{PRICE}) -$$
$$(\text{NUMBER ORDERED})\,(\text{COST}).$$

COST and PRICE refer to per unit values and we assume that unsold inventory has zero value. In the example we shall disregard the cost of unfilled demand; COST and PRICE are defined as parameters; and we shall assign the values: COST = $0.05; PRICE = $0.15.

The state variables NUMBER ORDERED and NUMBER SOLD must be generated. NUMBER ORDERED will take values determined by the evaluation of a decision rule which our newsboy elects to employ. The rule will be to order each day the number of papers demanded the preceding day. Thus each day:

$$\text{NUMBER ORDERED (DAY)} = \text{NUMBER DEMANDED (DAY} - 1).$$

where the value of the subscript (DAY) represents the current date. This illustrates the need for a system calendar variable, which we designate DAY, which takes on the values $1, 2, 3, \ldots, n.$ [9]

The variable, NUMBER SOLD, is determined in part by the exogenous event, CUSTOMER DEMAND. NUMBER SOLD also depends on the NUMBER ORDERED. If CUSTOMER DEMAND is equal to or less than NUMBER ORDERED, the newsboy can satisfy all customers. If CUSTOMER DEMAND is greater than NUMBER ORDERED, the newsboy can only sell an amount equal to NUMBER ORDERED. This relationship, used to determine NUMBER SOLD, can be expressed:

If CUSTOMER DEMAND $\leqslant$ NUMBER ORDERED,
then NUMBER SOLD = CUSTOMER DEMAND,

and

If CUSTOMER DEMAND $>$ NUMBER ORDERED,
then NUMBER SOLD = NUMBER ORDERED.

To generate values for CUSTOMER DEMAND we now resort to a shortcut. Suppose the newsboy knows from past experience that CUSTOMER DEMAND

---

[9] The notation used here anticipates the computer language, FORTRAN, which is introduced in the next chapter. Conventionally, we would write the subscripted variables as NUMBER ORDERED$_i$, NUMBER SOLD$_{i-1}$.

(daily) may be 15, 16, 17, 18, 19, or 20 newspapers. He also knows from his experience the relative frequency with which each value occurred and can thus construct the following table.

Customer Demand	Relative Frequency
15	1/12
16	2/12
17	4/12
18	3/12
19	1/12
20	1/12

He regards that the value of CUSTOMER DEMAND is determined by chance, but that in the long run the values occur with the frequencies noted. Therefore our newsboy constructs a type of roulette wheel in which the area is divided into six segments, each marked with a value of the variable, and each segment proportional in size to its relative frequency:

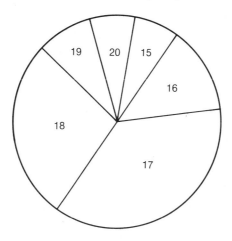

Each day the wheel is spun and the number of the segment taken to be the value of the variable, CUSTOMER DEMAND. He is now ready to simulate the system and test his proposed reorder rule. Table 1, which shows an average daily profit of $1.62, summarizes his activity for 10 days.

To begin the simulation, our newsboy spins his CUSTOMER DEMAND wheel and lets the first value represent demand the preceding day. This is necessary since his reorder rule requires a prior value (in our example this value was 18). Therefore the NUMBER ORDERED for DAY NUMBER 1 is 18. Next the wheel is used to generate CUSTOMER DEMAND for the first day. As we performed the simulation this value turned out to be 17. Comparing CUSTOMER DEMAND and NUMBER ORDERED for DAY NUMBER 1,

CUSTOMER DEMAND was less than NUMBER ORDERED. The NUMBER SOLD, employing our rule, is therefore 17 and AMOUNT is

$$(17)(0.15) - (18)(0.05) = \$1.65.$$

The variable "DAY" is given the value DAY = DAY + 1, which has the effect of moving us to the next day. The process is repeated, and the results are shown in Table 1.

The newsboy could now propose changes in the system, specifically in the reorder rule. He might wish to test a rule in which, for example, he orders an amount equal to average sales over perhaps the last three or five days. Other changes might be proposed. If he had reason to believe that the variable CUSTOMER DEMAND might change, he could model the anticipated change. We are not suggesting that a short, ten-day simulation run produces reliable information, nor that we have considered all properties of the system, but the

TABLE 1

Newsboy Simulation

Day	Customer Demand	Number Ordered	Customer Demand		Number Ordered	Customer Demand		Number Ordered	Number Sold	Amount	Amount (Cumulative
1	17	18		✓					17	1.65	1.65
2	17	17		✓					17	1.70	3.35
3	16	17		✓					16	1.55	4.90
4	17	16					✓		16	1.60	6.50
5	15	17		✓					15	1.40	7.90
6	17	15					✓		15	1.50	9.40
7	18	17					✓		17	1.70	11.10
8	20	18					✓		18	1.80	12.90
9	17	20		✓					17	1.55	14.45
10	18	17					✓		17	1.70	16.15

illustration serves to point out (in an elementary fashion) how the methodology is implemented. The meanings of such concepts as entities, attributes, state variables, parameters, decision rule, calendar, etc., are, hopefully, a little more meaningful.

The illustration points up another aspect of simulation. If we were to expand our model and propose a simulation run of several hundred or several thousand days for each of a series of system designs, we can readily appreciate the amount of effort involved. It is precisely for this reason that we call in the digital computer, and it is to the subject of computer programming that we turn in the next chapter.

Suggestions for Further Study

Forrester, Jay W., *Industrial Dynamics.* Cambridge, Mass., and New York: The M.I.T. Press and John Wiley & Sons, 1961.

Orcutt, G. H., M. Greenberger, J. Korbel, and A. H. Rivlin, *Micro-analysis of Socio-Economic Systems.* New York: Harper & Row, 1961.

Tocher, K. D., *The Art of Simulation.* Princeton, N. J.: D. Van Nostrand Co., 1963.

N. R. F. MAIER

Assets and Liabilities in Group Problem Solving: The Need for an Integrative Function

Research on group problem solving reveals that the group has both advantages and disadvantages over individual problem-solving. If the potentials for group problem-solving can be exploited and if its deficiencies can be avoided, it follows that group problem-solving can attain a level of proficiency not ordinarily achieved. The requirement for achieving this level of group performance seems to hinge on developing a style of discussion leadership which maximizes the group's assets and minimizes its liabilities. Since members possess the essential ingredients for the solutions, the deficiencies that appear in group solutions reside in the processes by which group solutions develop. These processes can determine whether the group functions effectively or ineffectively. The critical factor in a group's potential is organization and integration. With training, a leader can supply these functions and serve as the group's central nervous system, thus permitting the group to emerge as a highly efficient entity.

Source: Reprinted from *Psychological Review,* LXXIV, No. 4 (1967), pp. 239-49 with permission of the publisher, The American Psychological Association, Inc., and the author. The research reported here was supported by Grant No. MH-02704 from the United States Public Health Service. Grateful acknowledgment is made for the constructive criticism of Melba Colgrove, Junie Janzen, Mara Julius, and James Thurber.

A number of investigations have raised the question of whether group problem solving is superior, inferior, or equal to individual problem solving. Evidence can be cited in support of each position so that the answer to this question remains ambiguous. Rather than pursue this generalized approach to the question, it seems more fruitful to explore the forces that influence problem solving under the two conditions (9, 15). It is hoped that a better recognition of these forces will permit clarification of the varied dimensions of the problem-solving process, especially in groups.

The forces operating in such groups include some that are assets, some that are liabilities, and some that can be either assets or liabilities, depending upon the skills of the members, especially those of the discussion leader. Let us examine these three sets of forces.

Group Assets

GREATER SUM TOTAL OF KNOWLEDGE AND INFORMATION

There is more information in a group than in any of its members. Thus problems that require the utilization of knowledge should give groups an advantage over individuals. Even if one member of the group (e.g., the leader) knows much more than anyone else, the limited unique knowledge of lesser-informed individuals could serve to fill in some gaps in knowledge. For example, a skilled machinist might contribute to an engineer's problem-solving and an ordinary workman might supply information on how a new machine might be received by workers.

GREATER NUMBER OF APPROACHES TO A PROBLEM

It has been shown that individuals get into ruts in their thinking (6, 16, 44). Many obstacles stand in the way of achieving a goal, and a solution must circumvent these. The individual is handicapped in that he tends to persist in his approach and thus fails to find another approach that might solve the problem in a simpler manner. Individuals in a group have the same failing, but the approaches in which they are persisting may be different. For example, one researcher may try to prevent the spread of a disease by making man immune to the germ, another by finding and destroying the carrier of the germ, and still another by altering the environment so as to kill the germ before it reaches man. There is no way of determining which approach will best achieve the desired goal, but undue persistence in any one will stifle new discoveries. Since group members do not have identical approaches, each can contribute by knocking others out of ruts in thinking.

PARTICIPATION IN PROBLEM-SOLVING INCREASES ACCEPTANCE

Many problems require solutions that depend upon the support of others to be effective. Insofar as group problem solving permits participation and influence, it follows that more individuals accept solutions when a group solves the problem than when one person solves it. When one individual solves a problem he still has the task of persuading others. It follows, therefore, that when groups solve such problems, a greater number of persons accept and feel responsible for making the solution work. A low-quality solution that has good acceptance can be more effective than a higher-quality solution that lacks acceptance.

BETTER COMPREHENSION OF THE DECISION

Decisions made by an individual, which are to be carried out by others, must be communicated from the decision-maker to the decision executors. Thus individual problem solving often requires an additional stage—that of relaying the decision reached. Failures in this communication process detract from the merits of the decision and can even cause its failure or create a problem of greater magnitude than the initial problem that was solved. Many organizational problems can be traced to inadequate communication of decisions made by superiors and transmitted to subordinates, who have the task of implementing the decision.

The chances for communication failures are greatly reduced when the individuals who must work together in executing the decision have participated in making it. They not only understand the solution because they saw it develop, but they are also aware of the several other alternatives that were considered and the reasons why they were discarded. The common assumption that decisions supplied by superiors are arbitrarily reached therefore disappears. A full knowledge of goals, obstacles, alternatives, and factual information is essential to communication, and this communication is maximized when the total problem-solving process is shared.

Group Liabilities

SOCIAL PRESSURE

Social pressure is a major force making for conformity. The desire to be a good group member and to be accepted tends to silence disagreement and favors consensus. Majority opinions tend to be accepted regardless of whether or not their objective quality is logically and scientifically sound. Problems requiring solutions based upon facts, regardless of feelings and wishes, can suffer in group problem-solving situations.

It has been shown (32) that minority opinions in leaderless groups have little influence on the solution reached, even when these opinions are the correct ones. Reaching agreement in a group often is confused with finding the right answer, and it is for this reason that the dimensions of a decision's acceptance and its objective quality must be distinguished (22).

VALENCE OF SOLUTIONS

When leaderless groups (made up of three or four persons) engage in problem-solving, they propose a variety of solutions. Each solution may receive both critical and supportive comments, as well as descriptive and explorative comments from other participants. If the number of negative and positive comments for each solution are algebraically summed, each may be given a *valence index* (13). The first solution that receives a positive valence value of 15 tends to be adopted to the satisfaction of all participants about 85 percent of the time, regardless of its quality. Higher quality solutions introduced after the critical value for one of the solutions has been reached have little chance of achieving real consideration. Once some degree of consensus is reached, the jelling process seems to proceed rather rapidly.

The critical valence value of 15 appears not to be greatly altered by the nature of the problem or the exact size of the group. Rather, it seems to designate a turning point between the idea-getting process and the decision-making process (idea evaluation). A solution's valence index is not a measure of the number of persons supporting the solution, since a vocal minority can build up a solution's valence by actively pushing it. In this sense, valence becomes an influence in addition to social pressure in determining an outcome.

Since a solution's valence is independent of its objective quality, this group factor becomes an important liability in group problem-solving, even when the value of a decision depends upon objective criteria (facts and logic). It becomes a means whereby skilled manipulators can have more influence over the group process than their proportion of membership deserves.

INDIVIDUAL DOMINATION

In most leaderless groups a dominant individual emerges and captures more than his share of influence on the outcome. He can achieve this end through a greater degree of participation (valence), persuasive ability, or stubborn persistence (fatiguing the opposition). None of these factors is related to problem-solving ability, so that the best problem solver in the group may not have the influence to upgrade the quality of the group's solution (which he would have had if left to solve the problem by himself).

Hoffman and Maier (14) found that the mere fact of appointing a leader causes this person to dominate a discussion. Thus, regardless of his problem-solving ability a leader tends to exert a major influence on the outcome of a discussion.

CONFLICTING SECONDARY GOAL: WINNING THE ARGUMENT

When groups are confronted with a problem, the initial goal is to obtain a solution. However, the appearance of several alternatives causes individuals to have preferences and once these emerge the desire to support a position is created. Converting those with neutral viewpoints and refuting those with opposed viewpoints now enters into the problem-solving process. More and more the goal becomes that of winning the decision rather than finding the best solution. This new goal is unrelated to the quality of the problem's solution and therefore can result in lowering the quality of the decision (12).

Factors That Serve as Assets or Liabilities, Depending Largely upon the Skill of the Discussion Leader

DISAGREEMENT

The fact that discussion may lead to disagreement can serve either to create hard feelings among members or lead to a resolution of conflict and hence to an innovative solution (8, 10, 12, 20, 22, 30). The first of these outcomes of disagreement is a liability, especially with regard to the acceptance of solutions; while the second is an asset, particularly where innovation is desired. A leader can treat disagreement as undesirable and thereby reduce the probability of both hard feelings and innovation, or he can maximize disagreement and risk hard feelings in his attempts to achieve innovation. The skill of a leader requires his ability to create a climate for disagreement which will permit innovation without risking hard feelings. The leader's perception of disagreement is one of the critical factors in this skill area (30). Others involve permissiveness (19), delaying the reaching of a solution (24, 33), techniques for processing information and opinions (22, 25, 31), and techniques for separating idea getting from idea evaluation (21, 22, 31).

CONFLICTING INTERESTS VERSUS MUTUAL INTERESTS

Disagreement in discussion may take many forms. Often participants disagree with one another with regard to solutions, but when issues are explored one finds that these conflicting solutions are designed to solve different problems. Before one can rightly expect agreement on a solution, there should be agreement on the nature of the problem. Even before this, there should be agreement on the goal, as well as on the various obstacles that prevent the goal from being reached. Once distinctions are made between goals, obstacles, and solutions (which represent ways of overcoming obstacles), one finds increased opportunities for cooperative problem-solving and less conflict (11, 21, 22, 33, 40).

Often there is also disagreement regarding whether the objective of a solution is to achieve quality or acceptance (29), and frequently a stated problem reveals a complex of separate problems, each having separate solutions so that a search for a single solution is impossible (22). Communications often are inadequate because the discussion is not synchronized and each person is engaged in discussing a different aspect. Organizing discussion to synchronize the exploration of different aspects of the problem and to follow a systematic procedure increases solution quality (25, 31). The leadership function of influencing discussion procedure is quite distinct from the function of evaluating or contributing ideas (17, 19).

When the discussion leader aids in the separation of the several aspects of the problem-solving process and delays the solution-mindedness of the group (20, 22, 33), both solution quality and acceptance improve; when he hinders or fails to facilitate the isolation of these varied processes, he risks a deterioration in the group process (40). His skill thus determines whether a discussion drifts toward conflicting interests or whether mutual interests are located. Cooperative problem-solving can only occur after the mutual interests have been established and it is surprising how often they can be found when the discussion leader makes this his task (18, 22, 23).

RISK TAKING

Groups are more willing than individuals to reach decisions involving risks (42, 43). Taking risks is a factor in acceptance of change, but change may either represent a gain or a loss. The best guard against the latter outcome seems to be primarily a matter of a decision's quality. In a group situation this depends upon the leader's skill in utilizing the factors that represent group assets and avoiding those that make for liabilities.

TIME REQUIREMENTS

In general, more time is required for a group to reach a decision than for a single individual to reach one. Insofar as some problems require quick decisions, individual decisions are favored. In other situations acceptance and quality are requirements, but excessive time without sufficient returns also represents a loss.

On the other hand, discussion can resolve conflicts, whereas reaching consensus has limited value (42). The practice of hastening a meeting can prevent full discussion, but failure to move a discussion forward can lead to boredom and fatigue-type solutions, in which members agree merely to get out of the meeting. The effective utilization of discussion time (a delicate balance between permissiveness and control on the part of the leader), therefore, is needed to make the time factor an asset rather than a liability. Unskilled leaders tend to be too concerned with reaching a solution and therefore terminate a discussion before the group potential is achieved (24).

WHO CHANGES

In reaching consensus or agreement, some members of a group must change. Persuasive forces do not operate in individual problem-solving in the same way they operate in a group situation; hence, the changing of someone's mind is not an issue. In group situations, however, who changes can be an asset or a liability. If persons with the most constructive views are induced to change the end-product suffers; whereas if persons with the least constructive points of view change the end-product is upgraded. The leader can upgrade the quality of a decision because his position permits him to protect the person with a minority view and increase his opportunity to influence the majority position. This protection is a constructive factor because a minority viewpoint influences only when facts favor it (17, 18, 32).

The leader also plays a constructive role insofar as he can facilitate communications and thereby reduce misunderstandings (18, 40). The leader has an adverse effect on the end-product when he suppresses minority views by holding a contrary position and when he uses his office to promote his own views (24, 27, 32). In many problem-solving discussions the untrained leader plays a dominant role in influencing the outcome, and when he is more resistant to changing his views than are the other participants, the quality of the outcome tends to be lowered. This negative leader-influence was demonstrated by experiments in which untrained leaders were asked to obtain a second solution to a problem after they had obtained their first one (25). It was found that the second solution tended to be superior to the first. Since the dominant individual had influenced the first solution, he had won his point and therefore ceased to dominate the subsequent discussion which led to the second solution. Acceptance of a solution also increases as the leader sees disagreement as idea-producing rather than as a source of difficulty or trouble (30). Leaders who see some of their participants as troublemakers obtain fewer innovative solutions and gain less acceptance of decisions made than leaders who see disagreeing members as persons with ideas.

       Managerial Problem-Analysis

The Leader's Role for Integrated Groups

TWO DIFFERING TYPES OF GROUP PROCESS

In observing group problem-solving under various conditions it is rather easy to distinguish between cooperative problem-solving activity and persuasion or selling approaches. Problem-solving activity includes searching, trying out ideas on one another, listening to understand rather than to refute, making relatively short speeches, and reacting to differences in opinion as stimulating. The general pattern is one of rather complete participation, involvement, and interest. Persuasion activity includes the selling of opinions already formed, defending a position held, either not listening at all or listening in order to be able to refute, talking dominated by a few members, unfavorable reactions to disagreement, and a lack of involvement of some members. During problem solving the behavior observed seems to be that of members interacting as segments of a group. The interaction pattern is not between certain individual members, but with the group as a whole. Sometimes it is difficult to determine who should be credited with an idea. "It just developed," is a response often used to describe the solution reached. In contrast, discussions involving selling or persuasive behavior seem to consist of a series of interpersonal interactions with each individual retaining his identity. Such groups do not function as integrated units but as separate individuals, each with an agenda. In one situation the solution is unknown and is sought; in the other, several solutions exist and conflict occurs because commitments have been made.

THE STARFISH ANALOGY

The analysis of these two group processes suggests an analogy with the behavior of the rays of a starfish under two conditions; one with the nerve ring intact, the other with the nerve ring sectioned (7, 35, 36, 39). In the intact condition, locomotion and righting behavior reveal that the behavior of each ray is not merely a function of local stimulation. Locomotion and righting behavior reveal a degree of coordination and interdependence that is centrally controlled. However, when the nerve ring is sectioned, the behavior of one ray still can influence others, but internal coordination is lacking. For example, if one ray is stimulated, it may step forward, thereby exerting pressure on the sides of the other four rays. In response to these external pressures (tactile stimulation), these rays show stepping responses on the stimulated side so that locomotion successfully occurs without the aid of neural coordination. Thus integrated behavior can occur on the basis of external control. If, however, stimulation is applied to opposite rays, the specimen may be "locked" for a time, and in some species the conflicting locomotions may divide the animal, thus destroying it (5, 36).

Each of the rays of the starfish can show stepping responses even when sectioned and removed from the animal. Thus each may be regarded as an individual. In a starfish with a sectioned nerve ring the five rays become members of a group. They can successfully work together for locomotion purposes by being controlled by the dominant ray. Thus if uniformity of action is desired, the group of five rays can sometimes be more effective than the individual ray in moving the group toward a source of stimulation. However, if "locking" or the division of the organism occurs, the group action becomes less effective than individual action. External control, through the influence of a dominant ray, therefore can lead to adaptive behavior for the starfish as a whole, but it can also result in a conflict that destroys the organism. Something more than external influence is needed.

In the animal with an intact nerve ring, the function of the rays is coordinated by the nerve ring. With this type of internal organization the group is always superior to that of the individual actions. When the rays function as a part of an organized unit, rather than as a group that is physically together, they become a higher type of organization—a single intact organism. This is accomplished by the nerve ring, which in itself does not do the behaving. Rather, it receives and processes the data which the rays relay to it. Through this central organization, the responses of the rays become part of a larger pattern so that together they constitute a single coordinated total response rather than a group of individual responses.

THE LEADER AS THE
GROUP'S CENTRAL NERVOUS SYSTEM

If we now examine what goes on in a discussion group we find that members can problem-solve as individuals, they can influence others by external pushes and pulls, or they can function as a group with varying degrees of unity. In order for the latter function to be maximized, however, something must be introduced to serve the function of the nerve ring. In our conceptualization of group problem-solving and group decision, we see this as the function of the leader. Thus the leader does not serve as a dominant ray and produce the solution. Rather, his function is to receive information, facilitate communications between the individuals, relay messages, and integrate the incoming responses so that a single unified response occurs.

Solutions that are the product of good group discussions often come as surprises to discussion leaders. One of these is unexpected generosity. If there is a weak member, this member is given less to do, in much the same way as an organism adapts to an injured limb and alters the function of other limbs to keep locomotion on course. Experimental evidence supports the point that group decisions award special consideration to needy members of groups (11). Group decisions in industrial groups often give smaller assignments to the less gifted (18). A leader could not effectually impose such differential treatment on group members without being charged with discriminatory practices.

Another unique aspect of group discussion is the way fairness is resolved. In a simulated problem situation involving the problem of how to introduce a new truck into a group of drivers, the typical group solution involves a trading of trucks so that several or all members stand to profit. If the leader makes the decision the number of persons who profit is often confined to one (27, 34). In industrial practice, supervisors assign a new truck to an individual member of a crew after careful evaluation of needs. This practice results in dissatisfaction, with the charge of *unfair* being leveled at him. Despite these repeated attempts to do justice, supervisors in the telephone industry never hit upon the notion of a general reallocation of trucks, a solution that crews invariably reach when the decision is theirs to make.

In experiments involving the introduction of change, the use of group discussion tends to lead to decisions that resolve differences (18, 19, 26, 28, 29). Such decisions tend to be different from decisions reached by individuals because of the very fact that disagreement is common in group problem-solving and rare in individual problem-solving. The process of resolving differences in a constructive setting causes the exploration of additional areas and leads to solutions that are integrative rather than compromises.

Finally, group solutions tend to be tailored to fit the interests and per-sonalities of the participants; thus group solutions to problems involving fairness, fears, face-saving, etc., tend to vary from one group to another. An outsider cannot process these variables because they are not subject to logical treatment.

If we think of the leader as serving a function in the group different from that of its membership, we might be able to create a group that can function as an intact organism. For a leader, such functions as rejecting or promoting ideas according to his personal needs are out of bounds. He must be receptive to information contributed, accept contributions without evaluating them (posting contributions on a chalk board to keep them alive), summarize information to facilitate integration, stimulate exploratory behavior, create awareness of problems of one member by others, and detect when the group is ready to resolve differences and agree to a unified solution.

Since higher organisms have more than a nerve ring and can store informa-tion, a leader might appropriately supply information, but according to our model of a leader's role, he must clearly distinguish between supplying in-formation and promoting a solution. If his knowledge indicates the desirability of a particular solution, sharing this knowledge might lead the group to find this solution, but the solution should be the group's discovery. A leader's contri-butions do not receive the same treatment as those of a member of the group. Whether he likes it or not, his position is different. According to our conception of the leader's contribution to discussion, his role not only differs in influence, but gives him an entirely different function. He is to serve much as the nerve ring in the starfish and to further refine this function so as to make it a higher type of nerve ring.

This model of a leader's role in group process has served as a guide for many of our studies in group problem-solving. It is not our claim that this will lead to the best possible group function under all conditions. In sharing it we hope to indicate the nature of our guidelines in exploring group leadership as a function quite different and apart from group membership. Thus the model serves as a stimulant for research problems and as a guide for our analyses of leadership skills and principles.

Conclusions

On the basis of our analysis, it follows that the comparison of the merits of group versus individual problem-solving depends on the nature of the problem, the goal to be achieved (high quality solution, highly accepted solution, effective communication and understanding of the solution, innovation, a quickly reached solution, or satisfaction), and the skill of the discussion leader. If liabilities inherent in groups are avoided, assets capitalized upon, and conditions that can serve either favorable or unfavorable outcomes are effectively used, it follows that groups have a potential which in many instances can exceed that of a superior individual functioning alone, even with respect to creativity.

This goal was nicely stated by Thibaut and Kelley (41) when they:

> wonder whether it may not be possible for a rather small, intimate group to establish a problem-solving process that capitalizes upon the total pool of information and provides for great interstimulation of ideas without any loss of innovative creativity due to social restraints (p. 268).

In order to accomplish this high level of achievement, however, a leader is needed who plays a role quite different from that of the members. His role is analogous to that of the nerve ring in the starfish which permits the rays to execute a unified response. If the leader can contribute the integrative requirement, group problem - solving may emerge as a unique type of group function. This type of approach to group processes places the leader in a particular role in which he must cease to contribute, avoid evaluation, and refrain from thinking about solutions or group *products.* Instead he must concentrate on the group *process,* listen in order to understand rather than to appraise or refute, assume responsibility for accurate communication between members, be sensitive to unexpressed feelings, protect minority points of view, keep the discussion moving, and develop skills in summarizing.

References

1. Argyris, C., "T-Groups for Organizational Effectiveness," *Harvard Business Review*, XLII (1964), 60.

2. ——, "Explorations in Interpersonal Competence II," *Applied Behavioral Science*, 1, No. 3 (1965), 255.

3.——, *Organization and Innovation*. Homewood, Ill.: Richard D. Irwin, Inc., 1965.

4. Blake, R. R., J. S. Mouton, L. B. Barnes, and L. E. Greiner, "Break-through in Organization Development," *Harvard Business Review*, XLII (1964), 135.

5. Crozier, W. J., "Notes on Some Problems of Adaptation," *Biological Bulletin*, XXXIX (1920), 116-29.

6. Duncker, K., "On problem solving," *Psychological Monographs*, LVIII, No. 270 (1945).

7. Hamilton, W. F., "Coordination in the Starfish, III: The Righting Reaction as a Phase of Locomotion (Righting and Locomotion)," *Journal of Comparative Psychology*, II (1922), 81-94.

8. Hoffman, L. R., "Conditions for Creative Problem Solving," *Journal of Psychology*, LII (1961), 429-44.

9.——, "Group Problem Solving," in *Advances in Experimental Social Psychology*, Vol. II, ed. L. Berkowitz. New York: Academic Press, Inc., 1965, pp. 99-132.

10.——, E. Harburg, and N. R. F. Maier, "Differences and Disagreement as Factors in Creative Group Problem Solving," *Journal of Abnormal and Social Psychology*, LXIV (1962), 206-14.

11.——, and N. R. F. Maier, "The Use of Group Decision to Resolve a Problem of Fairness," *Personnel Psychology*, XII (1959), 545-59.

12.——, and——, "Quality and Acceptance of Problem Solutions by Members of Homogeneous and Heterogeneous Groups," *Journal of Abnormal and Social Psychology*, LXII (1961), 401-7.

13.——, and——, "Valence in the Adoption of Solutions by Problem-Solving Groups: Concept, Method, and Results," *Journal of Abnormal and Social Psychology*, LXIX (1964), 264-71.

14. ——, and——, "Valence in the Adoption of Solutions by Problem-Solving Groups: II. Quality and Acceptance as Goals of Leaders and Members" (Unpublished manuscript, 1967 [mimeo]).

15. Kelley, H. H., and J. W. Thibaut, "Experimental Studies of Group Problem Solving and Process," in *Handbook of Social Psychology*, ed. G. Lindzey. Cambridge, Mass.: Addison-Wesley Publishing Co., Inc., 1954, pp. 735-85.

16. Maier, N. R. F., "Reasoning in Humans. I: On Direction," *Journal of Comparative Psychology*, X (1930), 115-43.

17.——, "The Quality of Group Decisions as Influenced by the Discussion Leader," *Human Relations*, III (1950), 155-74.

18.——, *Principles of Human Relations*. New York: John Wiley & Sons, Inc., 1952.

19.——, "An Experimental Test of the Effect of Training on Discussion Leadership," *Human Relations*, VI (1953), 161-73.

20——, *The Appraisal Interview*. New York: John Wiley & Sons, Inc., 1958.

21.——, "Screening Solutions to Upgrade Quality: A New Approach to Problem Solving Under Conditions of Uncertainty," *Journal of Psychology*, IL (1960), 217-31.

22.——, *Problem Solving Discussions and Conferences: Leadership Methods and Skills*. New York: McGraw-Hill Book Company, 1963.

23.——, and J. J. Hayes, *Creative Management*. New York: John Wiley & Sons, Inc., 1962.

24. ——, and L. R. Hoffman, "Quality of First and Second Solutions in Group Problem Solving," *Journal of Applied Psychology*, XLIV (1960), 278-83.

25. ——, and ——, "Using Trained 'Developmental' Discussion Leaders to Improve Further the Quality of Group Decisions," *Journal of Applied Psychology*, XLIV (1960), 247-51.

26. ——, and ——, "Organization and Creative Problem Solving," *Journal of Applied Psychology*, XLV (1961), 277-80.

27. ——, and ——, "Group Decision in England and the United States," *Personnel Psychology*, XV (1962), 75-87.

28.——, and ——, "Financial Incentives and Group Decision in Motivating Change," *Journal of Social Psychology*, LXIV (1964), 369-78.

29.——, and ——, "Types of Problems Confronting Managers," *Personnel Psychology*, XVII (1964), 261-69.

30.——, and ——, "Acceptance and Quality of Solutions as Related to Leaders' Attitudes Toward Disagreement in Group Problem Solving," *Journal of Applied Behavioral Science*,I (1965), 373-86.

31.——, and R. A. Maier, "An Experimental Test of the Effects of 'Developmental' vs. 'Free' Discussions on the Quality of Group Decisions," *Journal of Applied Psychology*, XLI (1957), 320-23.

32.——, and A. R. Solem, "The Contribution of a Discussion Leader to the Quality of Group Thinking: The Effective Use of Minority Opinions," *Human Relations*, V (1952), 277-88.

33. ——, and ——, "Improving Solutions by Turning Choice Situations into Problems," *Personnel Psychology*, XV (1962), 151-57.

34.——, and L. F. Zerfoss, "MRP: A Technique for Training Large Groups of Supervisors and Its Potential Use in Social Research," *Human Relations*, V (1952), 177-86.

35. Moore, A. R., "The Nervous Mechanism of Coordination in the Crinoid Antedon Rosaceus," *Journal of Genetic Psychology*, VI (1924), 281-88.

36. ——, and M. Doudoroff, "Injury, Recovery, and Function in an Aganglionic Central Nervous System," *Journal of Comparative Psychology*, XXVIII (1939), 313-28.

37. Osborn, A. F., *Applied Imagination.* New York: Charles Scribner's Sons, 1953.

38. Schein, E., and W. Bennis, *Personal and Organizational Change Through Laboratory Methods.* New York: John Wiley & Sons, Inc., 1965.

39. Schneirla, T. C., and N. R. F. Maier, "Concerning the Status of the Starfish," *Journal of Comparative Psychology*, XXX (1940), 103-10.

40. Solem A. R., "1965: Almost Anything I Can Do, We Can Do Better," *Personnel Administration*, XXVIII (1965), 6-16.

41. Thibaut, J. W., and H. H. Kelley, *The Social Psychology of Groups.* New York: John Wiley & Sons, Inc., 1961.

42. Wallach, M. A., and N. Kogan, "The Roles of Information, Discussion, and Consensus in Group Risk Taking," *Journal of Experimental and Social Psychology*, I (1965), 1-19.

43.——, ——, and D. J. Bem, "Group Influence on Individual Risk Taking," *Journal of Abnormal and Social Psychology*, LXV (1962), 75-86.

44. Wertheimer, M., *Productive Thinking.* New York: Harper & Row, Publishers, 1959.

III

MANAGERIAL DECISION-MAKING

Primer:
The Notion of Goals

"...Life has a value only when it has something as its object...."—*Hegel*

Each model has, as one of its components, desired end states. These are the objectives of the model. They are the operationalization of the goals we wish to achieve.

These goals, or desired end states, are often thought of as derived from our needs in accordance with our values. That is, the manager has a host of needs and a host of values, and these act as a funnel as we select a path toward our desired end state.

The primary notion of this, Part III, of our text is the explication of the goals of a model on one hand and the values and needs of the manager on the other hand. That is, a very complex, reversible, feedback-like reaction exists. Our goals are at once a function of our values and needs and a determiner of our values and needs. Said on the other side of the mirror, our values and needs are concommitantly a cause and an effect of our goals.

My needs and values may lead me to pursue profit as a goal. But that pursuit will teach me to value an economic system in which the profit motive leads, in part, to societal utility maximization. And in the pursuit of profit, my needs whose gratifiers are most closely related to profit will more often be reinforced than other needs. And needs may be learned.

The circle continues. Decision-making is not a straight line or the branches of a tree. Rather, decision-making is better viewed as a friendly snake eating himself from behind.

The classical school is represented by an excerpt from Chester Barnard's classic book, *The Functions of the Executive.* This reading, which juxtaposes personal decisions and organization decision and delineates the environment of each, also acts as a major link between the approaches of the classical school and the behavioral sciences to decision-making. The quantitative sciences are represented by two articles which discuss alternative quantitative decision-making criteria. One article is prescriptive in that it demonstrates that an individual who satisfies the conditions for rationality outlined in the text should also use the decision criteria presented. Some drawbacks of serial decision-making from lower to higher managers are also discussed. The second reading discusses alternative quantitative decision-making criteria but leaves the choice of the "correct" criteria up to the subjective judgments of the manager. The Simon reading links the Q. S. and the B. S. approaches to decision-making by characterizing the ideas of multiple goals in the framework of a constrained optimization problem. The behavioral sciences are represented by an article which deals with alternative specification of rationality and their effects on decision-making.

HERBERT A. SIMON

On the Concept of
Organizational Goal

It is difficult to introduce the concept of organizational goal without
reifying the organization—treating it as something more than a system of
interacting individuals. On the other hand, the concept of goal appears
indispensable to organization theory. This paper proposes a definition of
"organizational goal" that resolves this dilemma.

The goal of an action is seldom unitary, but generally consists of a whole set
of constraints the action must satisfy. It appears convenient to use the term
"organizational goal" to refer to constraints, or sets of constraints, imposed
by the organizational role, that have only an indirect relation with the
personal motives of the individual who fills the role. More narrowly,
"organizational goal" may be used to refer particularly to the constraint sets
that define roles at the upper levels of the administrative hierarchy.

In actual organizations, the decision-making mechanism is a loosely coupled,
partially decentralized structure in which different sets of constraints may
impinge on decisions at different organizational locations. Although the

Source: Reprinted from *Administrative Science Quarterly,* Vol. 9, No. 1 (June, 1964),
pp. 1-22. Reprinted by permission of the author and the publisher.

description of organizational goals is consequently complex, the concept of goal can still be introduced in an entirely operational manner.[1]

Few discussions of organization theory manage to get along without introducing some concept of "organization goal." In the classical economic theory of the firm, where no distinction is made between an organizaton and a single entrepreneur, the organization's goal—the goal of the firm—is simply identical with the goal of the real or hypothetical entrepreneur. In general, it is thought not to be problematical to postulate that individuals have goals. If it is not, this solution raises no difficulties.

When we are interested in the internal structure of an organization, however, the problem cannot be avoided in this way. Either we must explain organizational behavior in terms of the goals of the individual members of the organization, or we must postulate the existence of one or more organization goals, over and above the goals of the individuals.[2]

The first alternative is an attractive one. It protects us from the danger of reifying the organization, of treating it as a superindividual entity having an existence and behavior independent of the behavior of its members. The difficulty with this alternative is that it is hard to carry off. The usual way it is attempted is by identifying the phrase "organization goals" with "goals of the firm's owners" or, alternatively, "goals of the firm's top management," or "goals of those who hold legitimate authority to direct the organization."

But this solution raises new difficulties, for we often have occasion to observe that the goals that actually underlie the decisions made in an organization do not coincide with the goals of the owners, or of top management, but have been modified by managers and employees at all echelons. Must we conclude, then, that it is the goals of the latter—of subordinate managers and employees—that are governing organizational behavior? Presumably not, because the kinds of behavior taking place are not those we would expect if the managers and employees were consulting only their personal goals. The whole concept of an informal organization, modified by, but not identical with, the goals either of management or of individual employees, becomes hazy and ambiguous if we follow this path.

Let us see if we can find a way between this Scylla and the Charybdis of reification. The first step toward clarification is to maintain a distinction between goals, on the one hand, and motives, on the other. By *goals* we shall

[1]This inquiry has been pursued under a grant from the Carnegie Corporation as part of a larger study on complex information processes. I am deeply indebted to Herbert Kaufman for persuading me of the need for the kind of clarification attempted here and for his helpful comments on a first draft.

[2]The present discussion is generally compatible with, but not identical to, that of my colleagues, R. M. Cyert and J. G. March, who discuss organizational goals in ch. iii of *A Behavioral Theory of the Firm* (Englewood Cliffs, N.J.: Prentice-Hall, Inc., 1963). Their analysis is most germane to the paragraphs of this paper that treat of motivation for goals and organizational survival.

mean value premises that can serve as inputs to decisions. By *motives* we mean the causes, whatever they are, that lead individuals to select some goals rather than others as premises for their decisions. In the next section we shall develop the concept of goal, defined as above. In subsequent sections we shall undertake to explicate the notion of *organization goal* and to clarify the relations between organization goals, and personal motives.

Before we can define "organization goals" we shall have to be clear on what we mean by "goals of an individual." We shall begin by considering the latter question.

Goals and Decisions: Multiple Criteria

Our discussion of goals will be much simplified if we have a definite model before us of the situation we are considering. In recent years in the field of management science or operations research, we have learned to build formal models to characterize even quite elaborate and complex decision situations, and to use these models to reach "optimal" decisions. Since many of these models make use of the tool of linear programming, we will employ a linear programming framework to describe the decision situation. No mathematical knowledge will be assumed beyond the ability to read algebraic notation.[3]

The optimal diet problem is a typical simple linear programming problem. We are given a list of foods, and for each item on the list its price, its calory content, and its proportions of each of the minerals and vitamins relevant to nutrition. Then we are given a set of nutritional requirements, which may include statements about minimum daily intake of minerals, vitamins, and calories, and may also put limits on maximum intake of some or all of these components.

The diet problem is to find that sublist of foods and their quantities that will meet the nutritional requirements at least cost. The problem can be formalized as follows:

Let the various foods be numbered from 1 through N, and the various nutritional components from 1 through M. Let x_i be the quantity of the ith food in the diet, y_j be the total quantity of the jth nutritional component in the diet, and p_i the price of the ith food. Let a_{ij} be the amount of the jth nutritional component in a unit quantity of the ith food; let b_j be the minimum requirement of the jth nutritional component, and c_j the maximum allowance. (Some of the b_j's may be zero, and some of the c_j's infinite.) Then:

$$\sum_i a_{ij}x_i = y_j, \qquad \text{for } j = 1, \ldots, M; \qquad (1)$$

[3]There are now a substantial number of elementary discussions of linear programming in the management science literature. For a treatment that develops the point of view proposed here, see A. Charnes and W. W. Cooper, *Management Models and Industrial Applications of Linear Programming* (New York, 1961), ch. i. See also Charnes and Cooper, "Deterministic Equivalents for Optimizing and Satisfying under Chance Constraints," *Operations Research*, 11 (1963), 18-39.

i.e., the total consumption of the jth nutritional element is the sum of the quantities of that element for each of the foods consumed. The nutritional requirements can be stated:

$$c_j \geq y_j \geq b_j, \qquad \text{for } j = 1, \ldots, M; \qquad (2)$$

i.e., the total quantity of the jth element must lie between b_j and c_j. The quantity of each food consumed must be non-negative, although it may be zero:

$$x_i \geq 0, \qquad i = 1, \ldots, N. \qquad (3)$$

Finally, the total cost of the diet is to be minimized; we are to find:

$$\operatorname*{Min}_{x} \sum_i x_i p_i. \qquad (4)$$

A diet (the solution is not necessarily unique) that satisfies all the relations (2), (3), (4) is called an *optimal* diet. A diet that satisfies the inequalities (2) and (3) (called *constraints*), but which is not necessarily a minimum cost diet, is called a *feasible* diet.

What is the goal of the diet decision? It would be an appropriate use of ordinary language to say that the goal is to minimize the cost of obtaining an adequate diet, for the condition (4) is the criterion we are minimizing. This criterion puts the emphasis on economy as the goal.

Alternatively, we might direct our attention primarily to the constraints, and in particular to the nutritional requirements (2). Then we might say that the goal is to find a nutritionally satisfactory diet that is economical. Although we still mention costs in this statement, we have clearly shifted the emphasis to the adequacy of the diet from a nutritional standpoint. The primary goal has now become good nutrition.

The relation between the criterion function (4) and the constraints (2) can be made even more symmetrical. Let us replace the criterion (4) with a new constraint:

$$\sum_i x_i p_i \leq k, \qquad (5)$$

that is to say, with the requirement that the total cost of the diet not exceed some constant, k. Now the set of feasible diets has been restricted to those that satisfy (5) as well as (2) and (3). But since the minimization condition has been removed, there is apparently no basis for choosing one of these diets over another.

Under some circumstances, we can, however, restrict the set of diets that deserve consideration to a subset of the feasible set. Suppose that all the nutritional constraints (2) are minimal constraints, and that we would always prefer, *ceteris paribus,* a greater amount of any nutritional factor to a smaller amount. We will say that diet A is dominated by diet B if the cost of diet B is no greater than the cost of diet A, and if diet B contains at least as much of each nutritional factor as does diet A, and more of at least one factor. We will call the set of diets in the feasible set that is undominated by other diets in that set the Pareto optimal set.

Our preference for one or the other of the diets in the Pareto optimal set will depend on the relative importance we assign to cost in comparison with amounts of nutritional factors, and to the amounts of these factors in relation with each other. If cost is the most important factor, then we will again choose the diet that is selected by criterion (4). On the other hand, if we attach great importance to nutritional factor j, we will generally choose a quite different feasible diet—one in which the quantity of factor j is as great as possible. Within the limits set by the constraints, it would be quite reasonable to call whatever criterion led us to select a particular member of the Pareto optimal set our goal. But if the constraints are strong enough, so that the feasible set and, *a fortiori*, the Pareto optimal set is very small, then the constraints will have as much or more influence on what diet we finally select than will the goal, so defined. For example, if we set one or more of the nutritional requirements very high, so that only a narrow range of diets also satisfy the budget constraint (5), then introducing the cost minimization criterion as the final selection rule will have relatively little effect on what diet we choose.

Under such circumstances it might be well to give up the idea that the decision situation can be described in terms of a simple goal. Instead, it would be more reasonable to speak of a whole set of goals—the whole set, in fact, of nutritional and budgetary constraints—that the decision-maker is trying to attain. To paraphrase a familiar epigram: "If you allow me to determine the constraints, I don't care who selects the optimization criterion."

Multiple Criteria in Organizations

To show the organizational relevance of our example it is only necessary to suppose that the decision we are discussing has arisen within a business firm that manufactures commercial stock feeds, that the nutritional requirements are requirements for hogs and the prices those of available feed ingredients, and that the finished feed prices facing the firm are fixed. Then minimizing the cost of feed meeting certain nutritional standards is identical with maximizing the profit from selling feed meeting those standards. Cost minimization represents the profit-maximizing goal of the company.

We can equally well say that the goal of the feed company is to provide its customers with the best feed possible, in terms of nutritional standards, at a given price, i.e., to produce feeds that are in the Pareto optimal set. Presumably this is what industry spokesmen mean when they say that the goal of business is not profit but efficient production of goods and services. If we had enlarged our model to give some of the prices that appear in the status of constraints, instead of fixing them as constants, we could have introduced goals, for example, the goal of suppliers' profits, or, if there were a labor input, the goal of high wages.[4]

We may summarize the discussion to this point as follows. In the decision-making situations of real life, a course of action, to be acceptable, must satisfy a whole set of requirements, or constraints. Sometimes one of these requirements is singled out and referred to as the goal of the action. But the choice of one of the constraints, from many, is to a large extent arbitrary. For many purposes it is more meaningful to refer to the whole set of requirements as the (complex) goal of the action. This conclusion applies both to individual and organizational decision-making.

Search for a Course of Action

Thus far, we have assumed that the set of possible actions is known in advance to the decision-maker. In many, if not most, real-life situations, possible courses of action must be discovered, designed, or synthesized. In the process of searching for a satisfactory solution, the goals of the action—that is, the constraints that must be satisfied by the solution—may play a guiding role in two ways. First, the goals may be used directly to synthesize proposed solutions (*alternative generation*). Second, the goals may be used to test the satisfactoriness of a proposed solution (*alternative testing*).[5]

We may illustrate these possibilities by considering what goes on in the mind of a chess player when he is trying to choose a move in a game. One requirement of a good move is that it put pressure on the opponent by attacking him in some way or by preparing an attack. This requirement suggests possible moves to an experienced player (alternative generation). For example, if the opponent's king is not well protected, the player will search for moves that attack the king, but after a possible move has been generated in this way (and thus automatically satisfies the requirement that it put pressure on the opponent), it must be tested against other requirements (alternative testing). For example, it will not be satisfactory if it permits a counterattack that is more potent than the attack or that can be carried out more quickly.

The decisions of everyday organizational life are similar to these decisions in chess. A bank officer who is investing trust funds in stocks and bonds may, because of the terms of the trust document, take as his goal increasing the capital value of the fund. This will lead him to consider buying common stock in

---

[4]See "A Comparison of Organization Theories," in my *Models of Man* (New York, 1957), pp. 170-182.

[5]For further discussion of the role of generators and tests in decision-making and problem-solving, see A. Newell and H. A. Simon, "The Processes of Creative Thinking," in H. E. Gruber, G. Terrell, and M. Wertheimer, eds., *Contemporary Approaches to Creative Thinking* (New York, 1962), particularly pp. 77-91.

firms in growth industries (alternative generation). But he will check each possible purchase against other requirements: that the firm's financial structure be sound, its past earnings record satisfactory, and so on (alternative testing). All these considerations can be counted among his goals in constructing the portfolio, but some of the goals serve as generators of possible portfolios, others as checks.[6]

The process of designing courses of action provides us, then, with another source of asymmetry between the goals that guide the actual synthesis and the constraints that determine whether possible courses of action are in fact feasible. In general, the search will continue until one decision in the feasible set is found, or, at most, a very few alternatives. Which member of the feasible set is discovered and selected may depend considerably on the search process, that is, on which requirements serve as goals or generators, in the sense just defined, and which as constraints or tests.

In a multiperson situation, one man's goals may be another man's constraints. The feed manufacturer may seek to produce feed as cheaply as possible, searching, for example, for possible new ingredients. The feed, however, has to meet certain nutritional specifications. The hog farmer may seek the best quality of feed, searching, for example, for new manufacturers. The feed, however, cannot cost more than his funds allow: if it is too expensive, he must cut quality or quantity. A sale will be made when a lot of feed is feasible in terms of the requirements of both manufacturer and farmer. Do manufacturer and farmer have the same goals? In one sense, clearly not, for there is a definite conflict of interest between them; the farmer wishes to buy cheap, the manufacturer to sell dear. On the other hand, if a bargain can be struck that meets the requirements of both—if the feasible set that satisfies both sets of constraints is not empty— then there is another sense in which they do have a common goal. In the limiting case of perfect competition, the constraints imposed by the market and the technology actually narrow down the feasible set to a single point, determining uniquely the quantity of goods they will exchange and the price.

The neatness and definiteness of the limiting case of perfect competition should not blind us to the fact that most real-life situations do not fit this case exactly. Typically, the generation of alternatives (e.g., product invention, development, and design) is a laborious, costly process. Typically, also, there is a practically unlimited sea of potential alternatives. A river valley development plan that aims at the generation of electric power, subject to appropriate provision for irrigation, flood control, and recreation will generally look quite different from a plan that aims at flood control, subject to appropriate provision for the other goals mentioned. Even though the plans generated in both cases will be examined for their suitability along all the dimensions mentioned, it is almost certain that quite different plans will be devised and proposed for consideration

[6]G. P. E. Clarkson, "A Model of Trust Investment Behavior," in Cyert and March, *op. cit.*

in the two cases, and that the plans finally selected will represent quite distinct points in the feasible set.

In later paragraphs we shall state some reasons for supposing that the total sets of constraints considered by decision-makers in different parts of an organization are likely to be quite similar, but that different decision-makers are likely to divide the constraints between generators and tests in quite different ways. Under these circumstances, if we use the phrase organization goals broadly to denote the constraint sets, we will conclude the organizations do, indeed, have goals (widely shared constraint sets). If we use the phrase organization goals narrowly to denote the generators, we will conclude that there is little commonality of goals among the several parts of large organizations and that subgoal formation and goal conflict are prominent and significant features of organizational life. The distinction we have made between generators and tests helps resolve this ambiguity, but also underlines the importance of always making explicit which sense of goal is intended.

Motivation for Goals

If by motivation we mean whatever it is that causes someone to follow a particular course of action, then every action is motivated—by definition. But in most human behavior the relation between motives and action is not simple; it is mediated by a whole chain of events and surrounding conditions.

We observe a man scratching his arm. His motive (or goal)? To relieve an itch.

We observe a man reaching into a medicine cabinet. His motive (or goal)? To get a bottle of lotion that, his wife has assured him, is very effective in relieving the itch of mosquito bites. Or have we misstated his motive? Is it to apply the lotion to his arm? Or, as before, to relieve the itch? But the connection between action and goal is much more complex in this case than in the previous one. There intervenes between them a means-end chain (get bottle, apply lotion, relieve itch), an expectation (that the lotion will relieve the itch), and a social belief supporting the expectation (that the wife's assurance is a reliable predictor of the lotion's efficacy). The relation between the action and the ultimate goal has become highly indirect and contingent, even in this simple case. Notice that these new complications of indirectness are superimposed on the complications we have discussed earlier—that the goal is pursued only within limits imposed by numerous side constraints (don't knock over the other bottles in the medicine cabinet, don't brush against the fresh paint, and so on).

Our point is identical with the point of the venerable story of the three bricklayers who were asked what they were doing. "Laying bricks," "Building a wall," "Helping to erect a great cathedral," were their respective answers. The investment trust officer whose behavior we considered earlier could answer in any of these modes, or others. "I am trying to select a stock for this investment portfolio." "I am assembling a portfolio that will provide retirement income for my client." "I am employed as an investment trust officer." Now it is the step of indirectness between the second and third answers that has principal interest for organization theory. The investment trust officer presumably has no "personal" interest in the retirement income of his client, only a "professional" interest in his role as trust officer and bank employee. He does have, on the other hand, a personal interest in maintaining that role and that employment status.

Role Behavior

Of course, in real life the line of demarcation between personal and professional interests is not a sharp one, for personal satisfactions may arise from the competent performance of a professional role, and both personal satisfactions and dissatisfactions may result from innumerable conditions that surround the employment. Nevertheless, it is exceedingly important, as a first approximation, to distinguish between the answers to two questions of motive: "Why do you keep (or take) this job?" and "Why do you make this particular investment decision?" The first question is properly answered in terms of the personal motives or goals of the occupant of the role, the second question in terms of goals that define behavior appropriate to the role itself.

Corresponding to this subdivision of goals into personal and role-defined goals, organization theory is sometimes divided into two subparts: (1) a theory of motivation explaining the decisions of people to participate in and remain in organizations; and (2) a theory of decision-making within organizations comprised of such people.[7]

In the motivational theory formulated by Barnard and me, it is postulated that the motives of each group of participants can be divided into *inducements* (aspects of participation that are desired by the participants) and *contributions* (aspects of participation that are inputs to the organization's production function but that generally have negative utility to participants). Each participant is motivated to maximize, or at least increase, his inducements while decreasing his contributions, and this motivation is a crucial consideration in explaining the decision to join (or remain). But "joining" means accepting an organizational role, and hence we do not need any additional motivational assumptions beyond those of inducements—contributions theory to explain the ensuing role-enacting behavior.

I hasten to repeat the caveat, introduced a few paragraphs above, that in thus separating our consideration of organizational role-enacting behavior from our consideration of personal motivation—allowing the decision to join as the

---

[7]For further discussion and references, see J. G. March and H. A. Simon, *Organizations* (New York, 1958), ch. iv.

only bridge between them—we are proposing an abstraction from the complexities of real life. A good deal of the significant research on human relations and informal organization, which has contributed heavily in the last generation to our understanding of organizational behavior, has been concerned specifically with the phenomena that this abstraction excludes. Thus, desire for power and concern for personal advancement represent an intrusion of personal goals upon organizational role, as do the social and craft satisfactions and dissatisfactions associated with work.

To say that the abstraction is sometimes untenable is not to deny that there may be many situations in which it is highly useful. There are, first of all, many organizational decisions that simply do not affect personal motives at all—where organizational goals and personal goals are orthogonal, so to speak. As a trivial example, the secretary's inducement-contribution balance is generally in no whit affected by the choice between typing a letter to A or a letter to B or by the content of the letter. Second, personal motives may enter the decision process as fixed constraints (only courses of action that satisfy the constraints are considered, but the constraints have no influence on the choice of action within the set). Thus, the terms of the employment contract may limit work to a forty-hour week but may have little to say about what goes on during the forty hours.[8]

The abstraction of organizational role from personal goals turns out to be particularly useful in studying the cognitive aspects of organizational decision-making, for the abstraction is consonant with some known facts about human cognitive processes. Of all the knowledge, attitudes, and values stored in a human memory, only a very small fraction are evoked in a given concrete situation. Thus, an individual can assume a wide variety of roles when these are evoked by appropriate circumstances, each of which may interact only weakly with the others. At one time he may be a father, at another a machinist, at another a chess player. Current information processing theories of human cognition postulate that there is only modest overlap of the subsets of memory contents—information and programs—that are evoked by these several roles. Thus, we might postulate that the day-to-day organizational environment evokes quite different associations out of the memory of the participant from those evoked when he is considering a change of jobs. To the extent this is so, it provides a further explanation of why his "personal" system of inducement and contributions, i.e., the utilities that enter into the latter decisions, will have no effect on his "organizational" decisions, i.e., those that are made while the first set is evoked.

The ability of a single individual to shift from one role to another as a function of the environment in which he finds himself thus helps explain the extent to which organizational goals become internalized, that is, are automatically evoked and applied during performance of the role. By whatever

[8]See "A Formal Theory of Employment Relation," in *Models of Man, op. cit.*

means the individual was originally motivated to adopt the role in the first place, the goals and constraints appropriate to the role become a part of the decision-making program, stored in his memory, that defines his role behavior.

Interpersonal Differences

Although the considerations introduced in the last section show that the uncoupling of organizational role from personal goals need not be complete, it may be useful to indicate a little more specifically how differences among individuals can affect their behavior in roles that are identical from an organizational standpoint.

A role must be understood not as a specific, stereotyped set of behaviors, but as a *program* (as that word is understood in computer technology) for determining the courses of action to be taken over the range of circumstances that arise. In previous sections we have given examples of such programs and have shown that they can be highly complex; for instance, a single decision may be a function of a large number of program instructions or premises.

Thus, while we may conceive of an ideal type of role that incorporates only organizational goals among its premises, the roles that members of organizations actually enact invariably incorporate both organizational and personal goals. We have already seen how both can be part of the total system of constraints.

But interpersonal differences in the enactment of roles go far beyond the incorporation of personal goals in the role. Role behavior depends on means-end premises as well as goal premises. Thus, particular professional training may provide an individual with specific techniques and knowledge for solving problems (accounting techniques, legal techniques, and so on), which are then drawn upon as part of the program evoked by his role. In this way, a chief executive with an accounting background may find different problem solutions from a chief executive, in the same position, with a legal background.

An individual may incorporate in his role not only a professional style but also a personal style. He may bring to the role, for example, habits and beliefs that provide him with crucial premises for his handling of interpersonal relations. Thus, an authoritarian personality will behave quite differently from a more permissive person when both are in the same organizational role and pursuing the same organizational goals.

The leeway for the expression of individual differences in role behavior is commonly narrowest in the handling of those matters that come to the role occupant at the initiative of others and is commonly broadest in his exercise of initiative and in selecting those discretionary matters to which he will attend and give priority. In terms used in earlier paragraphs, premises supplied by the organizational environment generally control alternative selection more closely than alternative generation.

The Organizational Decision-Making System

Let us limit ourselves for the present to the situations where occupational roles are almost completely divorced from personal goals and pursue the implications of this factoring of the behavior of organizational participants into its personal and organizational components. If we now consider the organizational decision-making programs of all the participants, together with the connecting flow of communication, we can assemble them into a composite description of the organizational decision-making system—a system that has been largely abstracted from the individual motives that determine participation.

In the simplest case, of a small, relatively unspecialized organization, we are back to a decision-making situation not unlike that of the optimal diet problem. The language of "goals," "requirements," "constraints," that we applied there is equally applicable to similarly uncomplicated organizational situations.

In more complicated cases, abstracting out the organizational decision-making system from personal motives does not remove all aspects of interpersonal (more accurately, interrole) difference from the decision-making process. For when many persons in specialized roles participate in making an organization's decisions, the total system is not likely to be monolithic in structure. Individual roles will differ with respect to the number and kinds of communications they receive and the parts of the environment from which they receive them. They will differ with respect to the evaluative communications they receive from other roles. They will differ in their search programs. Hence, even within our abstraction, which neglects personal motives, we can accommodate the phenomena of differential perception and subgoal formation.

To make our discussion more specific, let us again consider a specific example of an organizational decision-making system—in this case a system for controlling inventory and production. We suppose a factory in which decisions have to be made about (1) the aggregate rate of production, that is, the work force that will be employed and the hours employees will work each week, (2) the allocation of aggregate production facilities among the several products the factory makes, and (3) the scheduling of the sequence in which the individual products will be handled on the production facilities. Let us call these aggregate production decision, item allocation decision, and scheduling decision, respectively. The three sets of decisions may be made by different roles in the organization; in general, we would expect the aggregate decision to be handled at more central levels than the others. The real world situation will always include complications beyond those we have described, for it will involve decisions with respect to shipments to warehouses, decisions as to which products to hold in warehouse inventories, and many others.

Now we could conceive of an omniscient Planner (the entrepreneur of classical economic theory) who, by solving a set of simultaneous equations, would make each and all of these interrelated decisions. Decision problems of this kind have been widely studied during the past decade by management scientists, with the result that we now know a great deal about the mathematical structures of the problems and the magnitude of the computations that would be required to solve them. We know, in particular, that discovery of the optimal solution of a complete problem of this kind is well beyond the powers of existing or prospective computational equipment.

In actual organizational practice, no one attempts to find an optimal solution for the whole problem. Instead, various particular decisions, or groups of decisions, within the whole complex are made by specialized members or units of the organization. In making these particular decisions, the specialized units do not solve the whole problem, but find a "satisfactory" solution for one or more subproblems, where some of the effects of the solution on other parts of the system are incorporated in the definition of "satisfactory."

For example, standard costs may be set as constraints for a manufacturing executive. If he finds that his operations are not meeting those constraints, he will search for ways of lowering his costs. Longer production runs may occur to him as a means for accomplishing this end. He can achieve longer production runs if the number of style variations in product is reduced, so he proposes product standardization as a solution to his cost problem. Presumably he will not implement the solution until he has tested it against constraints introduced by the sales department—objections that refusal to meet special requirements of customers will lose sales.

Anyone familiar with organizational life can multiply examples of this sort, where different problems will come to attention in different parts of the organization, or where different solutions will be generated for a problem, depending on where it arises in the organization. The important point to be noted here is that we do not have to postulate conflict in personal goals or motivations in order to explain such conflicts or discrepancies. They could, and would, equally well arise if each of the organizational decision-making roles were being enacted by digital computers, where the usual sorts of personal limits on the acceptance of organizational roles would be entirely absent. The discrepancies arise out of the cognitive inability of the decision-makers to deal with the entire problem as a set of simultaneous relations, each to be treated symmetrically with the others.[9]

An aspect of the division of decision-making labor that is common to virtually all organizations is the distinction between the kinds of general, aggregative decisions that are made at high levels of the organization, and the kinds of specific, item-by-item decisions that are made at low levels. We have already alluded to this distinction in the preceding example of a system for controlling inventory and production. When executives at high levels in such a

[9]For some empirical evidence, see D. C. Dearborn and H. A. Simon, "Selective Perception: A Note on the Departmental Identification of Executives," *Sociometry,* 21 (1958), 140-144.

system make decisions about "aggregate inventory," this mode of factoring the decision-making problem already involves radical simplification and approximation. For example, there is no single, well-defined total cost associated with a given total value of aggregate inventories. There will generally be different costs associated with each of the different kinds of items that make up the inventory (for example, different items may have different spoilage rates or obsolescence rates), and different probabilities and costs associated with stock-outs of each kind of item. Thus, a given aggregate inventory will have different costs depending on its composition in terms of individual items.

To design a system for making decisions about the aggregate work force, production rate, and inventories requires an assumption that the aggregate inventory will never depart very far from a typical composition in terms of individual item types. The assumption is likely to be tolerable because subsidiary decisions are continually being made at other points in the organization about the inventories of individual items. These subsidiary decisions prevent the aggregate inventory from becoming severely unbalanced, hence make averages meaningful for the aggregate.

The assumption required for aggregation is not unlike that made by an engineer when he controls the temperature of a tank of water, with a single thermometer as indicator, knowing that sufficient mixing of the liquid in the tank is going on to maintain a stable pattern of temperature relations among its parts. Without such a stable pattern it would be infeasible to control the process by means of a measurement of the average temperature.

If one set of decisions is made, on this approximate basis, about aggregate work force, production rate, and inventories, then these decisions can be used as constraints in making detailed decisions at subsidiary levels about the inventory or production of particular items. If the aggregate decision has been reached to make one million gallons of paint next month, then other decisions can be reached as to how much paint of each kind to make, subject to the constraint that the production quotas for the individual items should, when added together, total one million gallons.[10]

This simple example serves to elucidate how the whole mass of decisions that are continually being made in a complex organization can be viewed as an organized system. They constitute a system in which (1) particular decision-making processes are aimed at finding courses of action that are feasible or satisfactory in the light of multiple goals and constraints, and (2) decisions reached in any one part of the organization enter as goals or constraints into the decisions being made in the other parts of the organization.

There is no guarantee that the decisions reached will be optimal with respect to any over-all organizational goal. The system is a loosely coupled one. Never-

---

[10]A system of this kind is developed in detail in "Determining Production Quantities under Aggregate Constraints," in C. Holt, F. Modigliani, J. Muth, and H. A. Simon, *Planning Production, Inventories, and Work Force* (Englewood Cliffs, N.J., 1960).

theless, the results of the over-all system can be measured against one or more organizational goals, and changes can be made in the decision-making structure when these results are adjudged unsatisfactory.

Further, if we look at the decision-making structure in an actual organization, we see that it is usually put together in such a way as to insure that the decisions made by specialized units will be made in cognizance of the more general goals. Individual units are linked to the total system by production schedules, systems of rewards and penalties based on cost and profit goals, inventory limits, and so on. The loose coupling among the parts has the positive consequence of permitting specific constraints in great variety to be imposed on subsystems without rendering their decision-making mechanisms inoperative.

The Decision-Making System and Organizational Behavior

In the previous sections great pains were taken to distinguish the goals and constraints (inducements and contributions) that motivate people to accept organizational roles from the goals and constraints that enter into their decision-making when they are enacting those organizational roles. On the one hand, the system of personal inducements and contributions imposes constraints that the organization must satisfy if it is to survive. On the other hand, the constraints incorporated in the organizational roles, hence in what I have called here the organizational decision-making system, are the constraints that a course of action must satisfy in order for the organization to adopt it.

There is no necessary *logical* connection between these two sets of constraints. After all, organizations sometimes fail to survive, and their demise can often be attributed to failure to incorporate all the important motivational concerns of participants among the constraints in the organizational decision-making system. For example, a major cause of small business failure is working capital shortage, a result of failure to constrain actions to those that are consistent with creditors' assumptions about the inducements important to consumers are reflected in the constraints that guide produce design. (It is widely believed that the troubles of the Chrysler Corporation stemmed from the design premise that car purchasers were primarily interested in buying a good piece of machinery.)

In general, however, there is a strong empirical connection between the two sets of constraints, for the organizations we will usually observe in the real world—those that have succeeded in surviving for some time—will be precisely those which have developed organizational decision-making systems whose constraints guarantee that their actions maintain a favorable balance of inducements to contributions for their participants. The argument, an evolutionary one, is the same one we can apply to biological organisms. There is no logical requirement that the temperatures, oxygen concentrations, and so on, maintained in the tissues of a bird by its physiological processes should lie within the ranges required for its survival. It is simply that we will not often have opportunities for observing birds whose physiological regulators do not reflect these external constraints. Such birds are soon extinct.[11]

Thus, what the sociologist calls the functional requisites for survival can usually give us good clues for predicting organizational goals; however, if the functional requisites resemble the goals, the similarity is empirical, not definitional. What the goals are must be inferred from observation of the organization's decision-making processes, whether these processes be directed toward survival or suicide.

Conclusions

We can now summarize our answers to the question that introduced this paper: What is the meaning of the phrase "organizational goal"? First, we discovered that it is doubtful whether decisions are generally directed toward achieving *a* goal. It is easier, and clearer, to view decisions as being concerned with discovering courses of action that satisfy a whole set of constraints. It is this set, and not any one of its members, that is most accurately viewed as the goal of the action.

If we select any of the constraints for special attention, it is (a) because of its relation to the motivations of the decision-maker, or (b) because of its relation to the search process that is generating or designing particular courses of action. Those constraints that motivate the decision-maker and those that guide his search for actions are sometimes regarded as more "goal-like" than those that limit the actions he may consider or those that are used to test whether a potential course of action he has designed is satisfactory. Whether we treat all the constraints symmetrically or refer to some asymmetrically as goals is largely a matter of linguistic or analytic convenience.

When we come to organizational decisions, we observe that many, if not most, of the constraints that define a satisfactory course of action are associated with an organizational role and hence only indirectly with the personal motives of the individual who assumes that role. In this situation it is convenient to use the phrase organization goal to refer to constraints, or sets of constraints, imposed by the organizational role, which has only this indirect relation to the motives of the decision-makers.

If we examine the constraint set of an organizational decision-making system, we will generally find it contains constraints that reflect virtually all the

[11]The relation between the functional requisites for survival and the actual constraints of the operating system is a central concept in W. R. Ashby's notion of a multistable system. See his *Design for a Brain* (2d ed.; New York, 1960).

inducements and contributions important to various classes of participants. These constraints tend to remove from consideration possible courses of action that are inimical to survival. They do not, of course, by themselves, often fully determine the course of action.

In view of the hierarchical structure that is typical of most formal organizations, it is a reasonable use of language to employ organizational goal to refer particularly to the constraint sets and criteria of search that define roles at the upper levels. Thus it is reasonable to speak of conservation of forest resources as a principal goal of the U. S. Forest Service, or reducing fire losses as a principal goal of a city fire department. For high-level executives in these organizations will seek out and support actions that advance these goals, and subordinate employees will do the same or will at least tailor their choices to constraints established by the higher echelons with this end in view.

Finally, since there are large elements of decentralization in the decision-making in any large organization, different constraints may define the decision prolems of different positions or specialized units. For example, "profit" may not enter directly into the decision-making of most members of a business organization. Again, this does not mean that it is improper or meaningless to regard profit as a principal goal of the business. It simply means that the decision-making mechanism is a loosely coupled system in which the profit constraint is only one among a number of constraints and enters into most subsystems only in indirect ways. It would be both legitimate and realistic to describe most business firms as directed toward profit-making—subject to a number of side constraints—operating through a network of decision-making processes that introduces many gross approximations into the search for profitable courses of action. Further, the goal ascription does not imply that any employee is motivated by the firm's profit goal, although some may be.

This view of the nature of organization goals leaves us with a picture of organizational decision-making that is not simple. But it provides us with an entirely operational way of showing, by describing the structure of the organizational decision-making mechanism, how and to what extent over-all goals, like "profit" or "conserving forest resources" help to determine the actual courses of action that are chosen.

CHESTER I. BARNARD

The Environment
of Decision

The acts of individuals may be distinguished in principle as those which are the result of deliberation, calculation, thought, and those which are unconscious, automatic, responsive, the results of internal or external conditions present or past. In general, whatever processes precede the first class of acts culminate in what may be termed "decision." Involved in acts which are ascribed to decision are many subsidiary acts which are themselves automatic, the processes of which are usually unknown to the actor.

When decision is involved there are consciously present two terms—the end to be accomplished and the means to be used. The end itself may be the result of logical processes in which the end is in turn a means to some broader or more remote end; or the immediate end, and generally the ultimate end, may not be a result of logical processes, but "given"—that is, unconsciously impressed—by conditions, including social conditions past or present, including orders of organizations. But whenever the end has been determined, by whatever process, the decision as to means is itself a logical process of discrimination, analysis,

Source: Chester I. Barnard, *The Functions of the Executive,* pp. 185-99. Copyright 1938 by the President and Fellows of Harvard College, all rights reserved. Reprinted with permission of the publisher, Harvard University Press.

choice—however defective either the factual basis for choice or the reasoning related to these facts.

The acts of organizations are those of persons dominated by organizational, not personal, ends. These ends, especially those which are most general or remote, since they represent a consensus of opinion, may be arrived at by nonlogical processes; but since they must usually be formulated in some degree, whereas individual ends more rarely need to be formulated, the ends of organization to a relatively high degree involve logical processes, not as rationalizations after decision, but as processes of decision. Moreover, when ends have been adopted, the coordination of acts as means to these ends is itself an essentially logical process. The discrimination of facts and the allocation of acts by specialization which coordination implies may quite appropriately be regarded as logical or deliberate thinking processes of organization, though not necessarily logical processes of thought of the individual participants. Generally, however, it will be observed that the more important *organization* acts of individuals are likely also to be logical—in that they require deliberate choice of means to accomplish ends which are not personal, and therefore cannot be directly automatic or responsive reactions.

This does not mean that unconscious, automatic, responsive, action is not involved in organization. On the contrary, the discussion of informal organization in Chapter IX has suggested that nonlogical organization processes are indispensable to formal organization. Moreover, much of the action of individuals as participating in organization is habitual, repetitive, and may be merely responsive by *organization design*—a result, for example, of specialization intended to enhance this nonlogical process. What is important here, however, is the superlative degree to which logical processes must and can characterize organization action as contrasted with individual action, and the degree to which decision is specialized in organization. It is the deliberate adoption of means to ends which is the essence of formal organization. This is not only required in order to make cooperation superior to the biological powers and senses of individuals, but it is possibly the chief superiority of cooperative to individual action in most of the important cases of enduring organizations.

From this analysis it follows that acts of decision are characteristic of organization behavior as contrasted with individual behavior, and that the description of the processes of decision are relatively more important to the understanding of organization behavior than in the case of individuals. Moreover, whereas these processes in individuals are as yet matters of speculation rather than of science in the various psychologies, they are in organizations much more open to empirical observation. In fact they are themselves matters of deliberate attention and subject to intentional specialization, as will appear later. The formulation of organization purposes or objectives and the more general decisions involved in this process and in those of action to carry them into effect are distributed in organizations, and are not, nor can they be, concentrated or specialized to individuals except in minor degree. The facts in this regard are obscured to many by the formal location of objective authority in various organization positions, the reasons for which have been discussed in Chapter XII; but it has already been indicated in that chapter that underlying the formal structure of authority and intraorganization communication are processes of interacting decisions distributed throughout the positions in the lines of communication. This may be regarded as the essential process of organization action which continually synthesizes the elements of cooperative systems into concrete systems.

Every effort that is a constituent of organization, that is, every coordinated cooperative effort, may involve two acts of decision. The first is the decision of the person affected as to whether or not he will contribute this effort as a matter of personal choice. It is a detail of the process of repeated personal decisions that determine whether or not the individual will be or will continue to be a contributor to the organization. The personal result here in question we have discussed in the chapters on the Economy of Incentives and the Theory of Authority. This act of decision is *outside* the system of efforts constituting organization, as it has been defined in Chapter VI, although it is, as we have seen, a subject for organized attention.

The second type of decisions has no direct or specific relation to personal results, but views the effort concerning which decision is to be made non-personally from the viewpoint of its organization effect and of its relation to organization purpose. This second act of decision is often made in a direct sense by individuals, but it is impersonal and organizational in its intent and effect. Very often it is also organizational in its process, as, for example, in legislatures, or when boards or committees determine action. The act of decision is a part of the organization itself.

This distinction between the two types of decision is frequently recognized in ordinary affairs. We very often say or hear sentences similar to this: "If this were my business, I think I would decide the question this way—but it is not my personal affair"; or, "I think the *situation* requires such and such an answer—but I am not in a position to determine what ought to be done"; or, "The decision should be made by someone else." This is in effect a restatement, with a different emphasis, of the suggestion in Chapter VII that a sort of dual personality is required of individuals contributing to organization action—the private personality, and the organization personality.

These two kinds of decisions—organization decisions and personal decisions—are chiefly to be distinguished as to process by this fact: that personal decisions cannot ordinarily be delegated to others, whereas organization decisions can often if not always be delegated. For example, what may be called a major decision by an individual may require numerous subsidiary decisions (or judgments) which he also must make. A similar important decision by an organization may in its final form be enunciated by one person and the corresponding subsidiary decisions by several different persons, all acting organizationally, not personally. Similarly, the execution of a decision by one person may require subsequent detailed decision by him as to various steps, whereas the execution of a similar decision in an organization almost always requires subsequent detailed decision by several different persons. Indeed, it may be said that often the responsibility for an organization decision is not a personal responsibility until assigned. Responsibility for organization decision must be assigned positively and definitely in many cases because the aptness of decision depends upon knowledge of facts and of organization purpose, and is therefore bound up with organization communication. Thus central or general organization decisions are best made at centers of the communication system of the organization, so that such decisions must be assigned to those located at these central positions. Persons located at such positions are known as executives; so that the necessities of communication as an essential element in organization imposes the assignment of responsibility for some kinds of organization decision to executives. In short, a characteristic of the services of executives is that they represent a specialization of the process of making organization decisions—and this is the essence of their functions.

The circumstances surrounding the making of concrete decisions are of course of indefinitely large variety, but we will give attention here only to certain general conditions, which may be presented under three headings: the occasions of decision, the evidences of decision, and the environment of decision.

I. The Occasions of Decision

The making of decisions, as everyone knows from personal experience, is a burdensome task. Offsetting the exhilaration that may result from correct and successful decision and the relief that follows the terminating of a struggle to determine issues is the depression that comes from failure or error of decision and the frustration which ensues from uncertainty. Accordingly, it will be observed that men generally try to avoid making decisions, beyond a limited degree when they are rather uncritical responses to conditions. The capacity of most men to make decisions is quite narrow,[1] although it is a capacity that may be considerably developed by training and especially by experience.

The executive is under the obligation of making decisions usually within approximately defined limits related to the position he has accepted; and is under the necessity of keeping within the limits of his capacity if he is continuously to discharge this obligation. He must, therefore, to be successful, distinguish between the occasions of decision in order to avoid the acceptance of more than he can undertake without neglecting the fields to which his position

[1]Why this is so will be presented at length in Chapter XVII.

relates. For the natural reluctance of other men to decide, their persistent disposition to avoid responsibility, and their fear of criticism, will lead them to overwhelm the executive who does not protect himself from excessive burdens of decision if he is not already protected by a well regulated and habitual distribution of responsibilities.

It is for this reason necessary in the making of decisions to maintain a balance between the fields from which the occasions of them arise. I suppose this is rarely a matter of conscious selection, and is probably subject to no general rules. It involves in itself important decisions. For our purposes, however, it may be helpful to note that the occasions for decision originate in three distinct fields: (a) from authoritative communications from superiors; (b) from cases referred for decision by subordinates; (c) from cases originating in the initiative of the executive concerned.

(a) Occasions for decision are frequently furnished by instructions or by general requirements of superior authority. Such decisions relate to the interpretation, application, and distribution of instructions. These occasions cannot be avoided, though the burden may be reduced by delegation of responsibility to subordinates. They involve serious decisions when the instructions seem morally wrong, harmful to the organization, or impossible of execution.

(b) The cases referred for decision may be called appellate cases. They arise from incapacity of subordinates, uncertainty of instructions, novelty of conditions, conflict of jurisdiction or conflicts of orders, or failure of subjective authority. The control of the number of appellate cases lies in adequacy of executive organization, of personnel, of previous decision; and the development of the processes of informal organization. The test of executive action is to make these decisions when they are important, or when they cannot be delegated reasonably, and to decline the others.

(c) The occasions of decision on the initiative of the executive are the most important test of his capacity. Out of his understanding of the situation, which depends upon his ability and initiative, and on the character of the communication system of his organization, it is to be determined whether something needs to be done or corrected. To decide that question involves not merely the ordinary elements but the executive's specific justification for deciding. For when the occasions for decision arise from above or below the position of the executive, others have in advance granted him authority; but when made on his own initiative, this always may be (and generally is) questioned, at least tacitly (in the form whether decision was necessary, or related to scope of obligations, etc.). Moreover, failure to decide is usually not specifically subject to attack, except under extreme conditions. Hence there is much incentive to avoid decision. Pressure of other work is the usual self-justification. Yet it is clear that the most important obligation is to raise and decide those issues which no one else is in a position to raise effectively.

From the point of view of the *relative* importance of specific decisions, those of executives properly call for first attention. From the point of view of *aggregate* importance, it is not decisions of executives but of nonexecutive participants in organization which should enlist major interest. Indeed it is precisely for this reason that many executive decisions are necessary—they relate to the facilitation of correct action involving appropriate decisions among others. In large measure this is a process of providing for the clear presentment of the issues or choices. At any event, it is easily evident merely from the inspection of the action of the nonexecutive participants in organization that coordination of action requires repeated organization decisions "on the spot" where the effective action or organization takes place. It is here that the final and most concrete objectives of purposes are found, with the maximum of definiteness. There is no further stage of organization action. The final selection of means takes place at this point.

It should be noted, however, that the types of decisions as well as the conditions change in character as we descend from the major executive to the nonexecutive positions in organization. At the upper limit decisions relating to ends to be pursued generally require the major attention, those relating to means being secondary, rather general, and especially concerned with personnel, that is, the development and protection of organization itself. At intermediate levels the breaking of broad purposes into more specific ends and the technical and technological problems, including economic problems, of action become prominent. At the low levels decisions characteristically relate to technologically correct conduct, so far as the action is organization action. But it is at these low levels, where ultimate authority resides, that the *personal* decisions determining willingness to contribute become of relatively greatest aggregate importance.

II. The Evidences of Decision

Not the least of the difficulties of appraising the executive functions or the relative merits of executives lies in the fact that there is little direct opportunity to observe the essential operations of decision. It is a perplexing fact that most executive decisions produce no direct evidence of themselves and that knowledge of them can only be derived from the cumulation of indirect evidence. They must largely be inferred from general results in which they are merely one factor, and from symptomatic indications of roundabout character.

Those decisions which are most directly known result in the emission of authoritative communications, that is, orders. Something is or is not to be done. Even in such cases the basic decision may not be evident; for the decision to attempt to achieve a certain result or condition may require several communications to different persons which appear to be complete in themselves but in which the controlling general decision may not be disclosed.

Again, a firm decision may be taken that does not result in any communication whatever for the time being. A decision properly timed must be made in advance of communicating it, either because the action involved must wait anticipated developments or because it cannot be authoritative without educational or persuasive preparation.

Finally, the decision may be not to decide. This is a most frequent decision, and from some points of view probably the most important. For every alert executive continually raises in his own mind questions for determination. As a result of his consideration he may determine that the question is not pertinent. He may determine that it is not now pertinent. He may determine that it is pertinent now, but that there are lacking adequate data upon which to base a final decision. He may determine that it is pertinent for decision now, but that it should or must be decided by someone else on the latter's initiative. He may determine that the question is pertinent, can be decided, will not be decided except by himself, and yet it would be better that it be not decided because his competence is insufficient.

The fine art of executive decision consists in not deciding questions that are not now pertinent, in not deciding prematurely, in not making decisions that cannot be made effective, and in not making decisions that others should make. Not to decide questions that are not pertinent at the time is uncommon good sense, though to raise them may be uncommon perspicacity. Not to decide questions prematurely is to refuse commitment of attitude or the development of prejudice. Not to make decisions that cannot be made effective is to refrain from destroying authority. Not to make decisions that others should make is to preserve morale, to develop competence, to fix responsibility, and to preserve authority.

From this it may be seen that decisions fall into two major classes: positive decisions—to do something, to direct action, to cease action, to prevent action; and negative decisions, which are decisions not to decide. Both are inescapable; but the negative decisions are often largely unconscious, relatively nonlogical, "instinctive," "good sense." It is because of the rejections that the selection is good. The best of moves may be offset by a false move. This is why time is usually necessary to appraise the executive. There is no current evidence of the all-important negative decisions. The absence of effective moves indicates failure of initiative in decision, but error of action probably often means absence of good negative decisions. The success of action through a period of time denotes excellence of selection and rejection of possible actions.

III. The Nature of the Environment

Whatever the occasions or the evidences of decision, it is clear that decisions are constantly being made. What is the nature of the environment of decisions, the materials with which they deal, the field to which they relate? It consists of two parts: (a) purpose; and (b) the physical world, the social world, the external things and forces and circumstances of the moment. All of these, including purpose, constitute the objective field of decision; but the two parts are of radically different nature and origin. The function of decision is to regulate the relations between these two parts. This regulation is accomplished either by changing the purpose or by changing the remainder of the environment.

(a) We may consider purpose first. It may seem strange perhaps that purpose should be included in the objective environment, since purpose of all things seems personal, subjective, internal, the expression of desire. This is true; but *at the moment of a new decision,* an existing purpose, the result of a previous decision under previous conditions, is an objective fact, and it is so treated at that moment insofar as it is a factor in new decision.

This is especially true because organization decisions do not relate to personal purposes, but to organization purposes. The purpose which concerns an organization decision may have been given as a fact to and accepted as such by the person who is responsible for making a new decision. But no matter how arrived at, when decision is in point, the purpose is fact already determined; its making is a matter of history; it may be as objective as another man's emotions may be to an observer.

We must next note, however, that purpose is essential to give any meaning to the rest of the environment.[2] The environment must be looked at from *some* point of view to be intelligible. A mere mass of things, atoms, movements, forces, noises, lights, could produce some response from a sensitive creature or certainly would have some effect on it, or on other things, but the reduction of this mass of everything to something significant requires a basis for discrimination, for picking out this and that as pertinent, relevant, interesting. This basis is that in *this* situation something is or is not to be done. The situation aids, obstructs, or is neutral from *this* point of view. The basis for this discrimination is a purpose, an end, an object to be accomplished.

Purpose itself has no meaning, however, except in an environment. It can only be defined in terms of an environment.[3] Even to want to go somewhere, anywhere, supposes some kind of environment. A very general purpose supposes a very general undifferentiated environment; and if the purpose is stated or thought of it must be in terms of that general environment. But when formed, it immediately (if it is not in suspense or dormant, so to speak) serves for reducing

[2] I am under the impression that in a general way both the form of expression and the concepts stated in the next several paragraphs were derived from or influenced by A. N. Whitehead's *Process and Reality.*

[3] Care should be taken to keep in mind that environment throughout does not mean merely physical aspects of the environment, but explicitly includes social aspects, although physical rather than other aspects are used for illustration as simpler. In many organizations, however, the physical aspects are constant and it is the social aspects which are pertinent. This is the case especially when the purpose is a concrete expression of social ideas or attitudes, as, for example, in ritualistic types of action whether religious or political.

that environment to more definite features; and the immediate result is to change purpose into a more specific purpose. Thus when I decide I want to go from A to B my idea of terrain is vague. But as soon as I have decided, the terrain becomes less vague; I immediately see paths, rocks, obstacles that are significant; and this finer discrimination results in detailed and smaller purposes. I not only want to go from A to B, but I want to go this way, that way, etc. This constant refinement of purpose is the effect of repeated decisions, in finer and finer detail, until eventually detailed purpose is contemporaneous accomplishment. But similarly with each new edition of purpose, a new discrimination of the environment is involved, until finally the last obstacle of progressive action represents a breaking up of a general purpose into many concrete purposes, each as it is made almost simultaneously associated with the action. The thing is done as soon as decided; it becomes a matter of history; it constitutes a single step in the process of experience.

Thus back-and-forth purpose and environment react in successive steps through successive decisions in greater and greater detail. A series of final decisions, each apparently trivial, is largely accomplished unconsciously and sums up into an effected general purpose and a route of experience.

(b) We may now consider the environment of decision exclusive of purpose. It consists of atoms and molecules, agglomerations of things in motion, alive; of men and emotions; of physical laws and social laws; social ideas, norms of action, of forces and resistances. Their number is infinite and they are all always present. They are also always changing. They are meaningless in their variety and changes except as discriminated in the light of purpose. They are viewed as static facts, if the change is not significant from the viewpoint of the purpose, or as both static and dynamic facts.

This discrimination divides the world into two parts; the facts that are immaterial, irrelevant, mere background; and the part that contains the facts that apparently aid or prevent the accomplishment of purpose. As soon as that discrimination takes place, decision is in bud. It is in the state of selecting among alternatives. These alternatives are either to utilize favorable factors, to eliminate or circumvent unfavorable ones, or to change the purpose. Note that if the decision is to deal with the environment, this automatically introduces new but more detailed purposes, the progeny, as it were, of the parent purpose; but if the decision is to change the purpose rather than deal with the environment, the parent is sterile. It is abandoned, and a new purpose is selected, thereby creating a *new* environment in the light of *that* purpose.

This looks like metaphysical speculation if one thinks of it as individual and personal—undemonstrable assumptions, speculative reasoning. But it can be observed in an organization, at least sufficiently to corroborate it roughly. Thus if the president of a telephone company for good reasons orders[4] two poles

---

[4]Partly to illustrate several statements in this essay I may say that it is necessary to imagine extreme conditions to suppose he would issue such an order. Ordinarily what he

carrying a cable removed from the north side of First Street between A and B Streets to the opposite side of First Street, it can, I think, be approximately demonstrated that carrying out that order involves perhaps 10,000 decisions of 100 men located at 15 points, requiring successive analyses of several environments, including social, moral, legal, economic, and physical facts of the environment, and requiring 9000 redefinitions and refinements of purpose, and 1000 changes of purpose. If inquiry be made of those responsible, probably not more than a half-a-dozen decisions will be recalled or deemed worthy of mention—those that seemed at the moment difficult or momentous, or that were subject to question or proved erroneous. The others will be "taken for granted," all a part of the business of knowing one's business. However, a large part of the decisions, purposes, and descriptions and analyses of the various environments will be a matter of record—short-cut, abbreviated, to be sure, but marking the routes of decisions with fair definiteness. Only in the case of individual workmen shall we be almost completely reduced to speculation as to the number and character of the decisions required, because many of them certainly will relate to physiological action.

The purpose of this chapter has been to suggest the climate of concrete decisions as they occur in organizations and to emphasize the radical difference between the process of decision in organizations, when decision is in its important aspects a social process, and the process of decision in individuals when it is a psychological process socially conditioned. Perhaps the most important inference to be drawn from this description is that within organizations, especially of complex types, there is a technique of decision, an organizational process of thinking, which may not be analogous to that of the individual. It would appear that such techniques differ widely among the various types of organization—for example, religious, political, industrial, commercial, etc. This is perhaps conveyed by the remark often made about the "differences in approach" to similar questions. It may be suspected that more than differences in technological character or even of the ends or purposes are involved.

At any event, it is evidently important to consider the principles of the decisive process as it actually takes place from the organizational viewpoint rather than from that of either psychology or systems of logic. This will be undertaken in the succeeding chapter.

---

would do would be to inquire whether it would be feasible to take the action suggested, or what would be involved in doing so, or he would state the problem and ask for its solution, etc. The executive art is nine-tenths inducing those who have authority to use it in taking pertinent action.

DAVID W. MILLER
MARTIN K. STARR

The Analysis
of Decisions

The Payoff Matrix

Mathematics suggests a convenient way to present our breakdown of the decision problem. This is to put it in the form of a matrix—called the *payoff matrix*. A matrix is simply a two-dimensional array of figures arranged in rows and columns. A matrix representation of the decision problem is particularly convenient because we can let the rows be the available strategies (one row for each strategy) and the columns be the states of nature (one column for each state of nature). When appropriate, the columns can reflect competitive actions as well.

The entry at the intersection of each row and column is the payoff—the measure of the utility of that specific outcome which occurs for a given strategy and a particular state of nature. Thus, the payoff matrix summarizes all of the characteristics of the decision problem which we have been discussing. Symbolically, the payoff matrix looks like Table 1—using N's to designate states of nature, S's to designate strategies, and P's to designate payoffs. The decision

Source: David W. Miller and Martin K. Starr, *The Structure of Human Decisions* (Englewood Cliffs, N. J.: Prentice-Hall, Inc., 1967). Reprinted with permission.

TABLE 1

	N_1	N_2	N_3	N_4	$\ldots$	N_j
S_1:	P_{11}	P_{12}	P_{13}	P_{14}	$\ldots$	$\ldots$
S_2:	P_{21}	P_{22}	P_{23}	P_{24}	$\ldots$	$\ldots$
$\ldots$	$\ldots$	$\ldots$		$\ldots$	$\ldots$	$\ldots$
S_i:	$\ldots$	$\ldots$		$\ldots$	$\ldots$	P_{ij}

problem is always the same—to select a specific strategy. The payoff matrix provides means of structuring and presenting the relevant information.

The payoff matrix representation of a decision problem seems so apt for its purpose that it is easy to overlook the question of whether it can always be constructed. Can every decision problem be put into a payoff matrix format? The answer is that the great majority of decision problems can be represented in payoff matrix form. However, in many instances how to do it is not obvious.

Difficulties arise as soon as it is necessary to consider a sequence of decisions as if they were one over-all decision. For example, consider the problem of sampling the quality of a production run to determine whether to accept the entire "lot." There is a preliminary decision to take a particular size sample. Then after determining how many defectives there are in the sample, a subsequent decision must be made to accept or to reject the lot. This is a typical problem involving a sequence of decisions. There are two separate decisions. (There are two sets of states of nature as well. *First* there is the unknown percentage of defectives that are actually in the lot. *Second,* there are different possible numbers of defectives which may be found in the sample—granting any specific number of defectives in the lot.) How can a problem such as this be put in payoff matrix form? As another example, remember that the columns of the payoff matrix can represent competitive actions. Consequently, any game with a sequence of moves creates similar difficulties.

It is our purpose to analyze decision problems in such a way that we can *recommend* to the manager a particular strategy which he should select for a specific case. It turns out that the payoff matrix provides a remarkably good structure for this analysis. We shall show how the payoff matrix representation is quite generally applicable. Nevertheless, it should be emphasized that the payoff matrix is simply a methodological convenience which in no way precludes the possibility that other bases for analyses can be found. Alternatives become especially important if the payoff matrix for a particular decision problem cannot be framed.

Returning now to the example of *acceptance sampling,* a difficulty occurs because the payoff matrix format requires the selection of *one* strategy, given that *one* state of nature holds, not several. Fortunately, the difficulty can be overcome by a suitable statement of what we mean by a strategy. Then, the lot acceptance example becomes straightforward. A strategy statement for the over-all decision problem becomes something like this.

Take a sample of size 10. Reject the lot if there is any defective product in the sample; otherwise accept it.

Redefinition of the states of nature is required. The effect of this transformation of terms is to increase drastically the number of strategies that must be considered. For our immediate purposes, this is only a technical problem. Indeed, the payoff matrix for this situation can be constructed. By means of this example, we have tried to emphasize that an appropriate payoff matrix can frequently be achieved—even in cases where, at first glance, it might seem otherwise.

Several Kinds of Decisions

There are many ways to classify decision problems. But for our purposes there is one kind of classification which is crucial. *This is a classification based on the amount of information available to the decision-maker about the likelihood of occurrence of the various states of nature.* Five main classes of decision problems exist in accord with this taxonomy. Important procedural differences are associated with each of these classes. Therefore, we must clearly distinguish between them.

Decision-making under certainty occurs when we have a problem where we know with certainty which state of nature will occur. This means that there is *only one column* in our payoff matrix. Alternatively, this kind of decision problem considers only one relevant payoff for each possible strategy. At first, this may seem like a trivial case. How can there be any difficulty in reaching the best decision if there is only one column? Simply read down the column to find the best payoff and that will be the optimum strategy. But it isn't quite that simple. The idea behind the suggestion is absolutely correct, but the difficulty is that there may be such an enormous number of strategy rows that it would be nearly impossible to list them.

Of what use then, is a payoff matrix which can't be written down? The answer is that in some cases, *when the actual payoff matrix can't be constructed, it still remains an effective means of conceptualizing the problem.* As we shall see, one of the contributions of operations research to decision-making is in this realm. For the present, it suffices to indicate that real *and important* decision problems of this type exist.

Suppose, for example, that you run a machine shop and have 20 contracts for machined parts. You also have 20 machines, any one of which could do any one of the contracts. But since the machines are of different designs, intended for different purposes, each type would require differing amounts of time for each contract—and, hence, would be more or less expensive. Quite naturally, you would like to assign the jobs to the machines so as to minimize the total cost. The first job could be assigned to any one of the 20 machines, the second job to any one of the remaining 19, the third job to any one of the remaining 18, and so forth. So the total number of ways in which you could assign the jobs is given by 20 X 19 X 18 X 17 X 16 X 15 . . . X 3 X 2 X 1. If one takes the trouble to do the arithmetic he will find that the total number of ways to assign the jobs to the machines is 2.4329 X 10^{18} (we have rounded off the number). Each way of assigning these jobs to machines is another possible strategy, so this decision problem's payoff matrix would have only one column (because the costs of the various machines are assumed known), but it would have almost 2½ quantillion rows.

That such a modest problem could produce so many rows in the payoff matrix may be surprising. It does serve to show that decision-making under certainty can be a genuine problem. And this sort of problem is by no means confined to machine shops. On the contrary, a great number of different kinds of organizational decision problems fall into the category of decision-making under certainty.

The *second* kind of decision problem occurs where there are a number of states of nature but where the decision-maker *knows* the probability of occurrence of each of the states of nature. This kind of situation is called *decision-making under risk.* For the purpose of illustration, consider the decision problem facing a gambler—where the possible states of nature are the various chance events, the probabilities of which can be calculated by probability theory. *Typically in many organizational problems, the probabilities of the various states of nature are known by virtue of determining how frequently they occurred in the past.* Thus, the decision problem of a manufacturer of antifreeze would involve various weather conditions. The probabilities of occurrence of these different states of nature might be determined from past experience. Similarly, inventory decision problems involving parts for factory or office equipment would include those states of nature that represent the various rates of failure of the parts, and these probabilities might be known from past experience. This kind of decision problem occurs frequently.

The *third* kind of decision problem is *decision-making under uncertainty,* where the probabilities of occurrence of the various states of nature are not known (or where, if one is an objectivist, the very idea of probabilitity descriptions for the states of nature is meaningless). *Such problems arise wherever there is no basis in past experience for estimating the probabilities of occurrence of the relevant states of nature.* The decision problems involved in marketing a new product would include various levels of demand as states of nature. Yet there is no past experience on which to base estimates of the relevant probabilities as there is in the case of established products. Decision problems concerning expansion of facilities may have states of nature including such events as war, depression, recession, and inflation. Believable probabilities cannot easily be estimated for these states of nature. Many decision problems of major importance are of this kind.

The huge gap in the availability of information between the second and the third categories suggests the need for a *fourth* category; *decision-making under partial information.* In reaching decisions under risk, we assume that the decision-maker knows the probability of occurrence of each state of nature. Consider an inventory problem. The states of nature are demand levels; the strategies are the quantities to order. For this to be a decision problem under risk it is necessary that the demand distribution be completely known. For the same problem under uncertainty we assume that nothing whatsoever is known about the demand distribution. What, then, about the intermediate cases, where *something,* but *not everything,* is known about the demand distribution? For example, some of the standard measures of descriptive statistics (such as averages, medians, or modes) might be known without knowing the whole demand distribution, e.g., the exact form of the distribution, such as normal, binomial, or Poisson. Thus, we could know that average demand was 100 units and that the standard deviation was 10 units—but nothing else. It is such cases as these that are included in the category of decision problems under partial information. *It may be the most common category of "real" decision problems. However, since somewhat more sophisticated procedures are required in dealing with this kind of decision problem, many decision-makers act as though the problem was one of risk, with varying degrees of penalty.* Although we shall not treat these kinds of problems, it was essential for classification purposes to mention them.[1]

The last category of decision problems that we shall mention is *decision-making under conflict.* Here the columns of the payoff matrix represent strategies of *rational opponents* rather than states of nature. The essence of this kind of decision problem is that the executive is involved in a competitive situation with an intelligent opponent. Military weapon and logistic systems and marketplace brand competition epitomize this class of decision-making—but even ordinary parlor games provide perfectly good illustrations. Decision-making under conflict is the subject studied in the theory of games. *The title, "theory of games," may suggest frivolity. Nothing could be further from the truth.* The essence of games (in the sense of the theory of games) is the presence of conflict of interest between two or more rational opponents. The grimness of war, the tensions of nuclear diplomacy, and the nature of business competition are all we need consider to deny the frivolity of the concept of games. There are many important and serious exemplifications of decision-making under conflict. And it is a particularly intractable domain.

Decision Criterion under Certainty

Now that we have outlined the various kinds of decision problems, we can turn to the basic question: How should a specific strategy be selected? In other

---

[1]This kind of decision problem is discussed at some length in Martin K. Starr and David W. Miller, *Inventory Control, Theory and Practice* (Englewood Cliffs, N.J.: Prentice-Hall, Inc., 1962).

words, how should the decision be made? What we want to investigate is the reasonable procedure or procedures by which a decision can be reached once we have developed the payoff matrix. We would like to find a *criterion* for each class of decision by which the decision-maker, given his payoff matrix, can select his strategy.

There is no difficulty, *in theory*, in determining the decision criterion under certainty. All we need do is find the strategy which has the best payoff and that is the strategy which should be selected. There is no possible reason for doing otherwise. Each strategy has one payoff, since there is only a single column in the payoff matrix when the state of nature is certainly known. The payoff (utility) represents the degree of achievement of the objective, so the largest payoff is the best one. The decision criterion, then, is: Select that strategy which has the largest payoff. The practical difficulty which arises when the number of strategies is enormous must be dealt with by such methods of operations research as *linear programming.*[2]

Decision Criterion under Risk

What happens in the case of decision-making under risk? Here we no longer have just one payoff for each strategy. Instead, there are a number of payoffs—one for each possible state of nature. So a decision criterion for risk will have to be based either on some suitable transformation of all of the possible payoffs for each strategy, or on one or more payoffs selected according to some rule.

Let us take a simple decision problem under risk as an example. Assume that a processor of frozen vegetables has to decide what crop to plant in a particular area. Suppose that the strategies are only two: to plant peas, or asparagus, and that the states of nature can be summarized in three possibilities: perfect weather, variable weather, and bad weather. On the basis of weather records it is determined that the probability of perfect weather is 0.25, the probability of variable weather is 0.50, and the probability of bad weather is 0.25. The dollar yields of the two crops under these different conditions are known and the organization's utility is assumed to be measured by the dollar amounts. All of this information can be summarized in a payoff matrix:

State of nature:	N_1	N_2	N_3
Probability:	0.25	0.50	0.25
Weather _____ _____:	*Perfect*	*Variable*	*Bad*
S_1: Plant peas	$40,000	$30,000	$20,000
S_2: Plant asparagus	$70,000	$20,000	$ 0

[2]See Chapter 10, Section 96.

What strategy should the decision-maker select? The rational individual, under these circumstances, will govern his selection of strategies by the *expected utility* of the strategies. He will select that strategy which has the largest expected utility.

We introduced the notion of expected values earlier. Using P_{ij} to designate the payoff for the ith strategy and the jth state of nature and p_j to designate the probability of the jth state of nature, it follows that the expected value of the payoff for the ith strategy, S_i, is

$$EV(S_i) = P_{i1}p_1 + P_{i2}p_2 + P_{i3}p_3 + \cdots + P_{in}p_n$$

$$= \sum_{j=1}^{j=n} P_{ij}\, p_j$$

where EV (S_i) designates the expected payoff for the strategy denoted by S_i. (Remember that an expected value is the simple arithmetic mean or average.)

Using the equation above, we can calculate the expected payoff for each of the two strategies in our example.

$$EV\ (S_1) = \$40,000(¼) + \$30,000(½) + \$20,000(¼) = \$30,000$$
$$EV\ (S_2) = \$70,000(¼) + \$20,000(½) + 0(¼) = \$27,500$$

The expected payoff for Strategy 1 is larger; this is the strategy that (all other things being equal) should be selected. The food processor should choose the alternative: plant peas. Why? Because if the same decision situation were presented to him a great number of times he would average $2500 more from Strategy 1 than he would from Strategy 2.

But, one may think, aren't there other factors to consider besides the expected value? For example, let us suppose that the probabilities were different. Suppose the probabilities were 1/2, 3/8, and 1/8, respectively, for the three states of nature. Then the expected payoffs for the two strategies would be:

$$EV\ (S_1) = \$40,000(½) + \$30,000(⅜) + \$20,000(⅛) = \$33,750$$
$$EV\ (S_2) = \$70,000(½) + \$20,000(⅜) + 0(⅛) = \$42,500$$

And, since the expected payoff for Strategy 2 is larger, this should be the choice of the food processor.

At this point one might say: On the face of it, I disagree! Look at the difference between the payoffs. If the processor chooses to plant asparagus (S_2), the expected payoff is higher because of the much higher return on asparagus with perfect weather. But if he plants asparagus and has bad weather, he doesn't make anything at all. Whereas, if he plants peas he may not make as much when the weather is perfect, but he never risks having no return at all. So why wouldn't a perfectly rational person prefer to forego a "slightly larger" expected payoff in order to avoid the possibility of no return at all? It might be said that he was paying the difference in expected payoffs as a premium on insurance against having no return.

This argument only appears to present a valid objection to the rule that the strategy with the highest expected payoff should be chosen. In fact, the objection is misplaced. A completely rational decision-maker might well reject Strategy 2 (plant asparagus), but it is because his utility for dollars is not properly measured by the dollar amounts that we have used. In short, for this case, the payoffs are wrong.

The same kind of problem was discussed in Chapter 4—the context being the self-insurance problem. It is an important point and deserves emphasis. *Any argument against the criterion of choosing the best expected value* (for a specific decision problem under risk) *implies that the executive has some other objective than just dollar amounts.* Here it is the objective of having some *control* over his income. In the self-insurance problem it was the objective of avoiding the possibility of ruin. Criticism of the expected value criterion (for risk) is directed against the wrong part of the analysis. *It is never a question of the criterion being wrong, but rather that the payoffs have been incorrectly measured to reflect the decision-maker's utilities for the outcomes.*

If the food processor was able to utilize a procedure for measuring his utility, he should then be able to demonstrate the correctness of the expected value criterion. In our present example, suppose that the dollar amounts do not adequately represent the decision-maker's utility. Consequently, he turns to the standard-gamble procedure to measure his utilities for the various outcomes. There are five possible outcomes; $70,000, $40,000, $30,000, $20,000, and 0. To determine this manager's utilities for the intermediate amounts we would present him with the usual choices. First, would he prefer $40,000 certainly to a lottery between $70,000 with probability $4/7$ and 0 dollars with probability of $3/7$? (note: $4/7 (70,000) + 3/7 (0) = $40,000). In this particular case, he would prefer the certainty of $40,000. So, we adjust the probability upward until he indicates no preference. This *might* occur at a probability of $6/7$ of getting the $70,000. We would proceed similarly with the other two outcomes and *might* find the *no-preference* probability for $30,000 at $p = 9/14$ and the *no-preference* probability for $20,000 at $p = 3/7$. This gives us the utilities for the five possible outcomes as follows:

Outcome	Utility
$70,000	1
$40,000	$6/7 = 0.857$
$30,000	$9/14 = 0.643$
$20,000	$3/7 = 0.429$
0	0

Our payoff matrix would be transformed:

$$0.857 \quad 0.643 \quad 0.429$$
$$1.000 \quad 0.429 \quad 0.000$$

We now proceed to calculate the expected payoffs as before (assuming that the second set of probabilities applies):

$$\text{EV } (S_1) = 0.857(\frac{1}{2}) + 0.643(\frac{3}{8}) + 0.429(\frac{1}{8}) = 0.723$$
$$\text{EV } (S_2) = 1.000(\frac{1}{2}) + 0.429(\frac{3}{8}) + 0(\frac{1}{8}) = 0.661$$

The executive should select Strategy 1, which has the larger expected payoff. For this example, the objection that had been raised seems reasonable, and in accord with the decision-maker's utility, as measured by the standard-gamble technique. *With a proper measure, there is no other rational decision criterion than the selection of that strategy associated with the largest expected payoff.*

Decision Criteria under Uncertainty

The case of decision-making under uncertainty is more complicated. For example, take the decision problem of an investor who has the objective of achieving the maximum possible rate of return. Assume that he has only three possible investments (his strategies): *speculative stocks, high-grade stocks, or bonds.* Further assume that only three possible states of nature can occur: *war, peace, or depression.* We will ignore the many nuances of capital gains, taxes on income, and so on.

The investor has determined his payoffs for each of the nine possible combinations of a strategy and a state of nature. He has expressed his payoffs *as rates of return on his investment* and his payoff matrix looks like this:

	N_1 War	N_2 Peace	N_3 Depression
S_1: Speculative stocks	20	1	−6
S_2: High-grade stocks	9	8	0
S_3: Bonds	4	4	4

The distinctive difference between this case and the preceding one is that the investor has no knowledge of the probabilities of the various states of nature. He has, therefore, no way to calculate an expected payoff for his strategies. What criterion should he use in selecting a strategy?

At the present time, *decision theory provides no one best criterion for selecting a strategy under conditions of uncertainty.* Instead, there are a number of different criteria, each of which has a perfectly good rationale to justify it. The choice among these criteria is determined by *organizational policy* and/or *the attitude of the executive.* As we shall see, *the use of different criteria can result in the selection of different strategies.* We shall discuss only some of the suggested criteria.

Criterion of Pessimism

First, the *maximin* criterion was suggested by Abraham Wald. (The reason for the name will become clear as we proceed.) Wald suggested that the decision-maker should be completely *pessimistic.* He should act as if Nature would always be malevolent, i.e., for whatever strategy he selected. Nature would choose a state that would minimize his payoff. Wald stated that the decision-maker should then select his strategy so that he would get as large a payoff as he could under these circumstances.

Let us return to our example. *If* the investor selects S_1, the worst that can happen is that a depression will occur, in which case his payoff would be -6. *Suppose* he selected S_2. Again, the worst that could happen would be a depression, in which case he would have a payoff of 0. *If* he selected S_3, however, he will always get a payoff of 4, no matter what state of nature occurred. In other words, the worst that could happen to him in this case would be a payoff of 4. We can arrange these conclusions in tabular form.

Strategy	Worst, or minimum, payoff
1	-6
2	0
3	4 ←

Following Wald's suggestion, the best that the investor can do, assuming that Nature will always be malevolent, is to select that strategy which has the *largest minimum* payoff—the *maximum minimum*—or *maximin.* The largest such payoff (the maximin payoff) is 4, which the investor will get if he selects Strategy 3 and invests his money in bonds. In this *particular* case the investor will always get 4 from Strategy 3. In general, the use of this criterion will *guarantee* the manager at least as large a payoff as the maximin payoff. Sometimes, of course, a larger payoff will result. The Wald maximin criterion dictates the selection of Strategy 3—investing in bonds. (If a cost matrix is used, then the best of the worsts would yield the *minimax* solution. See the regret criterion, below.)

The argument based on pessimism can be described as a conservative approach to an intrinsically difficult situation. There is further elucidation of this criterion, stemming from its application to the theory of games. This will be encountered subsequently. It is also interesting to note that this is the criterion professed by the majority of adherents to the objectivist approach in probability and statistics. Bear in mind that *this criterion is the sole one which can be defended rigorously if the payoffs can only be ranked.*

Criterion of Optimism

Hurwicz[3] suggested a variant of this criterion. He asks, essentially, why always assume that Nature will be malevolent? After all, we sometimes get good

[3]Leonid Hurwicz, *Optimality Criteria for Decision Making under Ignorance,* Cowles Commission discussion paper, *Statistics,* No. 370, 1951, mimeographed; cited in R. D. Luce and Howard Raiffa, *Games and Decisions* (New York: John Wiley & Sons, Inc., 1958).

breaks. Suppose an optimistic decision-maker felt "lucky" in a particular case about his chances of having a good state of nature occur? How might he be rational about this feeling? First let us assume that the executive is a *complete optimist*—the exact opposite to the Wald pessimist. He assumes that Nature will treat him kindly, selecting that state of nature which will yield the highest possible payoff for the strategy he has selected. How would he proceed?

He would look at the various payoffs for each strategy and select the largest payoff for each strategy. In this case he would find:

Strategy	Best, or maximum, payoff
1	20 ←
2	9
3	4

Since he thinks Nature will give him the largest payoff, he will select that strategy with the *largest maximum*—the *maximum maximum*—or, abbreviated, the *maximax*. In this case the maximax is the payoff of 20, which he will receive if he selects his first strategy and war occurs. (Admittedly, this makes him a strange kind of optimist.)

Now, Hurwicz didn't suggest that a rational decision-maker should be completely optimistic. He did suggest that if an individual felt "lucky" or optimistic he should be able to be rational about it. For this purpose he introduced the idea of a *coefficient of optimism.* As we have seen, the complete optimist takes account only of the largest payoff for each strategy. *The coefficient of optimism is a means by which the manager can take account of both the largest and the smallest payoffs—weighting their importance to his decision in accordance with his own feeling of optimism.* The coefficient of optimism is defined in terms of a lottery between the *largest* and *smallest* payoffs. In other words, the manager assigns to the maximum payoff a probability which he would be willing to accept in a lottery between that maximum payoff and the minimum payoff. This probability is his coefficient of optimism. Suppose, for example, that the executive chooses a coefficient of optimism of 3/5. This means that he would be satisfied to accept a lottery in which the maximum payoff had a probability of occurrence of 3/5 and the minimum payoff had a probability of occurrence of 2/5. By Hurwicz's criterion we must determine the expected payoff of each strategy, assuming that *either* the maximum *or* the minimum will occur and with the indicated probabilities. The calculations (using a coefficient of optimism of 3/5 = 0.6) are straightforward:

Strategy	Maximum payoff	Minimum payoff	Expected payoff
1	20	−6	20(0.6) + (−6)(0.4) = 9.6 ←
2	9	0	9(0.6) + (0)(0.4) = 5.4
3	4	4	4(0.6) + 4(0.4) = 4.0

According to the Hurwicz criterion, the investor should *select his first strategy*—investing in speculative stocks. (The same procedure can be used for a cost matrix where the coefficient of optimism is applied to the best, or minimum, cost. One minus this coefficient is multiplied by the worst, or maximum, cost. The criterion dictates the choice of the strategy with the lowest expected payoff.)

It may be noted that a coefficient of optimism of 1 leads to the procedure of the complete optimist, which we described above. Similarly, a coefficient of optimism of 0 leads to the Wald criterion—that of the complete pessimist. Suppose the manager doesn't know his coefficient of optimism. Luce and Raiffa suggest one way to determine what it is.[4] Consider the following simple decision payoff matrix. It reflects the values of the original matrix where the payoffs have been converted to the 0-1 utility scale:

	N_1 War	N_3 Depression
S_1: Speculative stocks	1	0
S_4:	x	x

The new strategy S_4 has been chosen so that *the payoffs will be the same* no matter which state of nature occurs. For example, in the present case, it might be the strategy of leaving the money in the savings bank rather than investing. (It should also be noticed that S_3 already conforms to this condition.) The strategy S_1 contains only the *maximum* and *minimum* payoffs in the original payoff matrix. Suppose, now, that the executive has a coefficient of optimism of k (an unknown which remains to be determined; we know only that, by definition, it must be at or between 0 and 1). With k as the coefficient of optimism the individual would calculate the expected values of the two strategies as before. In this case they are

Strategy	Expected payoff
1	k
2	x

For what value of x in the above payoff matrix would the executive be indifferent between the two strategies? Note that this is really the standard-gamble technique again (as illustrated in Figure 1). Suppose the investor is indifferent between S_1 and S_4 if x has the value 1/4. This means that the expected payoffs, in the Hurwicz sense, must be equal at $x = 1/4$, or else the decision-maker wouldn't be indifferent. We conclude, then, that for this investor the coefficient of optimism, k, must be 1/4.

Some say that this criterion is not as realistic as the one preceding or the

[4] Luce and Raiffa, *op. cit.,* p. 283.

FIGURE 1

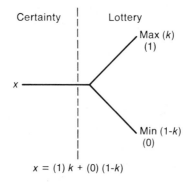

Certainty | Lottery

Max (k) (1)

x

Min (1-k) (0)

$$x = (1) k + (0) (1-k)$$

two that follow this discussion. It may even be that the Hurwicz criterion is less likely to be used in practice.[5] Nevertheless, it is enriching for our discussion. *First*, it shows how one can attempt to include more than one payoff in the decision criterion without using all of them. *Second*, since it is a perfectly reasonable argument it demonstrates further variety and the difficulty of unambiguously selecting a criterion for this class of decision problem. *With such variety, what does it mean to be rational in the face of uncertainty? Third*, the procedure for determining the coefficient of optimism is yet another example of how one can go about obtaining quantitative measures for subjective utilities and valuations. This is such a crucial problem that any illustrations of procedures for coping with it are worthy of consideration.

Criterion of Regret

A completely different criterion has been suggested by Savage.[6] This criterion requires an *alternative payoff measure* before it can be used. By "Savage criterion" we shall mean both the recommended payoff measure and the specific decision criterion applied to it.

We know that after a decision has been made and the state of nature has occurred—the executive receives the (indicated) payoff. Savage argues that after he knows the outcome the individual can experience regret because, now that he knows what state of nature occurred, he may wish he had selected a different

---

[5]None of these uncertainty criteria receive much use. Managers avoid decision problems under uncertainty. They do this by ignoring the existence of such problems and by deferring these decisions. Faced with the need to reach a decision under uncertainty, knowledge of these criteria can be illuminating, but it is unreasonable to expect them to replace intuition.

[6]Leonard J. Savage, "The Theory of Statistical Decision," *Journal of the American Statistical Association*, 46 (1951), 55-67.

strategy. Savage maintains that the decision-maker should attempt to minimize this regret which he can experience.

Exactly what is the nature of this regret? It resides in the fact that the best strategy may not have been selected for the particular state of nature that did occur. Savage suggests that *the amount of regret can be measured by the difference between the payoff actually received and the payoff that could have been received if the state of nature that was going to occur had been known.*

Thus, in our previous example, suppose war actually occurred. *If* the investor had selected his first strategy, he would experience no regret because he had already gotten the largest possible payoff. But if he had selected his second strategy he would have lost $20 - 9 = 11$, which he might otherwise have had. This measures his regret. *If* he had selected his third strategy he would experience regret of $20 - 4 = 16$.

Now, suppose peace prevailed. *If* the investor had selected his second strategy he would experience no regret because he would have obtained the largest possible payoff. But *if* he had selected his first strategy he would experience regret of $8 - 1 = 7$. And *if* he had chosen his third strategy he would experience regret of $8 - 4 = 4$.

Assuming that a depression occurred, the investor would experience no regret *if* he had selected his third strategy because it would have given him the largest possible payoff. *If* he had selected the first strategy, however, he would experience regret of $4 - (-6) = 10$. The selection of the second strategy in this case would give him regret of $4 - 0 = 4$. All of these measures can be conveniently presented in a *regret matrix*:

	N_1	N_2	N_3
S_1:	0	7	10
S_2:	11	0	4
S_3:	16	4	0

Savage then proposes to use a straightforward variant of the Wald criterion as the decision criterion for the regret matrix. Like Wald, he too chooses to be completely pessimistic about the state of nature that will occur. It will always be against the individual's best interests. The variant is required because the matrix measures regret, which (like costs) we want to make as small as possible. The original matrix represented (profit-type) payoffs, which we want to make as large as possible. But this difference is only procedural.

We ask: What is the worst that can happen to the decision-maker taking each of his strategies in turn? When we discussed the Wald criterion with respect to *profits* the answer was the minimum payoff for each strategy. Here it is *the maximum regret in each row*. We should note that this variant of the criterion is identical to that of the Wald criterion when applied to a cost matrix. We quickly obtain:

Strategy	Worst, or Maximum, regret
1	10 ←
2	11
3	16

The executive can insure himself against experiencing extreme regrets by selecting the strategy that has the *minimum maximum,* i.e., the *minimax.* In this case the minimax regret is 10. It is the maximum regret that the decision-maker must experience, assuming he selects his first strategy, which is to invest in speculative stocks. Of course, he may experience less regret, but 10 is the most regret he can possibly experience.

One could apply a criterion other than the minimax to the regret matrix. Either the Hurwicz of the Laplace criterion (to be discussed next) could be used instead of Wald's criterion. This is why it can be said that Savage's major contribution is the *regret measure of utility.* Nonetheless, for us the Savage criterion will describe both the development of the regret matrix and the application of the *Wald criterion* to it.

The Savage argument is applicable to either cost or profit matrices. If the original payoff matrix is expressed in "actual" dollars (whether of profits or costs), then the Savage regret calculation is equivalent to the determination of *opportunity costs* (which is a vitally important economic concept).[7] From all perspectives, *a regret matrix is an opportunity cost matrix.* This suggests that the regret matrix is rooted in fundamental economic truths which is further supported by the fact that a powerful empirical argument exists in favor of the Savage criterion. Namely, it is the only criterion that can make a "hedging" strategy optimal. *Hedging is the procedure for protecting oneself against fluctuations in the market price of commodities.* Since many businessmen hedge, we have empirical evidence of Savage's criterion in use.[8]

The Subjectivist Criterion

All three previous criteria operated without reference to the probabilities associated with the relevant states of nature. Consequently, they are well-suited for persons who subscribe to objective interpretations of probabilities. In the investor's case, this would be a crucial issue because it is clear that the states of nature in this problem do not lend themselves to objective probability assignments. After all, these states of nature are not part of a stable and repeatable system. Hence, they are not subject to frequency counts. In contrast, *the subjectivist would maintain that the manager has useful information in the form of degrees of belief concerning the likelihoods of occurrence of the relevant states*

---

[7]See page 251 for a discussion of the opportunity cost concept.

[8]See Problem 5g at the end of this chapter.

of nature. For the subjectivist, this problem is just like any other decision problem under risk.

It is evident that some problems which the objectivist considers classified under uncertainty will be considered classified under risk by the subjectivist. Are many problems affected in this way? The answer is yes—a very large number. And this explains why the dispute between objectivists and subjectivists is so important. *For the objectivist, a significant proportion of all decision problems* (particularly those which occur at higher organizational levels) *are cases of uncertainty. For the subjectivist, few decision problems exist under uncertainty.* To say that a decision problem is operating under uncertainty means to the subjectivist that the administrator has *absolutely no information* about the likelihoods of the states of nature. Most managers would agree that *such total ignorance is quite unlikely. So the subjectivist treats most decision problems as cases of risk. This has the important advantage that the decision criterion is not in dispute.*

There remain decision problems under uncertainty—even for the subjectivist. We shall now consider the criterion that the subjectivist recommends in this case. It is called the Laplace criterion,[9] and has been the subject of impassioned debate for many years.

The criterion is simple to state. *Since we don't know the probabilities with which the various states of nature will transpire, we will assume that they are all equal.* In other words, the inference is that every state of nature is equally likely to occur. Then we calculate the expected payoff for each strategy and select that strategy which has the largest expected payoff. That is, where there are n states of nature:

$$\text{EV } (S_i) = \frac{1}{n} \sum_{j=1}^{j=n} P_{ij}$$

This is straightforward. Why all the argument about it? One of the main reasons for contention is that the assumption of equal probabilities involves a famous doctrine called the *principle of insufficient reason.* The gist of this principle is: without specific cause a particular something won't happen. The relationship of the principle of insufficient reason to the problem at hand is direct. *Since we know of no reason for one state of nature to occur rather than another, we assume that one is as likely to occur as another.* The principle when used in this way *in connection with probabilities* is associated with the name of the eighteenth-century English clergyman Thomas Bayes. It is Bayes' *hypothesis* that if we have no reason to believe one probability to be different from another—we should assume them equal.

The principle has other uses in probability theory as well, and all of them are violently debated. For example, how do we know that a fair coin has a

<hr/>

[9]This criterion is named after Pierre Simon, Marquis de Laplace (1749-1827), a great French mathematician who first used this criterion in important ways.

probability of 1/2 of showing heads when it is tossed? One answer is that we know it because of the principle of insufficient reason. There is no specific reason why the coin should come up one way rather than another, so the probabilities must be equal (hence 1/2, since there are only two possibilities). Many probabilists reject this argument. They state that the only reason we think the probability of a head is 1/2 is the fact that we have observed it come up about half the time.

One of the best-known arguments of the Middle Ages has to do with this principle of insufficient reason. Jean Buridan, in the first half of the four-teenth century, invented an imaginary ass—known ever since as Buridan's Ass. This ass was supposed to be placed exactly in the middle between two identical bales of hay. Buridan maintained that the ass must starve to death because it would have no reason to go to one bale of hay rather than another—an interesting application of the principle.

Another famous, ancient use of the principle was with regard to the position of the earth in space. This argument ran to the effect that the earth couldn't be just any place in space because, if this were the case, God would have had no reason to put it one place rather than another. Therefore, He would never have put it anywhere. Starting from here, it was argued that the earth must be at the center of the universe.

Such uses of the principle as this sufficed to bring it into considerable disrepute. Nonetheless, the principle has many proponents who state that if used with caution, it is as legitimate as many other basic principles which underlie our efforts to understand the nature of reality.

The application of the subjectivist criterion is simple. Since there are three states of nature in our investor's example we assume that the probability of occurrence of each of them is 1/3. On this basis we can easily calculate the expected payoff for each strategy:

Strategy	Expected payoff	
1	$1/3[20 + 1 + (-6)]$	$= 5$
2	$1/3(9 + 8 + 0)$	$= 5.67 \leftarrow$
3	$1/3(4 + 4 + 4)$	$= 4$

The largest expected payoff is that of Strategy 2. This is the strategy which should be selected according to the Laplace criterion.

Other decision criteria have been suggested, but these four are among the best-known. It is interesting to note that every strategy in our example has been selected by one of the criteria. Strategy 1 (speculative stocks) was selected by the Savage criterion and by the Hurwicz criterion with coefficient of optimism of 3/5. Strategy 2 (high-grade stocks) was selected by the Laplace criterion. And Strategy 3 was selected by the Wald criterion. The selection of the decision criterion is obviously of crucial importance. So it must be emphasized that there is *no best criterion* in the sense that a conclusive argument can be offered for it.

As a matter of fact, there are examples that run counter to each of the criteria. By this we mean specific decision problems for which common sense would indicate a different selection of strategy than that indicated by the decision criterion. *It should not be construed, however, that common sense is the ultimate criterion. Common sense may work well enough when reality is uncomplicated.* Trouble starts when significant complexity exists and *common sense tells us that we can no longer rely on common sense.* In such cases the choice of criterion must be left to the decision-maker. It will be determined by individual attitudes or by company policy.

A Decision Criterion for Decision Criteria

A question might be raised at this point: If decision theory is so useful, why can't the problem of the decision criterion to be used be formulated as a decision problem and solved using decision theory? In other words, why not assume that the manager has four available strategies (say the four criteria discussed above), determine the possible states of nature, the objective, the payoff, and establish the payoff matrix. Then use decision theory to select a strategy—*viz.,* the decision criterion to be used for decision problems.

This question involves us with the *mirror problem* of how to decide how to decide (previously discussed in Chapter 2). Although we cannot completely unravel this knotty problem, there are several important aspects which will be worth considering. To begin with, how can we formulate the objective which is one step removed from our previous objective—to maximize the rate of return on our investment? Of course, we still want to maximize the return but we want something else in addition. In the investment example, all three strategies, under different criteria, held promise of maximizing our return. This seems like nonsense until we recognize the fact that uncertainty cannot be compromised. *Our problem in rendering decisions under uncertainty is to do it in such a way that our attitudes and state of mind are not jeopardized.*

Consequently, the formulation of our new objective must include consideration of the decision-maker's personality, attitudes, and way of life. The strategies are the four decision criteria. The states of nature become the range of values which the payoff measure (rate of return) could assume. For simplicity we can call them: win, lose, and draw. The new payoff measure must be some index of the *change* that will occur *in our state of mind* for any combination of strategy and state of nature. Let's see then what we have.

We must first characterize the individuals who would use the different decision criteria. We can call them: *cautious, adventurous, bad loser, and rational.* There are, of course, many other types of decision-makers and all shades between them. In this characterization we are taking some obvious liberties for the purpose of emphasizing the point. The four different kinds of decision-makers would now proceed to fill in the payoff measures for the matrix below:

	Win	Draw	Lose
Wald (cautious):			
Hurwicz (adventurous):			
Savage (bad loser):			
Laplace (rational):			

We can readily imagine that all four types of people will put different payoff measures into this matrix. For example, if an adventurous person decides to act cautiously and loses, he will be much more unhappy than if he had lost taking a sizable risk. The exact reverse will be true of the cautious person. The question now arises, assuming that we have filled in such a payoff matrix, how do we determine the probabilities of win, draw, and lose? Since they exist under uncertainty, we must choose a decision criterion (Wald, Hurwicz, Savage, or Laplace?), and we are back to the same problem with which we started. If we choose, we can pass on to the next mirror reflection. On the other hand, the adventurous person is likely to say: "I'm counting on luck," and he will rate "win" as more probable. The cautious person will say: "I can't count on luck," and he will lower the probability of win.

Sensitivity of the Criterion

There is still another way of looking at this problem. We shall disregard the influence of attitude and turn to the Laplace criterion, introducing small deviations from the assumption of equal probabilities. In other words, we are going to presume that we are not completely uncertain and that one of the states of nature is *just a little more likely* than any other state of nature. It will be recognized that even if we make small changes in all of the probabilities of the states of nature, we are no longer making decisions under uncertainty. We are now deciding under *risk*. Yet, if the changes that we have made are small, the formulation is almost identical with the Laplace criterion.

At some point, as we add little increments to the probability of one particular state of nature, while taking away an equivalent amount from the other probabilities, the strategy chosen by the Laplace criterion can be replaced by another strategy which has a larger expected value for the payoff. *The extent of change required to achieve such a shift reflects upon the sensitivity of this aspect of the system.*

Managerial Decision-Making

For example, the Laplace selection of Strategy 2 in the investment problem shifts to the selection of Strategy 1 when the first state of nature (war) goes from 0.33 probability to 0.37. (The other two states of nature are changed from 0.33 to 0.31.) On the other hand, the probability of depression must increase from 0.33 to 0.53 for Strategy 2 to shift to Strategy 3 (while war and peace go from 0.33 to 0.23). One way to interpret this is to say that if Strategy 1 is chosen by a particular criterion—except the Laplace—that criterion was chosen by the decision-maker because he had *more knowledge than he was aware he had.* That is why he chose a criterion other than the Laplace. In fact, he believed that war was more likely than peace or depression by an amount of 0.04. The required shift is small, and thereby *the system is sensitive to minor attitudinal biases* which support the contention that war will occur. Similarly, if the decision-maker's criterion selected Strategy 3 then we infer that he had reason to believe that a depression would occur and that he had as much as 0.20 additional belief in this outcome. This required shift is large. *The system is insensitive to minor biases* that a depression will occur.

The approach we are using is *sensitivity probing,* which is based on the question: How unbalanced must the relative uncertainties be before we stop calling them uncertainties? Since if we knew the probabilities of the states of nature we would use expected values, the Laplace criterion is the only one (of our four) that expresses *no attitude* except the desire to be rational. That is, *if we say we don't know the probabilities then we must act as if we don't know the probabilities.* That is why we characterize the Laplace criterion as rational. Therefore, the following observations about the attitude of the decision-maker seem relevant to the selection of the decision criterion.

1. States of nature may be equiprobable but it is unlikely that the individual has the chances of their occurring equally weighted *in his mind.*
2. It is possible that if you choose a criterion other than Laplace it is because you favor the probability that one or another state of nature will prevail. In any case, when it seems desirable, the Laplace criterion can permit the individual to think of the states of nature in equiprobable terms. Sensitivity testing can shed some light on the degree to which attitudes may affect results.

Decisions under Conflict

All previous discussion has been in terms of decisions against Nature. *The basic supposition has been that the state of nature which occurs will be independent of the selection of strategy of the manager.* When rational opponents are involved, we have decisions under conflict and this supposition is no longer true. On the contrary, usually the rational opponent (or opponents) will give careful thought to what the other executive can be expected to do before selecting his (or their) own courses of action. The essence of decision problems involving rational opponents is *conflict of interest*. For our discussion, the various opponents are all presumed to be rational. Therefore, they will be attempting to frustrate their opponents' wishes. As will be shown, *if one opponent exhibits nonrational behavior, he can only suffer for it*.

This part of decision theory is commonly known as *game theory*. It relates to a complex, highly developed body of knowledge. *Games* (in the general sense of game theory) *are customarily classified according to the number of opponents and the degree of conflict of interest*. The theory of games with only two opponents presents one of the simplest (but not simple!) cases. It is the variant most thoroughly developed. We shall confine our attention to this kind of game.

Games that have complete conflict of interest are ones in which what one opponent gains, the other loses. These are called *zero-sum games*. The nearest approximation to this kind of game in the business world would be a competitive battle for *share of the market*. One competitor can only increase his *share* of the market at the expense of his competitors. Political parties vying for Congressional seats is another illustration. Competitions for the award of fixed grants from foundations and for larger shares of a *given* budget also apply. Most recreational games that we play for fun are of this completely competitive type.

Games with less than complete conflict of interest are called *nonzero-sum games*. The majority of organization problems involving rational opponents are of this type. An example would be a competitive battle for sales. Here, the *size* of the market is involved. An advertising campaign might result in an increased share of the market, but it could also benefit the other competitors because of the tendency of advertising to stimulate sales for the product as well as for the brand. In other words, the gain of one competitor in terms of sales volume is not necessarily completely at the expense of the other competitors. The same reasoning applies to military conflicts and to conflicts between individuals and groups within and between organizations. The theory of nonzero-sum games is fascinating, but too elaborate for discussion here. We shall confine our attention to *two-person, zero-sum games* and the explanation of the decision criterion that is appropriate for this case.

Our concern is with competitive actions on the part of the opponent rather than with states of nature. So, instead of the *N's* we have been using we will use *C's* to represent the various possible competitive strategies. Since what one competitor wins, another loses (in a zero-sum game), we need use only one payoff matrix as before to represent the decision problem. We could not do this for a nonzero-sum game. In order to analyze nonzero-sum games we need a *separate payoff matrix for each opponent*.

Let us take as an example a decision problem involving a struggle for the share of the market against one opponent. Suppose that the manager has three strategies available and his competitor has four (there is no need for them to have the same number of possible strategies). The payoff matrix will be constructed in terms of the percentage-points increase in market share accruing to the manager.

Opponents' strategies

		C_1	C_2	C_3	C_4
Manager's	S_1:	0.6	−0.3	1.5	−1.1
Strategies	S_2:	0.7	0.1	0.9	0.5
	S_3:	−0.3	0.0	−0.5	0.8

This payoff matrix is read in exactly the same way as were the earlier ones. If the manager selects his first strategy and his opponent selects his third strategy, then the manager will increase his share of the market by 1.5 percentage points. And, of course, since this is a zero-sum game, the competitor will *lose* 1.5 percentage points of the market. Negative entries represent losses to the manager and gains to the competitor. The question is: How should the manager select his strategy? The difference from the cases where there was no rational opponent is that now, in reaching his decision, the manager must take into account what the opponent is likely to do. And, of course, vice versa holds.

It might appear that this would greatly increase the complexity of the decision problem and require some new kind of decision criterion. Actually, that isn't the case. In this kind of game it can be shown that the *only* rational decision criterion is the *Wald criterion*. Let us go through the reasoning to determine the strategy to be selected by using this criterion and then attempt to justify our statement that it is the *only* rational criterion.

The manager reasons, according to the Wald criterion, that if he selects S_1 he might lose as much as 1.1 (if his opponent selects C_4). If he selects S_2 he cannot do worse than to gain 0.1 (if his opponent selects C_2). If the manager selects S_3 he may lose 0.5 (if his opponent chooses C_3). Thus:

Strategy	Minimum payoff
S_1	−1.1
S_2	0.1 ◄──
S_3	−0.5

Following the Wald criterion we now select the maximum of these minimum payoffs, the *Maximin.* In this case it is 0.1, resulting from selecting S_2—which should therefore be the choice.

Remember, the opponent is rational. What is he thinking? He, too, elects to use the Wald criterion. From his standpoint the worst that can happen if he selects C_1 is that he will lose 0.7 (the maximum value in the column since the payoffs are stated in terms of *his opponent*). If he selects C_2 the worst that can happen is that he should lose 0.1 (if his opponent selects S_2). Proceeding similarly we obtain:

Competitor's action	Maximum loss
C_1	0.7
C_2	0.1 ◄──
C_3	1.5
C_4	0.8

According to the Wald criterion, the competitor will want to minimize his maximum loss, the *minimax* value. This minimax value is 0.1, achieved by selecting C_2. This, then, should be his choice. Thus, the best decisions on the part of the two competitors are that the manager should select S_2, his competitor should select C_2, and the result will be an increase of 0.1 percentage points in market share to the manager.

Why can we say that this is the only *rational* approach to such a competitive decision problem? Consider the situation from the standpoint of the manager. He knows that his opponent can minimize his maximum loss by selecting C_2. Assume that the opponent uses C_2. Then if the manager selected any other strategy but his S_2, he would do worse than he would by selecting S_2. If he selected S_1 he would lose 0.3 instead of winning 0.1. If he selected S_3 he would gain nothing instead of gaining 0.1. Similarly, the competitor knows that the manager can maximize his minimum gain by selecting S_2. If he does so the opponent does best by selecting his C_2. If he does anything else he loses more. Thus, with complete conflict of interest, the opponents are driven to use the Wald criterion.

If the manager *knows* that his competitor will not use C_2, or if he has any other pertinent information about what his competitor will do—other than what is expected of him—he will establish probabilities for the competitive strategies. From these, he can determine his own optimum strategy on the basis of decision-making under risk. *In such an event, the information he has obtained has measurable utility.* It will permit him to realize a greater payoff than he could otherwise expect. On the other hand, if he is unsure of his information he can continue to use his maximin strategy and *gain the advantage which must come to him if his competitor does not act in an entirely rational manner.*

It may be noted that in this payoff matrix the maximin value for the manager equaled the minimax value for his opponent—both of them being 0.1. This is by no means always the case. When the two values are different it develops that the use of *mixed strategies*—where the specific strategy to be used is selected randomly with a determined probability—will make them equal.[10] The proof of this fact is called the *fundamental theorem* of game theory. We shall not discuss this theorem further. It won't affect our point that the existence of a rational opponent can simplify the decision problem—converting it to a strictly deterministic situation (even when mixed strategies are involved).

Often, the information required to construct a payoff matrix is difficult to obtain. This may be especially true when the payoffs must represent the utilities of various outcomes to both participants in a competitive decision system. Frequently, we have recourse to the use of ranked data. This is well-illustrated by an example in Ch. 9, p. 224.

If the competitors do not have the same approximate utility then a

---

[10]The equal value is called a *saddlepoint*, whether it arises from mixed or pure strategies.

nonzero-sum game with *two payoff* matrices is required. And this assumes that *each* opponent is able to estimate his competitor's utilities. Otherwise, the matrix analysis loses its meaning. The common reason that competitive situations are of the nonzero-sum type is that the utilities of the opponents are not the same. Since *utilities are, by definition, subjective,* it may well be that the opponents do not know the utilities of their competitors for the various outcomes. As a matter of fact, one might expect that this would be the *usual case.*

Certain types of organizations often do have some degree of similarity in goals. In these cases, we would expect that the opponents might have some idea of the opposition's utility for the various outcomes. However, if a decision problem arose in which the executive really had no idea about the utility his opponent ascribed to the outcomes, then the decision problem would have to be treated under *uncertainty.* [11] This results because, not knowing the utilities of his opponent for the outcomes, the decision-maker has no way of knowing anything about the probabilities of the different competitive actions—which is an equivalent definition of decision-making under certainty.

In terms of actual organizational conditions, which decision situations are most likely to arise? It is clear that a large number of problems are primarily involved with states of nature. So the usefulness of our analysis concerning certainty, risk, and uncertainty is evident. But what about rational opponents? According to the classical conditions of *free enterprise* any decision problem is simply against nature because, by the definition of these conditions, no one business can have any effect on market conditions through any strategy which it might elect to follow. On the other hand, *wherever free-enterprise conditions do not exist in a specific market we are obliged to include competitive actions as part of the decision problem.* In short, under *oligopolistic* conditions in a particular market it is necessary to include competitive actions in the payoff matrix. Also, many problems of a *monopoly* can be construed as games against a rational opponent. In this case, they are the suppliers and consumers. Generally, *small organizations that deal in a large marketplace* can ignore the effects of a rational opponent. *This puts them in the position of deciding under conditions of risk or uncertainty. As the size of the company increases with respect to the market, the influence of rational opponents is felt.* As a rule, a particular management can evaluate its situation with respect to the importance of competition.

---

[11] And independent of the competitor in all respects.

RALPH O. SWALM

Utility Theory—
Insights into Risk-Taking

Preface. The term "cardinal utility theory" is new to most businessmen. But it is a term that will appear more and more regularly in management articles, books, meetings, and discussions in the future. It is a useful concept, may lead to surprising findings, and (just to clinch matters) is now being taught to students in business schools.

This article is the first one to explain for businessmen the rudiments of utility theory. The description of these principles comes in the first main section of the text. There follows a short discussion of some questions that elicit divided thought among scholars (this part may be of particular interest to those trying to evaluate current research efforts). In the final sections, the author describes some results and implications of a recent study employing utility theory concepts. These unusual findings bear on businessmen's attitudes toward risk and should be of quite general interest to policy makers.

Suppose that you were lucky enough to be offered the following alternatives.

Source: Ralph O. Swalm, "Utility Theory—Insights into Risk-Taking," *Harvard Business Review* (November-December, 1966). Copyright 1966 by the President and Fellows of Harvard College, all rights reserved. Reprinted with the permission of the publisher, Harvard University Press.

1. Accept the payment of a tax-free gift of $1 million.
2. Toss a fair coin. If heads comes up, you get nothing; if tails come up, you get a tax-free gift of $3 million.

Which would you choose? Would it be the certain $1 million, or the 50-50 chance of $3 million or nothing?

When confronted with this choice, most people say they would choose the certain $1 million, even though the gamble has what is called an "expected value" of $1.5 million. (The term "expected value," often used in quantitative analysis, is the product of the hoped-for gain and the probability of winning it—$3,000,000 X .50 in this case.) Said another way, the average winnings in this case, if you gamble repeatedly, are half again as large as your winnings if you take the certain $1 million.

Indeed, even when the winnings on the gamble increase to $5 million if tails come up, many people will still prefer the certain $1 million!

This is especially perplexing when one reads some of the articles about the application of decision theory to business decisions. Many writers assume, without apparent question, that a businessman will of course want to choose that alternative which maximizes his expected—or average—return.[1]

There is little or no recognition of the fact that rational people, whether they are businessmen or bartenders, sometimes prefer an alternative other than the one with the highest expected value. For these situations a different basis for the explanation and prediction of behavior needs to be found.

One theory that purports to describe man's behavior in such risk situations more adequately has been given the name *cardinal utility theory*. The formulation of cardinal utility theory was proposed by John von Neumann and Oskar Morgenstern in their monumental *Theory of Games and Economic Behavior*.[2] Oversimplifying a bit, this concept proposes that each individual attempts to optimize the expected value of something which is defined as utility, and that for each individual a relationship between utility and dollars can be found.

This article is, in a sense, a progress report aimed at exploring the usefulness of cardinal utility theory in understanding how businessmen make decisions in risk situations where the stakes are large. I use the term "progress report" advisedly, for research so far has raised as many questions as it has answered and much remains to be done in this area. After explaining cardinal utility theory, I shall raise the question of whether businessmen consider uncertainty in their decisions, and if so, how they might be expected to behave. Then I shall report some research findings on decision-making in the face of risks. These findings

[1]See, for example, David B. Hertz, "Risk Analysis in Capital Expenditure Decisions," *HBR*, January-February 1964, p. 95; and John F. Magee, "Decision Trees for Decision Making," *HBR*, July-August 1964, p. 126; and "How to Use Decision Trees in Capital Investment," *HBR*, September-October 1964, p. 79.
[2]Princeton, New Jersey, Princeton University Press, 1947.

cast serious doubts on the classical notion of the American businessman as a risk taker and on the validity of many control systems set up to monitor managers' behavior.

Nature of the Theory

To begin, what is cardinal utility theory all about? Let me try to explain the basic notions as simply as I can.

PERSONAL UTILITY FUNCTIONS

According to the theory, each individual has a measurable preference among various choices available in risk situations. This preference is called his utility. Utility is measured in arbitrary units which we will call "utiles." By suitable questioning we can determine for each individual a relationship between utility and dollars which is called his utility function. This plot offers a picture of his attitude toward taking risks.

In any decision involving risk, a man will choose that alternative which maximizes his utility. Once we know his utility function, the odds he assigns to events in a decision-making situation, and the consequences of each possible outcome, we should be able to predict his choice in that situation, since he will attempt to maximize his utility. Perhaps an example will make this clearer:

Suppose a decision-maker's utility function has been determined as shown in Exhibit 1. (I will explain how to determine the function later.) With such a diagram in hand, you should be able to predict the decision-maker's preference for alternatives such as these:

1. Receive a certain $100,000.
2. Have an 80% chance of winning $200,000 and a 20% chance of losing $50,000.

To make the prediction, you must calculate the decision-maker's expected utility for the two alternatives. First read from Exhibit 1 the utility for the three sums involved, as follows:

Sum	Utility
$100,000	15 utiles
$200,000	20 utiles
−$50,000	−10 utiles

Then calculate the expected utility of the two alternatives. The expected utility of the certain $100,000 is 15 utiles. The expected utility of the second alternative is 14 utiles—

$$.80 \ \text{X} \ [20 \ \text{utiles}] \ + \ .20 \ \text{X} \ [-10 \ \text{utiles}].$$

EXHIBIT 1

A Utility Curve

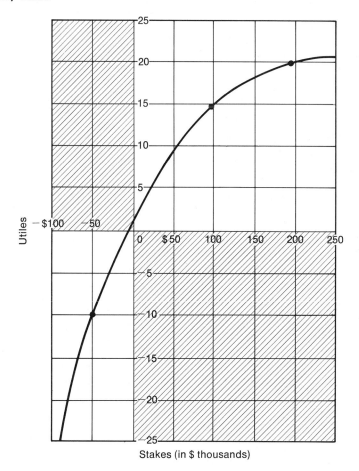

Stakes (in $ thousands)

Since the first alternative has the higher expected utility, utility theory would predict that the decision-maker in our example would prefer it over the second alternative.

Before showing how to determine an individual's utility function, let me mention that while relative utilities are measurable, absolute utility is not. That is, the scale on which utility is measured has no natural origin; instead, one is free to assign arbitrary utility values to any two sums of money. But, having done this, there will be for each individual a unique value for the utility that he would assign to any other sum of money. Thus, once we begin matching utiles and sums of money for the businessman in Exhibit 1, a curve or "profile" of his attitude toward risk is created which establishes his preferences for all stakes in the area described.

Our ordinary temperature scales are examples of this same sort of scale. We are free to define 32° F as the freezing point of water and 212° F as its boiling point, and then measure all other temperatures on this scale. But having defined two arbitrary points, we cannot logically say that a temperature of 80° F is twice as hot as one of 40° F, for if we transposed to the Centigrade scale, we would describe these same temperatures as about 27° C and 4½° C.

Unlike temperature scales, however, utility scales are postulated as personal and subjective. There is, therefore, no reason to expect one man's utility function (or plot of utility versus dollars) to agree with another's.

EQUATING ALTERNATIVES

How can we determine a person's utility function? The basic principle to use is this: if a decision-maker is indifferent between two alternatives, the expected utility of the alternatives is the same. To illustrate, suppose that Abner McGillicuty is one of those mentioned at the outset of this article who would choose a certain $1 million in preference to a 50-50 gamble on $3 million or nothing. The utility concept simply states that, on Abner's utility scale, the distance corresponding to the interval from 0 to $1 million is more than half of the distance corresponding to the interval from 0 to $3 million.

Suppose, further, that the winnings if tails come up can be increased until Abner becomes indifferent to taking the gamble or taking the certain $1 million. Assume, for the sake of argument, that he becomes indifferent when this amount reaches $5 million. In utility theory terms, the two alternatives then have equal utility.

Since each of the two possibilities in the coin-tossing example has a 50% likelihood of occurrence, the expected (or average) utility of the uncertain outcome can be calculated as:

$$.50 \times [\text{utility of } \$5,000,000] + .50 \times [\text{utility of } 0].$$

Now define the utility of any two of these points. For example, Abner's utility of $5 million might be defined as 10 utiles, and his utility of 0 as 0 utiles. Then determine the utility of the third point by simple algebra. Thus, if U represents the utility of a sum, then:

$$.5 \times U [\$5,000,000] + .5 \times U [0] = U [\$1,000,000].$$

Substituting the defined values leads to:

$$.5 [10 \text{ utiles}] = U [\$1,000,000]$$
$$5 \text{ utiles} = U [\$1,000,000].$$

Thus it can be seen that, on Abner's utility scale, the distance corresponding to the interval from 0 to $1 million is the same as the distance corresponding to the interval from $1 million to $5 million.

Note that it is tempting but incorrect to state that his utility for $5 million (10 utiles) is twice his utility for $1 million (5 utiles). For, as in the temperature example, it would be equally logical to define the utility of $5 million as 100 utiles and the utility of 0 as 90 utiles. In this case the utility of $1 million would be 95 utiles. The *distances* in utiles between 0 and $1 million would still be the same as that between $1 million and $5 million, but 95 would hardly be described as half of 100!

Plotting Abner's assigned utilities against dollars, there are three points on his utility function, as shown in Exhibit 2.

EXHIBIT 2

Three Points on Abner's Utility Function

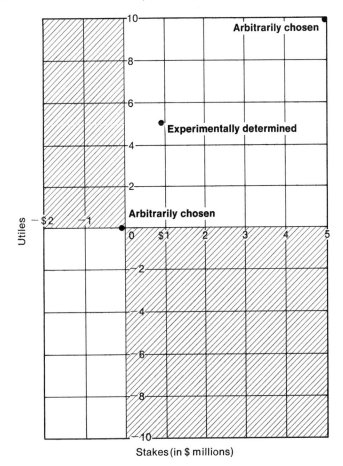

Stakes (in $ millions)

FURTHER DELINEATION

Clearly, Abner's "utility function" (or plot of utility versus dollars) is nonlinear, but three points can hardly be said to determine the outlines of the function. So it is necessary to seek more points.

Suppose Abner is asked the question: "You now have a contract offering a 50-50 chance of making $1,000,000 or nothing. Would you sell it for $400,000?" If he would, this indicates his utility for $400,000 is greater than his utility for the contract. To find the certain amount that has, for Abner, the same utility as the gamble, he might be asked if he would sell the contract for $200,000. If at this price he refuses to sell, it is known that his utility for $200,000 is less than that for the contract. Now the certain sum which has the same utility as the 50-50 chance at $1,000,000 has been fixed as being somewhere between $200,000 and $400,000. By continuing the "hunting" process, hopefully, the precise point at which he is indifferent can be determined. Assume it is found to be $300,000. This, then, is the monetary sum to which Abner would assign 2.5 utiles on a scale in which 0 equals 0 utiles and $1,000,000 equals 5 utiles. For:

$$.5 \times U\,[0] + .5 \times U\,[\$1,000,000] = U\,[\$300,000].$$

Substituting:

$$.5 \times [0 \text{ utiles}] + .5 \times [5 \text{ utiles}] = U\,[\$300,000]$$
$$2.5 \text{ utiles} = U\,[\$300,000].$$

So far Abner's behavior has been tested in situations where he can only gain. His behavior pattern in loss situations could be examined by asking questions such as: "Suppose you are asked to make a bid which, if successful, will net you $300,000 but which, if unsuccessful, will cost you $100,000. Would you choose to bid if you evaluated your chances of getting the bid as 3 to 1? (In this case the certainty option is to do nothing and, of course, gain or lose nothing.) Again, by successive probings, varying the amount of the loss or, alternatively, the odds assigned, one could eventually arrive at an indifference situation. Suppose, for Abner, this involves a loss of $100,000 at the original odds of 3 to 1. In this situation:

$$.75 \times U\,[\$300,000] + .25 \times U\,[-\$100,000] = U\,[0]$$
$$.75 \times 2.5 \text{ utiles} + .25\, U\,[-\$100,000] = 0 \text{ utiles}$$
$$U\,[-\$100,000] = -7.5 \text{ utiles}.$$

There are now five points on Abner's utility function, which can be tentatively connected by a smooth curve as shown in Exhibit 3.

Now some checkpoints should be tried to test the validity of the inferences made in connecting the points on Abner's utility function. If these points check out, we now, according to utility theory, should be able to predict Abner's

EXHIBIT 3

Abner's Completed Utility Function

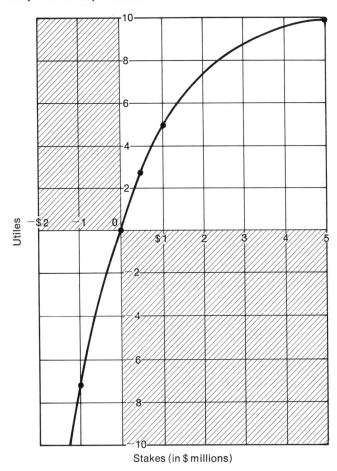

Stakes (in $ millions)

decisions in any risk situation in which the gains do not exceed $5,000,000 or the losses do not go below $100,000 provided we know the probabilities he attaches to the various outcomes of these situations.

Proper Role

What is the proper use of utility theory? As indicated, my own belief is that it will prove to be useful in *describing* and *predicting* executive behavior. Before substantiating this belief I want to point out, however, that some authorities question this position. They insist that the theory is *prescriptive* (or "normative"), that it indicates how executives *should* behave rather than how they *do* behave. Foremost among these authorities is Howard Raiffa. In reference to Savage's theory (which combines cardinal utility theory with subjective probability),[3] Raiffa has commented:

> Savage's theory is not a descriptive or predictive theory of behavior. It is a theory which purports to advise any one of its believers how he *should* behave in complicated situations, *provided* he can make choices in a coherent manner in relatively simple, uncomplicated situations.[4]

People do not always behave in a manner consistent with maximizing their utility, according to Raiffa, and this—

> . . . clearly demonstrates how important it is to have a theory which can be used to aid in the making of decisions under uncertainty. If most people behaved in a manner roughly consistent with [the] theory, then the theory would gain stature as a descriptive theory but would lose a good deal of its normative importance. We do not have to teach people what comes naturally. But as it is, we need to do a lot of teaching.[5]

A similar viewpoint has been expressed as follows by a person with whom I have had correspondence:

> The utility model is *not* a good descriptive theory for risk-taking situations. When people do what comes naturally, they are as inconsistent as can be. The real question is whether they want to act inconsistently or whether they wish to employ a methodology which would allow them to resolve their inconsistencies and allow them to analyze complex problems. But, alas, most businessmen are not perfectly rational men; rather, they are as inconsistent as all mortals are. There is no need to have a prescriptive theory of utility for the perfectly rational man. Just tell him to do what comes naturally. The *raison d'etre* for utility theory is that most of us are not supermen—we make errors of judgment and are inconsistent in our choices. And knowing this, some of us, when faced with an important and complex problem, might wish to employ, in a conscious manner, decision aids that will help police our inconsistencies and help guide us to an appropriate course of action. Utility theory purports to be such a decision aid.

Taking a contrary view are other authorities. Here are just a couple of samples from the literature (the emphasis on "predict" is mine):

> The von Neumann-Morgenstern measure of utility is a special type of

[3]See Leonard J. Savage, *Foundations of Statistics* (New York: John Wiley & Sons, Inc., 1954).

[4]"Risk, Ambiguity, and the Savage Axioms: Comment," *Quarterly Journal of Economics,* November 1961, p. 690.

[5]*Ibid.*

cardinal measure. .... The use of this utility measure enables us to *predict* which of certain lotteries a person will prefer. .... [6]

In the preceding chapters, we have discussed the rules which a rational person could be expected to observe when he has to make decisions under uncertainty. If we know these rules, we should be able to *predict* how a decision-maker will behave in a given situation.[7]

MORE USEFUL TESTS

The question of the degree to which businessmen *are* rational and of the extent to which utility theory *is* useful for predictive purposes should be determinable by experiment.

Indeed, experiments have been performed involving bets on drawing colored balls from several urns when varying degrees of information are available. These tests have shown that in risk situations many people do not behave in accordance with certain postulates (sometimes called Savage's Axioms) which rational people should be expected to follow. The prescriptive and descriptive schools each find the results consistent with their positions.[8]

It is my contention that results of experiments involving bets on colored balls in urns are much less relevant to industrial situations than is a direct examination of the degree to which a utility function derived from one set of reasonably realistic questions can be used to predict a businessman's answers to a different set of questions. One of the major purposes of the research reported later in this article is to make such an examination.

Utility theory, we have seen, is a refinement on methods which assume the desirability of optimizing expected dollar income in risk decisions. It suggests that a man will (or perhaps should) attempt to optimize expected *utility* rather than expected dollar gain—and that a function relating utility to dollar gain can be found for each rational individual.

Discovering such a function is not easy, and the results of hypothetical tests will always leave something to be desired. But surely we will get nearer the truth as we pose questions to businessmen which more closely approximate the day-to-day problems with which they have to deal on the job.

THEORY VS. REALITY

Do today's businessmen use approaches, such as those proposed by David

[6]Harold Bierman, Jr., Charles P. Bonini, Lawrence E. Fouraker, and Robert K. Jaedicke, *Quantitative Analysis for Business Decisions* (Homewood, Illinois: Richard D. Irwin, Inc., revised edition 1965), p. 194.

[7]Karl Borsch, "The Economics of Uncertainty," working paper no. 70 (Western Management Sciences Institute, University of California, Los Angeles, March 1965).

[8]See, for example, Daniel Ellsberg, "Risk, Ambiguity, and the Savage Axioms," *Quarterly Journal of Economics,* November 1961, p. 643.

Hertz and John Magee, which explicitly take risk into consideration in the making of day-to-day decisions?

The best available evidence indicates that very few do. In general, their approaches to decision-making can be described, to use technical phraseology, as "models under assumed certainty." In other words, in their approaches to or "models" of decision-making, probabilities seldom appear directly.

Why is this so? William T. Morris thinks that uncertainty gets suppressed in the analysis because of the fact that the human mind has limited information-handling capacities:

> The key to understanding any decision-making process is to discover the ways in which the decision-maker simplifies the complex fabric of the environment into workable conceptions of his decision problems. The human mind has limited information-handling capacities; thus both analysts and managers deal with decisions in terms of conceptual simplifications or models of reality. Perhaps the most obvious of these simplifications is that of suppressing one's necessary ignorance of the future and considering a decision *as if* only one possible future could occur. This is not to pretend that one *knows* the future with certainty but is simply an act of conceptual simplification. It allows one to answer the question, 'If this particular set of circumstances were to occur, what would be the reasonable course of action for management? If a manager does undertake the course of action which results, one may think of him as *acting as if* the set of circumstances in question were sure to occur.
>
> Likewise, when an analyst suppresses risk and uncertainty in making a management decision explicit, it does not imply that he claims knowledge of the future. It is one of the many ways in which science may simplify the real world in order to study it. None of us can know the future, but it is often very useful to ask questions about how we would act if we did. . . .
>
> It is traditional to study the great majority of managerial decisions as decisions under assumed certainty. Thus, in the selection of equipment, the selection of materials and designs, the choice of operating methods and policies, and so on, the assumption of certainty is widely used.[9]
>
> One should never lose sight of the fact, however, that such a model is a result of one's decision to simplify by suppressing uncertainties about the future. Its 'reasonableness' is a matter of judgment at first and what sort of results it leads to ultimately. It does not mean that the future is certain, only that one studies the decision *as if* the future were certain.[10]

There may be another reason for playing down uncertainty. Often risk is introduced late in the analysis on a somewhat ad hoc basis, instead of making specific probability statements about events in the analysis. Thus, in using methods such as the justly celebrated profitability index approach described by

---

[9]William T. Morris, *The Analysis of Management Decisions* (Homewood, Illinois: Richard D. Irwin, Inc., revised edition, 1964), pp. 49-50.

[10]*Ibid.,* p 10.

Ray I. Reul,[11] one elects to use a model that assumes that projected cash flows will be certain to occur, and later to interpret the resulting profitability index in the light of living in an uncertain world. Likewise, if a simple payback criterion is applied to test a proposed expenditure, the calculation assumes that the projected incomes and outgoes will be certain to occur, even though the selection of a cutoff point (such as a two-year payback) may be made in an attempt to take risk into consideration.

It is unusual to find examples of explicit probability statements in actual practice; yet modern theory increasingly deals with approaches or "models" requiring such statements. Texts and articles appear in greater and greater numbers on such subjects as decision trees, statistical inference, Monte-Carlo methods, and so forth. More and more businessmen, and particularly tomorrow's businessmen in today's schools, are exhorted to use sophisticated models that recognize risk explicitly.

When businessmen behave contrary to the way theorists urge them to behave, the reason is not always that the businessmen are unwise. Sometimes the theories are inadequate; more often, perhaps, logic lies somewhere between practice and theory. We can often refine our theories by looking a bit more closely at what the businessman has learned through experience and, perhaps intuitively, put into practice.

Attitudes toward Risk

How do businessmen act in situations where they recognize risks? In the research to be reported, utility theory was used to help answer this question. That is, we determined the utility functions (such as the ones in Exhibits 1 and 3) of a large number of executives, and used these functions as the basis of interpretation. The executives were in different lines of work and had diverse backgrounds.

Despite the fact that utility theory is urged on businessmen by the textbook writers, only two serious attempts to determine the utility functions of businessmen have been reported.[12] Together, these reports attempt to find utility functions for 32 businessmen, of whom half are in a single large but unnamed chemical company and half in the oil exploration field.

It is true that there have been a number of very carefully planned experiments testing utility functions of graduate students and other suitable warm bodies faced with gambles involving, quite literally, pennies. But such ex-

[11]See, for instance, "Profitability Index for Investments," *HBR,* July-August 1957, p. 116.

[12]See P. E. Green, "Risk Attitudes and Chemical Investment Decisions," *Chemical Engineering Progress,* January 1963, p. 35; and C. Jackson Grayson, Jr., *Decisions Under Uncertainty* (Division of Research, Harvard Business School, 1960).

periments have limited relevance to the world of business. As Jacob Marchak says:

> Tentative explorations performed . . . on graduate students or by these students on their wives do supply some preliminary evidence that deserves to be treated in a more rigorous way. It would be worthwhile to perform such experiments on mature executives, rather than on students.[13]

RESEARCH APPROACH

Ideally we would have liked to have our subjects deal with real sums in real situations. However, even the wealthiest foundation could not be expected to underwrite repeated million-dollar experiments, and few businesses would allow their executives to participate in experiments whose possible outcomes might require their treasurer to pay out large sums! So we were forced to ask a number of businessmen how they would behave in risk situations as described to them. We did our best to make the situations seem real and to get realistic replies.

We sought to find the utility functions displayed in making corporate, rather than private, decisions. We were able to question a rather wide range of decision-makers (though most had an engineering background) in one company—I shall call it "Company A"—and a smaller number of decision-makers in a cross section of industries. Altogether, about 100 executives were tested.

Except in a few cases, each man was interviewed individually; this consumed one to two hours per man. After first introducing the utility theory concept (in much the same way as in this article), we set the stage for the experimental evaluation of his corporate utility function with an explanation such as that shown in Exhibit 4 (which is a somewhat abridged version of that actually used). Sometimes the construction of the question was varied, but the reader will recognize that the approach used was very similar to that employed in deriving Exhibit 3.

EXHIBIT 4

Instructions to Participants in Tests

"We are about to perform a series of experiments; in each of these you will be asked to make a decision in a situation involving risk. Although real-life risk situations often involve a continuum of possible alternatives, we shall, to simplify matters, look only at simple cases in which you are asked to choose between a choice that leads to a certain gain (or loss) of a known amount and a course of action that could lead to either of two outcomes, each of which is considered—on the basis of the best information available at the time you are required to make your decision—to have a 50-50 chance of occurring.

"In all cases we will assume that all incomes or outgoes will take place in the very near future, or, alternatively, that these can be

---

[13]Actual vs. Consistent Decision Behavior," *Behavioral Science,* April 1964, p. 104.

considered the present worths of all future cash flows that are affected by your decision. All amounts are considered to be net after taxes.

"You are asked to make these choices in your capacity as a corporate decision-maker, not as a private individual dealing with your own funds. Try to give replies that represent the actual action you would take if presented with this choice at work *today*. We want to know what you would actually *do*, not what you feel you should do or what the speaker might expect you to do.

"Conceptually, all of the questions you will be asked are of this general form:

> "Suppose you are faced with choosing between one of two alternative courses of action. The first involves undertaking to bid on a new project. If the bid is successful, your company will make a net gain of, say, $100,000. If unsuccessful, you will be reimbursed for the costs of making the bid, making your net gain zero. Your best available information leads you to assign a 50-50 chance to these possible events.
>
> "'Your second possible course of action is to put the manpower you might spend in making the bid into cost-reduction efforts. Based on past experience, you are certain that this would result in a net gain. How large would this certain gain have to be to make you indifferent as to which choice to make? In other words, at what certain income would you be indifferent to your company's getting that income or getting a 50-50 chance of making $100,000 or nothing?

"In all of the questions you are asked, the following will hold true. You will always be presented with two mutually exclusive choices. One will always involve a 50-50 chance between two possible outcomes; the second will always involve a certain outcome. The dollar amounts of two of your three possible final outcomes will be given; you will be asked to fix the amount of the third in such a way that you would be indifferent to the choice between the gamble and the certain outcome."

Because of the possible confounding of utility and subjective probabilities, and because there was considerable evidence that few could sense fine distinctions between one course of action that had, say, a 90% probability of success and another that had, say, a 95% probability, we limited all our risks to those involving a 50-50 chance. These were easily understood as equivalent to a flip of a coin. (Nevertheless, the 50-50 chance caused many respondents difficulty because, as they put it, "We just don't go into an investment unless the chances of success are much better than 50-50." The concept that many bids are made when the odds of success are 50-50 or less helped a bit here. Interestingly, several research administrators in the same companies as the participants objected that their odds were never this good!)

After discussing our instructions thoroughly, we then asked each man what the maximum single amount that he might recommend be spent in any one year might be. We defined his "planning horizon" as twice this amount. We did this to examine the hypothesis that a man's corporate utility function was more a function of his own corporate planning horizon than it was of the actual resources of the corporation. This also enabled us to ask each man questions regarding sums that had meaning to him.

We then started a line of questioning, similar to the questions in the instructions, involving sums of money up to the man's planning horizon. For examples of such questions see Exhibit 5.

EXHIBIT 5

Examples of Questions Asked

Suppose a man's planning horizon is $1 million. Our first question would be structured somewhat as follows (the situation was varied to some degree to fit the man's own background):

> "Suppose you are faced with two choices. The first is to recommend that your company commit a certain amount of engineering manpower to making a bid. If successful, the bid will result in a net profit, after tax, of $1 million. If unsuccessful, you will be reimbursed for the expenses incurred, so that your net return will be zero. Your best estimate of the odds favoring success is 50-50.

> "Your second alternative is to recommend that the engineering manpower be employed in developing a new plant layout. You are certain that this would result in an after-tax income of, say, $300,000. These are mutually exclusive alternatives; that is, acceptance of one precludes the possibility of accepting the other. Either opportunity will be lost if not accepted now. Which would you recommend?"

If he recommended the bid, the $300,000 figure was increased; if he said he would recommend the layout, the question was repeated with a lower income (say $200,000) postulated as the income from the revised layout. This process was repeated until a value was found at which the respondent was indifferent to the choice of recommending the investment in the bid or the layout. (It was recognized, of course, that in the real world, an *area* of indifference, rather than a unique point, would be found.)

The value of the certainty option at this point of indifference was noted and used as the basis for a second question. Suppose, for the respondent, that this amount were $250,000. The next question might be:

> "Suppose you planned to purchase a general-purpose machine but a colleague proposed, instead, to buy a more efficient special-

purpose machine. Both cost the same; the difficulty is that the contract for which the special-purpose machine would be required has only a 50-50 probability of being received. If it is received, the special-purpose machine will yield a profit of $250,000. If not, your net income will be zero. On the other hand, the general-purpose machine will produce a certain savings of, say, $100,000. Which would you recommend?"

(In actual practice, this question would take longer to state and explain; here we offer only the bare essentials.)

Again, the "certain savings" would be manipulated until a point of indifference was reached. This same sort of question would be asked repeatedly to establish a number of points which would, hopefully, define the respondent's utility curve; additional questions would be asked to establish still more points that would act as checks on the curve.

In some questions, losses were involved. For example, one question might take this form:

"Suppose your company is being sued for patent infringement. Your lawyer's best judgment is that your chances of winning the suit are 50-50; if you win, you will lose nothing, but if you lose, it will cost the company $1,000,000. Your opponent has offered to settle out of court for $200,000. Would you fight or settle?"

If this situation could not be envisaged by the decision-maker, or if he indicated a special reaction to a question involving a suit, a question involving a different context, but the same sum of money, would be tried.

Finally, the points determined by this series of questions were plotted to yield a utility function for a man. In each case, the horizontal scale (gains and losses) was plotted in terms of the planning horizon rather than actual dollar amounts. The vertical scale was established by defining the utility of the planning horizon as 120 utiles, and the utility of 0 dollars as 0 (120 was used to permit a sequence of even numbers when the figure was repeatedly halved). About half the points plotted were "checkpoints" to test the consistency of the replies.

FINDINGS AND CONTRASTS

Some sample utility functions from the research are shown in Exhibit 6. The numbers refer to the designations used in the original research. All but Man #1 are from Company A.

The first observation is that in most cases the points do not lie on a smooth

EXHIBIT 6

Samples of Utility Functions

GROUP A

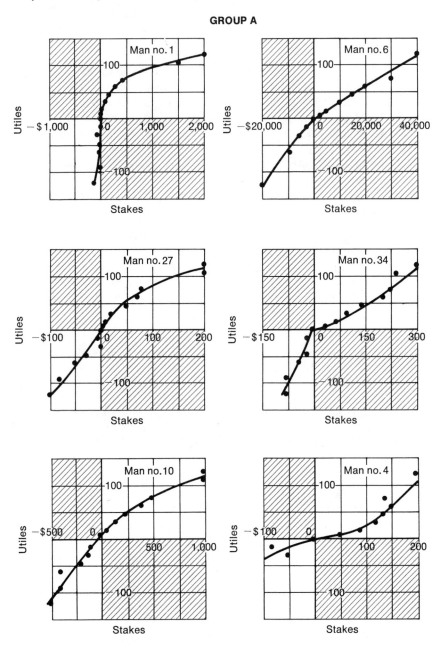

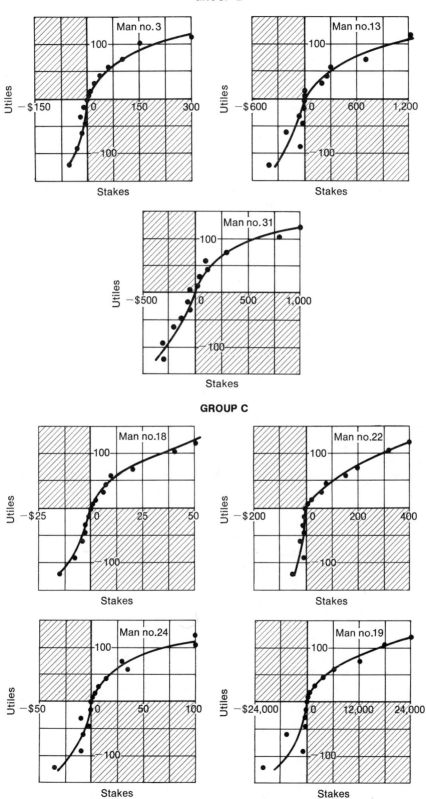

curve. However, although there is scatter, the points show a trend sufficiently clear for a curve to be fitted through them in much the same way that an engineer fits a curve to experimental data.

Reasonably accurate predictions can be made about answers to questions involving risk and sums of money within the range covered by the curve, as shown by the closeness of most of the points to the curve.

Now consider some of the differences in attitude which these utility functions reveal. For example, consider Group A. One could characterize Man #1 as extremely conservative, #27 as conservative, #10 as moderately conservative, #6 as linear, #34 as inclined toward risk, and #4 as a gambler.

To illustrate more specifically, contrast Man #4, a gambler, with Man #27, a conservative. Both have a planning horizon of $200,000 (to which, as earlier mentioned, we have arbitrarily assigned a utility of 120 utiles on a scale in which 0 dollars is assigned to 0 utiles). Suppose each of these men was faced with a decision of whether or not he should recommend taking a 50-50 chance of making $200,000 or nothing (this gamble is easily shown to be worth 60 utiles to either) in preference to recommending a line of action that would lead with certainty to an income of $100,000 (or 50% of the man's planning horizon). Man #4 would recommend the gamble, and Man #27 the certain $100,000. For the first, $100,000 has a utility of only about 25 utiles (reading from the curve); for the second, it has a utility of more than 80 utiles, well in excess of the 60 which the gamble is worth. In fact, proceeding across the 60-utile line in each case, we find that Man #4 would still want to gamble until the certainty option rose to about 75% ($150,000) of his planning horizon, whereas Man #27 would not gamble if the certainty option were about 30% ($60,000) of his planning horizon.

In short, one executive values the gamble at less than $60,000; the other, at $150,000. Yet both are employed by the same corporation and are making decisions that involve the same corporate funds! Does this raise some interesting questions? If you were their common supervisor, would you wish to know of this difference? Would you be curious as to how these utility functions compared with your own—or to those of your company president?

While Group A shows how different and how personal utility functions usually are, Group B shows how similar some can be. Note that all the men represented in Group B can be termed quite conservative.

SOME DISTURBING RESULTS

A finding that will disturb many businessmen is that the men's utility functions appear to be more closely related to the amounts with which they are accustomed to deal as individuals than to the financial position of the company. To see this, look at Group C, showing the utility functions of four men. Note that these men have planning horizons ranging from $50,000 to $24,000,000;

however, their utility functions, when plotted against amounts shown in terms of their planning horizons, are roughly comparable. Plotted on an absolute scale, they clearly would not be.

Yet another disturbing phenomenon is a fairly consistent pattern of sharp slopes found in the negative quadrants. Man #3 (Group B) is fairly typical. Note that if we assign 120 utiles to his planning horizon of $300,000, we must assign −120 utiles to a loss of only about $55,000. This means that he would not recommend a proposal that had a 50-50 chance of either making his company $300,000 or losing $60,000. But it seems rather clear that Company A, being an industrial giant, would gain if its managers took such favorable gambles.

We would pay little attention if Man #3 were a maverick, but he is not. If you look over the rest of the curves, you will agree that he is not atypical. These curves certainly do not portray the risk-takers of which we hear so much folklore. They portray decision-makers quite unwilling to take what, for the company, would seem to be rather attractive risks. One cannot help wondering if this might be due to control procedures that bias managers against making any decision which might lead to a loss. Do our control procedures unduly reward the man who recommends the low but certain return alternative at the expense of the man who is willing to gamble when the potential gain makes the risk worthwhile?

Evidence that this may be so is offered by the fact that in our study several respondents stated quite clearly that they were aware that their choices were not in the best interests of the company, but that they felt them to be in their own best interests as aspiring executives, and therefore they represented the choices they would actually make. From an experimenter's viewpoint this was encouraging, for it indicated the respondents were truly trying to give answers that represented what they *would* do, and not what they felt they *should* do. But it raises a vast and fundamental question regarding control procedures now in use.

Even the thought that our research involved recommendations rather than decisions and that top decision-makers would behave more in the best interests of the company is not comforting. If the lower echelons screen out all proposals but the low-risk, low-gain type, the top decision-makers never get to rule on many potentially desirable opportunities. Furthermore, some of our respondents are themselves heads of major divisions of one of our country's industrial giants. We would say that this research indicates that a good hard look at existing control systems is in order.

FURTHER QUESTIONS

Returning to the utility curves shown, note that, in general, the points in the positive quadrant appear to come closer to falling on a smooth, continuous curve than do those in the negative quadrant. This may be due to the questions asked, or it may be a reflection of the fact that the respondents simply are not accustomed to consider loss situations, or that they become frustrated and less rational when faced with decisions involving potential loss. Certainly more research is required before an explanation of this phenomenon can be made with any degree of confidence.

Actually, many questions like this might be raised; a great deal more research needs to be done. For example, would the same curves have resulted if we had varied the probabilities? How stable, over time, are these results? (The limited data we have obtained thus far show surprising stability, but more research is needed.) In cases where incomes are spread over long time periods, are the appropriate utilities based on the present worth of the incomes—or should we take the present worths of the utilities of each cash flow?

Indeed, the research performed thus far raises more questions than it has given definitive answers to. But the questions it raises would seem to demand answers, and so it is confidently expected that this will be but one of a series of progress reports offered by many researchers. The alert businessman will want to keep abreast of these reports, and perhaps even to support some studies, for they may help him to better understand his own and others' decisions and thus perhaps help him to make better ones.

Conclusion

Cardinal utility theory is not a completely satisfactory predictor of executive behavior when decisions involving risks must be made, nor is it a completely satisfactory method of describing such behavior. Authorities like Ward Edwards have pointed to various weaknesses or possible weaknesses in the theory—its assumption that man is rational, for instance, its overlooking of the possibility that people exhibit preferences for different probabilities, and the difficulties of measurement.[14] Nevertheless, it seems to me that the study reported shows that utility theory has much to offer businessmen as a tool of prediction and description. The results for the businessmen participating in the study were reasonably consistent and useful, and point to individual characteristics that were not otherwise apparent. And future studies along similar lines could be even more helpful. Moreover, since (as our experiments show) the criterion of expected value tends to be rejected by businessmen, we have no other good basis for prescribing or predicting decisions that involve risk if we reject utility theory.

What broad conclusions can be drawn from the research project? Six stand out:

[14]See "The Theory of Decision Making," *Psychological Bulletin,* July 1954; reprinted as Chapter 33 in *Some Theories of Organization,* edited by Albert H. Rubenstein and Chadwick J. Haverstroh (Homewood, Illinois: Richard D. Irwin, Inc., 1960), pp. 385-430.

Managerial Decision-Making

(1) Businessmen do *not* attempt to optimize the expected dollar outcome in risk situations involving what, to them, are large amounts. As a result, methodologies which assume they do will tend to be rejected by such businessmen. More acceptable approaches are therefore needed. Cardinal utility theory offers at least a step in the right direction.

(2) Cardinal utility theory offers a reasonable basis for judging the internal consistency of a series of decisions made by an executive dealing with risks, and can be an aid in increasing the consistency of such decisions.

(3) The theory offers a relatively simple way of classifying many types of industrial decision-makers. For example, a supervisor may learn that, in decisions involving significant risks, one man tends to be quite conservative, a second tends to be a gambler, and a third tends to be moderately conservative. If he is moderately conservative himself, he will be happier delegating decisions to the third than to either of the other two. Does he need cardinal utility theory to see these differences? Not always, but much of the time it *will* reveal characteristics that are not otherwise apparent. It does this because it allows comparability (in real life, different executives usually face different problems and risks), shows a range of feeling about risk (in real life the boss is likely to get but one recommendation on a question), offers more objectivity (the subordinate's manner, his reputation, and other factors do not color the situation), and makes more precision possible (the risk taker's ideas are pinned to specific numbers).

(4) The action a junior executive recommends in a risk situation is a function of his own "planning horizon" (that is, it is related to the largest single amount he would recommend to be spent) rather than to the financial condition and position of his company. If top management deems this undesirable (and to me this would almost certainly seem to be the case), then the utility theory concept offers a promising way to begin corrective action.

(5) Attitudes toward risk decisions vary even more widely among various decision-makers in a given company than we are inclined to think. Indeed, what one man calls white, another will swear is black. The risk one man would recommend, another would shun as the plague. Utility theory offers a means of determining the degree to which this is true among decision makers in a company.

(6) If the decision-makers interviewed are at all representative of U.S. executives in general, our managers are surely not the takers of risk so often alluded to in the classical defense of the capitalistic system. Rather than seeking risks, they shun them, consistently refusing to recommend risks that, from the overall company viewpoint, would almost surely be attractive.

In "The Change Seekers," Patrick H. Irwin and Frank W. Langham, Jr. observed:

"Top management must expect some changes to fail. If *all* changes succeed, it can only mean lack of imaginative, competitive striving. Some failures should be anticipated rather than penalized. . . . Above all, top management needs the courage to take carefully considered risks. Without such courage, much is lost."[15]

The executive who agrees with this statement will be concerned over the results of the research reported in this article. He may well find himself asking questions like these: Is management sufficiently aware of the degree to which, for one reason or another, company decision-makers avoid situations offering good chances for large gains because of the possibility of loss? Is the risk-shunning behavior of managers a product of corporate control procedures? Should management reexamine these procedures and consider possibilities for revising them?

Cardinal utility theory offers one method of answering these questions in a factual way. Why not use it?

[15]*HBR,* January-February 1966, p. 91.

J. G. MARCH
H. A. SIMON

Cognitive Limits
on Rationality

In the three previous chapters, we have considered how motivations and goals affect human behavior in organizations. The content of these chapters constitutes an important amendment to the "classical" theory of organization, which regards the employee as an "instrument." In the present chapter and the following one we shall focus on a different set of qualities of the organization member—his characteristics—as a rational man. When, at the end of Chapter 7, we conclude our study of these characteristics and their implications for organization theory, we will have completed the main tasks we set ourselves:

1. to eliminate, one by one, the artificialities of the classical description of the employee as an instrument;

2. to replace this abstraction with a new one that recognizes that members of organizations have wants, motives, and drives, and are limited in their knowledge and in their capacities to learn and to solve problems.

First, we take note of some characteristics of human rationality that bear upon decision-making processes in organizations. Next, we see how organiza-

Source: J. G. March and H. A. Simon, *Organizations* (New York: John Wiley & Sons, 1966), pp. 136-71. Reprinted with permission.

tional decision-making is organized into "programs" or strategies. In the third section we re-examine the phenomenon of organizational identification in the light of the introductory analysis to see to what extent identification is an intellective rather than a motivational process. The fourth section considers the implications of the decision-making process for the division of work; and the fifth section discusses the communications requirements and processes that arise out of the division of work. In the final section we state some of the broader propositions about organization structure that can be derived from the analysis of decision-making processes.

6.1 The Concept of Rationality

How does the rationality of "administrative man" compare with that of classical "economic man" or with the rational man of modern statistical decision theory? The rational man of economics and statistical decision theory makes "optimal" choices in a highly specified and clearly defined environment:

1. When we first encounter him in the decision-making situation, he already has laid out before him the whole set of alternatives from which he will choose his action. This set of alternatives is simply "given"; the theory does not tell how it is obtained.

2. To each alternative is attached a set of consequences—the events that will ensue if that particular alternative is chosen. Here the existing theories fall into three categories: (a) *Certainty*: theories that assume the decision-maker has complete and accurate knowledge of the consequences that will follow on each alternative. (b) *Risk:* theories that assume accurate knowledge of a probability distribution of the consequences of each alternative. (c) *Uncertainty:* theories that assume that the consequences of each alternative belong to some subset of all possible consequences, but that the decision maker cannot assign definite probabilities to the occurrence of particular consequences.

3. At the outset, the decision maker has a "utility function" or a "preference-ordering" that ranks all sets of consequences from the most preferred to the least preferred.

4. The decision-maker selects the alternative leading to the preferred set of consequences. In the case of *certainty*, the choice is unambiguous. In the cask of *risk*, rationality is usually defined as the choice of that alternative for which the expected utility is greatest. Expected utility is defined here as the average, weighted by the probabilities of occurrence, of the utilities attached to all possible consequences. In the case of *uncertainty*, the definition of rationality becomes problematic. One proposal that has had wide currency is the rule of "minimax risk": consider the worst set of consequences that may follow from each alternative, then select the alternative whose "worst set of consequences" is preferred to the worst sets

attached to other alternatives. There are other proposals (e.g., the rule of "minimax regret"), but we shall not discuss them here.

SOME DIFFICULTIES IN THE CLASSICAL THEORY

There are difficulties with this model of rational man. In the first place, only in the case of certainty does it agree well with common-sense notions of rationality. In the case of uncertainty, especially, there is little agreement, even among exponents of statistical decision theory, as to the "correct" definition, or whether, indeed, the term "correct" has any meaning here. (Marschak, 1950).

A second difficulty with existing models of rational man is that it makes three exceedingly important demands upon the choice-making mechanism. It assumes (1) that all the alternatives of choice are "given"; (2) that all the consequences attached to each alternative are known (in one of the three senses corresponding to certainty, risk, and uncertainty respectively); (3) that the rational man has a complete utility-ordering (or cardinal function) for all possible sets of consequences.

One can hardly take exception to these requirements in a normative model—a model that tells people how they *ought* to choose. For if the rational man lacked information, he might have chosen differently "if only he had known." At best, he is "subjectively" rational, not "objectively" rational. But the notion of objective rationality assumes there is some objective reality in which the "real" alternatives, the "real" consequences, and the "real" utilities exist. If this is so, it is not even clear why the cases of choice under risk and under uncertainty are admitted as rational. If it is not so, it is not clear why only limitations upon knowledge of consequences are considered, and why limitations upon knowledge of alternatives and utilities are ignored in the model of rationality.

From a phenomenological viewpoint we can only speak of rationality relative to a frame of reference; and this frame of reference will be determined by the limitations on the rational man's knowledge. We can, of course, introduce the notion of a person observing the choices of a subject, and can speak of the rationality of the subject relative to the frame of reference of the observer. If the subject is a rat and the observer is a man (especially if he is the man who designed the experimental situation), we may regard the man's perception of the situation as objective and the rat's as subjective. (We leave out of account the specific difficulty that the rat presumably knows his own utility function better than the man does.) If, however, both subject and observer are men—and particularly if the situation is a natural one not constructed for experimental purposes by the observer—then it becomes difficult to specify the objective situation. It will be safest, in such situations, to speak of rationality only relative to some specified frame of reference.

The classical organization theory described in Chapter 2, like classical economic theory, failed to make explicit this subjective and relative character of rationality, and in so doing, failed to examine some of its own crucial premises. The organizational and social environment in which the decision-maker finds himself determines what consequences he will anticipate, what ones he will not; what alternatives he will consider, what ones he will ignore. In a theory of organization these variables cannot be treated as unexplained independent factors, but must themselves be determined and predicted by the theory.

ROUTINIZED AND PROBLEM-SOLVING RESPONSES

The theory of rational choice put forth here incorporates two fundamental characteristics: (1) Choice is always exercised with respect to a limited, approximate, simplified "model" of the real situation [A-6.1]. We call the chooser's model his "definition of the situation." (2) The elements of the definition of the situation are not "given"—that is, we do not take these as data of our theory—but are themselves the outcome of psychological and sociological processes, including the chooser's own activities and the activities of others in his environment [A-6.2]. (Simon, 1947, 1955; March, 1955a; Cyert and March, 1955, 1956; Newell, Shaw, and Simon, 1958).

Activity (individual or organizational) can usually be traced back to an environmental stimulus of some sort, e.g., a customer order or a fire gong. The responses to stimuli are of various kinds. At one extreme, a stimulus evokes a response—sometimes very elaborate—that has been developed and learned at some previous time as an appropriate response for a stimulus of this class. This is the "routinized" end of the continuum, where a stimulus calls forth a performance program almost instantaneously.

At the other extreme, a stimulus evokes a larger or smaller amount of problem-solving activity directed toward finding performance activities with which to complete the response. Such activity is distinguished by the fact that it can be dispensed with once the performance program has been learned. Problem-solving activities can generally be identified by the extent to which they involve *search:* search aimed at discovering alternatives of action or consequences of action. "Discovering" alternatives may involve inventing and elaborating whole performance programs where these are not already available in the problem solver's repertory (Katona, 1951).

When a stimulus is of a kind that has been experienced repeatedly in the past, the response will ordinarily be highly routinized [A-6.3]. The stimulus will evoke, with a minimum of problem-solving or other computational activity, a well-structured definition of the situation that will include a repertory of response programs, and programs for selecting an appropriate specific response from the repertory. When a stimulus is relatively novel, it will evoke problem-solving activity aimed initially at constructing a definition of the situation and then at developing one or more appropriate performance programs [A-6.4].

Psychologists (e.g., Wertheimer, Duncker, de Groot, Maier) and observant laymen (e.g., Poincaré, Hadamard) who have studied creative thinking and problem-solving have been unanimous in ascribing a large role in these phenomena to search processes. Search is partly random, but in effective problem-solving it is not blind. The design of the search process is itself often an object of rational decision. Thus, we may distinguish substantive planning—developing new performance programs—from procedural planning—developing programs for the problem-solving process itself. The response to a particular stimulus may involve more than performance—the stimulus may evoke a spate of problem-solving activity—but the problem-solving activity may itself be routinized to a greater or lesser degree. For example, search processes may be systematized by the use of check lists.

SATISFACTORY VERSUS OPTIMAL STANDARDS

What kinds of search and other problem-solving activity are needed to discover an adequate range of alternatives and consequences for choice depends on the criterion applied to the choice. In particular, finding the optimal alternative is a radically different problem from finding a satisfactory alternative. An alternative is *optimal* if: (1) there exists a set of criteria that permits all alternatives to be compared, and (2) the alternative in question is preferred, by these criteria, to all other alternatives. An alternative is *satisfactory* if: (1) there exists a set of criteria that describes minimally satisfactory alternatives, and (2) the alternative in question meets or exceeds all these criteria.

Most human decision-making, whether individual or organizational, is concerned with the discovery and selection of satisfactory alternatives; only in exceptional cases is it concerned with the discovery and selection of optimal alternatives [A-6.5]. To optimize requires processes several orders of magnitude more complex than those required to satisfice. An example is the difference between searching a haystack to find the *sharpest* needle in it and searching the haystack to find a needle sharp enough to sew with.

In making choices that meet satisfactory standards, the standards themselves are part of the definition of the situation. Hence, we need not regard these as given—any more than the other elements of the definition of the situation—but may include in the theory the processes through which these standards are set and modified. The standard-setting process may itself meet standards of rationality: for example, an "optimizing" rule would be to set the standard at the level where the marginal improvement in alternatives obtainable by raising it would be just balanced by the marginal cost of searching for alternatives meeting the higher standard. Of course, in practice the "marginal improvement" and the "marginal cost" are seldom measured in comparable units, or with much accuracy. Nevertheless, a similar result would be automatically attained if the standards were raised whenever alternatives proved easy to discover, and lowered whenever they were difficult to discover. Under these circumstances, the alternatives chosen would not be far from the optima, if the cost of search were taken into consideration. Since human standards tend to have this characteristic under many conditions, some theorists have sought to maintain the optimizing model by introducing cost-of-search considerations. Although we doubt whether this will be a fruitful alternative to the model we are proposing in very many situations, neither model has been used for predictive purposes often enough to allow a final judgment.

PERFORMANCE PROGRAMS

We have seen that under certain circumstances the search and choice processes are very much abridged. At the limit, an environmental stimulus may evoke immediately from the organization a highly complex and organized set of responses. Such a set of responses we call a *performance program*, or simply a *program*. For example, the sounding of the alarm gong in a fire station initiates such a program. So does the appearance of a relief applicant at a social worker's desk. So does the appearance of an automobile chassis in front of the work station of a worker on the assembly line.

Situations in which a relatively simple stimulus sets off an elaborate program of activity without any apparent interval of search, problem-solving, or choice are not rare. They account for a very large part of the behavior of all persons, and for almost all of the behavior of persons in relatively routine positions. Most behavior, and particularly most behavior in organizations, is governed by performance programs.

The term "program" is not intended to connote complete rigidity. The content of the program may be adaptive to a large number of characteristics of the stimulus that initiates it. Even in the simple case of the fire gong, the response depends on the location of the alarm, as indicated by the number of strokes. The program may also be conditional on data that are independent of the initiating stimuli. It is then more properly called a *performance strategy*. For example, when inventory records show that the quantity on hand of a commodity has decreased to the point where it should be reordered, the decision rule that governs the behavior of the purchasing agent may call upon him to determine the amount to be ordered on the basis of a formula into which he inserts the quantity that has been sold over the past 12 months. In this case, search has been eliminated from the problem, but choice—of a very routinized kind, to be sure—remains.

We will regard a set of activities as routinized, then, to the degree that choice has been simplified by the development of a fixed response to defined stimuli. If search has been eliminated, but a choice remains in the form of a clearly defined and systematic computing routine, we will still say that the activities are routinized. We will regard activities as unroutinized to the extent that they have to be preceded by program-developing activities of a problem-solving kind.

6.2 Performance Programs in Organizations

There are several ways to determine what programs a particular organization uses:

1. Observing the behavior of organization members. In relatively routine positions, where the same situations recur repetitively and are handled in terms of fairly definite programs, it is easy to infer the program from behavior. This is a common method for inducting new members of an organization into its procedures.

2. Interviewing members of the organization. Most programs are stored in the minds of the employees who carry them out, or in the minds of their superiors, subordinates, or associates. For many purposes, the simplest and most accurate way to discover what a person does is to ask him.

3. Examining documents that describe standard operating procedures. Programs may be written down, more or less completely and more or less accurately. The relation of a written operating procedure to the actual program that is carried out is complex, for the program may have been written down: (a) as an instruction to initiate a new program and communicate it to those who will carry it out; (b) as a description of an existing program to instruct new organization members; or (c) as an exposition (with or without amendments) of an existing program to legitimize or "formalize" it. There are other possibilities besides these three. In any event, when a document is used as a source of information about a program, the purposes for which it was prepared are relevant to its interpretation.

A person who has been trained in the observation of organizations can extract by these and other techniques a large part of the program that governs routine behavior. This is such a common-sense fact that its importance has been overlooked: Knowledge of the program of an organization permits one to predict in considerable detail the behavior of members of the organization. And the greater the *programming* (6.1) of individual activities in the organization, the greater the *predictability* (6.2) of those activities [6.2:6.1].

To be sure, prediction of behavior from the knowledge of a program has none of the element of "surprise" that we commonly associate with scientific prediction—any more than prediction of the lines that will be uttered by a Hamlet on the stage. It is no less important for its common-sense obviousness.

In general, we would anticipate that programs will be generated by past experience and in expectation of future experience in a given situation. Thus, the greater the *repetitiveness* (6.3) of individual activities, the greater the programming [6.1;6.3]. From this one would predict that programming will be most complete for clerical and factory jobs, particularly when the work is organized largely by process.

The prediction of behavior from a program when tasks are relatively simple and routine is illustrated by findings of Guetzkow and Simon (1955) using five-man experimental groups in the Bavelas network. Employing methods-analysis techniques, they were able to predict average trial times of groups to within 10 percent from a knowledge of the methods the groups were using to perform the task.

If the program determines in some detail the behavior of individuals and groups performing relatively routine tasks, then we can predict behavior to the extent that we can answer the following questions: (1) What motivates members of the organization to accept a program as a determinant of their behavior? What processes, other than motivation, are involved in implementation of programs? This question has already been examined in earlier chapters. (2) What determines the content of a program? To what extent can the program be predicted uniquely from the requirements of the task? How are programs invented and developed, and what are the determinants of this process (3) What are the consequences of programs, as developed and executed, for the goal and subgoal structure of the organization? (4) What are the predictors of behavior in areas that are not routinized and are unprogrammed? This question will be taken up in the next chapter.

We turn now to the second and third of these questions.

PROGRAM CONTENT

The extent to which many human activities, both manual and clerical, can be programmed is shown by the continuing spread of automation to encompass a wider and wider range of tasks. In order to substitute automatic processes for human operatives, it is necessary to describe the task in minute detail, and to provide for the performance of each step in it. The decomposition of tasks into their elementary program steps is most spectacularly illustrated in modern computing machines which may carry out programs involving thousands of such steps. The capabilities of computers have now been extended to many tasks that until recently have been thought to be relatively complex, involving problem-solving activities of a fairly high order. Some examples are several existing computer programs for the automatic design of small electric motors and transformers, a program that enables a computer to discover proofs for certain kinds of mathematical theorems, and a program for translating languages.

Even on routine jobs, *program content* (6.4) varies. We have already mentioned the extreme case: the detailed specification of output, methods, and pace in a man-paced assembly operation. But not all programs are of this type. They may not contain detailed time specifications (e.g., in typical machine-paced operations). In fact, programs usually specify the content of an activity more closely than its timing [A-6.6]. They may specify the properties of the product (e.g., in blueprints, tolerances, etc.) rather than the detail of the methods to be used. We need propositions that will explain variations in program content along these dimensions:

(a) The extent to which pacing rules are built into the program.
(b) The extent to which work activities are detailed in the program.
(c) The extent to which product specifications are detailed in the program.

Since performance programs are important aspects of the organizational system, their content will presumably tend to be related to the functions they perform. We can identify two major functions that such programs fulfill, or at least are intended to fulfill. First, they are a part of the control system in the organization. Organizations attempt to control employees by specifying a standard operating procedure and attaching organizational rewards and penalties to it. Second, performance programs are important parts of the coordination system in the organization. They help fulfill the needs for interdepartmental predictability [A-6.7] (Blau, 1955).

Insofar as they are to function as controls, the programs must be linked to variables that are observable and measurable. We would expect program content to be a function of the *ease of observing job activities* (6.5), the *ease of observing job output* (6.6), and the *ease of relating activities to output* (6.7) [6.4:6.5, 6.6, 6.7]. Thus, we would predict that programs will contain activity specifications in preference to product specifications to the extent that: (a) the activity pattern is easily observed and supervised; (b) the quantity and quality of output are not easily observed and supervised; (c) the relations between activity pattern and output are highly technical, and are matters of scientific and engineering knowledge, better known to specialists in the organization than to the operatives (Ridley and Simon, 1938).

Conversely, programs will contain specifications of quality and quantity of output to the extent that: (a) the activity pattern is difficult to observe and supervise; (b) the quantity and quality of output are easily observed and supervised; (c) the relations between activity pattern and output are matters of common sense, are matters of skill in the specific occupation for which the operatives are trained, or are highly variable, depending upon circumstances of the individual situation that are better known to the operatives than to supervisors and specialists.

For performance programs to serve as coordinative devices, they must be linked to the coordination needs that are felt by the organization. Consequently, we would hypothesize that program content will be a function of the *need for activity coordination* (6.8) and the *need for output coordination* (6.9) [6.4:6.8, 6.9]. The more minutely other members of the organization need to synchronize or coordinate their activities with the activities of a particular member, the more completely will the program specify the activity pattern and/or the pacing of those activities. But to the extent that the activities of the former depend on the characteristics of the output of the latter, rather than on his activities, the program will specify product characteristics.

These propositions about program content are derived from the assumption that the program will be rationally adapted to the organization's objectives. To the extent that this assumption actually determines program, program content becomes a technological question in exactly the same way as the form of the production function is a technological question. In the experiment with the Bavelas network, mentioned previously, determining the most efficient program for performing the task is an exercise in methods study resting upon knowledge of human physiological constants—the times required to perform certain simple acts. If we assume that over some period of time an organization will actually arrive at an efficient program, we can predict its long-run behavior from our technical analysis.

Suppose, however, that we substitute for the maximizing assumption implicit in this method of prediction the assumption that behavior is rational in the more limited sense described earlier: that programs are sought that will operate "satisfactorily," and that the "best" program is not necessarily sought or found. In this case, predicting the program becomes more difficult. Which of the (presumably numerous) satisfactory potential programs the organization will adopt depends, under these circumstances, upon the procedures it employs to construct new programs and to improve existing ones. These procedures will provide the principal subject matter for the next chapter.

THE STRUCTURE OF PROGRAMS

To illustrate further the structure of programs for handling recurrent events, we will describe some formal procedures often used by business concerns for controlling inventory. We will analyze first the common "two-bin" system of inventory control, then a more elaborate system.

In the two-bin system of inventory control, two quantities are established for each item kept in stock: (1) the order quantity (the amount to be purchased on a single order), (2) the buffer stock (the amount that should be on hand when a new order is placed). The program is very simple:

1. When material is drawn from stock, note whether the quantity that remains equals or exceeds the buffer stock. If not:
2. Write a purchase order for the specified order quantity.

Let us call the first step the "program-evoking" step, and the second step the "program-execution" step. The bifurcation is characteristic of programs—a program includes a specification of the circumstances under which the program is to be evoked [A-6.8]. In the example just cited, the program specifies certain observations, which are to be made (whether the buffer stock is intact) whenever a certain event occurs (withdrawal of material from stock). A decision to act or not to act (to apply or not to apply the program) is based on the result of the observation.

The program-evoking step may involve only observation auxiliary to some other activity (as in this example), or it may invoke systematic scanning of some part of the environment (e.g., the activity of a quality inspector). Further, a program-execution step by one member of an organization may serve as a program-evoking step for another member. In the example above, the receipt of a purchase order from the inventory clerk is a program-evoking step for the purchasing department.

In our very simple example, the program-execution step requires neither discretion nor problem-solving. In more complicated situations, the program will be a strategy; i.e., action will be contingent on various characteristics of the situation. For example, in a more elaborate inventory control scheme the purchase quantity may depend on a forecast of sales. Then the program might look like this:

1. When material is drawn from stock, note whether the quantity that remains equals or exceeds the buffer stock. If not:

2. Determine from the sales forecast provided by the sales department the sales expected in the next k months.

3. Insert this quantity in the "order quantity formula," and write a purchase order for the quantity thus determined.

This program, although it is contingent on certain changing facts (the sales forecast), does not allow discretion to the person who executes it—at least in ordinary meanings of the word "discretion." If, however, the organization does not provide the inventory clerk with an official sales forecast, or does not establish a specific order quantity, we would say that the clerk's activity was, to that extent, discretionary. We might discover by observation and interview that the clerk was in fact following a very definite and invariable program, but one stored in his own memory and not recorded in official instructions.

THE NATURE OF DISCRETION

The amounts and kinds of *discretion* (6.10) available to the organizational participant are a function of his performance program and in particular the extent to which the program specifies activities (means) and the extent to which it specifies product or outcome (ends) [6.10:6.4]. The further the program goes in the latter direction, the more discretion it allows for the person implementing the program to supply the means-end connections. Compare the programs cited earlier with the following alternative program:

1. It is the duty of the inventory clerk to determine when each item should be recorded and in what quantity, and to place orders with the purchasing department. He should perform this function with attention to the costs of holding inventories, the costs of shortages, and the economies associated with bulk orders.

If we interpret the last sentence as enjoining the clerk to minimize the sum of the specified costs, we see that this program specifies a goal, but leaves the means undetermined. To construct a "rational" program starting from these premises requires the following steps: (1) defining the total cost function in specific terms; (2) estimating the coefficients that appear in the cost function; (3) deriving a formula or "strategy" that specifies the ordering rules as functions of: (a) the coefficients that appear in the cost function, (b) the sales forecasts (i.e., finding the policy that minimizes step 1), and (4) inserting in the formula the coefficients estimated in step 2, and the sales forecasts.

It is difficult to find a place for discretion within the framework of traditional theories of rational behavior. In the present theory, however, a whole host of phenomena fall under this heading.

First, when a program involves search activities, the actual course of action depends on what is found. We may regard the choice of a course of action after search as discretionary.

Second, when a program describes a strategy, application of the strategy to specific circumstances requires forecasts or other estimates of data. We may regard the application of the strategy to select a course of action as discretionary.

Third, a program may exist in the memory of the individual who is to apply it, having arrived there either as a result of extraorganizational training (e.g., professional training or apprenticeship), or as a product of learning from experience rather than as a result of formal instructions. Under these circumstances we often regard him as behaving in a discretionary fashion.

In all of the cases listed above, the decision process may in fact be highly routinized—the term "discretionary" referring in these instances to the form of the performance program or the source from which it was acquired. These cases need to be distinguished from a fourth meaning of "discretionary": A program may specify only general goals, and leave unspecified the exact activities to be used in reaching them. Moreover, knowledge of the means-ends connections may be sufficiently incomplete and inexact that these cannot be very well specified in advance. Then "discretion" refers to the development and modification of the performance program through problem-solving and learning processes. Although it is difficult to draw a perfectly sharp line between changing a program and changing a datum in applying a strategy, we have already argued that there is an important difference of degree here. With these several meanings of the term "discretionary" in mind, we do not need separate propositions about the amount of discretion, for these will be subsumed under the propositions already noted that specify the form, content, and completeness of programs.

INTERRELATION OF PROGRAMS

A program, whether simple or complex, is initiated when it is evoked by some stimulus. The whole pattern of programmed activity in an organization is a complicated mosaic of program executions, each initiated by its appropriate program-evoking step [A-6.9].

Insofar as the stimuli that evoke programs come from outside the organization, the individual pieces of this mosaic are related to each other only in making claims on the same time and resources, and hence in posing an allocation problem. Nevertheless, if the goal of optimizing is taken seriously, this allocation problem will usually complicate the problem-solving process greatly, for it requires the marginal return from activity in response to any particular stimulus to be equated with the marginal return from activities in response to all other stimuli. Hence, all programs must be determined simultaneously.

When the goal is to respond to stimuli in a satisfactory, but not necessarily optimal, fashion, choice is much simpler; for the standards may be set at levels that permit a satisficing response to each stimulus without concern for the others. The organization, under these circumstances, normally has some slack that reduces the interdependence among its several performance programs.

Apart from resource-sharing, there may be other and more integral connections among programs. Program A may be a *higher-level* program, i.e., a problem-solving activity whose goal is to revise other programs, either by constructing new ones, reconstructing existing ones, or simply modifying individual premises in existing programs. In this case, the *content* of the lower-level programs that are related to A will depend on A. Or, program A may be a program one of whose execution steps serves as an initiating stimulus for program B.

The inventory example illustrates both possibilities. As to the first, program A may be a forecasting program, or a program for periodic revision of the coefficients in the cost function. As to the second possibility, the order that goes from the inventory clerk to the purchasing department serves to initiate one of the purchasing programs of the latter.

PROGRAM AND ORGANIZATION STRUCTURE

In organizations there generally is a considerable degree of parallelism between the hierarchical relations among members of the organization and the hierarchical relations among program elements. That is to say, the programs of members of higher levels of the organization have as their main output the modification or initiation of programs for individuals at lower levels [A-6.10].

Any organization possesses a repertory of programs that, collectively, can deal in a goal-oriented way with a range of situations. As new situations arise, the construction of an entirely new program from detailed elements is rarely contemplated. In most cases, adaptation takes place through a recombination of lower-level programs that are already in existence [A-6.11]. An important objective of standardization is to widen as far as possible the range of situations that can be handled by combination and recombination of a relatively small number of elementary programs.

Limitation of high-level action to the recombination of programs, rather than the detailed construction of new programs out of small elements, is extremely important from a cognitive standpoint. Our treatment of rational behavior rests on the proposition that the "real" situation is almost always far too complex to be handled in detail. As we move upwards in the supervisory and executive hierarchy, the range of interrelated matters over which an individual has purview becomes larger and larger, more and more complex. The growing complexity of the problem can only be matched against the finite powers of the individual if the problem is dealt with in grosser and more aggregative form. One way in which this is accomplished is by limiting the alternatives of action that are considered to the recombination of a repertory of programs (Simon, 1953b).

We may again illustrate this point with the inventory example. Top management decides upon the total dollar inventories without controlling the distribution of inventories among individual items. Specific inventory control programs are found at lower levels of the organization.

6.3 Perception and Identifications

We have seen that humans, whether inside or outside administrative organizations, behave rationally, if at all, only relative to some set of "given" characteristics of the situation. These "givens" include knowledge or assumptions about future events or probability distributions of future events, knowledge of alternatives available for action, knowledge of consequences attached to alternatives—knowledge that may be more or less complete—and rules or principles for ordering consequences or alternatives according to preference.

These four sets of givens define the situation as it appears to the rational actor. In predicting his behavior, we need this specification and not merely a specification of the situation as it "really" is, or, more precisely, as it appears to an outside observer.

The steps that lead, for an actor, to his defining the situation in a particular way involve a complex interweaving of affective and cognitive processes. What a person wants and likes influences what he sees; what he sees influences what he wants and likes.

Managerial Decision-Making

In the three previous chapters we have examined primarily motivational and affective factors. We have considered the relation between individual goals and organizational goals, the ways in which goals are acquired from reference groups, and the motivational bases for conformity with group goals. Cognition enters into the definition of the situation in connection with goal attainment—determining what means will reach desired ends. But cognition enters into the goal-formation process also, because the goals used as criteria for choice seldom represent "final" or "ultimate" values. Instead, they too reflect the perceived relations of means to ends and hence are modified by changing beliefs about these relations. Since goals provide the principal bridge between motivations and cognition, we will begin our consideration of cognitive elements in the definition of the situation with the topic of subgoal formation.

COGNITIVE ASPECTS OF SUBGOAL FORMATION

An individual can attend to only a limited number of things at a time. The basic reason why the actor's definition of the situation differs greatly from the objective situation is that the latter is far too complex to be handled in all its detail. Rational behavior involves substituting for the complex reality a model of reality that is sufficiently simple to be handled by problem-solving processes.

In organizations where various aspects of the whole complex problem are being handled by different individuals and different groups of individuals, a fundamental technique for simplifying the problem is to factor it into a number of nearly independent parts, so that each organizational unit handles one of these parts and can omit the others from its definition of the situation [A-6.12]. This technique is also prominent in individual and small-group behavior. A large complex task is broken down into a sequence of smaller tasks, the conjunction of which adds up to the accomplishment of the larger. The factorization of a large task into parts can be more elaborate for an organization than for an individual, but the underlying reason is the same: the definition of the situation at any one moment must be sufficiently simple to be encompassed by a human mind.

The principal way to factor a problem is to construct a means-end analysis. The means that are specified in this way become subgoals which may be assigned to individual organizational units [A-6.13]. This kind of jurisdictional assignment is often called "organization by purpose" or "departmentalization by purpose."

The motivational aspect of this particular process of subgoal formation is rather simple. Whatever will motivate individuals and groups to accept the tasks assigned them through the legitimate (formal and informal) processes of the organization will provide motivation for subgoals. For the subgoals are implicit or explicit in the definition of the situation as it is incorporated in the task assignment.

When tasks have been allocated to an organizational unit in terms of a subgoal, other subgoals and other aspects of the goals of the larger organization tend to be ignored in the decisions of the subunit. In part, this bias in decision-making can be attributed to shifts in the *focus of attention* (6.11). The definition of the situation that the subunit employs is simplified by omitting some criteria and paying particular attention to others. In particular, we expect the focus of attention to be a function of the *differentiation of subgoals* (6.12) and the *persistence of subgoals* (6.13) [6.11:6.12, 6.13].

The tendency of members of an organizational unit to evaluate action only in terms of subgoals, even when these are in conflict with the goals of the larger organization, is reinforced by at least three cognitive mechanisms. The first of these is located within the individual decision-maker, the second within the organizational unit, and the third in the environment of the organizational unit.

In the individual there is reinforcement through selective perception and rationalization. That is, the persistence of subgoals is furthered by the focus of attention it helps to generate [6.13:6.11]. The propensity of individuals to see those things that are consistent with their established frame of reference is well established in individual psychology. Perceptions that are discordant with the frame of reference are filtered out before they reach consciousness, or are reinterpreted or "rationalized" so as to remove the discrepancy. The frame of reference serves just as much to validate perceptions as the perceptions do to validate the frame of reference.

Within the organizational unit there is reinforcement through the *content of in-group communication* (6.14). Such communication affects the *focus of information* (6.15) [6.15:6.14], and thereby increases subgoal persistence [6.13:6.15]. The vast bulk of our knowledge of fact is not gained through direct perception but through the second-hand, third-hand, and *n*th-hand reports of the perceptions of others, transmitted through the channels of social communication. Since these perceptions have already been filtered by one or more communicators, most of whom have frames of reference similar to our own, the reports are generally consonant with the filtered reports of our own perceptions, and serve to reinforce the latter. In organizations, two principal types of in-groups are of significance in filtering: in-groups with members in a particular organizational unit, and in-groups with members in a common profession [A-6.14]. Hence, we may distinguish *organizational* identifications and *professional* identifications. There are others, of course, but empirically these appear to be the most significant.

Finally, there is reinforcement through selective exposure to environmental stimuli. The *division of labor in the organization* (6.16) affects the information that various members receive [6.15:6.16]. This differentiation of information contributes to the differentiation of subgoals [6.12:6.15]. Thus perceptions of the environment are biased even before they experience the filtering action of the frame of reference of the perceiver. Salesmen live in an environment of customers; company treasurers in an environment of bankers; each sees a quite distinct part of the world (Dearborn and Simon, 1958).

There is one important distinction between this source of reinforcement and the two mentioned previously. Reinforcement through selective perception and rationalization and reinforcement through in-group communication serve to explain how a particular definition of this situation, once it becomes established in an individual or group, maintains itself with great stability and tenacity. These mechanisms do not explain, however, what particular definitions of the situation will *become* established in particular environments—they explain behavior persistence and not the origins of behavior. In order to predict what particular subgoals we are likely to find in particular parts of an organization, we must take as our starting point (a) the system of subgoal assignment that has resulted from analysis of the organization's goals, and (b) the kinds of stimuli to which each organizational unit is exposed in carrying out its assignments. Under the last heading we must include the selective feedback to organizational units of those consequences of action that relate to their particular subgoals.

Through these mechanisms of subgoal formation and subgoal perception, there is selective attention to particular consequences of proposed alternatives, and selective inattention to others. The magnitude of these effects depends in part on variations in the "capacity" of the individual participants in the organization. The smaller the *span of attention* (6.17), the narrower the focus of attention and the more critical the screening mechanisms cited above [6.11:6.17]. One variable of particular importance in determining the span of attention is, of course, the *time pressure* (6.18) involved [6.17:6.18]. In general, we would expect selective perception to be most acute where time is shortest. The relations among these variables are indicated in Figure 1.

OTHER COGNITIVE ASPECTS
OF THE DEFINITION OF THE SITUATION

All the statements of the last section apply, *mutatis mutandis,* to the other elements of the definition of the situation besides goals and values. That is to say, the definition of the situation represents a simplified, screened, and biassed model of the objective situation, and filtering affects all of the "givens" that enter into the decision process: knowledge of assumptions about future events; knowledge of sets of alternatives available for action; knowledge of consequences attached to alternatives; goals and values (Levin, 1956; Gore, 1956).

Consider just knowledge and assumptions about future and present events—"stipulated facts," "absorption of uncertainty." What the sales of the ABC Company are going to be in 1961 is a question of fact. But this matter of fact may become a matter of organizational stipulation—all action within the organization to which the 1961 sales figure is relevant being based upon an

FIGURE 1

Some Factors Affecting Selective Attention to Subgoals

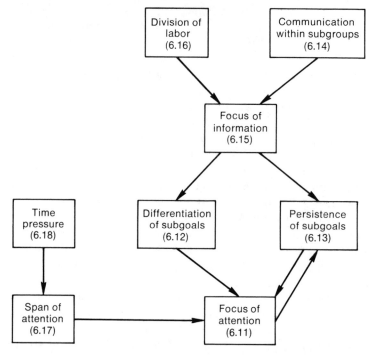

"official" sales forecast. Organizational techniques for dealing with uncertain future and present facts will be discussed in a later section of this chapter.

A related phenomenon is the summarizing of raw information to communicate it further in the organization. The weatherman makes observations of temperature, humidity, barometric pressure, but may communicate only his conclusions in the form of a weather forecast. In organizational communication evidence is replaced with conclusions drawn from that evidence, and these conclusions then become the "facts" on which the rest of the organization acts [A-6.15]. One particular form or summarization is classification. When a particular thing has been classified as belonging to a species, all the attributes of the species can be ascribed to the individual instance of it. Priority systems are an example of an important kind of formal classification device.

Similarly, individuals and organizations develop repertories of programs of action suited to different situations. These are frequently combined with classification systems so that once a situation has been assigned to a particular class the appropriate action program can be applied to it. Such repertories of performance programs, and the requisite habits and skills for their use, appear to make up the largest part of professional and vocational training.

Managerial Decision-Making

Knowledge of consequences is intimately related to selective attention to subgoals, and does not require further elaboration here.

The goals that are included in the definition of the situation influence choice only if there are some means, valid or illusory, for determining the connections between alternative actions and goal satisfaction—only if it can somehow be determined whether and to what extent these goals will be realized if particular courses of action are chosen. When a means of testing actions is perceived to relate a particular goal or criterion with possible courses of action, the criterion will be called operational. Otherwise the criterion will be called nonoperational. This distinction has already been made in discussing the effects of organizational reward systems.

For some purposes we will need to make the further distinction between cases where means-end relations can be evaluated prior to action, and those where they can be evaluated only after the fact. We will call operational goals in the former case *operational ex ante,* in the latter case *operational ex post.*

The goal of "promoting the general welfare" is frequently a part of the definition of the situation in governmental policy-making. It is a nonoperational goal because it does not provide (either *ex ante* or *ex post*) a measuring rod for comparing alternative policies, but can only be related to specific actions through the intervention of subgoals. These subgoals, whose connection with the broader "general welfare" goal is postulated but not testable, become the operational goals in the actual choice situation. (Speaking strictly, whether a goal is operational or nonoperational is not a yes-no question. There are all degrees of "operationality." It will often be convenient, however, to refer simply to the two ends of the continuum.)

An important circumstance causing the substitution of subgoals for more general goals as criteria of decision is that the former are perceived as operational, the latter as nonoperational [A-6.16]. For example, a business firm may understand to some degree how its specific actions affect its share of market, but may understand less surely how its actions affect long-range profits. Then the subgoal of maintaining a particular share of market may become the effective criterion of action—the operational goal.

The distinction between operational and nonoperational goals, combined with the generalization that behavior in organizations is intendedly rational, leads to the consideration of two qualitatively different decision-making processes associated with these two kinds of goals. When a number of persons are participating in a decision-making process, and these individuals have the same operational goals, differences in opinion about the course of action will be resolved by predominately analytic processes, i.e., by the analysis of the expected consequences of courses of action for realization of the shared goals. When either of the postulated conditions is absent from the situation (when goals are not shared, or when the shared goals are not operational and the operational subgoals are not shared), the decision will be reached by predominately bargaining processes. These are, of course, a distinction and prediction made in Chapter 5 and lead to a proposition previously suggested: Rational, analytic processes take precedence over bargaining processes to the extent that the former are feasible. The condition of feasibility is that there be shared operational goals. The proposition, while it has not been much tested, is eminently testable. The goal structure of participants in a decision-making process can be determined by observation of their interaction or by interviewing or opinion-polling techniques. Their understanding of the means-end connections, and of possible methods for testing these connections, can be ascertained in the same way. It is not difficult to code their actual interaction in such a way as to detect the amount of bargaining.

The distinction between operational and nonoperational goals has been made the basis for the distinction between unitary and federal organization units (Simon, Smithburg, and Thompson, 1950, pp. 268-72). This distinction will be explored in the next chapter.

The distinction between operational and nonoperational goals also serves to explain why a theory of public expenditures has never developed a richness comparable to that of the theory of public revenues. The economic approach to a theory of public expenditures would postulate some kind of "utility" or "welfare" function. A rational expenditure pattern would be one in which the marginal dollar of expenditure in each direction would make an equal marginal contribution to welfare. Although statements of this kind are encountered often enough in the literature of public finance, they are infrequently developed. The reason is that, in the absence of any basis for making the welfare maximization goal operational (because of the absence of an operational common denominator among the subgoals of governmental service), the general statement leads neither to description nor to prescription of behavior (Simon, 1943).

In the literature on organizations, identification with subgoals has generally been attributed to motivation. Hence, in an analysis of conflict among organizational units, the affective aspects of the conflict have been stressed. In the present section, we have seen that cognitive processes are extremely important in producing and reinforcing subgoal identification. Subgoals may replace broader goals as a part of the whole process of replacing a complex reality with a simplified model of reality for purposes of decision and action (Blau, 1955).

What difference does it make whether subgoal identification is motivationally or cognitively produced—whether the attachment to the subgoal has been internalized or is only indirect, through a cognitive link to some other goal? It may make very little or no difference in the short run; indeed, it may be difficult to find evidence from shortrun behavior that would distinguish between these mechanisms. But it may make a great deal of difference in the processes for changing identifications. The greater *the dependence of the identification on cognitive links* to other goals (6.19), the greater the *effectiveness of attention-directing simuli in changing goal emphasis* (6.20) [6.20:6.19]. By the same token, where identification depends on cognitive links, the invention of new techniques for evaluating the means-ends connections between action alternatives and goals will transform bargaining processes into processes of rational analysis. These hypotheses can be tested empirically.

The Division of Work

Insofar as tasks are highly programmed, the division of work is a problem of efficient allocation of activities among individuals and among organizational units—a version of the assignment problem already discussed in Chapter 2. However, we need to make two distinctions that tend to be overlooked in the classical theory: First, there is a problem of specialization among individual employees, and a problem of specialization among organizational units. There is no reason to suppose that both sets of problems have the same answers or that the same general principles apply to both. Second, the division of work that is most effective for the performance of relatively programmed tasks need not be the same as that which is most effective for the performance of relatively unprogrammed tasks. In the present discussion, we shall be concerned primarily with programmed tasks; the subject of unprogrammed tasks will be reserved for the next chapter.

The economies of individual specialization arise principally from opportunities for using programs repetitively [A-6.17]. To develop in a person the capacity to carry out a particular program requires an investment in training. In automatic operations, there is an analogous capital investment in machinery capable of carrying out the program. In the case of a computing machine, a substantial part of this investment actually consists of the cost of programming the machine for the particular operations in question. In all of these cases there are economies to be derived, *ceteris paribus,* from assigning the work so as to minimize this investment cost per unit of program execution.

Programs that are built into machines or acquired by humans usually take the form of generalized means—skills or processing capacities that can be used in executing a wide variety of tasks. Typing skill, for example, is a skill of transforming any manuscript into typewritten form, and typing occurs as a subprogram in a wide range of programs. Similarly, a drill press is a bundle of capacities for drilling holes; the program can be called into play whenever the fabrication of some product requires holes to be drilled.

This rather obvious point underlies the central problem in specializing highly programmed activities. Consider an organization that performs a large number of tasks, each consisting of the fabrication of a product. If we analyze the fabrication process into subprograms, we find that it becomes economical to arrange the work so that there will be specialized means (machines and trained employees) for performing some of these subprograms. But since a number of these specialties will be required for the manufacture of each product, we create in this way considerable interdependence and need for coordination among them. The greater the *specialization by subprograms* (6.21) (process specialization), the greater the *interdependencies among organizational subunits* (6.22) [6.22:6.21].

Interdependence does not by itself cause difficulty if the pattern of interdependence is stable and fixed. For in this case, each subprogram can be designed to take account of all the other subprograms with which it interacts. Difficulties arise only if program execution rests on contingencies that cannot be predicted perfectly in advance. In this case, coordinating activity is required to secure agreement about the estimates that will be used as the basis for action, or to provide information to each subprogram unit about the relevant activities of the others. Hence, we arrive at the proposition that the more repetitive and predictable the situation, the greater the *tolerance for interdependence* (6.23) [6.23:6.3]. Conversely, the greater the elements of variability and contingency, the greater is the burden of coordinating activities that are specialized by process (MacMahon, Millet, and Ogden, 1941).

Thus, we predict that process specialization will be carried furthest in stable environments, and that under rapidly changing circumstances specialization will be sacrificed to secure greater self-containment of separate programs [A-6.18] A second prediction is that organizations, in order to permit a greater degree of process specialization, will devise means for increasing stability and predictability of the environment [A-6.19].

Three important devices come under this heading. All of these devices may be regarded as instances of the more general practice of standardization—of reducing the infinite number of things in the world, potential and actual—to a moderate number of well-defined varieties. The greater the *standardization of the situation* (6.24), the greater the tolerance for subunit interdependencies [6.23:6.24].

The first step in almost all major manufacturing sequences that lead from natural raw materials to finished goods is refining. In steel manufacture, a complex of natural materials—ores, coke, and flux—is reduced to a relatively homogeneous, standard material—pig iron. In the natural textile industries, fibers are transformed into threads of uniform size, strength, and elasticity by carding and spinning processes. In all such cases, the complexity of subsequent manufacturing processes and their contingency on raw materials is reduced by transforming highly variable natural materials into much more homogeneous semimanufactured products [A-6.20]. After homogeneity has been attained, subsequent steps in the manufacturing process may again produce great variety in the product—alloy steels in the first example, dyed fabrics in the second. But it is often difficult and expensive to program this subsequent elaboration unless the processing begins with a simple, homogeneous material of known properties.

A second important device for dealing with the interdependencies created by specialization is the use of interchangeable parts [A-6.21]. When the fit of two parts is assured by setting minimum and maximum size limits, the interdependency between the units that make them is decreased and the burden of coordination partly removed.

Third, the need for coordinated timing between successive process steps is reduced by holding buffer inventories [A-6.22]. If process A precedes process B in the manufacture of some item, then the effect of variations in the rate of process A upon process B can be removed largely by maintaining an inventory of products on which process A has been completed.

Even with such devices, the need for coordination typically remains. The most common device for securing coordination among subprograms where there is a high degree of process specialization is scheduling. A schedule is simply a plan, established in advance, that determines what tasks will be handled and when. It may have greater or less detail, greater or less precision. The *type of coordination* (6.25) used in the organization is a function of the extent to which the situation is standardized [6.25:6.24]. To the extent that contingencies arise, not anticipated in the schedule, coordination requires communication to give notice of deviations from planned or predicted conditions, or to give instructions for changes in activity to adjust to these deviations. We may label coordination based on pre-established schedules *coordination by plan,* and coordination that involves transmission of new information *coordination by feedback.* The more stable and predictable the situation, the greater the reliance on coordination by plan; the more variable and unpredictable the situation, the greater the reliance on coordination by feedback.

Insofar as coordination is programmed and the range of situations sufficiently circumscribed, we would not expect any particularly close relation between the coordinative mechanisms and the formal organizational hierarchy. That is to say, scheduling information and feedback information required for coordination are not usually communicated through hierarchical channels. Hierarchy may be important in establishing and legitimizing programs, but the communication involved in the execution of highly programmed activities does not generally follow the "lines of command" [A-6.23] (Bakke, 1950).

In addition, from the standpoint of any particular organization, specialization and the structure of subprograms is as much sociological as it is technological. The organization depends to a great extent upon the training that employees bring to it—training acquired by apprenticeship or in schools. Hence the boundaries of specialization of individual jobs tend to be determined by the structure of trades and professions in the broader social environment [A-6.24].

COMMUNICATION

On the basis of the foregoing analysis, we may classify the occasions for communication as follows:

1. Communication for nonprogrammed activity. This is a catchall category that will need further analysis later.

2. Communication to initiate and establish programs, including day-to-day adjustment or "coordination" of programs.

3. Communication to provide data for application of strategies (i.e., required for the execution of programs).

4. Communication to evoke programs (i.e., communications that serve as "stimuli").

5. Communication to provide information on the results of activities.

The distinction between the first two categories and the last three is the familiar distinction between communication relating to procedural matters and communication relating to substantive content.

Empirical evidence for the distinction among the last three categories was obtained from a study of the use of accounting data by operating departments in manufacturing concerns. It was found that accounting information was used at various executive levels to answer three different kinds of questions: (a) Problem-solving questions: Which course of action is better? This corresponds to our category 3. (b) Attention-directing questions: What problems shall I look into? This corresponds to category 4. (c) Score-card questions: How well am I (or is he) doing? This corresponds to category 5. Some of the accounting information was also used in connection with less programmed activity (Simon, Guetzkow, Kozmetsky, and Tyndall, 1954). We will consider this point below.

COMMUNICATION AND COORDINATION

The capacity of an organization to maintain a complex, highly interdependent pattern of activity is limited in part by its capacity to handle the communication required for coordination. The greater the *efficiency of communication* (6.26) within the organization, the greater the tolerance for interdependence [6.23:6.26]. The problem has both quantitative and qualitative aspects.

As we noted earlier, it is possible under some conditions to reduce the volume of communication required from day to day by substituting coordination by plan for coordination by feedback. By virtue of this substitution, organizations can tolerate very complex interrelations among their component parts in the performance of repetitive activities. The coordination of parts is incorporated in the program when it is established, and the need for continuing communication is correspondingly reduced. Each specific situation, as it arises, is largely covered by the standard operating procedure.

A different method for increasing the organization's tolerance for interdependence is to increase the efficiency of communication by making it possible to communicate large amounts of information with relatively few symbols. An obvious example is the blueprint, which provides a common plan stated in extreme detail. The blueprint employs a carefully defined, highly developed "language" or set of symbolic and verbal conventions. Because of this standardized language, it can convey large quantities of information. The same attention to standardization of language is seen in accounting systems and other reporting systems that employ numerical data.

Accounting definitions and blueprint conventions are examples of a still more general phenomenon: technical languages, whose symbols have definite and common meanings to the members of an organization. Prominent in these technical languages are categories for classifying situations and events.

The role of unambiguous technical terms in permitting coordination by feedback is shown by the Christie-Luce-Macy experiments (Macy, Christie, and Luce, 1953) with "noisy marbles" in the Bavelas network. Participants in the experiment were given some colored marbles, and they were required to discover what color was held by all of them. Control groups were given marbles that had solid colors like "red," "yellow," etc. Experimental groups were given streaked marbles whose colorings did not correspond in any simple way to color designations in common language. Comparison of the performance of the control with the experimental groups showed (a) that the latter were much hindered by the lack of adequate technical vocabulary, and (b) that their performance became comparable to that of the control groups only when they succeeded in inventing such a vocabulary and securing its acceptance throughout the group.

Classification schemes are of particular significance for the program-evoking aspects of communication. When an event occurs that calls for some kind of organization response, the question is asked, in one form or other: "What *kind* of event is this?" The organization has available a repertory of programs, so that once the event has been classified the appropriate program can be executed without further ado. We can make this process more specific with a pair of examples.

The oil gauge on the dashboard of an automobile is an example of the use of classification in program-evoking. For most drivers, the oil pressure is either "all right" or "low." In the first case, no action is taken; in the second case a remedial program is initiated (e.g., taking the automobile to a repair shop). Some auto manufacturers have substituted a red light, which turns on when the oil pressure is not in the proper range, for the traditional gauge. This example also illustrates how substituting standards of satisfactory performance for criteria of optimization simplifies communication.

Similarly, inspection activities often involve dichotomous decisions. In these cases, the choice is not usually between evoking a program or not evoking one (action or inaction), but between different programs. Thus, if the item being inspected meets the standards, one program is evoked (it is passed on for further processing); if it fails to meet standards, another program is evoked (scrapping, or reworking, as the case may be).

One reason that classifying is so economical of communication is that most of the coordination can be preprogrammed; the organization has a repertory of responses to stimuli, and it only needs to know what kind of stimulus it is confronted with in order to execute an elaborate program. On the other hand, if the communication system could handle a more complete description of the program-evoking event, and if the action part of the organization had the capacity to develop programs on the spot to meet present needs, no doubt one could conceive tailor-made programs that would be more accurately adapted to each separate situation than are the preprogrammed responses.

Here again the normative or adaptive problem of organization design is one of balance. If its model of reality is not to be so complex as to paralyze it, the organization must develop radical simplifications of its responses. One such simplification is to have (a) a repertory of standard responses, (b) a classification of program-evoking situations, (c) a set of rules to determine what is the appropriate response for each class of situations. The balance of economies and efficiencies here is exactly the same as it is in all cases of standardization. Note that what we have described in an organizational framework is quite comparable to discrimination learning in individuals. In the individual case, as in the organizational, there is a close relationship between the categories used in the cognitive code and the operational decision rules (Whorf, 1956).

In our culture, language is well developed for describing and communicating about concrete objects. The blueprint has already been mentioned as an important technical device for this purpose. Language is also very effective in communicating about things that can be classified and named, even if they are intangible. Thus, when there are standard repertories of programs, it is easy to refer to them.

On the other hand, it is extremely difficult to communicate about intangible objects and nonstandardized objects. Hence, the heaviest burdens are placed on the communications system by the less structured aspects of the organization's tasks, particularly by activity directed toward the explanation of problems that are not yet well defined. We shall see in the next chapter that this difference in communication difficulty has important implications for the organization of nonprogrammed activities.

Where the available means of communication are primitive—relative to the communication needs—so will be the system of coordination. There will tend to be less self-containment of organizational units and a greater reliance on coordination through communication the greater the efficiency of communication [6.12:6.26]. This relation may sometimes be obscured by the fact that pressure toward coordination (e.g., under conditions of rapid change) may compel attempts at feedback coordination even though available communication is inefficient. It should also be noted that self-containment decreases and interdependencies increase the likelihood of developing an efficient communication code [6.26:6.21].

THE ABSORPTION OF UNCERTAINTY

The use of classification schemes in communication has further consequences, some of which go back to our earlier discussion of perception and identification. The technical vocabulary and classification schemes in an organization provide a set of concepts that can be used in analyzing and in communicating about its problems. Anything that is easily described and discussed in terms of these concepts can be communicated readily in the organization; anything that does not fit the system of concepts is communicated only with difficulty. Hence, the world tends to be perceived by the organization members in terms of the particular concepts that are reflected in the organization's vocabulary. The particular categories and schemes of classification it employs are reified, and become, for members of the organization, attributes of the world rather than mere conventions (Blau, 1955).

The reification of the organization's conceptual scheme is particularly noticeable in *uncertainty absorption* (6.27). Uncertainty absorption takes place when inferences are drawn from a body of evidence and the inferences, instead of the evidence itself, are then communicated. The successive editing steps that transform data obtained from a set of questionnaires into printed statistical tables provide a simple example of uncertainty absorption.

Through the process of uncertainty absorption, the recipient of a communication is severely limited in his ability to judge its correctness. Although there may be various tests of apparent validity, internal consistency, and consistency with other communications, the recipient must, by and large, repose his confidence in the editing process that has taken place, and, if he accepts the communication at all, accept it pretty much as it stands. To the extent that he can interpret it, his interpretation must be based primarily on his confidence in the source and his knowledge of the biases to which the source is subject, rather than on a direct examination of the evidence.

By virtue of specialization, most information enters an organization at highly specific points. Direct perception of production processes is limited largely to employees in a particular operation on the production floor. Direct perception of customer attitudes is limited largely to salesmen. Direct evidence of the performance of personnel is restricted largely to immediate supervisors, colleagues, and subordinates.

In all of these cases, the person who summarizes and assesses his own direct perceptions and transmits them to the rest of the organization becomes an important source of informational premises for organizational action. The "facts" he communicates can be disbelieved, but they can only rarely be checked. Hence, by the very nature and limits of the communication system, a great deal of discretion and influence is exercised by those persons who are in direct contact with some part of the "reality" that is of concern to the organization. Both the amount and the *locus of uncertainty absorption* (6.28) affect the *influence structure of the organization* (6.29) [6.29:6.27,6.28].

Because of this, uncertainty absorption is frequently used, consciously and unconsciously, as a technique for acquiring and exercising power. In a culture where direct contradiction of assertions of fact is not approved, an individual who is willing to make assertions, particularly about matters that do not contradict the direct perceptions of others, can frequently get these assertions accepted as premises of decision.

We can cite a number of more or less "obvious" variables that affect the absorption of uncertainty. The more complex the data that are perceived and the less adequate the organization's language, the closer to the source of the information will the uncertainty absorption take place, and the greater will be the amount of summarizing at each step of transmission. The locus of absorption will tend to be a function of such variables as: (a) the needs of the recipient for raw as against summarized information (depending upon the kinds of data used in selecting the appropriate program), (b) the need for correction of biases in the transmitter, (c) the distribution of technical competence for interpreting and summarizing raw data, and (d) the need for comparing data from two or more sources in order to interpret it.

The way in which uncertainty is absorbed has important consequences for coordination among organizational units. In business organizations, expected sales are relevant to decisions in many parts of the organization: purchasing decisions, production decisions, investment decisions, and many others. But if each organizational unit were permitted to make its own forecast of sales, there might be a wide range of such estimates with consequent inconsistencies among the decisions made by different departments—the purchasing department, for example, buying raw materials that the production department does not expect to process. It may be important in cases of this kind to make an *official* forecast and to use this official forecast as the basis for action throughout the organization.

Where it is important that all parts of an organization act on the same premises, and where different individuals may draw different conclusions from the raw evidence, a formal uncertainty absorption point will be established, and the inferences drawn at that point will have official status in the organization as "legitimate" estimates. The greater the need for coordination in the organization, the greater the *use of legitimized "facts"* (6.30) [6.30:6.8, 6.9].

THE COMMUNICATION NETWORK

Associated with each program is a set of information flows that communicate the stimuli and data required to evoke and execute the program. Generally this communication traverses definite channels, either by formal plan or by the gradual development of informal programs. Information and stimuli move from sources to points of action; information of results moves from points of action to points of decision and control.

Managerial Decision-Making

Rational organization design would call for the arrangement of these channels so as to minimize the communication burden. But insofar as the points of origin of information and the points of action are determined in advance, the only mobile element is the point of decision. Whatever may be the position in the organization holding the formal authority to legitimize the decision, to a considerable extent the effective discretion is exercised at the points of uncertainty absorption.

In large organizations, specialization of communication functions will be reflected in the division of work itself. Among the specialized communication units we find are (a) units specializing in the actual physical transmission of communications: a telephone and teletype unit, messenger group, or the like; (b) units specializing in recording and report preparation: bookkeeping and other record-keeping units; (c) units specializing in the acquisition of raw information, usually referred to as intelligence units, sometimes as research units; (d) units specializing in the provision of technical premises for decision: research units, technical specialists; (e) units specializing in the interpretation of policy and organizational goals, a function usually not much separated from the main stem of the hierarchy; and (f) units specializing in the retention of information: files, archives units [A-6.25].

In part, communication channels are deliberately and consciously planned in the course of programming. In part, they develop through usage. We will make two hypotheses about such development. First, the greater the communication efficiency of the channel, the greater the *communication channel usage* (6.31) [6.31:6.26]. The possession by two persons, or two organization units, of a common, efficient language facilitates communication. Thus, links between members of a common profession tend to be used in the communication system. Similarly, other determinants of language compatibility—ethnic background, education, age, experience—will affect what channels are used in the organization.

Second, channel usage tends to be self-reinforcing [6.31:6.31]. When a channel is frequently used for one purpose, its use for other unrelated purposes is encouraged. In particular, formal hierarchical channels tend to become general-purpose channels to be used whenever no special-purpose channel or informal channel exists or is known to the communicator. The self-reinforcing character of channel usage is particularly strong if it brings individuals into face-to-face contact. In this case (the Homans hypothesis) informal communication, much of it social in character, develops side-by-side with task-oriented formal communication, and the use of the channel for either kind of communication tends to reinforce its use for the other.

In part, the communication network is planned; in part, it grows up in response to the need for specific kinds of communication; in part, it develops in response to the social functions of communication. At any given stage in its development, its gradual change is much influenced by the pattern that has already become established. Hence, although the structure of the network will be considerably influenced by the structure of the organization's task, it will not be completely determined by the latter.

Once a pattern of communication channels has become established, this pattern will have an important influence on decision-making processes, and particularly upon nonprogrammed activity. We may anticipate some of the analysis of the next chapter by indicating briefly the nature of this influence.

The existing pattern of communication will determine the relative frequency with which particular members of the organization will encounter particular stimuli, or kinds of stimuli, in their search processes [6.11:6.31]. For example, a research and development unit that has frequent communication with sales engineers and infrequent communication with persons engaged in fundamental research will live in a different environment of new product ideas than a research and development unit that has the opposite communication pattern.

The communication pattern will determine how frequently and forcefully particular consequences of action are brought to the attention of the actor. The degree of specialization, for example, between design engineers, on the one hand, and installation and service engineers, on the other, will have an important influence on the amount of awareness of the former as to the effectiveness of their designs.

From our previous propositions concerning time pressure effects, we would predict that the pattern of communication would have a greater influence on nonprogrammed activities carried out with deadlines and under time pressure than upon activities that involve relatively slow and deliberate processes of decision. For, given sufficient time, if particular information is available anywhere in an organization, its relevance to any particular decision is likely to be noticed. Where decisions are made relatively rapidly, however, only the information that is locally available is likely to be brought to bear. We see here another reason why specialization (in this case specialization with respect to possession of information) is tolerated to a greater degree under "steady-state" conditions than when the organization is adapting to a rapidly changing environment.

ORGANIZATION STRUCTURE AND THE BOUNDARIES OF RATIONALITY

It has been the central theme of this chapter that the basic features of organization structure and function derive from the characteristics of human problem-solving processes and rational human choice. Because of the limits of human intellective capacities in comparison with the complexities of the problems that individuals and organizations face, rational behavior calls for simplified models that capture the main features of a problem without capturing all its complexities.

The simplifications have a number of characteristic features: (1) Optimizing is replaced by satisficing—the requirement that satisfactory levels of the criterion variables be attained. (2) Alternatives of action and consequences of action are discovered sequentially through search processes. (3) Repertories of action programs are developed by organizations and individuals, and these serve as the alternatives of choice in recurrent situations. (4) Each specific action program deals with a restricted range of situations and a restricted range of consequences. (5) Each action program is capable of being executed in semi-independence of the others—they are only loosely coupled together [A-6.26].

Action is goal-oriented and adaptive. But because of its approximating and fragmented character, only a few elements of the system are adaptive at any one time; the remainder are, at least in the short run, "givens." So, for example, an individual or organization may attend to improving a particular program, or to selecting an appropriate program from the existing repertory to meet a particular situation. Seldom can both be attended to simultaneously.

The notion that rational behavior deals with a few components at a time was first developed extensively in connection with economic behavior by John R. Commons, who spoke of "limiting factors" that become the foci of attention and adaptation. Commons' theory was further developed by Chester I. Barnard, who preferred the term "strategic factor."

This "one-thing-at-a-time" or "*ceteris paribus*" approach to adaptive behavior is fundamental to the very existence of something we can call "organization structure." Organization structure consists simply of those aspects of the pattern of behavior in the organization that are relatively stable and that change only slowly. If behavior in organizations is "intendedly rational," we will expect aspects of the behavior to be relatively stable that either (a) represent adaptations to relatively stable elements in the environment, or (b) are the learning programs that govern the process of adaptation.

An organization is confronted with a problem like that of Archimedes: in order for an organization to behave adaptively, it needs some stable regulations and procedures that it can employ in carrying out its adaptive practices. Thus, at any given time an organization's programs for performing its tasks are part of its structure, but the least stable part. Slightly more stable are the switching rules that determine when it will apply one program, and when another. Still more stable are the procedures it uses for developing, elaborating, instituting, and revising programs.

The matter may be stated differently. If an organization has a repertory of programs, then it is adaptive in the short run insofar as it has procedures for selecting from this repertory a program appropriate to each specific situation that arises. The process used to select an appropriate program is the "fulcrum" on which short-run adaptiveness rests. If, now, the organization has processes for adding to its repertory of programs or for modifying programs in the repertory, these processes become still more basic fulcra for accomplishing longer-run adaptiveness. Short-run adaptiveness corresponds to what we ordinarily call problem-solving, long-run adaptiveness to learning.

There is no reason, of course, why this hierarchy of mechanisms should have only three levels—or any specified number. In fact, the adaptive mechanisms need not be arranged hierarchically. Mechanism A may include mechanism B within its domain of action, and vice versa. However, in general there is much asymmetry in the ordering, so that certain elements in the process that do not often become strategic factors (the "boundaries of rationality") form the stable core of the organization structure.

We can now see the relation between Commons' and Barnard's theories of the "limiting" or "strategic" factor and organization structure. Organization will have structure, as we have defined the term here, insofar as there are boundaries of rationality—insofar as there are elements of the situation that must be or are in fact taken as givens, and that do not enter into rational calculations as potential strategic factors. If there were not boundaries to rationality, or if the boundaries varied in a rapid and unpredictable manner, there could be no stable organization structure. Some aspects of structure will be more easily modified than others, and hence we may need to distinguish short-run and long-run structure.

In this chapter, we have been concerned mostly with short-run structure—with programs to respond to sequences of situations requiring adaptive action. The "boundaries of rationality" that have been the source of our propositions have consisted primarily of the properties of human beings as organisms capable of evoking and executing relatively well-defined programs but able to handle programs only of limited complexity.

In the next chapter, we will shift our attention to long-run considerations, and particularly to the processes in organizations that bring programs into existence and that modify them.

IV

MANAGERIAL SOLUTION IMPLEMENTATION

Primer:
The Notion of Influence

"... We cannot live only for ourselves. A thousand fibers connect us with our fellow-men; and along those fibers, as sympathetic threads, our actions run as causes, and they come back to us as effects . . ."—Melville

This part of the text comprises what has been considered by some to be all of management. Here we are concerned with getting things done through people. The manager has a model; he has decided upon a course of action; he must now implement that action program.

But implementation, by the nature of our society and the organizations within which most of us operate, requires influencing others. So the big issue in implementation is the issue of influence. We advocate a social critical path methodology: a plan which points to the spot where influence will be most effective.

The spectrum of topics to be covered such that the totality of this area might be included is so large as to make any such attempt unfeasible. Thus, for Part IV, we selected a shotgun approach, using as our pellets the articles we felt were most smoothly rounded.

But it must not go unsaid that Part IV ties back to Parts II and III as promised in our first chapter. For any act at influence really means acting on the models and the goals of other individuals. That is, as we wish to change the behavior of others such that it comes to be more in accordance with our desires, we consciously or unconsciously operate upon the models and goals of those we wish to influence. One of the hopes of this text is to bring this phenomenon to the surface.

Solution implementation is the area most talked about in management, and yet so little has been scientifically accomplished. We believe that consideration of the concepts of Parts II and III of this text are a necessary, concomitant condition for success with the issues of Part IV. That is, a model—a game plan—for the implementation of the chosen solution is as important as the model developed to analyze the original problem.

The classical school is represented by a reading which discusses many of the principles of management which have become the hallmark of the classical school. The quantitative sciences are represented by two articles. One discusses an analytical method for determining choke (congestive) points of a system. Once identified, these points can then become the place for heightened managerial attention. The other article deals with the systematic controlling and reporting of information by digital computers. The use of computer-based management information systems allows the manager to better understand and more rapidly obtain the consequences of his decisions and the viability of his implementation program. The behavioral sciences are represented by three articles which approach the notion of influence and implementation from different vantage points within the organization. Points discussed are as follows: how the organization itself influences management development, how management task descriptions might be changed to better conform to the influence of leadership style of a particular manager; how, by their very nature, complex organizations allow lower-level employees to become sources of power and influence beyond their orgizational rank.

EDGAR H. SCHEIN[1]

Management Development as a Process of Influence

The continuing rash of articles on the subject of developing better managers suggests, on the one hand, a continuing concern that existing methods are not providing the talent which is needed at the higher levels of industry and, on the other hand, that we continue to lack clear-cut formulations about the process by which such development occurs. We need more and better managers and we need more and better theories of how to get them.

In the present paper I would like to cast management development as the problem of how an organization can influence the beliefs, attitudes, and values (hereafter simply called attitudes) of an individual for the purpose of "developing" him, i.e., changing him in a direction which the organization regards to be in his own and the organization's best interests. Most of the existing conceptions of the development of human resources are built upon assumptions of how people learn and grow, and some of the more strikingly contrasting theories of

Source: *Industrial Management Review*, Vol. 2, No. 2 (May, 1961) © 1961 by the Industrial Management Review Association; all rights reserved.

[1] I am greatly indebted to Warren Bennis and Douglas McGregor, whose helpful comments on the first draft of this paper have helped me to refine many of the ideas in it.

management development derive from disagreements about such assumptions.[2] I will attempt to build on a different base: instead of starting with assumptions about learning and growth, I will start with some assumptions from the social psychology of influence and attitude change.

Building on this base can be justified quite readily if we consider that adequate managerial performance at the higher levels is at least as much a matter of attitudes as it is a matter of knowledge and specific skills, and that the acquisition of such knowledge and skills is itself in part a function of attitudes. Yet we have given far more attention to the psychology which underlies change in the area of knowledge and abilities than we have to the psychology which underlies change in attitudes. We have surprisingly few studies of how a person develops loyalty to a company, commitment to a job, or a professional attitude toward the managerial role; how he comes to have the motives and attitudes which make possible the rendering of decisions concerning large quantities of money, materials, and human resources; how he develops attitudes toward himself, his co-workers, his employees, his customers, and society in general which give us confidence that he has a sense of responsibility and a set of ethics consistent with his responsible position, or at least which permit us to understand his behavior.

It is clear that management is becoming increasingly professionalized, as evidenced by increasing emphasis on undergraduate and graduate education in the field of management. But professionalization is not only a matter of teaching candidates increasing amounts about a set of relevant subjects and disciplines; it is equally a problem of preparing the candidate for a role which requires a certain set of attitudes. Studies of the medical profession (Merton, Reader, and Kendall, 1957), for example, have turned their attention increasingly to the unravelling of the difficult problem of how the medical student acquires those attitudes and values which enable him to make responsible decisions involving the lives of other people. Similar studies in other professions are sorely needed. When these are undertaken, it is likely to be discovered that much of the training of such attitudes is carried out implicitly and without a clearly formulated rationale. Law schools and medical schools provide various kinds of experiences which insure that the graduate is prepared to fulfill his professional role. Similarly, existing approaches to the development of managers probably provide ample opportunities for the manager to learn the attitudes he will need to fulfill high-level jobs. But in this field, particularly, one gets the impression that such opportunities are more the result of intuition or chance than of clearly formulated policies. This is partly because the essential or pivotal aspects of the managerial role have not as yet been clearly delineated, leaving ambiguous both the area of knowledge to be mastered and the attitude to be acquired.

---

[2]An excellent discussion of two contrasting approaches—the engineering vs. the agricultural—deriving from contrasting assumptions about human behavior can be found in McGregor, 1960, Chapter 14.

implies that the individual must perceive some need for change in himself, must be able to change, and must perceive the influencing agent as one who can facilitate such change in a direction acceptable to the individual. A model of the influence process, then, must account for the development of the motivation to change as well as the actual mechanisms by which the change occurs.

It is usually assumed that pointing out to a person some of his areas of deficiency, or some failure on his part in these areas, is sufficient to induce in him a readiness to change and to accept the influencing agent's guidance or recommendations. This assumption may be tenable if one is dealing with deficiencies in intellectual skills or technical knowledge. The young manager can see, with some help from his superiors, that he needs a greater knowledge of economics, or marketing, or production methods, and can accept the suggestion that spending a year in another department or six weeks at an advanced management course will give him the missing knowledge and/or skills.

However, when we are dealing with attitudes, the suggestion of deficiency or the need for change is much more likely to be perceived as a basic threat to the individual's sense of identity and to his status position vis-a-vis others in the organization. Attitudes are generally organized and integrated around the person's image of himself, and they result in stabilized, characteristic ways of dealing with others. The suggestion of the need for change not only implies some criticism of the person's image of himself, but also threatens the stability of his working relationships because change at this level implies that the expectations which others have about him will be upset, thus requiring the development of new relationships. It is not at all uncommon for training programs in human relations to arouse resistance or to produce, at best, temporary change because the expectations of co-workers operate to keep the individual in his "normal" mold. Management development programs which ignore these psychological resistances to change are likely to be self-defeating, no matter how much attention is given to the actual presentation of the new desired attitudes.

Given these general assumptions about the integration of attitudes in the person, it is appropriate to consider influence as a process which occurs over time and which includes three phases:

(1) *Unfreezing*[3]: an alteration of the forces acting on the individual, such that his stable equilibrium is disturbed sufficiently to motivate him and to make him ready to change; this can be accomplished either by increasing the pressure to change or by reducing some of the threats or resistances to change.

(2) *Changing*: the presentation of a direction of change and the actual process of learning new attitudes. This process occurs basically by one of

[3]These phases of influence are a derivation of the change model developed by Lewin (1947).

Managerial Solution Implementation

Existing practice in the field of management development involves a[c]
such as: indoctrination and training programs conducted at various point[s]
manager's career; systematic job rotation involving changes both in the na[ture of]
the functions performed (e.g., moving from production into sales), in p[hysical]
location, and in the individual's superiors; performance appraisal pr[ocedures]
including various amounts of testing, general personality assessmen[t, and]
counseling both within the organization and through the use of outsid[e con-]
sultants; apprenticeships, systematic coaching, junior management boar[ds,]
special projects to facilitate practice by the young manager in functions [he will]
have to perform later in his career; sponsorship and other comparable ac[tivities]
in which a select group of young managers is groomed systematically fo[r higher]
level jobs (i.e., made into "crown princes"); participation in special confe[rences]
and training programs, including professional association meetings, [human]
relations workshops, advanced management programs conducted in bu[siness]
schools or by professional associations like the American Management [Asso-]
ciation, regular academic courses like the Sloan programs offered at Sta[nford]
and MIT, or liberal arts courses like those offered at the University of Pe[nnsyl-]
vania, Dartmouth, Northwestern, etc. These and many other specific educa[tional]
devices, along with elaborate schemes of selection, appraisal, and place[ment,]
form the basic paraphernalia of management development.

Most of the methods mentioned above stem from the basic conceptio[n that]
it is the responsibility of the business enterprise, as an institution, to define [what]
kind of behavior and attitude change is to take place and to con[struct]
mechanisms by which such change is to occur. Decisions about the ki[nd of]
activity which might be appropriate for a given manager are usually ma[de by]
others above him or by specialists hired to make such decisions. Where he [is to]
be rotated, how long he is to remain on a given assignment, or what kind of [re-]
training he should undertake, is masterminded by others whose conce[rn is]
"career development." In a sense, the individual stands alone against the [insti-]
tution where his own career is concerned, because the basic assumption is [that]
the institution knows better than the individual what kind of man it nee[ds and]
wants in its higher levels of management. The kind of influence model whi[ch is]
relevant, then, is one which considers the whole range of resources availabl[e to]
an organization.

In the remainder of this paper I will attempt to spell out these ge[neral]
themes by first presenting a conceptual model for analyzing influence, t[hen]
providing some illustrations from a variety of organization influence situati[ons,]
and then testing its applicability to the management development situation.

A Model of Influence and Change

Most theories of influence or change accept the premise that change d[oes]
not occur unless the individual is *motivated* and *ready* to change. This statem[ent]

two mechanisms: (a) *identification*[4]—the person learns new attitudes by identifying with and emulating some other person who holds those attitudes; or (b) *internalization*—the person learns new attitudes by being placed in a situation where new attitudes are demanded of him as a way of solving problems which confront him and which he cannot avoid; he discovers the new attitudes essentially for himself, though the situation may guide him or make it probable that he will discover only those attitudes which the influencing agent wishes him to discover.

(3) *Refreezing*: the integration of the changed attitudes into the rest of the personality and/or into ongoing significant emotional relationships.

In proposing this kind of model of influence we are leaving out two important cases—the individual who changes because he is *forced* to change by the agent's direct manipulation of rewards and punishments (what Kelman calls "compliance") and the individual whose strong motivation to rise in the organizational hierarchy makes him eager to accept the attitudes and acquire the skills which he perceives to be necessary for advancement. I will ignore both of these cases for the same reason—they usually do not involve genuine, stable change, but merely involve the adoption of overt behaviors which imply to others that attitudes have changed, even if they have not. In the case of compliance, the individual drops the overt behavior as soon as surveillance by the influence agent is removed. Among the upwardly mobile individuals, there are those who are willing to be unfrozen and to undergo genuine attitude change (whose case fits the model to be presented below) and those whose overt behavior change is dictated by their changing perception of what the environment will reward, but whose underlying attitudes are never really changed or refrozen.

I do not wish to emply that a general reward-punishment model is incorrect or inappropriate for the analysis of attitude change. My purpose, rather, is to provide a more refined model in terms of which it becomes possible to specify the differential effects of various kinds of rewards and punishments, some of which have far more significance and impact than others. For example, as I will try to show, the rewarding effect of approval from an admired person is very different in its ultimate consequences from the rewarding effect of developing a personal solution to a difficult situation.

The processes of unfreezing, changing, and refreezing can be identified in a variety of different institutions in which they are manifested in varying degrees or intensity. The content of what may be taught in the influence process may vary widely from the values of Communism to the religious doctrines of a nun, and the process of influence may vary drastically in its intensity. Nevertheless there is value in taking as our frame of reference a model like that proposed and testing its utility in a variety of different organizational contexts, ranging from

[4]These mechanisms of attitude change are taken from Kelman (1958).

Communist "thought reform" centers to business enterprises' management development programs. Because the value system of the business enterprise and its role conception of the manager are not as clear-cut as the values and role prescriptions in various other institutions, one may expect the processes of unfreezing, changing, and refreezing to occur with less intensity and to be less consciously rationalized in the business enterprise. But they are structurally the same as in other organizations. One of the main purposes of this paper, then, will be to try to make salient some features of the influence of the organization on the attitudes of the individual manager by attempting to compare institutions in which the influence process is more drastic and explicit with the more implicit and less drastic methods of the business enterprise.

Illustrations of Organizational Influence

UNFREEZING

The concept of unfreezing and the variety of methods by which influence targets can be unfrozen can best be illustrated by considering examples drawn from a broad range of situations. The Chinese Communists in their attempt to inculcate Communist attitudes into their youth or into their prisoners serve as a good prototype of one extreme. First and most important was the removal of the target person from those situations and social relationships which tended to confirm and reinforce the validity of the old attitudes. Thus the targets, be they political prisoners, prisoners of war, university professors, or young students, were isolated from their friends, families, and accustomed work groups and cut off from all media of communication to which they were accustomed. In addition, they were subjected to continuous exhortations (backed by threats of severe punishment) to confess their crimes and adopt new attitudes, and were constantly humiliated in order to discredit their old sense of identity.

The isolation of the target from his normal social and ideological supports reached its height in the case of Western civilians who were placed into group cells with a number of Chinese prisoners who had already confessed and were committed to reforming themselves and their lone Western cell mate. In the prisoner of war camps such extreme social isolation could not be produced, but its counterpart was created by the fomenting of mutual mistrust among the prisoners, by cutting off any supportive mail from home, and by systematically disorganizing the formal and informal social structure of the POW camp (by segregation of officers and noncommissioned officers from the remainder of the group, by the systematic removal of informal leaders or key personalities, and by the prohibition of any group activity not in line with the indoctrination program) (Schein, 1960, 1961).

The Chinese did not hesitate to use physical brutality and threats of death and/or permanent nonrepatriation to enforce the view that only by collaboration and attitude change could the prisoner hope to survive physically and psychologically. In the case of the civilians in group cells, an additional and greater stress was represented by the social pressure of the cell mates who would harangue, insult, revile, humiliate, and plead with the resistant Westerner twenty-four hours a day for weeks or months on end, exhorting him to admit his guilt, confess his crimes, reform, and adopt Communist values. This combination of physical and social pressures is perhaps a prototype of the use of coercion in the service of unfreezing a target individual in attitude areas to which he is strongly committed.

A somewhat milder, though structurally similar, process can be observed in the training of a nun (Hulme, 1956). The novice enters the convent voluntarily and is presumably ready to change, but the kind of change which must be accomplished encounters strong psychological resistances because, again, it involves deeply held attitudes and habits. Thus the novice must learn to be completely unselfish and, in fact, selfless; she must adapt to a completely communal life; she must give up any source of authority except the absolute authority of God and of those senior to her in the convent; and she must learn to curb her sexual and aggressive impulses. How does the routine of the convent facilitate unfreezing? Again a key element is the removal of the novice from her accustomed routines, sources of confirmation, social supports, and old relationships. She is physically isolated from the outside world, surrounded by others who are undergoing the same training as she, subjected to a highly demanding and fatiguing physical regimen, constantly exhorted toward her new role and punished for any evidence of old behaviors and attitudes, and subjected to a whole range of social pressures ranging from mild disapproval to total humiliation for any failure.

Not only is the novice cut off from her old social identity, but her entry into the convent separates her from many aspects of her physical identity. She is deprived of all means of being beautiful or even feminine; her hair is cut off and she is given institutional garb which emphasizes formlessness and sameness; she loses her old name and chronological age in favor of a new name and age corresponding to length of time in the convent; her living quarters and daily routine emphasize an absolute minimum of physical comfort and signify a total devaluation of anything related to the body. At the same time the threat associated with change is minimized by the tremendous support which the convent offers for change and by the fact that everyone else either already exhibits the appropriate attitudes or is in the process of learning them.

If we look at the process by which a pledge comes to be a full-fledged member of a fraternity, we find in this situation also a set of pressures to give up old associations and habits, a devaluation of the old self by humiliations ranging from menial, senseless jobs to paddling and hazing, a removal of threat through sharing of training, and support for good performance in the pledge role. The evangelist seeking to convert those who come to hear him attempts to unfreeze his audience by stimulating guilt and by devaluating their former selves as sinful and unworthy. The teacher wishing to induce motivation to learn sometimes points out the deficiencies in the student's knowledge and hopes at the same time to induce some guilt for having those deficiencies.

Some of the elements which all unfreezing situations have in common are the following: (1) the physical removal of the influence target from his accustomed routines, sources of information, and social relationships; (2) the undermining and destruction of all social supports; (3) demeaning and humiliating experience to help the target see his old self as unworthy and thus to become motivated to change; (4) the consistent linking of reward with willingness to change and of punishment with unwillingness to change.

CHANGING

Once the target has become motivated to change, the actual influence is most likely to occur by one of two processes. The target finds one or more models in his social environment and learns new attitudes by identifying with them and trying to become like them; or the target confronts new situations with an experimental attitude and develops for himself attitudes which are appropriate to the situation and which remove whatever problem he faces. These two processes—*identification* and *internalization*—probably tend to occur together in most concrete situations, but it is worthwhile, for analytical purposes, to keep them separate.[5]

The student or prisoner of the Chinese Communists took his basic step toward acquiring Communist attitudes when he began to identify with his more advanced fellow student or prisoner. In the group cell it was the discovery by the Western prisoner that his Chinese cell mates were humans like himself, were rational, and yet completely believed in their own and his guilt, which forced him to re-examine his own premises and bases of judgment and led him the first step down the path of acquiring the Communist point of view. In other words, he began to identify with his cell mates and to acquire their point of view as the only solution to getting out of prison and reducing the pressure on him. The environment was, of course, saturated with the Communist point of view, but it is significant that such saturation by itself was not sufficient to induce genuine attitude change. The prisoner kept in isolation and bombarded with propaganda was less likely to acquire Communist attitudes than the one placed into a group cell with more reformed prisoners. Having a personal model was apparently crucial.

In the convent the situation is essentially comparable except that the novice

[5]Both are facilitated greatly if the influence agent saturates the environment with the new message or attitude to be learned.

Managerial Solution Implementation

is initially much more disposed toward identifying with older nuns and has a model of appropriate behavior around her all the time in the actions of the others. It is interesting to note also that some nuns are singled out as particularly qualified models and given the appropriate name of "the living rule." It is also a common institution in initiation or indoctrination procedures to attach to the target individual someone who is labelled a "buddy" or "big brother," whose responsibility it is to teach the novice "the ropes" and to communicate the kinds of attitudes expected of him.

In most kinds of training and teaching situations, and even in the sales relationship, it is an acknowledged fact that the process is facilitated greatly if the target can identify with the influence agent. Such identification is facilitated if the social distance and rank difference between agent and target are not too great. The influence agent has to be close enough to the target to be seen as similar to the target, yet must be himself committed to the attitudes he is trying to inculcate. Thus, in the case of the Chinese Communist group cell, the cell-mates could be perceived as sharing a common situation with the Western prisoner and this perception facilitated his identification with them. In most buddy systems, the buddy is someone who has himself gone through the training program in the recent past. If the target is likely to mistrust the influence attempts of the organization, as might be the case in a management-sponsored training program for labor or in a therapy program for delinquents in a reformatory, it is even more important that the influence agent be perceived as similar to the target. Otherwise he is dismissed as a "company man" or one who has already sold out, and hence is seen as someone whose message or example is not to be taken seriously.

Internalization, the discovery of attitudes which are the target's own solutions to his perceived dilemmas, can occur at the same time as identification. The individual can use the example of others to guide him in solving his own problems without necessarily identifying with them to the point of complete imitation. His choice of attitude remains ultimately his own in terms of what works for him, given the situation in which he finds himself. Internalization is only possible in an organizational context in which, from the organization's point of view, a number of different kinds of attitudes will be tolerated. If there is a "party line," a company philosophy, or a given way in which people have to feel about things in order to get along, it is hardly an efficient procedure to let trainees discover their own solutions. Manipulating the situation in such a way as to make the official solution the only one which is acceptable can, of course, be attempted, but the hazards of creating real resentment and alienation on the part of the individual when he discovers he really had no choice may outweigh the presumed advantages of letting him think he had a choice.

In the case of the Chinese Communists, the convent, the revival meeting, the fraternity, or the institutional training program, we are dealing with situations where the attitudes to be learned are clearly specified. In this kind of situation, internalization will not occur unless the attitudes to be learned happen to fit uniquely the kind of personal problem the individual has in the situation. For example, a few prisoners of the Communists reacted to the tremendous unfreezing pressures with genuine guilt when they discovered they held certain prejudices and attitudes (e.g. when they realized that they had looked down on lower class Chinese in spite of their manifest acceptance of them). These prisoners were then able to internalize certain portions of the total complex of Communist attitudes, particularly those dealing with unselfishness and working for the greater good of others. The attitudes which the institution demanded of them also solved a personal problem of long standing for them. In the case of the nun, one might hypothesize that internalization of the convent's attitudes will occur to the extent that asceticism offers a genuine solution to the incumbent's personal conflicts.

Internalization is a more common outcome in those influence settings where the direction of change is left more to the individual. The influence which occurs in programs like Alcoholics Anonymous, in psychotherapy or counseling for hospitalized or incarcerated populations, in religious retreats, in human relations training of this kind pursued by the National Training Laboratories (1953), and in certain kinds of progressive education programs is more likely to occur through internalization or, at least, to lead ultimately to more internalization.

REFREEZING

Refreezing refers to the process by which the newly acquired attitude comes to be integrated into the target's personality and ongoing relationships. If the new attitude has been internalized while being learned, this has automatically facilitated refreezing because it has been fitted naturally into the individual's personality. If it has been learned through identification, it will persist only so long as the target's relationship with the original influence model persists unless new surrogate models are found or social support and reinforcement is obtained for expressions of the new attitude.[6]

In the case of the convent such support comes from a whole set of expectations which others have of how the nun should behave, from clearly specified role prescriptions, and from rituals. In the case of individuals influenced by the Chinese Communists, if they remained in Communist China they received constant support for their new attitudes from superiors and peers; if they returned to the West, the permanence of their attitude change depended on the degree of support they actually received from friends and relations back home,

---

[6]In either case the change may be essentially permanent, in that a relationship to a model or surrogate can last indefinitely. It is important to distinguish the two processes, however, because if one were to try to change the attitude, different strategies would be used depending upon how the attitude had been learned.

or from groups which they sought out in an attempt to get support. If their friends and relatives did not support Communist attitudes, the repatriates were influenced once again toward their original attitudes or toward some new integration of both sets.

The importance of social support for new attitudes was demonstrated dramatically in the recent Billy Graham crusade in New York City. An informal survey of individuals who came forward when Graham called for converts indicated that only those individuals who were subsequently integrated into local churches maintained their faith. Similar kinds of findings have been repeatedly noted with respect to human relations training in industry. Changes which may occur during the training program do not last unless there is some social support for the new attitudes in the "back home" situation.

The kind of model which has been discussed above might best be described by the term "coercive persuasion." The influence of an organization on an individual is coercive in the sense that he is usually forced into situations which are likely to unfreeze him, in which there are many overt and covert pressures to recognize in himself a need for change, and in which the supports for his old attitudes are in varying degrees coercively removed. It is coercive also to the degree that the new attitudes to be learned are relatively rigidly prescribed. The individual either learns them or leaves the organization (if he can). At the same time, the actual process by which new attitudes are learned can best be described as persuasion. In effect, the individual is forced into a situation in which he is likely to be influenced. The organization can be highly coercive in unfreezing its potential influence targets, yet be quite open about the direction of attitude change it will tolerate. In those cases where the direction of change is itself coerced (as contrasted with letting it occur through identification or internalization), it is highly unlikely that anything is accomplished other than surface behavioral change in the target. And such surface change will be abandoned the moment the coercive force of the change agent is lessened. If behavioral changes are coerced at the same time as other unfreezing operations are undertaken, actual influence can be facilitated if the individual finds himself having to learn attitudes to justify the kinds of behavior he has been forced to exhibit. The salesman may not have an attitude of cynicism toward his customers initially. If, however, he is forced by his boss to behave as if he felt cynical, he might develop real cynicism as a way of justifying his actual behavior.

Management Development: Is It Coercive Persuasion?

Do the notions of coercive persuasion developed above fit the management development situation? Does the extent to which they do or do not fit such a model illuminate for us some of the implications of specific management development practices?

UNFREEZING

It is reasonable to assume that the majority of managers who are being "developed" are not ready or able to change in the manner in which their organization might desire and therefore must be unfrozen before they can be influenced. They may be eager to change at a conscious motivation level, yet still by psychologically unprepared to give up certain attitudes and values in favor of untried, threatening new ones. I cannot support this assumption empirically, but the likelihood of its being valid is high because of a related fact which is empirically supportable. Most managers do not participate heavily in decisions which affect their careers, nor do they have a large voice in the kind of self-development in which they wish to participate. Rather, it is the man's superior or a staff specialist in career development who makes the key decisions concerning his career (Alfred, 1960). If the individual manager is not trained from the outset to take responsibility for his own career and given a heavy voice in diagnosing his own needs for a change, it is unlikely that he will readily be able to appreciate someone else's diagnosis. It may be unclear to him what basically is wanted of him or, worse, the ambiguity of the demands put upon him combined with his own inability to control his career development is likely to arouse anxiety and insecurity which would cause even greater resistance to genuine self-assessment and attitude change.[7] He becomes preoccupied with promotion in the abstract and attempts to acquire at a surface level the traits which he thinks are necessary for advancement.

If the decisions made by the organization do not seem valid to the manager, or if the unfreezing process turns out to be quite painful to him, to what extent can he leave the situation? His future career, his financial security, and his social status within the business community all stand to suffer if he resists the decisions made for him. Perhaps the most coercive feature is simply the psychological pressure that what he is being asked to do is "for his own ultimate welfare." Elementary loyalty to his organization and to his managerial role demands that he accept with good grace whatever happens to him in the name of his own career development. In this sense, then, I believe that the business organization has coercive forces at its disposal which are used by it in a manner comparable to the uses made by other organizations.

Given the assumption that the manager who is to be developed needs to be unfrozen, and given that the organization has available coercive power to accomplish such unfreezing, what mechanisms does it actually use to unfreeze potential influence targets?

The essential elements to unfreezing are the removal of supports for the old attitudes, the saturation of the environment with the new attitudes to be

---

[7]An even greater hazard, of course, is that the organization communicates to the manager that he is not expected to take responsibility for his own career at the same time that it is trying to teach him how to be able to take responsibility for important decisions!

acquired, a minimizing of threat, and a maximizing of support for any change in the right direction. In terms of this model it becomes immediately apparent that training programs or other activities which are conducted in the organization at the place of work for a certain number of hours per day or week are far less likely to unfreeze and subsequently influence the participant than those programs which remove him for varying lengths of time from his regular work situation and normal social relationships.

Are appraisal interviews, used periodically to communicate to the manager his strengths, weaknesses and areas for improvement, likely to unfreeze him? Probably not, because as long as the individual is caught up in his regular routine and is responding, probably quite unconsciously, to a whole set of expectations which others have about his behavior and attitudes, it is virtually impossible for him to hear, at a psychological level, what his deficiencies or areas needing change are. Even if he can appreciate what is being communicated to him at an intellectual level, it is unlikely that he can emotionally accept the need for change, and even if he can accept it emotionally, it is unlikely that he can produce change in himself in an environment which supports all of his old ways of functioning. This statement does not mean that the man's co-workers necessarily approve of the way he is operating or like the attitudes which he is exhibiting. They may want to see him change, but their very expectations concerning how he normally behaves operate as a constraint on him which makes attitude change difficult in that setting.

On the other hand, there are a variety of training activities which are used in management development which approximate more closely the conditions necessary for effective unfreezing. These would include programs offered at special training centers such as those maintained by IBM on Long Island and General Electric at Crotonville, N. Y.; university-sponsored courses in management, liberal arts, and/or the social sciences; and especially, workshops or laboratories in human relations such as those conducted at Arden House, N. Y., by the National Training Laboratories. Programs such as these remove the participant for some length of time from his normal routine, his regular job, and his social relationships (including his family in most cases), thus providing a kind of moratorium during which he can take stock of himself and determine where he is going and where he wants to go.

The almost total isolation from the pressures of daily life in the business world which a mountain chateau such as Arden House provides for a two-week period is supplemented by other unfreezing forces. The de-emphasis on the kind of job or title the participant holds in his company and the informal dress remove some of the symbolic or status supports upon which we all rely. Sharing a room and bath facilitates with a roommate requires more than the accustomed exposure of private spheres of life to others. The total involvement of the participant in the laboratory program leaves little room for reflection about the back home situation. The climate of the laboratory commununciates tremendous support for any efforts at self-examination and attempts as much as possible to reduce the threats inherent in change by emphasizing the value of experimentation, the low cost and risk of trying a new response in the protected environment of the lab, and the high gains to be derived from finding new behavior patterns and attitudes which might improve back home performance. The content of the material presented in lectures and the kind of learning model which is used in the workshop facilitates self-examination, self-diagnosis based on usable feedback from other participants, and rational planning for change.[8]

The practice of rotating a manager from one kind of assignment to another over a period of years can have some of the same unfreezing effects and thus facilitate attitude change. Certainly his physical move from one setting to another removes many of the supports to his old attitudes, and in his new job the manager will have an opportunity to try new behaviors and become exposed to new attitudes. The practice of providing a moratorium in the form of a training program prior to assuming a new job would appear to maximize the gains from each approach, in that unfreezing would be maximally facilitated and change would most probably be lasting if the person did not go back to a situation in which his co-workers, superiors, and subordinates had stable expectations of how he should behave.

Another example of how unfreezing can be facilitated in the organizational context is the practice of temporarily reducing the formal rank and responsibilities of the manager by making him a trainee in a special program, or an apprentice on a special project, or an assistant to a high ranking member of the company. Such temporary lowering of formal rank can reduce the anxiety associated with changing and at the same time serves officially to destroy the old status and identity of the individual because he could not ordinarily return to his old position once he had accepted the path offered by the training program. He would have to move either up or out of the organization to maintain his sense of self-esteem. Of course, if such a training program is perceived by the trainee as an indication of his failing rather than a step toward a higher position, his anxiety about himself would be too high to facilitate effective change on his part. In all of the illustrations of organizational influence we have presented above, change was defined as being a means of gaining status—acceptance into Communist society, status as a nun or a fraternity brother, salvation, etc. If participants come to training programs believing they are being punished, they typically do not learn much.

The above discussion is intended to highlight the fact that some management development practices do facilitate the unfreezing of the influence target, but that such unfreezing is by no means automatic. Where programs fail, therefore, one of the first questions we must ask is whether they failed because they did not provide adequate conditions for unfreezing.

[8]Although, as I will point out later, such effective unfreezing may lead to change which is not supported or considered desirable by the "back home" organization.

CHANGING

Turning now to the problem of the mechanisms by which changes actually occur, we must confront the question of whether the organization has relatively rigid prescribed goals concerning the direction of attitude change it expects of the young manager, or whether it is concerned with growth in the sense of providing increasing opportunities for the young manager to learn the attitudes appropriate to ever more challenging situations. It is undoubtedly true that most programs would claim growth as their goal, but the degree to which they accomplish it can only be assessed from an examination of their actual practice.

Basically the question is whether the organization influences attitudes primarily through the mechanism of identification or the mechanism of internalization. If the development programs stimulate psychological relationships between the influence target and a member of the organization who has the desired attitudes, they are thereby facilitating influence by identification but, at the same time, are limiting the alternatives available to the target and possibly the permanence of the change achieved. If they emphasize that the target must develop his own solutions to ever more demanding problems, they are risking that the attitudes learned will be incompatible with other parts of the organization's value system but are producing more permanent change because the solutions found are internalized. From the organization's point of view, therefore, it is crucial to know what kind of influence it is exerting and to assess the results of such influence in terms of the basic goals which the organization may have. If new approaches and new attitudes toward management problems are desired, for example, it is crucial that the conditions for internalization be created. If rapid learning of a given set of attitudes is desired, it is equally crucial that the conditions for identification with the right kind of models be created.

One obvious implication of this distinction is that programs conducted within the organization's orbit by its own influence agents are much more likely to facilitate identification and thereby the transmission of the "party line" or organization philosophy. On the other hand, programs like those conducted at universities or by the National Training Laboratories place much more emphasis on the finding of solutions by participants which fit their own particular needs and problems. The emphasis in the human relations courses is on "learning how to learn" from the participant's own interpersonal experiences and how to harness his emotional life and intellectual capacities to the accomplishment of his goals, rather than on specific principles of human relations. The nearest thing to an attitude which the laboratory staff, acting as influence agents, does care to communicate is an attitude of inquiry and experimentation, and to this end the learning of skills of observation, analysis, and diagnosis of interpersonal situations is given strong emphasis. The training group, which is the acknowledged core of the laboratory approach, provides its own unfreezing forces by being unstructured as to the content of discussion. But it is strongly committed to a method of learning by analysis of the member's own experiences in the group, which facilitates the discovery of the value of an attitude of inquiry and experimentation.

Mutual identification of the members of the group with each other and member identifications with the staff play some role in the acquisition of this attitude, but the basic power of the method is that the attitude of inquiry and experimentation *works* in the sense of providing for people valuable new insights about themselves, groups, and organizations. To the extent that it works and solves key problems for the participants, it is internalized and carried back into the home situation. To the extent that it is learned because participants wish to emulate a respected fellow member or staff member, it lasts only so long as the relationship with the model itself, or a surrogate of it, lasts (which may, of course, be a very long time).

The university program in management or liberal arts is more difficult to categorize in terms of an influence model, because within the program there are usually opportunities both for identification (e.g., with inspiring teachers) and internalization. It is a safe guess in either case, however, that the attitudes learned are likely to be in varying degrees out of phase with any given company's philosophy unless the company has learned from previous experience with a given course that the students are taught a point of view consistent with its own philosophy. Of course, universities, as much as laboratories, emphasize the value of a spirit of inquiry and, to the extent that they are successful in teaching this attitude, will be creating potential dissidents or innovators, depending on how the home company views the result.

Apprenticeships, special jobs in the role of "assistant to" somebody, job rotation, junior management boards, and so on stand in sharp contrast to the above methods in the degree to which they facilitate, indeed almost demand, that the young manager learn by watching those who are senior or more competent. It is probably not prescribed that in the process of acquiring knowledge and skills through the example of others he should also acquire their attitudes, but the probability that this will happen is very high if the trainee develops any degree of respect and liking for his teacher and/or supervisor. It makes little difference whether the teacher, coach, or supervisor intends to influence the attitudes of his trainee or not. If a good emotional relationship develops between them, it will facilitate the learning of knowledge and skills, and will, at the same time, result in some degree of attitude change. Consequently, such methods do not maximize the probability of new approaches being invented to management problems, nor do they really by themselves facilitate the growth of the manager in the sense of providing opportunities for him to develop solutions which fit his own needs best.

Job rotation, on the other hand, can facilitate growth and innovation provided it is managed in such a way as to insure the exposure of the trainee to a broad range of points of view as he moves from assignment to assignment. The practice of shifting the developing manager geographically as well as functionally both facilitates unfreezing and increases the likelihood of his being exposed to new attitudes. This same practice can, of course, be merely a convenient way of indoctrinating the individual by sending him on an assignment, for example, "in order to acquire the sales point of view from Jim down in New York," where higher management knows perfectly well what sort of a view Jim will communicate to his subordinates.

REFREEZING

Finally, a few words are in order about the problem of refreezing. Under what conditions will changed attitudes remain stable, and how do existing practices aid or hinder such stabilization? Our illustrations from the nonindustrial setting highlighted the importance of social support for any attitudes which were learned through identification. Even the kind of training emphasized in the National Training Laboratories programs, which tends to be more internalized, does not produce stable attitude change unless others in the organization, especially superiors, peers, and subordinates, have undergone similar changes and give each other stimulation and support, because lack of support acts as a new unfreezing force producing new influence (possibly in the direction of the original attitudes).

If the young manager has been influenced primarily in the direction of what is already the company philosophy, he will, of course, obtain strong support and will have little difficulty maintaining his new attitudes. If, on the other hand, management development is supposed to lead to personal growth and organizational innovation, the organization must recognize the reality that new attitudes cannot be carried by isolated individuals. The lament that we no longer have strong individualists who are willing to try something new is a fallacy based on an incorrect diagnosis. Strong individuals have always gained a certain amount of their strength from the support of others, hence the organizational problem is how to create conditions which make possible the nurturing of new ideas, attitudes, and approaches. If organizations seem to lack innovators, it may be that the climate of the organization and its methods of management development do not foster innovation, not that its human resources are inadequate.

An organizational climate in which new attitudes which differ from company philosophy can nevertheless be maintained cannot be achieved merely by an intellectual or even emotional commitment on the part of higher-ranking managers to tolerance of new ideas and attitudes. Genuine support can come only from others who have themselves been influenced, which argues strongly that at least several members of a given department must be given the same training before such training can be expected to have effect. If the superior of the people involved can participate in it as well, this strengthens the group that much more, but it would not follow from my line of reasoning that this is a necessary condition. Only some support is needed, and this support can come as well from peers and subordinates.

From this point of view, the practice of sending more than one manager to any given program at a university or human relations workshop is very sound. The National Training Laboratories have emphasized from the beginning the desirability of having organizations send teams. Some organizations like Esso Standard have created their own laboratories for the training of the entire management complement of a given refinery, and all indications are that such a practice maximizes the possibility not only of the personal growth of the managers, but of the creative growth of the organization as a whole.

Conclusion

In the above discussion I have deliberately focused on a model of influence which emphasizes procedure rather than content, interpersonal relations rather than mass media, and attitudes and values rather than knowledge and skills. By placing management development into a context of institutional influence procedures which also include Chinese Communist thought reform, the training of a nun, and other more drastic forms of coercive persuasion, I have tried to highlight aspects of management development which have remained implicit yet which need to be understood. I believe that some aspects of management development are a mild form of coercive persuasion, but I do not believe that coercive persuasion is either morally bad in any *a priori* sense or inefficient. If we are to develop a sound theory of career development which is capable of including not only many of the formal practices, some of which are more and some of which are less coercive than those discussed, we need to suspend moral judgments for the time being and evaluate influence models solely in terms of their capacity to make sense of the data and to make meaningful predictions.

References

Alfred, T. M., *Personal communication,* 1960.

Hulme, K., *The Nun's Story.* Boston: Little Brown, 1957.

Kelman, H. C., "Compliance, identification, and internalization: three processes of attitude change," *Conflict Resolution,* II (1958), 51-60.

Lewin, K., "Frontiers in group dynamics: concept, method and reality in social science," *Hum. Relat.,* I, (1947) 5-42.

McGregor, D., *The human side of enterprise.* New York: McGraw-Hill, 1960.

Merton, R. K., G. G. Reader, and Patricia L. Kendall, *The student-physician* Cambridge, Mass.: Harvard University Press, 1957.

National Training Laboratory in Group Development, *Explorations in human relations training: an assessment of experience, 1947-1953.* Washington, D.C.: National Education Association, 1953.

Schein, E. H., *Brainwashing.* Cambridge, Mass.: Center for International Studies, M.I.T., 1961.

Schein, E. H., "Interpersonal communication, group solidarity, and social influence," *Sociometry*, 23 (1960), 148-61.

ERNEST DALE

Fayol
the Universalist

At what moment in my life I became convinced that social phenomena are, like physical phenomena, subject to natural laws independent of our will, I cannot say. It seems to me that I have never doubted it.

Henri Fayol, *L'Eveil de L'Esprit public*

Taylor and Gilbreth were concerned mainly with *techniques* that management might use and on the rank-and-file level at that. So, too, was Elton Mayo, although his approach to the problem was different. Harrington Emerson considered the subject from the viewpoint of higher management and the direction of the business as a whole, but he was also concerned mainly with techniques: dispatching, cost accounting, standardization, and so on. None of them attempted to deal with management as a function entirely separate from the various specialties. That task has been undertaken by others.

One of the most famous of the analyses of management itself is that made by Henri Fayol, a French engineer born in 1841. Fayol was chief executive (Directeur General) of a large coal and steel combine from 1888 to 1918, and

Source: Ernest Dale, *Management: Theory and Practice,* 2nd ed. Copyright 1969 by Ernest Dale. Reprinted with permission of McGraw-Hill Book Company.

during that time brought it from the verge of bankruptcy to high success. As a mining engineer, he had become accustomed to working with principles and techniques that embodied scientific truth. When he became a manager, he sought to develop something similar for management, and he eventually came to the conclusion that there was a single "administrative science" whose principles could be used in all management situations no matter what type of organization was being managed.

Fayol emphasized, however, that he used the word "principle" only for convenience. His principles, he said, were not immutable laws but rules of thumb to be used as the occasion demanded.

Thus he was a universalist only in that he thought the principles would be useful to all types of managers; he did not consider that a manager needs nothing more than a knowledge of management principles in order to manage successfully. At higher and higher levels, he said, a manager depends less and less on technical knowledge of what he is managing and more and more on knowledge of administration, but even at the very top he needs some technical knowledge and familiarity with the field.

In 1916, Fayol published a paper embodying his conclusions in the bulletin of a French trade association, under the title "Administration industrielle et générale" (General and Industrial Management). This was later published in book form, and is now considered one of the classics of management literature. It has had considerable influence not only on the theories of management current today, but on the actions and aims of many managers in important positions. Many who have never read Fayol's book have learned his principles at second or third hand and applied them to their own organizations.

Fayol defined the functions of administration as:

1. To plan
2. To organize (both men and materials)
3. To command—that is, to tell subordinates what to do
4. To coordinate
5. To control

Four Important Principles

He laid down a number of principles for the administrator, the most famous of which are the following:

1. *Authority is not to be conceived of apart from responsibility*. In explaining this maxim, Fayol stressed that those who have authority to issue orders should be willing to accept responsibility for the consequences. "Generally speaking," he wrote, "responsibility is feared as much as authority is sought

after."[1] Today the converse of this proposition is often stressed: *Authority should be equal to responsibility.* That is, if a man is responsible for the results of a given operation, he should be given enough authority to take the actions necessary to ensure success.

2. There should be *unity of command.* That is, for any action whatsoever, an employee should receive orders from one superior only. This principle, of course, runs directly contrary to Taylor's recommendation that workers be directed by several functional foremen, each of whom would be a specialist in one particular phase of the operation, "I do not think," Fayol wrote, "that a shop can be well run in flagrant violation of this [the unity of command]. Nevertheless, Taylor successfully managed large-scale concerns. . . . I imagine that in practice Taylor was able to reconcile functionalism with the principle of unity of command, but that is a supposition whose accuracy I am not in a position to verify."[2]

3. There should be *unity of direction.* There should be "one head and one plan" for a group of activities having the same objective. How this differs from the preceding principle can be shown by a simple illustration: A company could conceivably split up a sales force of twenty men, all selling the same product in the same territories, and have two sales managers, each in charge of ten men. Each of the salesmen would take orders from only one man, but there would be no unity of direction unless all sales plans were coordinated at a higher level.

4. *Gangplanks should be used* to prevent the *scalar chain* from bogging action down. What Fayol meant by this is illustrated by the following diagram taken from his book:

A on the diagram represents the top man in the organization, who is directly over *B* and *L. B,* in turn, is over *C,* and *L* is the immediate superior of *M,* and so on down the line. In a strict observance of "channels," any communication from *F* to *P* would go all the way up one side of the triangle to *A* and down the other side, a time-consuming process.

Fayol suggested that a "gangplank" (the dotted line) could be thrown across without weakening the chain of command. It would only be necessary for the superiors of *F* and *P* to authorize them to treat directly with each other, provided each informed his superior of any action taken. Fayol wrote:

---

[1]*General and Industrial Management,* trans. Constance Storrs, Sir Isaac Pitman & Sons, Ltd., London, 1949, p. 22.
[2]*Ibid.,* p. 69.

It allows the two employees F and P to deal . . . in a few hours, with some question or other which via the scalar chain would pass through twenty transmissions, inconvenience many people, involve masses of paper, lose weeks or months to get to a conclusion less satisfactory generally than the one which could have been obtained via direct contact. . . .

Is it possible that such practices, as ridiculous as they are devastating, could be in current use? Unfortunately there can be little doubt of it in government department affairs. It is usually acknowledged that the chief cause is fear of responsibility. I am rather of the opinion that it is insufficient executive capacity on the part of those in charge. If supreme authority A insisted that his assistants B and L made use of the "gang plank" themselves and made its use incumbent upon their subordinates . . . the habit . . . of taking responsibility would be established.[3]

Other Principles

In addition to these, Fayol listed the following ten principles:

1. *Division of work,* or specialization. He wrote:

Specialization belongs to the natural order. . . . The worker always on the same part, the manager concerned always with the same matters, acquire an ability, sureness, and accuracy which increase their output. Each change of work brings in its train an adaptation which reduces output . . . yet division of work has its limits which experience and a sense of proportion teach us may not be exceeded.[4]

2. *Discipline:*

General opinion is deeply convinced that discipline [obedience, application, energy, and outward marks of respect] is absolutely essential for the smooth running of business. . . . I would approve unreservedly of this . . . were it followed by this other: "Discipline is what leaders make it." . . . Experience and tact on the part of a manager are put to the proof in the choice and degree of sanctions to be used, such as remonstrances, warnings, fines, suspensions, demotion, dismissal. Individual people and attendant circumstances must be taken into account.[5]

The best means of maintaining discipline, he said, are to have (a) good superiors at all levels; (b) agreements (made either with the individual employees or with a union, as the case might be) that are as clear and fair as possible; (c) penalties judiciously applied.

3. *Subordination of individual interest to general interest.* "The interest of one

[3]*Ibid.,* pp. 35-36.
[4]*Ibid.,* p. 20.
[5]*Ibid.,* pp. 22-23.

employee or group of employees should not prevail over that of the concern."[6] To ensure this, he added, there must be firmness and good example on the part of superiors, agreements that are as fair as possible, and constant supervision.

4. Remuneration. Wages and salaries, Fayol stated, should be fair. They should depend both on circumstances (the cost of living, general economic conditions, the demand for labor, the economic state of the business) and on the value of the employee. The plan should reward well-directed effort, but should not lead to overpayment "going beyond reasonable limits."[7] The method of payment—by the day, by the job, by the piece, or by the day plus bonuses—would depend on the circumstances; each method had advantages and disadvantages. As to profit-sharing plans, which were to some extent in use in his day, he was extremely dubious, though he thought such a plan might be useful in some instance, particularly for managers. Profits, he pointed out, often depended on many factors other than individual capability even on the part of the highest managers. He was generally in favor of nonfinancial incentives (good working conditions, housing, etc.), though he believed they were possible only for large-scale concerns.

5. Centralization. Like division of work, Fayol felt, centralization belonged to the natural order. "In every organism . . . sensations converge towards the brain or directive part, and from the brain or directive part orders are sent out which set all parts of the organism in movement."[8] The question of centralization or decentralization, he said, is a simple question of proposition. In small firms, where the managers give orders directly to subordinates, there is absolute centralization; in large concerns, where a long scalar chain is interposed between managers and the lower grades, orders and counterinformation too have to go through a series of intermediaries.

> What appropriate share of initiative may be left to intermediaries depends on the personal character of the manager, on his moral worth, on the reliability of his subordinates, and also on the condition of the business. . . . Seeing that both absolute and relative value of manager and employees are constantly changing, it is understandable that the degree of centralization or decentralization may itself vary constantly.[9]

6. Order. By order Fayol meant a place for everything and everything in its place, a place for everyone and everyone in his place—and the right man in the

---

[6]*Ibid.*, p. 26.
[7]*Ibid.*, p. 27.
[8]*Ibid.*, p. 33.
[9]*Ibid.*, p. 33.

right place. Moreover, he believed that this kind of order "demands precise knowledge of the human requirements and resources of the concern and a constant balance between these requirements and resources. Now this balance is ... the more difficult the bigger the business."[10]

7. Equity. This Fayol defined as "justice tempered with kindness."

8. Stability of tenure of personnel. Both managers and employees, and especially managers, he pointed out, need time to learn their jobs; if they leave or are removed within a short time, the learning time has been wasted. Generally, he said, the managerial personnel of prosperous concerns is stable; that of unsuccessful ones is unstable. But since—aside from the changes inevitable because of death or retirement—the incompetent must be removed and some of those who do well must be promoted, stability of tenure is also a matter of proportion.

9. Initiative. The manager must sacrifice his own vanity to encourage and inspire those under him to show initiative, within the limits of respect for authority and for discipline. The plans and proposals made will contribute to the success of the business and to morale.

10. Esprit de corps. The manager must encourage cohesiveness and *esprit de corps* among his subordinates. Here Fayol cautioned particularly against two temptations the manager may be subject to: (1) divide and rule, and (2) abuse of written communications. Dividing up enemy forces may be clever, he said, but to apply the same tactics to one's own team is not. And a manager should give his subordinates oral rather than written directions and explanations whenever possible, because face-to-face contacts make for speed, clarity, and harmony.

Summary

Fayol believed that there is an "administrative science" applicable to all kinds of administration in any type of industry or in government.

He defined the functions of administration as planning, organizing, commanding, coordinating, and controlling. Among the more important principles or guides he developed for the administrator were unity of command, unity of direction, responsibility equal to authority, and the use of "gangplanks" in cases where going through the channels of the scalar chain would take too much time.

[10]*Ibid.,* p. 37.

Case Study:
The French Postal, Telephone, and Telegraph (the P.T.T.)[11]

After Henri Fayol retired from business in 1918, he devoted his time to writing and speaking on the science of administration. He was particularly concerned with what he considered the absence of good management in the public service. Hence he devoted some study to the French Postal, Telephone, and Telegraph Services, which were run by the government. He summarized their shortcomings as follows:

1. The services were headed by an undersecretary of state, a political appointee chosen by the Cabinet subject to parliamentary confirmation. Since the undersecretary was a political appointee, his tenure was uncertain: he would be out of a job whenever the Cabinet fell, which happened quite often under the Third Republic. His superior was the Minister of Public Works.

2. There was no long-range plan.

3. There was no budget.

4. There was excessive and abusive intervention by members of Parliament.

5. There was no incentive for effort and insufficient compensation for services rendered.

6. Since the undersecretary usually did not remain in office very long, he could not be held accountable for the shortcomings of the services.

The functions of the undersecretary were the preparation of laws and decrees, the signing of numerous orders and instructions, collection and expenditure of funds, approval of legislative bills and budgets, and the appointment of members of P.T.T. committees. He was assisted by a chief executive officer, a chief of service, and a central service, and worked with many committees: a management committee, a technical committee, an improvement committee, an organization committee, a marketing committee, a building committee, an examination committee, a promotion committee, and a disciplinary committee.

The following services reported to the chief executive officer: the central service, personnel and accounting, postal service, telegraph service, telephone service, postal checks and postal savings, and the inspection service.

1. In the light of Fayol's theories, what would he consider the principal shortcomings in the setup?

2. What would his principal recommendations for improvement probably be?

---

[11]From *L'incapacite' industrielle de l'etat: Les P.T.T.,* Dunod, Paris, 1921.

Selected Readings

Foreword by L. Urwick to *General and Industrial Management,* Henri Fayol (trans. Constance Storrs). Sir Isaac Pitman & Sons, Ltd., London, 1949. An account of the life, work, and significance of Henri Fayol.

Oliver Sheldon, *The Philosophy of Management.* Sir Isaac Pitman & Sons, Ltd., London, 1923. Another view of administration as a science in itself, applicable to all types of organizations.

FERDINAND K. LEVY
GERALD L. THOMPSON
JEROME D. WIEST

The ABCs* of
the Critical Path Method

Recently added to the growing assortment of quantitative tools for business decision-making is the Critical Path Method—a powerful but basically simple technique for analyzing, planning, and scheduling large, complex projects. In essence, the tool provides a means of determining (1) which jobs or activities, of the many that comprise a project, are "critical" in their effect on total project time, and (2) how best to schedule all jobs in the project in order to meet a target date at a minimum cost. Widely diverse kinds of projects lend themselves to analysis by CPM, as is suggested in the following list of applications:

—The construction of a building (or a highway).

*Avoid bottlenecks, Best production schedule, Comprehensive look at the work ahead.
Source: *Harvard Business Review,* Vol. 41, No. 5 (September-October, 1963), pp. 98-108.
Copyright 1963 by the President and Fellows of Harvard College, all rights reserved. Reprinted with permission of the publisher, Harvard University Press.
   Authors' note: The preparation of this article was supported by the Office of Naval Research and the Bureau of Ships through grants to the Graduate School of Industrial Administration, Carnegie Institute of Technology. A different version of this material appears as Chapter 20 in *Industrial Scheduling,* edited by J.F. Muth and G.L. Thompson (Englewood Cliffs, N.J.: Prentice-Hall, Inc., 1963). The job list and project graph for the house-building example were developed by Peter R. Winters.

—Planning and launching a new project.

—A turnaround in an oil refinery (or other maintenance projects).

—Installing and debugging a computer system.

—Research and engineering design projects.

—Scheduling ship construction and repairs.

—The manufacture and assembly of a large generator (or other job-lot operations).

—Missile countdown procedures.

Each of these projects has several characteristics that are essential for analysis by CPM:

(1) The project consists of a well-defined collection of jobs (or activities) which, when completed, mark the end of the project.

(2) The jobs may be started and stopped independently of each other, within a given sequence. (This requirement eliminates continuous-flow process activities, such as oil refining, where "jobs" or operations necessarily follow one after another with essentially no slack.)

(3) The jobs are ordered—that is, they must be performed in technological sequence. (For example, the foundation of a house must be constructed before the walls are erected.)

What Is the Method?

The concept of CPM is quite simple and may best be illustrated in terms of a project graph. The graph is not an essential part of CPM; computer programs have been written which permit necessary calculations to be made without reference to a graph. Nevertheless, the project graph is valuable as a means of depicting, visually and clearly, the complex of jobs in a project and their inter-relations:

First of all, each job necessary for the completion of a project is listed with a unique identifying symbol (such as a letter or number), the time required to complete the job, and its immediate prerequisite jobs. For convenience in graphing, and as a check on certain kinds of data errors, the jobs may be arranged in "technological order," which means that no job appears on the list until all of its predecessors have been listed. Technological ordering is impossible if a cycle error exists in the job data (e.g., job a precedes b, b precedes c, and c precedes a).

Then each job is drawn on the graph as a circle, with its identifying symbol and time appearing within the circle. Sequence relationships are indicated by arrows connecting each circle (job) with its immediate successors, with the arrows pointing to the latter. For convenience, all circles with no predecessors are connected to a circle marked "Start"; likewise, all circles with no successors are connected to a circle marked "Finish." (The "Start" and "Finish" circles may be considered pseudo jobs of zero time length.)

Typically, the graph then depicts a number of different "arrow paths" from Start to Finish. The time required to traverse each path is the sum of the times associated with all jobs on the path. The critical path (or paths) is the longest path (in time) from Start to Finish; it indicates the minimum time necessary to complete the entire project.

This method of depicting a project graph differs in some respects from that used by James E. Kelley, Jr., and Morgan R. Walker, who, perhaps more than anyone else, were responsible for the initial development of CPM. (For an interesting account of its early history see their paper, "Critical-Path Planning and Scheduling."[1]) In the widely used Kelley-Walker form, a project graph is just the opposite of that described above: jobs are shown as arrows, and the arrows are connected by means of circles (or dots) that indicate sequence relationships. Thus all immediate predecessors of a given job connect to a circle at the tail of the job arrow, and all immediate successor jobs emanate from the circle at the head of the job arrow. In essence, then, a circle marks an event—the completion of all jobs leading into the circle. Since these jobs are the immediate prerequisites for all jobs leading out of the circle, they must all be completed before *any* of the succeeding jobs can begin.

In order to accurately portray all predecessor relationships, "dummy jobs" must often be added to the project graph in the Kelley-Walker form. The method described in this article avoids the necessity and complexity of dummy jobs, is easier to program for a computer, and also seems more straightforward in explanation and application.

In essence, the critical path is the bottleneck route. Only by finding ways to shorten jobs along the critical path can the over-all project time be reduced; the time required to perform noncritical jobs is irrelevant from the viewpoint of total project time. The frequent (and costly) practice of "crashing" *all* jobs in a project in order to reduce total project time is thus unnecessary. Typically, only about 10 percent of the jobs in large projects are critical. (This figure will naturally vary from project to project.) Of course, if some way is found to shorten one or more of the critical jobs, then not only will the whole project time be shortened but the critical path itself may shift and some previously noncritical jobs may become critical.

Example: Building a House

A simple and familiar example should help to clarify the notion of critical path scheduling and the process of constructing a graph. The project of building

[1]*Proceedings of the Eastern Joint Computer Conference,* Boston (December 1-3, 1959); see also James E. Kelley, Jr., "Critical-Path Planning and Scheduling: Mathematical Basis," *Operations Research* (May-June 1961), pp. 296-320.

Managerial Solution Implementation

a house is readily analyzed by the CPM technique and is typical of a large class of similar applications. While a contractor might want a more detailed analysis, we will be satisfied here with the list of major jobs (together with the estimated time and the immediate predecessors for each job) shown in Exhibit 1.

Sequence and Time Requirements of Jobs *EXHIBIT 1*

	Description	Immediate predecessors	
	Start		
	Excavate and pour footers	a	
	Pour concrete foundation	b	
	Erect wooden frame including rough roof	c	
	Lay brickwork	d	
	Install basement drains and plumbing	c	
	Pour basement floor	f	
	Install rough plumbing	f	
	Install rough wiring	d	
	Install heating and ventilating	d, g	
	Fasten plaster board and plaster (including drying)	i, j, h	
	Lay finish flooring	k	
	Install kitchen fixtures	l	
	Install finish plumbing	l	
	Finish carpentry	l	
	Finish roofing and flashing	e	
	Fasten gutters and downspouts	p	
	Lay storm drains for rain water	c	
	Sand and varnish flooring	o, t	
	Paint	m, n	
	Finish electrical work	t	
	Finish grading	q, r	
	Pour walks and complete landscaping	v	
	Finish	s, u, w	

In that exhibit, the column "immediate predecessors" determines the sequence relationships of the jobs and enables us to draw the project graph, Exhibit 2. Here, in each circle the letter before the comma identifies the job and the number after the comma indicates the job time.

Following the rule that a "legal" path must always move in the direction of

EXHIBIT 2

Project Graph

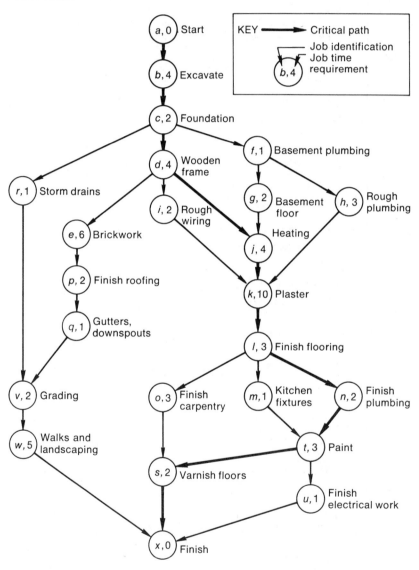

the arrows, we could enumerate 22 unique paths from Start to Finish, with associate times ranging from a minimum of 14 days (path *a-b-c-r-v-w-x*) to a maximum of 34 days (path *a-b-c-d-j-k-l-n-t-s-x*). The latter is the critical path; it determines the over-all project time and tell us which jobs are critical in their effect on this time. If the contractor wishes to complete the house in less than 34 days, it would be useless to shorten jobs not on the critical path. It may seem to him, for example, that the brickwork (*e*) delays progress, since work on a whole series of jobs (*p-q-v-w*) must wait until it is completed. But it would be fruitless to rush the completion of the brickwork, since it is not on the critical path and so is irrelevant in determining total project time.

SHORTENING THE CP

If the contractor were to use CPM techniques, he would examine the critical path for possible improvements. Perhaps he could assign more carpenters to job *d,* reducing it from four to two days. Then the critical path would change slightly, passing through jobs *f* and *g* instead of *d*. Notice that total project time would be reduced only one day, even though two days had been shaved off job *d.* Thus the contractor must watch for possible shifting of the critical path as he affects changes in critical jobs.

Shortening the critical path requires a consideration of both engineering problems and economic questions. Is it physically possible to shorten the time required by critical jobs (by assigning more men to the job, working overtime, using different equipment, and so on)? If so, would the costs of speedup be less than the savings resulting from the reduction in over-all project time? CPM is a useful tool because it quickly focuses attention on those jobs that are critical to the project time, it provides an easy way to determine the effects of shortening various jobs in the project, and it enables the user to evaluate the costs of a "crash" program.

Two important applications of these features come to mind:

Du Pont, a pioneer in the application of CPM to construction and maintenance projects, was concerned with the amount of downtime for maintenance at its Louisville works, which produces an intermediate product in the neoprene process. Analyzing the maintenance schedule by CPM, Du Pont engineers were able to cut downtime for maintenance from 125 to 93 hours. CPM pointed to further refinements that were expected to reduce total time to 78 hours. As a result, performance of the plant improved by about one million pounds in 1959, and the intermediate was no longer a bottleneck in the neoprene process.

PERT (i.e., Program Evaluation Review Technique), a technique closely related to the critical path method, is widely credited with helping to shorten by two years the time originally estimated for completion of the engineering and development program for the Navy's Polaris missile. By pinpointing the longest paths through the vast maze of jobs necessary for completion of the missile design, PERT enabled the program managers to concentrate their efforts on those activities that vitally affected total project time.[2]

Even with our small house-building project, however, the process of enumerating and measuring the length of every path through the maze of jobs is tedious. A simple method of finding the critical path and, at the same time, developing useful information about each job is described next.

Critical Path Algorithm

If the start time or date for the project is given (we denote it by S), then there exists for each job an earliest starting time (ES), which is the earliest possible time that a job can begin, if all its predecessors are also started at their ES. And if the time to complete the job is t, we can define, analogously, its earliest finish time (EF) to be ES + t.

There is a simple way of computing ES and EF times using the project graph. It proceeds as follows:

(1) Mark the value of S to the left and to the right of Start.

(2) Consider any new unmarked job *all of whose predecessors have been marked,* and mark to the left of the new job the *largest* number marked to the right of any of its *immediate* predecessors. This number is its early start time.

(3) Add to this number the job time and mark the result (EF time) to the right of the job.

(4) Continue until Finish has been reached, then stop.

Thus, at the conclusion of this calculation the ES time for each job will appear to the left of the circle which identifies it, and the EF time will appear to the right of the circle. The number which appears to the right of the last job, Finish, is the early finish time (F) for the entire project.

To illustrate these calculations let us consider the following simple production process:

An assembly is to be made from two parts, A and B. Both parts must be turned on the lathe, and B must be polished while A need not be. The list of jobs to be performed, together with the predecessors of each job and the time in minutes to perform each job, is given in Exhibit 3.

The project graph is shown in Exhibit 4. As previously, the letter identifying each job appears before the comma and its job time after the comma. Also

[2]See Robert W. Miller, "How to Plan and Control with PERT," *HBR,* March-April 1962, p. 93.

EXHIBIT 3

Data for Production Process

Job No.	Description	Immediate Predecessors	Normal Time (minutes)
a	Start		0
b	Get materials for A	a	10
c	Get materials for B	a	20
d	Turn A on lathe	b, c	30
e	Turn B on lathe	b, c	20
f	Polish B	e	40
g	Assemble A and B	d, f	20
h	Finish	g	0

EXHIBIT 4

Calculation of Early Start and Early Finish Times for Each Job

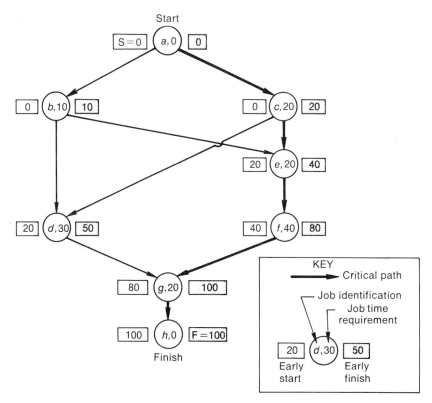

shown on the graph are the ES and EF times for each job, assuming that the start time, S, is *zero*. The ES time appears to the left of the circle representing a job, and the EF time appears to the right of the circle. Note that F = 100. The reader may wish to duplicate the diagram without these times and carry out the calculations for himself as a check on his understanding of the computation process described above.

LATEST START AND FINISH TIMES

Suppose now that we have a target time (T) for completing the project. T may have been originally expressed as a calendar date, e.g., October 1 or February 15. When is the latest time that the project can be started and finished?

In order to be feasible it is clear that T must be greater (later) than or equal to F, the early finish time for the project. Assuming this is so, we can define the concept of late finish (LF), or the latest time that a job can be finished, without delaying the total project beyond its target time (T). Similarly, late start (LS) is defined to be LF $- T$, where t is the job time.

These numbers are determined for each job in a manner similar to the previous calculations except that we work from the end of the project to its beginning. We proceed as follows:

(1) Mark the value of T to the right and left of Finish.

(2) Consider any new unmarked job *all of whose successors have been marked,* and mark to the right of the new job the *smallest* LS time marked to the left of any of its immediate successors.

The logic of this is hard to explain in a few words, although apparent enough by inspection. It helps to remember that the smallest LS time of the successors of a given job, if translated into calendar times, would be the latest finish time of that job.

(3) Subtract from this number the job time and mark the result to the left of the job.

(4) Continue until Start has been reached, then stop.

At the conclusion of this calculation the LF time for a job will appear to the right of the circle which identifies it, and the LS time for the job will appear to the left of the circle. The number appearing to the right of Start is the latest time that the entire project can be started and still finish at the target time T.

In Exhibit 5 we carry out these calculations for the example of Exhibit 3. Here T = F = 100, and we separate early start and finish and late start and finish times by semicolons so that ES;LS appears to the left of the job and EF;LF to the right. Again the reader may wish to check these calculations for himself.

EXHIBIT 5

Calculation of Late Start and Late Finish Times for Each Job

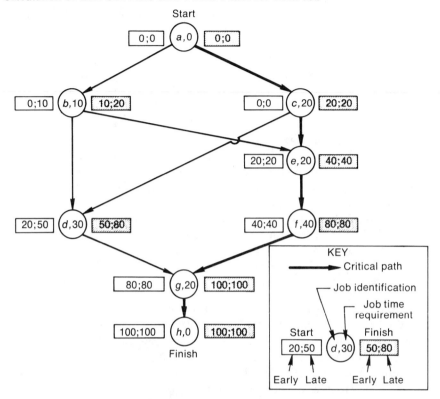

Concept of Slack

Examination of Exhibit 5 reveals that some jobs have their early start equal to late start, while others do not. The difference between a job's early start and its late start (or between early finish and late finish) is called total slack (TS). Total slack represents the maximum amount of time a job may be delayed beyond its early start without necessarily delaying the project completion time.

We earlier defined critical jobs as those on the longest path through the project. That is, critical jobs *directly* affect the total project time. We can now relate the critical path to the concept of slack.

FINDING THE CRITICAL PATH

If the target date (T) equals the early finish date for the whole project (F), then all critical jobs will have *zero* total slack. There will be at least one path going from Start to Finish that includes critical jobs only, i.e., the *critical path*. If T is greater (later) than F, then the critical jobs will have total slack equal to T minus F. This is a minimum value; since the critical path includes only critical jobs, it includes those with the smallest TS. All noncritical jobs will have *greater* total slack.

In Exhibit 5, the critical path is shown by darkening the arrows connecting critical jobs. In this case there is just one critical path, and all critical jobs lie on it; however, in other cases there may be more than one critical path. Note that T = F; thus the critical jobs have zero total slack. Job b has TS = 10, and job d has TS = 30; either or both of these jobs could be delayed by these amounts of time without delaying the project.

Another kind of slack is worth mentioning. Free slack (FS) is the amount a job can be delayed without delaying the early start of any other job. A job with positive total slack may or may not also have free slack, but the latter never exceeds the former. For purposes of computation, the free slack of a job is defined as the difference between the job's EF time and the *earliest* of the ES times of all its immediate successors. Thus, in Exhibit 5, job b has FS of 10, and job d has FS of 30. All other jobs have zero free slack

SIGNIFICANCE OF SLACK

When a job has zero total slack, its scheduled start time is automatically fixed (that is, ES = LS); and to delay the calculated start time is to delay the whole project. Jobs with positive total slack, however, allow the scheduler some discretion in setting their start times. This flexibility can usefully be applied to smoothing work schedules. Peak loads that develop in a particular shop (or in a machine, or within an engineering design group, to cite other examples) may be relieved by shifting jobs on the peak days to their late starts. Slack allows this kind of juggling without affecting project time.[3]

Free slack can be used effectively at the operating level. For example, if a job has free slack, the foreman may be given some flexibility in deciding when to start the job. Even if he delays the start by an amount equal to (or less than) the free slack, the delay will not affect the start times or slack of succeeding jobs (which is not true of jobs that have no free slack). For an illustration of these notions, we return to our house-building example.

BACK TO THE CONTRACTOR

In Exhibit 6, we reproduce the diagram of house-building jobs, marking the ES and LS to the left, and the EF and LF to the right of each job (for example,

---

[3]For a method for smoothing operations in a job shop, based on CPM and the use of slack, see F. K. Levy, G. L. Thompson, and J. D. Wiest, "Multi-Ship, Multi-Shop Production Smoothing Algorithm," *Naval Logistics Research Quarterly,* March 9, 1962.

"0;3" and "4;7" on either side of the b,4 circle). We assume that construction begins on day zero and must be completed by day 37. Total slack for each job is not marked, since it is evident as the difference between the pairs of numbers ES and LS or EF and LF. However, jobs that have positive free slack are so marked.

EXHIBIT 6

Project Graph with Start and Finish Times

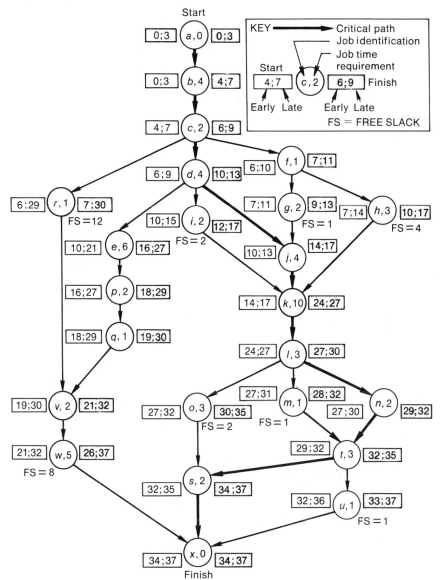

There is one critical path, which is shown darkened in the diagram. All critical jobs on this path have total slack of three days.

Several observations can be drawn immediately from the diagram:

(1) The contractor could postpone starting the house three days and still complete it on schedule, barring unforeseen difficulties (see the difference between early and late times at the Finish). This would reduce the total slack of all jobs by three days, and hence reduce TS for critical jobs to zero.

(2) Several jobs have free slack. Thus the contractor could delay the completion of i (rough wiring) by two days, g (the basement floor) by one day, h (rough plumbing) by four days, r (the storm drains) by 12 days, and so on—without affecting succeeding jobs.

(3) The series of jobs e (brickwork), p (roofing), q (gutters), v (grading), and w (landscaping) have a comfortable amount of total slack (nine days). The contractor can use these and other slack jobs as "fill in" jobs for workers who become available when their skills are not needed for currently critical jobs. This is a simple application of workload smoothing: juggling the jobs with slack in order to reduce peak demands for certain skilled workers or machines.

If the contractor were to effect changes in one or more of the critical jobs, by contrast, the calculations would have to be performed again. This he can easily do; but in large projects with complex sequence relationships, hand calculations are considerably more difficult and liable to error. Computer programs have been developed, however, for calculating ES, LS, EF, LF, TS, and FS for each job in a project, given the set of immediate prerequisites and the job times for each job.[4]

Handling Data Errors

Information concerning job times and predecessor relationships is gathered, typically, by shop foremen, scheduling clerks, or others closely associated with a project. It is conceivable that several kinds of errors may occur in such job data:

1. The estimated job times may be in error.

2. The predecessor relationship may contain cycles: e.g., job a is a predecessor for b, b is a predecessor for c, and c is a predecessor for a.

3. The list of prerequisites for a job may include more than the immediate

---

[4]An algorithm on which one such computer program is based is discussed by F. K. Levy, G. L. Thompson, and J. D. Wiest, in chapter 22, "Mathematical Basis of the Critical Path Method," *Industrial Scheduling* (see Authors' Note, p. 98).

prerequisites; e.g., job *a* is a predecessor of *b*, *b* is a predecessor of *c*, and *a* and *b* both are predecessors of *c*.

4. Some predecessor relationships may be overlooked.

5. Some predecessor relationships may be listed that are spurious.

How can management deal with these problems? We shall examine each briefly in turn.

Job times. An accurate estimate of total project time depends, of course, on accurate job-time data. CPM eliminates the necessity (and expense) of careful time studies for *all* jobs. Instead the following procedure can be used:

—Given rough time estimates, construct a CPM graph of the project.

—Then those jobs that are on the critical path (together with jobs that have very small total slack, indicating that they are nearly critical) can be more closely checked, their times reestimated, and another CPM graph constructed with the refined data.

—If the critical path has changed to include jobs still having rough time estimates, then the process is repeated.

In many projects studied, it has been found that only a small fraction of jobs are critical; so it is likely that refined time studies will be needed for relatively few jobs in a project in order to arrive at a reasonably accurate estimate of the total project time. CPM thus can be used to reduce the problem of Type I errors at a small total cost.

Prerequisites. A computer algorithm has been developed to check for errors of Types 2 and 3 above. The algorithm (mentioned in footnote 4) systematically examines the set of prerequisites for each job and cancels from the set all but immediate predecessor jobs. When an error of Type 2 is present in the job data, the algorithm will signal a "cycle error" and print out the cycle in question.

Wrong or missing facts. Errors of Types 4 and 5 cannot be discovered by computer routines. Instead, manual checking (perhaps by a committee) is necessary to see that prerequisites are accurately reported.

Cost Calculations

The cost of carrying out a project can be readily calculated from the job data if the cost of doing each job is included in the data. If jobs are done by crews, and the speed with which the job is done depends on the crew size, then it is possible to shorten or lengthen the project time by adding or removing men from crews. Other means for compressing job times might also be found; but any speedup is likely to carry a price tag. Suppose that we assign to each job a "normal time" and a "crash time" and also calculate the associated costs necessary to carry the job in each time. If we want to shorten the project, we can assign some of the critical jobs to their crash time, and compute the corresponding direct cost. In this way it is possible to calculate the cost of completing the project in various total times, with the direct costs increasing as the over-all time decreases.

Added to direct costs are certain overhead expenses which are usually allocated on the basis of total project time. Fixed costs per project thus decrease as project time is shortened. In ordinary circumstances a combination of fixed and direct costs as a function of total project time would probably fall into the pattern shown in Exhibit 7. The minimum total cost (point A) would likely fall to the left of the minimum point on the direct cost curve (point B) indicating that the optimum project time is somewhat shorter than an analysis of direct costs only would indicate.

EXHIBIT 7

Typical Cost Pattern

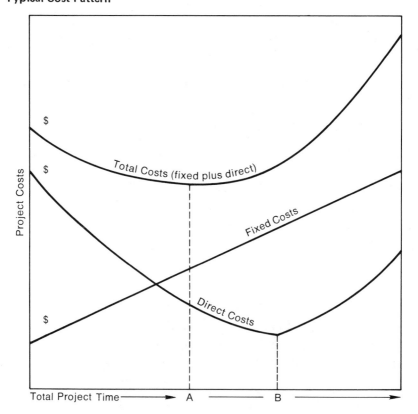

Managerial Solution Implementation

Other economic factors, of course, can be included in the analysis. For example, pricing might be brought in:

> A large chemical company starts to build a plant for producing a new chemical. After the construction schedule and completion date are established an important potential customer indicates a willingness to pay a premium price for the new chemical if it can be made available earlier than scheduled. The chemical producer applies techniques of CPM to its construction schedule and calculates the additional costs associated with "crash" completion of jobs on the critical path. With a plot of costs correlated with total project time, the producer is able to select a new completion date such that the increased costs are met by the additional revenue offered by the customer.

New Developments

Because of their great potential for applications, both CPM and PERT have received intensive development in the past few years. This effort is sparked, in part, because of the Air Force (and other governmental agency) requirements that contractors use these methods in planning and monitoring their work. Here are some illustrations of progress made:

> One of the present authors (Wiest) has developed extensions of the workload smoothing algorithm. These extensions are the so-called SPAR (for Scheduling Program for Allocating Resources) programs for scheduling projects having limited resources.

> A contemporaneous development by C-E-I-R, Inc., has produced RAMPS (for Resource Allocation and Multi-Project Scheduling), which is similar but not identical.

> The most recent version of PERT, called PERT/COST, was developed by the armed services and various businesses for use on weapon-systems development projects contracted by the government. Essentially, PERT/COST adds the consideration of resource costs to the schedule produced by the PERT procedure. Indications of how smoothing can be accomplished are also made. Other recent versions are called PERT II, PERT III, PEP, PEPCO, and Super PERT.

Conclusion

For the manager of large projects, CPM is a powerful and flexible tool, indeed, for decision making:

> —It is useful at various stages of project management, from initial planning or analyzing of alternative programs, to scheduling and controlling the jobs (activities) that comprise a project.

—It can be applied to a great variety of project types—from our house-building example to the vastly more complicated design project for the Polaris—and at various levels of planning—from scheduling jobs in a single shop, or shops in a plant, to scheduling plants within a corporation.

—In a simple and direct way it displays the interrelations in the complex of jobs that comprise a large project.

—It is easily explainable to the layman by means of the project graph. Data calculations for large projects, while tedious, are not difficult, and can readily be handled by a computer.

—It pinpoints attention to the small subset of jobs that are critical to project completion time, thus contributing to more accurate planning and more precise control.

—It enables the manager to quickly study the effects of "crash" programs and to anticipate potential bottlenecks that might result from shortening certain critical jobs.

—It leads to reasonable estimates of total project costs for various completion dates, which enable the manager to select an optimum schedule.

Because of the above characteristics of CPM—and especially its intuitive logic and graphic appeal—it is a decision-making tool which can find wide appreciation at all levels of management.[5] The project graph helps the foreman to understand the sequencing of jobs and the necessity of pushing those that are critical. For the manager concerned with day-to-day operations in all departments, CPM enables him to measure progress (or lack of it) against plans and to take appropriate action quickly when needed. And the underlying simplicity of CPM and its ability to focus attention on crucial problem areas of large projects make it an ideal tool for the top manager. On his shoulders falls the ultimate responsibility for overall planning and coordination of such projects in the light of company-wide objectives.

[5]See A. Charnes and W. W. Cooper, "A Network Interpretation and a Directed Sub-Dual Algorithm for Critical Path Scheduling," *Journal of Industrial Engineering,* July-August 1962, pp. 213-219.

ROBERT V. HEAD

Management Information Systems: A Critical Appraisal

The subject of "management information systems" has been much discussed, and much maligned by both systems professionals and management people over the past few years. Both groups agree, though, that there has been a good deal of significant progress over the last two years or so, and it is the purpose of this paper to comment on these recent developments.

It seems appropriate to begin with a discussion of some of the basic concepts and design objectives of management information systems. This will be followed by comments on the approaches being taken by large organizations that seem to best characterize contemporary information systems development. Finally, there will be a brief discussion of some of the current problems in this volatile field. For although we have found solutions to many of the technical problems in management information systems, there remain others, largely nontechnical, that threaten to inhibit the dramatic progress that might otherwise be achieved.

Source: *Datamation* (Barrington, Ill.: Technical Publishing Co., 1967). Reprinted with permission.

The Concept

Let us begin by describing what a "management information system" really is. To do so, it may be useful to look back over the past ten years at the ways in which companies have been utilizing their data processing equipment. The bottom portion of Figure 1 indicates some of the data processing applications that the typical large company has successfully developed. All these application areas have been attacked, one by one, and converted to automatic processing equipment. As a class, these applications have provided the capability of processing the massive volume of accounting transactions of an organization, and producing, as a result of this processing, reports scheduled according to some predetermined cycle.

This is by and large what companies have been doing up to now. The concept that has been arousing increased interest in recent years has to do not only with the processing of information by computer for accounting purposes but with using this same information in different and more imaginative ways. This involves, for one thing, the use of information for management control purposes. Here the emphasis is not on historical record-keeping but on the processing of information requests and the providing of reports "as required" on a demand basis. The upward-pointing arrows in Figure 1 are meant to suggest that the same data obtained for routine accounting purposes can be selected and transformed for such management control purposes.

At a higher level of management usage, there is the opportunity, and

FIGURE 1

Management Information System

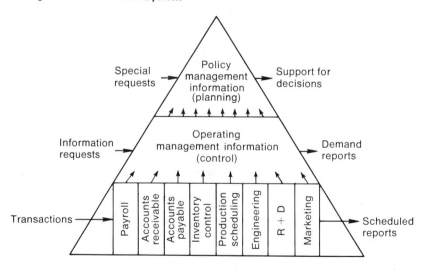

attendant design objective, in an information system to use the same data not only for middle management control but to aid policy-level decision-makers. The apex of the Figure 1 diagram suggests that special requests can be directed to the information system by executive management, with the system providing support for decision making at this level.[1] This can be defined as a planning type of usage of the information system.

Thus we are evolving from conventional or traditional applications to the use of the same information at the middle management level for control purposes and at the general management or executive level for planning purposes.[2]

Many practitioners refer to the information identified at the bottom of Figure 1 as the organization's data base. Another way of looking at this data base is to think not in terms of separate or discrete applications but instead to view the data base as consisting of elements of information as shown in Figure 2. The bottom of this figure can be likened to a "soup" in which numerous data elements are floating around, not well-structured or well-organized but all present. In a large system, there may be hundreds or thousands of different kinds of data elements floating around in this data base soup.

In order to accomplish anything useful with these elements, it is necessary to give the data base an organization and structure. This structuring requires at least three things to be done: one is that the *information requirements* of management have to be identified. We need to know which of the elements potentially available are actually required. We need then to define them by providing a *data description*, in technical terms, of the data elements: how large they are, what their meaning is, where they are stored, how one can get at them. Then finally, it is of great importance to identify *data relationships* among the

---

[1]Note the phrase "support for decision-making." This is employed deliberately to avoid the implication that the computer itself is a decision-maker in any important respect. While it is true that many lower order decisions have been programmed for the computer (e.g., inventory replenishment), the computer's primary role in a management information system is to provide data adequate to abet the decision-making function. For a general discussion of programmed and nonprogrammed decision-making, see Herbert A. Simon's *The New Science of Management Decision,* (Harper & Brothers, 1960).

[2]Although the terminology differs, the usages of information discussed in this paper generally correspond to the levels of planning and control identified by Robert N. Anthony in his authoritative work, *Planning and Control Systems: A Framework for Analysis* (Harvard, 1965). Anthony's three levels are defined as follows: Strategic Planning: the process of deciding on objectives of the organization, on changes in these objectives, on the resources used to attain these objectives, and on the policies that are to govern the acquisition, use, and disposition of these resources.

Management Control: the process by which managers assure that resources are obtained and used effectively and efficiently in the accomplishment of the organization's objectives.

Operational Control: the process of assuring that specific tasks are carried out effectively and efficiently.

From the point of view of this paper, business data processing has heretofore concentrated on accomplishing the specific day-to-day tasks of the company, i.e., operational control.

FIGURE 2

Management Information System Data Base

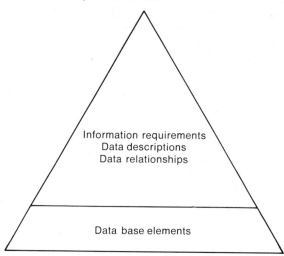

data base elements. An employee skill number might, for example, be a data element. This data element would be referenced in payroll compilation, the maintaining of personnel records, in industrial relations. Thus the same data element could be related to many different files or, putting it another way, to many different management usages of information.

Not only is the organization of information changing significantly from what it has been in the past but the utilization of this information is also changing. Companies engaged in developing management information systems are going beyond the use of computers simply to maintain records; they are exploring much more imaginative and ambitious applications. A few of these new uses are identified in Figure 3. They include graphics capability to display the elements retrieved from the data base, as well as modeling and simulation. They extend to linking the information system to other systems dedicated to on-line process control, and involve the application of specialized retrieval techniques to pull information from the data base. Most of these innovations in information systems encourage, and in some instances require, a close interaction between manager and machine.

Considerations in Systems Design

A fundamental question confronting the system designer when he begins to think about the data base aspect of management information systems is: how many levels of data base are there going to be in the organization? There exists,

FIGURE 3

Information System Utilization

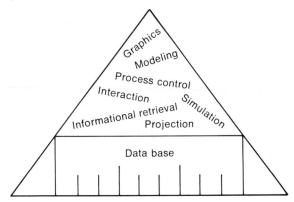

of course, a management hierarchy with different information needs at its various levels, and so the question arises whether the information system can serve all these levels in an organization with but a single data base.

The bottom of Figure 4 reflects the continuing need to maintain the details of each business transaction, facts having to do with individual customer accounts and kindred information. All these details of transactions still have to be maintained much as they have been in the past, and information about them will typically constitute a fundamental part of the data base. Operating management obviously does not need all this detail, but it does need some portion or subset of it, as indicated by the center section of Figure 4. And at the top, policy management needs yet another subset of the overall data base. So the

FIGURE 4

How Many Levels of Data Base?

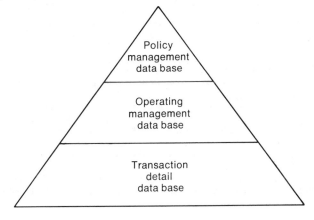

question must be answered: can these varying needs be served by a single data base, or will the system designer be forced to structure three different data bases? If he has to fragment the information system by level, then there is necessarily going to be some redundancy in the data elements maintained. Consider a specific example. In a commercial banking system it is necessary for the teller to have access to the details pertaining to each account—i.e., the current balance, the amounts of the checks drawn against the account, and so on. But this is really not of interest at the operating management level. This level is interested in cumulative information about groups of accounts, say all those under a branch manager's supervision. And at the policy-management level, the information needs are even broader, having to do with loan-to-deposit ratios, and deposit growth expectancy. Thus the designer is confronted with the problem of structuring the data base to accommodate these varying levels of information seekers.

A similar problem, but one having a "vertical" rather than a "horizontal" nature, is suggested by Figure 5. For not only does the system designer have to structure horizontally, but he has also to determine whether different functional portions of the company can share a common data base—i.e., whether he must chop the data base into vertical as well as horizontal segments. Can the marketing department use the same data base as the production or accounting people, or is each intent on having one of its own? There seems to be some tendency in the latter direction, as there exist today systems dedicated, for example, to marketing information and serving the marketing part of the organization only. A major challenge to the information system designer lies in trying to integrate the company data base so that it can be useful to all major organizational levels and components.[3]

Another difficulty confronting the system designer concerns management's "information threshold." This has to do with the level to which a given executive may want to descend into the data base for information. The top horizontal line in Figure 6 indicates what the system designer may regard as the "appropriate" information threshold for policy-level management. Executive "A", however, does not want to be confronted with the degree of detail envisaged in such a system design. An example that comes to mind is that of

[3]Anthony takes a pessimistic view with respect to the satisfaction of top management's information needs. After asserting, rightfully, in this author's opinion, that "the data needed for strategic planning depend on the nature of the problem being studied" and that "not all these problems can be forseen," he concludes: It is because of the varied and unpredictable nature of the data required for strategic planning that an attempt to design an all-purpose internal information system is probably hopeless. For the same reason, the dream of some computer specialists of a gigantic data bank, from which planners can obtain all the information they wish by pressing some buttons, is probably no more than a dream.

The author of this paper is more optimistic, holding the view that contemporary data base design concepts, which facilitate the retrieval of data elements in response to un-structured and nonpredetermined management requests, can contribute significantly to the realization of such a dream.

FIGURE 5

How Many Specialized Data Bases?

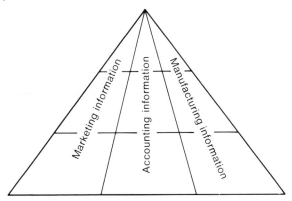

FIGURE 6

The Information Threshold Problem-I

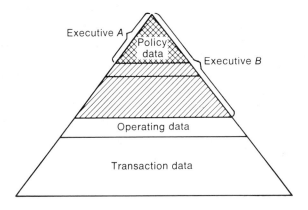

General Eisenhower. When he was President, his preference was said to lie in having all problems brought to him summarized very succinctly. Thus, he might be representative of that kind of chief executive who does not want to delve very far down into the data base, but instead desired summary presentations of information.

But if the system is developed to accommodate such an executive's information threshold, the system designer must determine what should be done when his chief is succeeded by another executive who has an entirely different information threshold. Consider executive "B" in Figure 6, who frequently wishes to examine information that has to do with day-to-day control of the business—i.e., operating data. Secretary of Defense McNamara is regarded as this type of executive in that he has a very low information threshold and demands many detailed facts before making a decision.

Now, the systems analyst does not want to have to restructure, and more importantly, reimplement, the system each time there is a transition from one chief executive to another. He wishes instead to have, as a design objective, a system that is sufficiently *adaptable* to accommodate the information needs of different types of executives. This is certainly another of the challenges in information systems design.

An additional aspect of this information threshold problem, or perhaps another way of looking at it, becomes evident when executive "A" has, let us say, a marketing background, so that when marketing transactions are involved he wants to go all the way down to the bottom of the data base as evidenced by the shaded left hand portion of Figure 7. Such an executive may call for all the details of a particular customer order, asking "How long was this order delayed?" "What was the amount of the order?" Management experts may assert that this executive is violating sound organizational principles by doing so, but the systems man must recognize that in a real life situation this is the way executives operate and, consequently, he must design systems to accommodate these needs. Otherwise, management simply will not make use of the system.

And, of course, systems can be tailored in this manner. The designer can allow hypothetical executive "A" to satisfy his personal need to know, but it must be remembered that this executive is not going to be in charge forever and may be succeeded by someone from, say, the engineering sector. This could turn out to be executive "B", as represented by the shaded right hand side of Figure 7, who in general wishes much more detail, but will want to go down to the very lowest level in the data base only when engineering or R & D problems are

FIGURE 7

The Threshold Problem-II

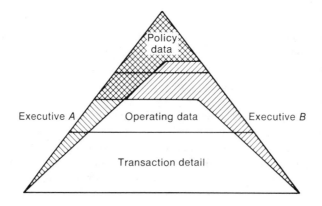

involved. It is essential to design a system that does not have to be reworked completely when such changes in management information thresholds occur.

These are some of the considerations that systems people must be concerned with, whether they work for an equipment manufacturer interested in seeing his equipment used in an information systems context, or for a user seeking to install an up-to-date management information system.

Trends

Now that we have established a conceptual framework, let us examine some current industry developments. What are companies actually doing today? Some of the concepts just presented have been in the public domain for some time, but do not necessarily or entirely reflect what is actually happening in terms of the things companies are spending good money on in the information systems field.

APPLICATIONS REWORKING

Commercial applications programmed in the past are today being reworked by many companies in a very drastic and far-reaching way. Existing applications are being redone, not so much because of a conscious decision by management to develop an integrated information system but simply because third-generation computers are being widely installed. Most companies that had in the past a tape oriented, second-generator computer are now installing larger, third-generation gear. This third-generation equipment offers features not readily available to system designers in the past, including mass direct access storage, a variety of on-line terminal devices, and substantial remote processing capability.

Though it is usually possible for a company to retain existing applications by using emulation or simulation, most companies recognize that they can best exploit the more powerful new computers by rethinking their applications from the bottom up. And in the course of such rethinking, there is an unprecedented opportunity to provide more effectively for the information needs of management. Thus, the fact that new equipment is forcing applications to be redone is giving impetus to the development of management information systems.

FORMALIZED SYSTEMS PLANNING

Accompanying, and related to, the phenomenon of applications reworking is the growth of a formalized approach to systems planning. This is largely a reflection of the experience gained in the recent past, when a computer was installed in the company initially for one purpose—to automate the major accounting routines. Thus, public utilities first automated revenue accounting and insurance companies, premium accounting. But now that they have committed themselves to the expensive and time-consuming task of reworking their key applications, companies have become interested in devising some sort of "road-map" of the future in order to avoid yet another wave of rework a few years hence. A five-year planning period is typical, although some go out longer. All seek to anticipate the systems capability that should exist in the organization over the planning period.

These plans are truly formalized, documented and presented to management for endorsement and reviewed and updated periodically. If, for example, a company has no corporate planning staff, the information systems group trying to develop a long-range systems plan lacks the necessary guidance to establish its plan. For the systems plan depends importantly on the firm's overall strategy concerning such matters as new products, mergers and acquisitions, and geographic expansion. When management's own insight into these future possibilities is not clear, the systems group can only build its long-term plan on assumptions about company growth. And by so proceeding, the systems people tend to become, by default, the corporate planning staff.

MANAGEMENT SCIENCE EMPHASIS

As the focus of technological interest in many companies comes to bear on management information systems, there is heightened emphasis on the employment of management science techniques—i.e., the usage of the computer in a scientific approach to business problem solving. Looking at this development in historical perspective, it is evident that, with the repetitive accounting tasks already automated. further exploitation of the computer must draw heavily upon statistical and mathematical techniques to assist management decision-making. It is not by accident that some of the major computer manufacturers have moved to unify their product line, bridging the traditional distinction between so-called "scientific" data processing, using binary machines, and "commercial" data processing, using decimal machines. These manufacturers are striving to supply equipment that can be applied to whatever purposes are appropriate for business usage at this point in time.

REGIONAL INFORMATION PROCESSING

The design philosophy associated with the development of a broadly applicable company data base would appear to provide a strong motivation towards centralizing the company's information processing systems. In practice, though, there is a tendency to regionalize data processing capability, with a

Managerial Solution Implementation

number of large companies proceeding actively along these lines. One diversified manufacturing company presently has data processing capability located in more than 25 decentralized operating departments. These departments, each of which has profit and loss responsibility, in the past had pretty much of a free hand to determine their data processing equipment needs. This company now plans to centralize its computing equipment, though not to the extent of pooling it in one headquarters location. There will be instead four regional centers, serving groups of these decentralized departments.

Another example is that of a large bank that presently operates several centers for processing checks, handling hundreds of thousands of items per day. They are now in the process of closing these centers, but will not pull everything into the bank's headquarters. Instead, this bank will convert to two regional centers.

Why take a regional approach? Perhaps management is reluctant at this time to make the ultimate commitment of concentrating all its data processing capability in one place. Possibly what is now happening represents an intermediate step, and another generation of systems technology will see further centralization.

INFORMATION MANAGEMENT SYSTEMS

Concentration on management information systems has encouraged an important collateral effort to develop "information management systems." Some practitioners call these "file management systems," others call them "management inquiry systems," or "data base systems." Basically, an information management system is a software tool useful in organizing, processing, and presenting information. Companies engaged in developing management information systems are showing increasing interest in these programs which help organize and manage information more effectively. Recalling the notion of the data base as a "soup," with data elements floating around in it, the role of an information management system is to coalesce these data elements into records and files suitable for processing and inquiry purposes. The concept of an information management system is of sufficient importance to warrant a brief discussion of the functions performed by such systems.

System Functions

File creation. Perhaps the most basic thing they can do is establish files. This involves the identification of the data elements that must appear in a given file. These elements are described to the information management system, which then creates files in accordance with stated requirements for data element and file usage. Storage allocation is controllable by the system, and a file can be set up in whatever physical storage medium is appropriate to the use of the information in the file.

File maintenance. Another of the classical tasks in data processing now being assumed by information management software is file maintenance. Here, transaction processing requirements set forth by the systems analyst are transformed by the information management system into routines to accomplish the updating of master files.

Report generation. The idea of using software to assist in generating management reports is not new. Report generators have been around for a long time, but today's information management systems incorporate them as a function within an integrated and internally consistent software package. Thus, having set up a file, the analyst can now direct the system to generate reports tailored to management specifications.

On-line inquiry. The three information management functions just mentioned would be adequate for conventional, off-line, sequential processing. Many information management systems go beyond this, however, to permit operation in an on-line mode. The files established and maintained by the system thus are made available for direct management inquiry. Such inquiry capability requires the design of an inquiry language and the development of interpretive programs to analyze the inquiries and set up the file search logic required to obtain the data elements needed to satisfy the inquiry.

Information retrieval. The final major function of information management software has to do with information retrieval. If a system is to accept real-time queries against the data base, it is necessary to structure the files in such a way that the system can be immediately responsive to requests for information. Information management systems are thus beginning to borrow from the field of information retrieval. As a consequence, information retrieval techniques have begun moving out of the field of library science and into business organization as an important part of information management software.

Consider the difference between the rigidly structured and carefully prescheduled computer reports that management is now accustomed to receiving, and the capability of asking the system to retrieve and display, in real-time, answers to such queries as the following: "Which branches in our banking system have more than 2,000 loan accounts *and* a loan-to-deposit ration of 1.2 *or* have more than 10 percent of their deposit accounts with an average of over $10,000. Advanced information management software can help the designer provide this kind of inquiry and information retrieval capability.

Problems in Systems Planning

Thus far we have discussed some key notions in information systems design and looked briefly at major developments taking place in leading companies. While these provide signs of substantial progress, many serious problems remain. The list of problems is perhaps not quite so long as it was before the advent of third-generation computers, with their mass direct access storage and inquiry devices. Similarly, the type of software technology epitomized by the new information management systems has helped markedly. The problems remaining are less technical in nature than before. They have to do with introducing the technology that has become available into the company environment.

The most immediate problem of this kind centers around the fact that management information systems cost more than predecessor systems. If a company president studies his system costs, he will soon discover that the equipment and software necessary to support a management information system cost a lot more than the company had to invest in the past in more conventional applications. It is undeniable that there is a higher price tag associated with management information systems than the already considerable cost burden that companies have been carrying for data processing technology. Despite the fact that unit costs have been declining, e.g. cost per bit stored, cost per item processed, hardware and software costs are both rising in an absolute sense, reflecting the more ambitious objectives of today's information systems design. As a result, management is taking a closer look at new equipment proposals, and challenging each new systems project more vigorously.

Associated with the problem of rising developmental and operating costs is that of system justification. Even though a proposed system may be very costly, an enlightened company management may be willing to support it if the proponents of the system can demonstrate what the benefits are going to be. In the past, when a computer was installed for repetitive accounting tasks, there were almost invariably demonstrable savings resulting from clerical worker displacement. This was usually a very tangible cost-justification, and most companies are proud of the fact that they have been very objective and have never installed a computer without the off-setting cost benefits. But this approach is no longer appropriate for companies that have *already* obtained these tangible cost benefits by means of systems presently installed. Today, the question is not what it may be worth, for instance, to an investment company to update its portfolios and otherwise process the paperwork, but rather what it is worth to provide an investment manager with a cathode-ray tube display device and the underlying mathematical techniques to aid in security analysis and portfolio selection. These are benefits that in the past were referred to, a trifle cavalierly, as "intangible." But *most* of the benefits of a management information system are of this intangible nature. Clearly, what is needed are new methods of justifying information system costs by quantifying somehow these heretofore "intangible" benefits. Until this can be done, it is difficult to see how management can be persuaded to commit substantial company resources to truly effective information systems development.

In seeking to chart a course of action, management men sometimes become understandably confused about just what their systems people are trying to do in the field of information technology. All too frequently management is caught in the crosstalk between two schools of thought: on the one extreme there are the enthusiasts, who point to the very powerful and sophisticated results that can be obtained with computers. It is easy, they assert, to develop a management information system. If only a particular piece of hardware is purchased or software applied, you are well on the way to achieving tremendous progress. There has unquestionably been a great deal of overzealousness, and overselling, but at the other extreme lies undue disillusion. There are people who say: "This is all baloney. There really is no such thing as a management information system, it is a sort of chimera. We must be more practical and abandon these grandiose concepts." And management has been caught in the middle.

Also contributing to management's difficulty in trying to understand information systems technology is the communications gap that frequently exists between the systems professionals in the company and the management people responsible for determining where the company is going in information systems. This communications gap has always existed, but it has become more evident now that it concerns systems that have an immediate impact on decision-making. These are foremost among the problems associated with the introduction of management information systems. While much has been accomplished in the technological sphere and in the refinement of important concepts, much remains to be done before these systems become operational on a broad scale. The challenges to be faced are many, and the exploitation of the technical tools now available will require the best efforts of systems professionals, coupled with an unprecedented level of management support.

DORWIN CARTWRIGHT
RONALD LIPPITT

Group Dynamics and the Individual

How should we think of the relation between individuals and groups? Few questions have stirred up so many issues of metaphysics, epistemology, and ehtics. Do groups have the same reality as individuals? If so, what are the properties of groups? Can groups learn, have goals, be frustrated, develop, regress, begin and end? Or are these characteristics strictly attributable only to individuals? If groups exist, are they good or bad? How *should* an individual behave with respect to groups? How *should* groups treat their individual members? Such questions have puzzled man from the earliest days of recorded history.

In our present era of "behavioral science" we like to think that we can be "scientific" and proceed to study human behavior without having to take sides on these problems of speculative philosophy. Invariably, however, we are guided by certain assumptions, stated explicitly or not, about the reality or irreality of groups, about their observability, and about their good or bad value.

Usually these preconceptions are integral parts of one's personal and

Source: *International Journal of Group Psychotherapy*, Vol. 7 (January 1957), pp. 86-102. Reprinted by permission of the authors and International Universities Press.

scientific philosophy, and it is often hard to tell how much they derive from emotionally toned personal experiences with other people and how much from coldly rational and "scientific" considerations. In view of the fervor with which they are usually defended, one might suspect that most have a small basis at least in personally significant experiences. These preconceptions, moreover, have a tendency to assume a homogeneous polarization—either positive or negative.

Consider first the completely negative view. It consists of two major assertions: first, groups don't really exist. They are a product of distorted thought processes (often called "abstractions"). In fact, social prejudice consists precisely in acting as if groups, rather than individuals, were real. Second, groups are bad. They demand blind loyalty, they make individuals regress, they reduce man to the lowest common denominator, and they produce what *Fortune* magazine has immortalized as "group-think."

In contrast to this completely negative conception of groups, there is the completely positive one. This syndrome, too, consists of two major assertions: first, groups really do exist. Their reality is demonstrated by the difference it makes to an individual whether he is accepted or rejected by a group and whether he is part of a healthy or sick group. Second, groups are good. They satisfy deep-seated needs of individuals for affiliation, affection, recognition, and self-esteem; they stimulate individuals to moral heights of altruism, loyalty, and self-sacrifice; they provide a means, through cooperative interaction, by which man can accomplish things unattainable through individual enterprise.

This completely positive preconception is the one attributed most commonly, it seems, to the so-called "group dynamics movement." Group dynamicists, it is said, have not only *reified* the group but also *idealized* it. They believe that everything should be done by and in groups—individual responsibility is bad, man-to-man supervision is bad, individual problem-solving is bad, and even individual therapy is bad. The only good things are committee meetings, group decisions, group problem-solving, and group therapy. "If you don't hold the group in such high affection," we were once asked, "why do you call your research organization the Research Center *for* Group Dynamics? And, if you are *for* groups and group dynamics, mustn't you therefore be *against* individuality, individual responsibility, and self-determination?"

Five Propositions about Groups

This assumption that individuals and groups must necessarily have incompatible interests is made so frequently in one guise or another that it requires closer examination. Toward this end we propose five related assertions about individuals, groups, and group dynamics, which are intended to challenge the belief that individuals and groups must necessarily have incompatible, or for that matter, compatible interests.

1. Groups do exist; they must be dealt with by any man of practical affairs, or indeed by any child, and they must enter into any adequate account of human behavior. Most infants are born into a specific group. Little Johnny may be a welcome or unwelcome addition to the group. His presence may produce profound changes in the structure of the group and consequently in the feelings, attitudes, and behavior of various group members. He may create a triangle where none existed before or he may break up one which has existed. His development and adjustment for years to come may be deeply influenced by the nature of the group he enters and by his particular position in it—whether, for example, he is a first or second child (a personal property which has no meaning apart from its reference to a specific group).

There is a wealth of research whose findings can be satisfactorily interpreted only by assuming the reality of groups. Recall the experiment of Lewin, Lippitt, and White (15) in which the level of aggression of an individual was shown to depend upon the social atmosphere and structure of the group he is in and not merely upon such personal traits as aggressiveness. By now there can be little question about the kinds of results reported from the Western Electric study (18) which make it clear that groups develop norms for the behavior of their members with the result that "good" group members adopt these norms as their *personal* values. Nor can one ignore the dramatic evidence of Lewin, Bavelas, and others (14) which shows that group decisions may produce changes in individual behavior much larger than those customarily found to result from attempts to modify the behavior of individuals *as* isolated individuals.

2. Groups are inevitable and ubiquitous. The biological nature of man, his capacity to use language, and the nature of his environment which has been built into its present form over thousands of years require that man exist in groups. This is not to say that groups must maintain the properties they now display, but we cannot conceive of a collection of human beings living in geographical proximity under conditions where it would be correct to assert that no groups exist and that there is no such thing as group membership.

3. Groups mobilize powerful forces which produce effects of the utmost importance to individuals. Consider two examples from rather different research settings. Seashore (22) has recently published an analysis of data from 5,871 employees of a large manufacturing company. An index of group cohesiveness, developed for each of 228 work groups, permitted a comparison of members working in high and in low cohesive groups. Here is one of his major findings: "Members of high cohesive groups exhibit less anxiety than members of low cohesive groups, using as measures of anxiety: (a) feeling 'jumpy' or 'nervous,' (b) feeling under pressure to achieve higher productivity (with actual productivity held constant), and (c) feeling a lack of support from the company" (p.98). Seashore suggests two reasons for the relation between group cohesiveness and individual anxiety: "(1) that the cohesive group provides effective support for the individual in his encounters with anxiety-provoking aspects of his environment, thus allaying anxiety, and

(2) that group membership offers direct satisfaction, and this satisfaction in membership has a generalized effect of anxiety-reduction" (p. 13). Perhaps a more dramatic account of the powerful forces generated in groups can be derived from the publication by Stanton and Schwartz (24) of their studies of a mental hospital. They report, for example, how a patient may be thrown into an extreme state of excitement by disagreements between two staff members over the patient's care. Thus, two doctors may disagree about whether a female patient should be moved to another ward. As the disagreement progresses, the doctors may stop communicating relevant information to one another and start lining up allies in the medical and nursing staff. The patient, meanwhile, becomes increasingly restless until, at the height of the doctors' disagreement, she is in an acute state of excitement and must be secluded, put under sedation, and given special supervision. Presumably, successful efforts to improve the interpersonal relations and communications among members of the staff would improve the mental condition of such a patient.

In general, it is clear that events occurring in a group may have repercussions on members who are not directly involved in these events. A person's position in a group, moreover, may affect the way others behave toward him and such personal qualities as his levels of aspiration and self-esteem. Group membership itself may be a prized possession or an oppressive burden: tragedies of major proportions have resulted from the exclusion of individuals from groups, and equally profound consequences have stemmed from enforced membership in groups.

4. Groups may produce both good and bad consequences. The view that groups are completely good and the view that they are completely bad are both based on convincing evidence. *The only fault with either is its one-sidedness.* Research motivated by one or the other is likely to focus on different phenomena. As an antidote to such one-sidedness it is a good practice to ask research questions in pairs, one stressing positive aspects and one negative: What are the factors producing conformity? *and* what are the factors producing nonconformity? What brings about a breakdown in communication? *and* what stimulates or maintains effective communication? An exclusive focus on pathologies or upon positive criteria leads to a seriously incomplete picture.

5. A correct understanding of group dynamics permits the possibility that desirable consequences from groups can be deliberately enhanced. Through a knowledge of group dynamics, groups can be made to serve better ends, for knowledge gives power to modify human beings and human behavior. At the same time, recognition of this fact produces some of the deepest conflicts within the behavioral scientist, for it raises the whole problem of social manipulation. Society must not close its eyes to Orwell's horrible picture of life in 1984, but it cannot accept the alternative that in ignorance there is safety.

To recapitulate our argument: groups exist; they are inevitable and ubiquitous; they mobilize powerful forces having profound effects upon individuals; these effects may be good or bad; and through a knowledge of group dynamics there lies the possibility of maximizing their good value.

A Dilemma

Many thoughtful people today are alarmed over one feature of groups: the pressure toward conformity experienced by group members. Indeed, this single "bad" aspect is often taken as evidence that groups are bad in general. Let us examine the specific problem of conformity, then, in order to attain a better understanding of the general issue. Although contemporary concern is great, it is not new. More than one hundred years ago Alexis de Tocqueville wrote: "I know of no country in which there is so little independence of mind and real freedom of discussion as in America. . . . In America the majority raises formidable barriers around the liberty of opinion. . . . The master (majority) no longer says: 'You shall think as I do or you shall die'; but he says: 'You are free to think differently from me and to retain your life, your property, and all that you possess, but they will be useless to you, for you will never be chosen by your fellow citizens if you solicit their votes; and they will affect to scorn you if you ask for their esteem. You will remain among men, but you will be deprived of the rights of mankind. Your fellow creatures will shun you like an impure being; and even those who believe in your innocence will abandon you, lest they should be shunned in their turn' " (25, pp. 273-75).

Before too readily accepting such a view of groups as the whole story, let us invoke our dictum that research questions should be asked in pairs. Nearly everyone is convinced that individuals should not be blind conformers to group norms, that each group member should not be a carbon copy of every other member, but what is the other side of the coin? In considering why members of groups conform, perhaps we should also think of the consequences of the removal of individuals from group membership or the plight of the person who really does not belong to any group with clear-cut norms and values. The state of anomie, described by Durkheim, is also common today. It seems as if people who have no effective participation in groups with clear and strong value systems either crack up (as in alcoholism or suicide) or they seek out groups which will demand conformity. In discussing this process, Talcott Parsons writes: "In such a situation it is not surprising that large numbers of people should . . . be attracted to movements which can offer them membership in a group with a vigorous esprit de corps with submission to some strong authority and rigid system of belief, the individual thus finding a measure of escape from painful perplexities or from a situation of anomie" (17, pp. 128-29).

The British anthropologist, Adam Curle, has stressed the same problem when he suggested that in our society we need not four, but five freedoms, the fifth being freedom from that neurotic anxiety which springs from a man's isolation from his fellows, and which, in turn, isolates him still further from them.

We seem, then, to face a dilemma: the individual needs social support for his values and social beliefs; he needs to be accepted as a valued member of some group which *he* values; failure to maintain such group membership produces anxiety and personal disorganization. But, on the other hand, group membership and group participation tend to cost the individual his individuality. If he is to receive support from others and, in turn, give support to others, he and they must hold in common some values and beliefs. Deviation from these undermines the possibility of group support and acceptance.

Is there an avenue of escape from this dilemma? Certainly, the issue is not as simple as we have described it. The need for social support for some values does not require conformity with respect to all values, beliefs, and behavior. Any individual is a member of several groups, and he may be a successful deviate in one while conforming to another (think of the visitor in a foreign country or of the psychologist at a convention of psychiatrists). Nor should the time dimension be ignored; a person may sustain his deviance through a conviction that his fate is only temporary. These refinements of the issue are important and should be examined in great detail, but before we turn our attention to them, we must assert that we do *not* believe that the basic dilemma can be escaped. To avoid complete personal disorganization man must conform to at least a minimal set of values required for participation in the groups to which he belongs.

Pressures to Uniformity

Some better light may be cast on this problem if we refer to the findings of research on conformity. What do we know about the way it operates?

COGNITIVE PROCESSES

Modern psychological research on conformity reflects the many different currents of contemporary psychology, but the major direction has been largely determined by the classic experiment of Sherif (23) on the development of social norms in perceiving autokinetic movement and by the more recent study of Asch (1) of pressures to conformity in perceiving unambiguous visual stimuli.

What does this line of investigation tell us about conformity? What has it revealed, for instance, about the conditions that set up pressures to conformity? Answers to this question have taken several forms, but nearly all point out that social interaction would be impossible if some beliefs and perceptions were not commonly shared by the participants. Speaking of the origin of such cognitive pressures to uniformity among group members, Asch says: "The individual comes to experience a world that he shares with others. He perceives that the surroundings include him, as well as others, and that he is in the same relation to the surroundings as others. He notes that he, as well as others, is converging upon the same object and responding to its identical properties. Joint action and mutual understanding require this relation of intelligibility and structural simplicity. In these terms the 'pull' toward the group becomes understandable" (1, p. 484).

Consistent with this interpretation of the origin of pressures to uniformity in a perceptual or judgmental situation are the findings that the major variables influencing tendencies to uniformity are (a) the quality of the social evidence (particularly the degree of unanimity of announced perceptions and the subject's evaluation of the trustworthiness of the other's judgments), (b) the quality of the direct perceptual evidence (particularly the clarity or ambiguity of the stimuli), (c) the magnitude of the discrepancy between the social and the perceptual evidence, and (d) the individual's self-confidence in the situation (as indicated either by experimental manipulations designed to affect self-confidence or by personality measurements).

The research in this tradition has been productive, but it has emphasized the individual and his cognitive problems and has considered the individual apart from any concrete and meaningful group membership. Presumably any trustworthy people adequately equipped with eyes and ears could serve to generate pressures to conformity in the subject, regardless of his specific relations to them. The result of this emphasis has been to ignore certain essential aspects of the conformity problem. Let us document this assertion with two examples.

First, the origin of pressures to uniformity has been made to reside in the person whose conformity is being studied. Through eliminating experimentally any possibility that pressures might be exerted by others, it has been possible to study the conformity of people as if they existed in a world where they can see or hear others but not be reacted to by others. It is significant, indeed, that conformity does arise in the absence of direct attempts to bring it about. But this approach does not raise certain questions about the conditions which lead to *social* pressures to conformity. What makes some people try to get them to conform? The concentration of attention on the conformer has diverted attention away from the others in the situation who may insist on conformity and make vigorous efforts to bring it about or who may not exert any pressures at all on deviates.

A second consequence of this emphasis has been to ignore the broader social meaning of conformity. Is the individual's personal need for a social validation of his beliefs the only reason for conforming? What does deviation do to a person's acceptance by others? What does it do to his ability to influence others? Or, from the group's point of view, are there reasons to insist on certain common values, beliefs, and behavior? These questions are not asked nor answered by an approach which limits itself to the cognitive problems of the individual.

GROUP PROCESSES

The group dynamics orientation toward conformity emphasizes a broader range of determinants. Not denying the importance of the cognitive situation, we want to look more closely at the nature of the individual's relation to particular groups with particular properties. In formulating hypotheses about the origin of pressures to uniformity, two basic sources have been stressed. These have been stated most clearly by Festinger and his co-workers (5), who propose that when differences of opinion arise within a group, pressures to uniformity will arise (a) if the validity or "reality" of the opinion depends upon agreement with the group (essentially the same point as Asch's), or (b) if locomotion toward a group goal will be facilitated by uniformity within the group.

This emphasis upon the group, rather than simply upon the individual, leads one to expect a broader set of consequences from pressures to uniformity. Pressures to uniformity are seen as establishing: (a) a tendency on the part of each group member to change his own opinion to conform to that of the other group members, (b) a tendency to try to change the opinions of others, and (c) a tendency to redefine the boundaries of the group so as to exclude those holding deviate opinions. The relative magnitudes of these tendencies will depend on other conditions which need to be specified.

This general conception of the nature of the processes that produce conformity emerged from two early field studies conducted at the Research Center for Group Dynamics. It was also influenced to a considerable extent by the previous work of Newcomb (16) in which he studied the formation and change of social attitudes in a college community. The first field study, reported by Festinger, Schachter and Back (7), traced the formation of social groups in a new student housing project. As each group developed, it displayed its own standards for its members. The extent of conformity to the standards of a particular group was found to be related directly to the degree of cohesiveness of that group as measured by sociometric choices. Moreover, those individuals who deviated from their own group's norms received fewer sociometric choices than those who conformed. A process of rejection for nonconformity had apparently set in. The second field study, reported by Coch and French (3), observed similar processes. This study was conducted in a textile factory and was concerned with conformity to production standards set by groups of workers. Here an individual worker's reaction to new work methods was found to depend upon the standards of his group and, here too, rejection for deviation was observed.

The next phase of this research consisted of a series of experiments with groups created in the laboratory. It was hoped thereby to be able to disentangle the complexity of variables that might exist in any field setting in order to understand better the operations of each. These experiments have been reported in various publications by Festinger, Back, Gerard, Hymovitch, Kelley, Raven, Schachter, and Thibaut (2, 6, 8, 9, 11, 20). We shall not attempt to describe these studies in detail, but draw upon them and other research in an effort to summarize the major conclusions.

First, a great deal of evidence has been accumulated to support the hypothesis that pressures to uniformity will be greater the more members want to remain in the group. In more attractive or cohesive groups, members attempt more to influence others and are more willing to accept influence from others. Note that here pressures to conformity are high in the very conditions where satisfaction from group membership is also high.

Second, there is a close relation between attempts to deviate and tendencies to reject him. If persistent attempts to change the deviate fail to produce conformity, then communication appears to cease between the majority and the deviate, and rejection of the deviate sets in. These two processes, moreover, are more intense the more cohesive the group. One of the early studies which documented the process of rejection was conducted by Schachter (20) on college students. It has recently been replicated by Emerson (4) on high school students, who found essentially the same process at work, but he discovered that among his high school students efforts to influence others continued longer, there was a greater readiness on the part of the majority to change, and there was a lower level of rejection within a limited period of time. Yet another study, conducted in Holland, Sweden, France, Norway, Belgium, Germany, and England, found the same tendency to reject deviates in all of these countries. This study, reported by Schachter, et al. (21), is a landmark in cross-cultural research.

Third, there is the question of what determines whether or not pressures to uniformity will arise with respect to any particular opinion, attitude, and behavior. In most groups there are no pressures to uniformity concerning the color of necktie worn by the members. Differences of opinion about the age of the earth probably would not lead to rejection in a poker club, but they might do so in certain fundamentalist church groups. The concept of *relevance* seems to be required to account for such variations in pressures to uniformity. And, if we ask, "relevance for what?" we are forced again to look at the group and especially at the goals of the group.

Schachter (20) has demonstrated, for example, that deviation on a given issue will result much more readily in rejection when the issue is relevant to the group's goals than when it is irrelevant. And the principle of relevance seems to be necessary to account for the findings of a field study reported by Ross (19). Here attitudes of fraternity men toward restrictive admission policies were studied. Despite the fact that there was a consistent policy of exclusion in these fraternities, there was, surprisingly, little evidence for the existence of pressures toward uniformity of attitudes. When, however, a field experiment was conducted in which the distribution of actual opinions for each fraternity house was reported to a meeting of house members together with a discussion of the relevance of these opinions for fraternity policy, attitudes then tended to change to conform to the particular model position of each house. Presumably the experimental treatment made uniformity of attitude instrumental to group locomotion where it had not been so before.

Sources of Heterogeneity

We have seen that pressures to uniformity are stronger the more cohesive the group. Shall we conclude from this that strong, need-satisfying, cohesive groups must always produce uniformity on matters that are important to the group? We believe not. We cannot, however, cite much convincing evidence since research has focused to date primarily upon the sources of pressures to uniformity and has ignored the conditions which produce heterogeneity. Without suggesting, then, that we can give final answers, let us indicate some of the possible sources of heterogeneity.

GROUP STANDARDS ABOUT UNIFORMITY

It is important, first, to make a distinction between conformity and uniformity. A group might have a value that everyone should be as different from everyone else as possible. Conformity to this value, then, would result not in uniformity of behavior but in nonuniformity. Such a situation often arises in therapy groups or training groups where it is possible to establish norms which place a high value upon "being different" and upon tolerating deviant behavior. Conformity to this value is presumably greater the more cohesive the group and the more it is seen as relevant to the group's objectives. Unfortunately, very little is known about the origin and operation of group standards about conformity itself. We doubt that the pressure to uniformity which arises from the need for "social reality" and for group locomotion can simply be obliterated by invoking a group standard of tolerance, but a closer look at such processes as those of group decision-making will be required before a deep understanding of this problem can be achieved.

FREEDOM TO DEVIATE

A rather different source of heterogeneity has been suggested by Kelley and Shapiro (12). They reason that the more an individual feels accepted by the other members of the group, the more ready he should be to deviate from the beliefs of the majority under conditions where objectively correct deviation would be in the group's best interest. They designed an experiment to test this hypothesis. The results, while not entirely clear because acceptance led to greater cohesiveness, tend to support this line of reasoning.

It has been suggested by some that those in positions of leadership are freer to deviate from group standards than are those of lesser status. Just the opposite conclusion has been drawn by others. Clearly, further research into group properties which generate freedom to deviate from majority pressures is needed.

SUBGROUP FORMATION

Festinger and Thibaut (8) have shown that lower group-wide pressures to uniformity of opinion result when members of a group perceive that the group is composed of persons differing in interest and knowledge. Under these conditions subgroups may easily develop with a resulting heterogeneity within the group as a whole though with Asch's (1) finding that the presence of a partner for a deviate greatly strengthens his tendency to be independent. One might suspect that such processes, though achieving temporarily a greater heterogeneity, would result in a schismatic subgroup conflict.

POSITIONS AND ROLES

A more integrative achievement of heterogeneity seems to arise through the process of role differentiation. Established groups are usually differentiated according to "positions" with special functions attached to each. The occupant of the position has certain behaviors prescribed for him by the others in the group. These role prescriptions differ, moreover, from one position to another, with the result that conformity to them produces heterogeneity within the group. A group function, which might otherwise be suppressed by pressures to uniformity, may be preserved by the establishment of a position whose responsibility is to perform the function.

Hall (10) has recently shown that social roles can be profitably conceived in the context of conformity to group pressures. He reasoned that pressures to uniformity of prescriptions concerning the behavior of the occupant of a position and pressures on the occupant to conform to these prescriptions should be greater the more cohesive the group. A study of the role of aircraft commander in bomber crews lends strong support to this conception.

In summary, it should be noted that in all but one of these suggested sources of heterogeneity we have assumed the process of conformity—to the norms of a subgroup, to a role, or to a group standard favoring heterogeneity. Even if the price of membership in a strong group be conformity, it need not follow that strong groups will suppress differences.

More Than One Group

Thus far our analysis has proceeded as though the individual were a member of only one group. Actually we recognize that he is, and has been, a member of many groups. In one of our current research projects we are finding that older adolescents can name from twenty to forty "important groups and persons that influence my opinions and behavior in decision situations." Indeed, some personality theorists hold that personality should be viewed as an "internal society" made up of representations of the diverse group relationships which the individual now has and has had. According to this view, each individual has a unique internal society and makes his own personal synthesis of the values and behavior preferences generated by these affiliations.

The various memberships of an individual may relate to one another in various ways and produce various consequences for the individual. A past group may exert internal pressures toward conformity which are in conflict with a present group. Two contemporaneous groups may have expectations for the person which are incompatible. Or an individual may hold a temporary membership (the situation of a foreign student, for example) and be faced with current conformity pressures which if accepted will make it difficult to readjust when returning to his more permanent memberships.

This constant source of influence from other memberships toward deviancy of every member of every group requires that each group take measures to preserve its integrity. It should be noted, however, that particular deviancy pressures associated with a given member may be creative or destructive when evaluated in terms of the integrity and productivity of the group, and conformity pressures from the group may be supportive or disruptive of the integrity of the individual.

Unfortunately there has been little systematic research on these aspects of multiple group membership. We can only indicate two sets of observations concerning (a) the intrapersonal processes resulting from multiple membership demands, and (b) the effects on group processes of the deviancy pressures which arise from the multiple membership status of individual members.

MARGINAL MEMBERSHIP

Lewin (13), in his discussion of adolescence and of minority group membership, has anlyzed some of the psychological effects on the person of being "between two groups" without a firm anchorage in either one. He says: "The transition from childhood to adulthood may be a rather sudden shift (for instance, in some of the primitive societies), or it may occur gradually in a setting where children and adults are not sharply separated groups. In the case of the so-called 'adolescent difficulties,' however, a third state of affairs is often

prevalent: children and adults consitute two clearly defined groups; the adolescent does not wish any longer to belong to the children's group and, at the same
time, knows that he is not really accepted in the adult group. He has a position
similar to what is called in sociology the 'marginal man' . . . a person who stands
on the boundary between two groups. He does not belong to either of them, or
at least he is not sure of his belongingness in either of them" (p. 143). Lewin
goes on to point out that there are characteristic maladjustive behavior patterns
resulting from this unstable membership situation: high tension, shifts between
extremes of behavior, high sensitivity, and rejection of low status members of
both groups. This situation, rather than fostering strong individuality, makes
belonging to closely knit, loyalty-demanding groups very attractive. Dependency
and acceptance are a welcome relief. Probably most therapy groups have a
number of members who are seeking relief from marginality.

OVERLAPPING MEMBERSHIP

There is quite a different type of situation where the person does have a
firm anchorage in two or more groups but where the group standards are not
fully compatible. Usually the actual conflict arises when the person is physically
present in one group but realizes that he also belongs to other groups to which
he will return in the near or distant future. In this sense, the child moves
between his family group and his school group every day. The member of a
therapy group has some sort of time perspective of "going back" to a variety of
other groups between each meeting of the therapy group.

In their study of the adjustment of foreign students both in this country
and after returning home, Watson and Lippitt (26) observed four different ways
in which individuals cope with this problem of overlapping membership.

1. Some students solved the problem by "living in the present" at all times.
When they were in the American culture all of their energy and attention
was directed to being an acceptable member of this group. They avoided
conflict within themselves by minimizing thought about and contact with
the other group "back home." When they returned to the other group they
used the same type of solution, quickly shifting behavior and ideas to fit
back into the new present group. Their behavior appeared quite inconsistent, but it was a consistent approach to solving their problem of multiple
membership.
2. Other individuals chose to keep their other membership the dominant
one while in this country. They were defensive and rejective every time the
present group seemed to promote values and to expect behavior which they
felt might not be acceptable to the other group "back home." The strain of
maintaining this orientation was relieved by turning every situation into a
"black and white" comparison and adopting a consistently rejective posture
toward the present, inferior group. This way of adjusting required a con-

siderable amount of distorting of present and past realities, but the return to the other group was relatively easy.

3. Others reacted in a sharply contrasting way by identifying whole-heartedly with the present group and by rejecting the standards of the other group as incorrect or inferior at the points of conflict. They were, of course, accepted by the present group, but when they returned home they met rejection or felt alienated from the standards of the group (even when they felt accepted).

4. Some few individuals seemed to achieve a more difficult but also more creative solution. They attempted to regard membership in both groups as desirable. In order to succeed in this effort, they had to be more realistic about perceiving the inconsistencies between the group expectations and to struggle to make balanced judgments about the strong and weak points of each group. Besides taking this more objective approach to evaluation, these persons worked on problems of how the strengths of one group might be interpreted and utilized by the other group. They were taking roles of creative deviancy in both groups, but attempting to make their contributions in such a way as to be accepted as loyal and productive members. They found ways of using each group membership as a resource for contributing to the welfare of the other group. Some members of each group were of course threatened by this readiness and ability to question the present modal ways of doing things in the group.

Thus it seems that the existence of multiple group memberships creates difficult problems both for the person and for the group. But there are also potentialities and supports for the development of creative individuality in this situation, and there are potentialities for group growth and achievement in the fact that the members of any group are also members of other groups with different standards.

Some Conclusions

Let us return now to the question raised at the beginning of this paper. How should we think of the relation between individuals and groups? If we accept the assumption that individuals and groups are both important social realities, we can then ask a pair of important questions. What kinds of effects do groups have on the emotional security and creative productivity of the individual? What kinds of effects do individuals have on the morale and creative productivity of the group? In answering these questions it is important to be alerted to both good and bad effects. Although the systematic evidence from research does not begin to provide full answers to these questions, we have found evidence which tends to support the following general statements.

Strong groups do exert strong influences on members toward conformity.

These conformity pressures, however, may be directed toward uniformity of thinking and behavior, or they may foster heterogeneity.

Acceptance of these conformity pressures, toward uniformity or heterogeneity, may satisfy the emotional needs of some members and frustrate others. Similarly, it may support the potential creativity of some members and inhibit that of others.

From their experiences of multiple membership and their personal synthesis of these experiences, individuals do have opportunities to achieve significant bases of individuality.

Because each group is made up of members who are loyal members of other groups and who have unique individual interests, each group must continuously cope with deviancy tendencies of the members. These tendencies may represent a source of creative improvement in the life of the group or a source of destructive disruption.

The resolution of these conflicting interests does not seem to be the strengthening of individuals and the weakening of groups, or the strengthening of groups and the weakening of individuals, but rather a strengthening of both by qualitative improvements in the nature of interdependence between integrated individuals and cohesive groups.

References

1. Asch, S. E., *Social Psychology*. Englewood Cliffs, N.J.: Prentice-Hall, Inc., 1952.
2. Back, K. W., "Influence through Social Communication," *J. Abn. & Soc. Psychol.,* 46 (1951), pp. 9-23.
3. Coch, L. and J. R. P. French, "Overcoming Resistance to Change," *Hum. Relat.,* 1 (1948), 512-32.
4. Emerson, R. M., "Deviation and Rejection: An Experimental Replication," *Am. Sociol. Rev.,* 19 (1954), pp. 688-93.
5. Festinger, L., "Informal Social Communication," *Psychol. Rev.,* 57 (1950), 271-92.
6. Festinger L., H. B. Gerard, B. Hymovitch, H. H. Kelley, and B. Raven, "The Influence Process in the Presence of Extreme Deviates," *Hum. Relat.,* 5 (1952), 327-46.
7. Festinger L., S. Schachter, and K. Back, *Social Pressures in Informal Groups.* New York: Harper & Row, Publishers, 1950.
8. Festinger, L. and J. Thibaut, "Interpersonal Communication in Small Groups," *J. An. & Soc. Psychol.,* 46 (1951), pp. 92-99.
9. Gerard, H. B., "The Effect of Different Dimensions of Disagreement on the Communication Process in Small Groups," *Hum. Relat.,* 6 (1953), 249-71.

10. Hall, R. L., "Social Influence on the Aircraft Commander's Role," *Am. Sociol. Rev.*, 20 (1955), 292-99.

11. Kelley, H. H., "Communication in Experimentally Created Hierarchies," *Hum. Relat.*, 4 (1951), 39-56.

12. Kelley, H. H. and M. M. Shapiro "An Experiment on Conformity to Group Norms Where Conformity is Detrimental to Group Achievement," *Am. Sociol. Rev.*, 19 (1954), 667-77.

13. Lewin, K., *Field Theory in Social Science.* New York: Harper & Row, Publishers, 1951.

14. Lewin, K., "Studies in Group Decision," *Group Dynamics: Research and Theory*, ed. D. Cartwright and A. Zander. Evanston, Ill.: Row, Peterson, 1953.

15. Lewin, K., R. Lippitt, and R. White, "Patterns of Aggressive Behavior in Experimentally Created 'Social Climates.' " *J. Soc. Psychol.*, 10:271-99, 1939.

16. Newcomb, T. M., *Personality and Social Change.* New York: Dryden, 1943.

17. Parsons, T., *Essays in Sociological Theory*, rev. ed. Glencoe: Free Press, 1954.

18. Roethlisberger, F. J. and W. J. Dickson, *Management and the Worker.* Cambridge: Harvard University Press, 1939.

19. Ross, I., "Group Standards Concerning the Admission of Jews," *Soc. Prob.*, 2 (1955), 133-40.

20. Schachter, S., "Deviation, Rejection, and Communication," *J. Abn. & Soc. Psychol.*, 46 (1951), 190-207.

21. Schachter, S., *et al.*, "Cross-cultural Experiments on Threat and Rejection," *Hum. Relat.*, 7 (1954), 403-39.

22. Seashore, S. E., *Group Cohesiveness in the Industrial Group.* Ann Arbor, Mich.: Institute for Social Research, 1954.

23. Sherif, M., *The Psychology of Social Norms.* New York: Harper & Row, Publishers, 1936.

24. Stanton, A. H., and M. S. Schwartz, *The Mental Hospital.* New York: Basic Books, 1954.

25. de Tocqueville, A., *Democracy in America*, Vol. 1. New York: Alfred A. Knopf, 1945 (original publication, 1835).

26. Watson, J. and R. Lippitt, *Learning across Cultures.* Ann Arbor, Mich.: Institute for Social Research, 1955.

DAVID MECHANIC

Sources of Power of
Lower Participants in
Complex Organizations

It is not unusual for lower participants[1] in complex organizations to assume and wield considerable power and influence not associated with their formally defined positions within these organizations. In sociological terms they have considerable personal power but no authority. Such personal power is often attained, for example, by executive secretaries and accountants in business firms, by attendants in mental hospitals, and even by inmates in prisons. The personal power achieved by these lower participants does not necessarily result from unique personal characteristics, although these may be relevant, but results rather from particular aspects of their location within their organizations.

Source: David Mechanic, "Sources of Power of Lower Participants in Complex Organizations," *Administrative Science Quarterly,* Vol. 7, No. 3 (December, 1962), pp. 349-364. Reprinted with permission.

[1]The term "Lower participants" comes from Amitai Etzioni, *A Comparative Analysis of Complex Organizations* (New York, 1961) and is used by him to designate persons in positions of lower rank: employees, rank-and-file, members, clients, customers, and inmates. We shall use the term in this paper in a relative sense denoting position vis-a-vis a higher-ranking participant.

Informal Versus Formal Power

Within organizations the distribution of authority (institutionalized power) is closely if not perfectly correlated with the prestige of positions. Those who have argued for the independence of these variables[2] have taken their examples from diverse organizations and do not deal with situations where power is clearly comparable.[3] Thus when Bierstedt argues that Einstein had prestige but no power, and the policeman power but no prestige, it is apparent that he is comparing categories that are not comparable. Generally persons occupying high-ranking positions within organizations have more authority than those holding low-ranking positions.

One might ask what characterizes high-ranking positions within organizations. What is most evident, perhaps, is that lower participants recognize the right of higher-ranking participants to exercise power, and yield without difficulty to demands they regard as legitimate. Moreover, persons in high-ranking positions tend to have considerable access and control over information and persons both within and outside the organization, and to instrumentalities or resources. Although higher supervisory personnel may be isolated from the task activities of lower participants, they maintain access to them through formally established intermediary positions and exercise control through intermediary participants. There appears, therefore, to be a clear correlation between the prestige of positions within organizations and the extent to which they offer access to information, persons, and instrumentalities.

Since formal organizations tend to structure lines of access and communication, access should be a clue to institutional prestige. Yet access depends on variables other than those controlled by the formal structure of an organization, and this often makes the informal power structure that develops within organizations somewhat incongruent with the formally intended plan. It is these variables that allow work groups to limit production through norms that contravene the goals of the larger organization, that allow hospital attendants to thwart changes in the structure of a hospital, and that allow prison inmates to exercise some control over prison guards. Organizations, in a sense, are continuously at the mercy of their lower participants, and it is this fact that makes organizational power structure especially interesting to the sociologist and social psychologist.

CLARIFICATION OF DEFINITIONS

The purpose of this paper is to present some hypotheses explaining why lower participants in organizations can often assume and wield considerable

---

[2]Robert Bierstedt, An Analysis of Social Power, *American Sociological Review* 15 (1950), 730-738.

[3]Robert A. Dahl, The Concept of Power, *Behavioral Science,* 2 (1957), 201-213.

power which is not associated with their positions as formally defined within these organizations. For the purposes of this analysis the concepts "influence," "power," and "control" will be used synonymously. Moreover, we shall not be concerned with type of power, that is, whether the power is based on reward, punishment, identification, power to veto, or whatever.[4] Power will be defined as *any force that results in behavior that would not have occurred if the force had not been present.* We have defined power as a force rather than a relationship because it appears that much of what we mean by power is encompassed by the normative framework of an organization, and thus any analysis of power must take into consideration the power of norms as well as persons.

I shall also argue, following Thibaut and Kelley,[5] that power is closely related to dependence. To the extent that a person is dependent on another, he is potentially subject to the other person's power. Within organizations one makes others dependent upon him by controlling access to information, persons, and instrumentalities which I shall define as follows:

Information includes knowledge of the organization, knowledge about persons, knowledge of the norms, procedures, techniques, and so forth.

Persons include anyone within the organization or anyone outside the organization upon whom the organization is in some way dependent.

Instrumentalities include any aspect of the physical plant of the organization or its resources (equipment, machines, money, and so on). Power is a function not only of the extent to which a person controls information, persons, and instrumentalities, but also the importance of the various attributes he controls.[6]

Finally, following Dahl,[7] we shall agree that comparisons of power among persons should, as far as possible, utilize comparable units. Thus we shall strive for clarification by attempting to oversimplify organizational processes; the goal is to set up a number of hypothetical statements of the relationship between variables taken two at a time, "all other factors being assumed to remain constant." . . .

To state the hypothesis suggested, somewhat more formally:

Other factors remaining constant, organizational power is related to access to persons, information, and instrumentalities.

[4]One might observe, for example, that the power of lower participants is based primarily on the ability to "veto" or punish. For a discussion of bases of power, see John R. P. French, Jr., and Bertram Raven, "The Bases of Social Power," in D. Cartwright and A. Zander, eds., *Group Dynamics* (Evanston, Ill., 1960), pp. 607-623.

[5]John Thibaut and Harold H. Kelley, *The Social Psychology of Groups* (New York: 1959). For a similar emphasis on dependence, see Richard M. Emerson, Inter-Dependence Relationships, *American Sociological Review,* 27 (1962), 31-41.

[6]Although this paper will not attempt to explain how access may be measured, the author feels confident that the hypotheses concerned with access are clearly testable.

[7]*Op. cit.*

Other factors remaining constant, as a participant's length of time in an organization increases, he has increased access to persons, information, and instrumentalities.

While these hypotheses are obvious, they do suggest that a careful scrutiny of the organizational literature, especially that dealing with the power or counterpower of lower participants, might lead to further formalized statements, some considerably less obvious than the ones stated.

Sources of Power of Lower Participants

The most effective way for lower participants to achieve power is to obtain, maintain, and control access to persons, information, and instrumentalities. To the extent that this can be accomplished, lower participants make higher-ranking participants dependent upon them. Thus dependence together with the manipulation of the dependency relationship is the key to the power of lower participants.

A number of examples can be cited which illustrate the preceding point. Scheff, for example, reports on the failure of a state mental hospital to bring about intended reform because of the opposition of hospital attendants.[8] He noted that the power of hospital attendants was largely a result of the dependence of ward physicians on attendants. This dependence resulted from the physician's short tenure, his lack of interest in administration, and the large amount of administrative responsibility he had to assume. An implicit trading agreement developed between physicians and attendants, whereby attendants would take on some of the responsibilities and obligations of the ward physician in return for increased power in decision-making processes concerning patients. Failure of the ward physician to honor his part of the agreement resulted in information being withheld, disobedience, lack of cooperation, and unwillingness of the attendants to serve as a barrier between the physician and a ward full of patients demanding attention and recognition. When the attendant withheld cooperation, the physician had difficulty in making a graceful entrance and departure from the ward, in handling necessary paper work (officially his responsibility), and in obtaining information needed to deal adequately with daily treatment and behavior problems. When attendants opposed change, they could wield influence by refusing to assume responsibilities officially assigned to the physician.

Similarly, Sykes describes the dependence of prison guards on inmates and the power obtained by inmates over guards.[9] He suggests that although guards

[8]Thomas J. Scheff, Control over Policy by Attendants in a Mental Hospital, *Journal of Health and Human Behavior*, 2 (1961), 93-105.

[9]Gresham M. Sykes, "The Corruption of Authority and Rehabilitation," in A. Etzioni, ed., *Complex Organizations* (New York, 1961), pp. 191-97.

could report inmates for disobedience, frequent reports would give prison officials the impression that the guard was unable to command obedience. The guard, therefore, had some stake in ensuring the good behavior of prisoners without the use of formal sanctions against them. The result was a trading agreement whereby the guard allowed violations of certain rules in return for cooperative behavior. A similar situation is found in respect to officers in the Armed Services or foremen in industry. To the extent that they require formal sanctions to bring about cooperation, they are usually perceived by their superiors as less valuable to the organization. For a good leader is expected to command obedience, at least, if not commitment.

Factors Affecting Power

EXPERTISE

Increasing specialization and organizational growth has made the expert or staff person important. The expert maintains power because high-ranking persons in the organization are dependent upon him for his special skills and access to certain kinds of information. One possible reason for lawyers obtaining many high governmental offices is that they are likely to have access to rather specialized but highly important means to organizational goals.[10]

We can state these ideas in hypotheses, as follows:

H3 Other factors remaining constant, to the extent that a low-ranking participant has important expert knowledge not available to high-ranking participants, he is likely to have power over them.

Power stemming from expertise, however, is likely to be limited unless it is difficult to replace the expert. This leads to two further hypotheses:

H4 Other factors remaining constant, a person difficult to replace will have greater power than a person easily replaceable.

H5 Other factors remaining constant, experts will be more difficult to replace than nonexperts.

While persons having expertise are likely to be fairly high-ranking partici-pants in an organization, the same hypotheses that explain the power of lower participants are relevant in explaining the comparative power positions of intermediate- and high-ranking persons. . . .

[10]As an example, it appears that 6 members of the cabinet, 30 important subcabinet officials, 63 senators, and 230 congressmen are lawyers (*New Yorker,* April 14, 1962, p. 62). Although one can cite many reasons for lawyers holding political posts, an important one appears to be their legal expertise.

As a result of growing specialization, expertise is increasingly important in organizations. As the complexity of organizational tasks increases, and as organizations grow in size there is a limit to responsibility that can be efficiently exercised by one person. Delegation of responsibility occurs, experts and specialists are brought in to provide information and research, and the higher participants become dependent upon them. Experts have tremendous potentialities for power by withholding information, providing incorrect information, and so on, and to the extent that experts are dissatisfied, the probability of organizational sabotage increases.

EFFORT AND INTEREST

The extent to which lower participants may exercise power depends in part on their willingness to exert effort in areas where higher-ranking participants are often reluctant to participate. Effort exerted is directly related to the degree of interest one has in an area.

> *H6* Other factors remaining constant, there is a direct relationship between the amount of effort a person is willing to exert in an area and the power he can command.

For example, secretarial staffs in universities often have power to make decisions about the purchase and allocation of supplies, the allocation of their services, the scheduling of classes, and, at times, the disposition of student complaints. Such control may in some instances lead to sanctions against a professor by polite reluctance to furnish supplies, ignoring his preferences for the scheduling of classes, and giving others preference in the allocation of services. While the power to make such decisions may easily be removed from the jurisdiction of the lower participant, it can only be accomplished at a cost—the willingness to allocate time and effort to the decisions dealing with these matters. To the extent that responsibilities are delegated to lower participants, a certain degree of power is likely to accompany the responsibility. Also, should the lower participant see his perceived rights in jeopardy, he may sabotage the system in various ways.

Let us visualize a hypothetical situation where a department concludes that secretarial services are being allocated on a prejudicial basis as a result of complaints to the chairman of the department by several of the younger faculty. Let us also assume that, when the complaint is investigated, it is found to be substantially correct; that is, some of the younger faculty have difficulty obtaining secretarial services because of preferences among the secretarial staff. If in attempting to eliminate discretion by the secretarial staff, the chairman establishes a rule ordering the allocation of services on the basis of the order in which work appears, the rule can easily be made ineffective by complete conformity to it. Deadlines for papers, examinations, and the like will occur, and flexibility in the allocation of services is required if these deadlines are to be met. Thus the need for flexibility can be made to conflict with the rule by a staff usually not untalented in such operations.

When an organization gives discretion to lower participants, it is usually trading the power of discretion for needed flexibility. The cost of constant surveillance is too high, and the effort required too great; it is very often much easier for all concerned to allow the secretary discretion in return for cooperation and not too great an abuse of power.

> *H7* Other factors remaining constant, the less effort and interest higher-ranking participants are willing to devote to a task, the more likely are lower participants to obtain power relevant to this task.

ATTRACTIVENESS

Another personal attribute associated with the power of low-ranking persons in an organization is attractiveness or what some call "personality." People who are viewed as attractive are more likely to obtain access to persons, and, once such access is gained, they may be more likely to succeed in promoting a cause. But once again dependence is the key to the power of attractiveness, for whether a person is dependent upon another for a service he provides, or for approval or affection, what is most relevant is the relational bond which is highly valued.

> *H8* Other factors remaining constant, the more attractive a person, the more likely he is to obtain access to persons and control over these persons.

LOCATION AND POSITION

In any organization the person's location in physical space and position in social space are important factors influencing access to persons, information, and instrumentalities.[11] Propinquity affects the opportunities for interaction, as well as one's position within a communication network. Although these are some-

---

[11]There is considerable data showing the powerful effect of propinquity on communication. For summary, see Thibaut and Kelley, *op. cit.,* pp. 39-42.

what separate factors, we shall refer to their combined effect as centrality[12] within the organization.

> *H9* Other factors remaining constant, the more central a person is in an organization, the greater is his access to persons, information, and instrumentalities.

Some low participants may have great centrality within an organization. An executive's or university president's secretary not only has access, but often controls access in making appointments and scheduling events. Although she may have no great formal authority, she may have considerable power.

COALITIONS

It should be clear that the variables we are considering are at different levels of analysis: some of them define attributes of persons, while others define attributes of communication and organization. Power processes within organizations are particularly interesting in that there are many channels of power and ways of achieving it.

In complex organizations different occupational groups attend to different functions, each group often maintaining its own power structure within the organization. Thus hospitals have administrators, medical personnel, nursing personnel, attendants, maintenance personnel, laboratory personnel, and so on. Universities, similarly, have teaching personnel, research personnel, administrative personnel, maintenance personnel, and so on. Each of these functional tasks within organizations often becomes the sphere of a particular group that controls activities relating to the task. While these tasks usually are coordinated at the highest levels of the organization, they often are not coordinated at intermediate and lower levels. It is not unusual, however, for coalitions to form among lower participants in these multiple structures. A secretary may know the man who manages the supply of stores, or the person assigning parking stickers. Such acquaintances may give her the ability to handle informally certain needs that would be more time-consuming and difficult to handle formally. Her ability to provide services informally makes higher-ranking participants in some degree dependent upon her, thereby giving her power, which increases her ability to bargain on issues important to her.

---

[12]The concept of centrality is generally used in a more technical sense in the work of Bavelas, Shaw, Gilchrist, and others. For example, Bavelas defines the central region of a structure as the class of all cells with the smallest distance between one cell and any other cell in the structure, with distance measured in link units. Thus, the most central position in a pattern is the position closest to all others, Cf. Harold Leavitt, "Some Effects of Certain Communication Patterns on Group Performance," in E. Maccoby, T. N. Newcomb, and E. L. Hartley, eds., *Readings in Social Psychology* (New York, 1958), p. 559.

Rules

In organizations with complex power structures lower participants can use their knowledge of the norms of the organization to thwart attempted change. In discussing the various functions of bureaucratic rules, Gouldner maintains that such rules serve as excellent substitutes for surveillance, since surveillance in addition to being expensive in time and effort arouses considerable hostility and antagonism.[13] Moreover, he argues, rules are a functional equivalent for direct, personally given orders, since they specify the obligations of workers to do things in specific ways. Standardized rules, in addition, allow simple screening of violations, facilitate remote control, and to some extent legitimize punishment when the rule is violated. The worker who violates a bureaucratic rule has little recourse to the excuse that he did not know what was expected, as he might claim for a direct order. Finally, Gouldner argues that rules are "the 'chips' to which the company staked the supervisors and which they could use to play the game";[14] that is, rules established a punishment which could be withheld, and this facilitated the supervisors' bargaining power with lower participants.

While Gouldner emphasizes the functional characteristics of rules within an organization, it should be clear that full compliance to all the rules at all times will probably be dysfunctional for the organization. Complete and apathetic compliance may do everything but facilitate achievement of organizational goals. Lower participants who are familiar with an organization and its rules can often find rules to support their contention that they not do what they have been asked to do, and rules are also often a rationalization for inaction on their part. The following of rules becomes especially complex when associations and unions become involved, for there are then two sets of rules to which the participant can appeal.

What is suggested is that rules may be chips for everyone concerned in the game. Rules become the "chips" through which the bargaining process is maintained. Scheff, as noted earlier, observed that attendants in mental hospitals often took on responsibilities assigned legally to the ward physician, and when attendants refused to share these responsibilities the physician's position became extremely difficult.[15]

The ward physician is legally responsible for the care and treatment of each ward patient. This responsibility requires attention to a host of details. Medicine, seclusion, sedation and transfer orders, for example, require the doctor's signature. Tranquilizers are particularly troublesome in this regard since they require frequent adjustment of dosage in order to get the desired effects. The physician's

---

[13]Alvin W. Gouldner, *Patterns of Industrial Bureaucracy* (Glencoe, Ill., 1954).

[14]*Ibid.*, p. 173.

[15]Scheff, *op. cit.*

order is required to each change in dosage. With 150 patients under his care on tranquilizers, and several changes of dosages a week desirable, the physician could spend a major portion of his ward time in dealing with this single detail.

Given the time-consuming formal chores of the physician, and his many other duties, he usually worked out an arrangement with the ward personnel, particularly the charge (supervisory attendant), to handle these duties. On several wards, the charge called specific problems to the doctor's attention, and the two of them, in effect, would have a consultation. The charge actually made most of the decisions concerning dosage change in the back wards. Since the doctor delegated portions of his formal responsibilities to the charge, he was dependent on her good will toward him. If she withheld her cooperation, the physician had absolutely no recourse but to do all the work himself.[16]

In a sense such delegation of responsibility involves a consideration of reward and cost, whereby the decision to be made involves a question of what is more valuable—to retain control over an area, or to delegate one's work to lower participants.

There are occasions, of course, when rules are regarded as illegitimate by lower participants, and they may disregard them. Gouldner observed that, in the mine, men felt they could resist authority in a situation involving danger to themselves.[17] They did not feel that they could legitimately be ordered to do anything that would endanger their lives. It is probably significant that in extremely dangerous situations organizations are more likely to rely on commitment to work than on authority. Even within nonvoluntary groups dangerous tasks are regarded usually as requiring task commitment, and it is likely that commitment is a much more powerful organizational force than coercive authority.

Summary

The preceding remarks are general ones, and they are assumed to be in part true of all types of organizations. But power relationships in organizations are likely to be molded by the type of organization being considered, the nature of organizational goals, the ideology of organizational decision-making, the kind of commitment participants have to the organization, the formal structure of the organization, and so on. In short, we have attempted to discuss power processes within organizations in a manner somewhat divorced from other major organizational processes. We have emphasized variables affecting control of access to persons, information, and facilities within organizations. Normative definitions, perception of legitimacy, exchange, and coalitions have all been viewed in

[16]*Ibid.,* p. 97.
[17]Gouldner, *op. cit.*

relation to power processes. Moreover, we have dealt with some attributes of persons related to power: commitment, effort, interest, willingness to use power, skills, attractiveness, and so on. And we have discussed some other variables: time, centrality, complexity of power structure, and replaceability of persons. It appears that these variables help to account in part for power exercised by lower participants in organizations.

V

MANAGERIAL
ALTERNATIVE
FUTURES

Chapter:
The Manager as
an Adaptive Integrator

In trying to place the role and form of the manager in the future we must
first speculate on the organization of which he or she is a part. While no ultimate
agreement can be reached on an exact form of the future organization, some
agreement can be reached on what many feel will be the major characteristics of
future organizations. The weight given to each characteristic, not their identification, is the major forecasting problem. In this section we will briefly
summarize the consensus views of many authors on some of these characteristics: size, turbulence, performance measurement, and roles of individuals
and groups, and then try to place our view of the future manager in this
proposed future environment.

Organizations will tend to diffuse themselves toward both ends of the size
spectrum. The giants of today will continue to grow, though probably at a
slower rate, as will the current middle-size companies that survive. These giants
of the future will also take on more of a public image if not actually entering the
public sector. Administered and maintained corporate educational and medical
systems and facilities are currently appearing and corporate involvement in fire
protection and sanitation is not out of the reach of imagination. If not directly
entering the public sector all future giants will be more in the public light than

today, either by increased governmental regulation or increased activity of consumer-oriented "watchdog" committees. The future giant will also tend toward multinationality and conglomeration. Single or similar product firms, other than service organizations, will tend to disappear. Setting aside intermittent occurences of protectionism, the world will become the marketplace not only for goods and raw material resouces for the giant firm but also for its diversification and personnel resources. We will see multinational not international companies. At the other end of the size spectrum we will see the growth of the small firm, highly specialized in product, service, or technology. These will be drawn from those small firms that currently exist and from the profitable residue of our current medium-size firms which do not survive. These firms will thrive servicing both individuals whose environment has grown more complex and the giant firms whose desire for making and servicing all that they produce will wane. We will also see the growth of the individually owned craft/unusual commodity store as the trend toward self-actualization increases.

The increased availability of information and the exponential growth of technology will combine to make the future environment anything but static. Due to advanced technology and size, the complexity of the organization will grow. As the complexity increases, changes are bound to be more radical and occur more frequently. The growth of technology continues unabated and few forecast any appreciable decline in the rate of this growth. Rapid change in technology is synonymous with increased turbulence of the organization's environment. As computerized information systems become more common, huge masses of pertinent and impertinent data will be available throughout the organization. It is not only the amount of information but the phenomenal speed at which it will be available that will increase turbulence. Managers who had to wait weeks for data on which to make a decision will in the future have it in minutes. This will increase the number of decisions made per unit of time. Increased numbers of decisions almost always leads to increases in turbulence. Lastly, organizations will become more responsive to the needs and desires of the public. As these needs and desires change so will the organization and again turbulence will increase.

At this point in time, it is not clear whether profit is or is not an adequate measure of a firm's effectiveness and efficiency to society. What seems clear is that firms will adopt other measures of performance in the future and that these measures will be more highly correlated with social well-being. It is also thought that government will play a greater role in organizational goal-setting. This will come about through increased governmental control over environmental quality, workmen's compensation, and other standards, or by governmental regulation of the entire firm and thus its performance measure, as for utilities today, or the total incorporation of the firm into the government. Other suggestions call for a system of national social accounting rather than gross national product as a measure of the total performance of the economy, while others have suggested that a valid measure would be the percentage of the population in each level of Maslow's need hierarchy, with the national goal being to have as many people moving toward self-actualization as possible.

Scientific management and bureaucratic structures have governed the role of individuals and groups within organizations since the turn of this century. It is not clear whether these techniques will be able to sustain the organization as its environment becomes more turbulent. With the expected increase in turbulence, organizations will have to become more adaptive and their employees more innovative and creative. The need for a hierarchical structure will be reduced as tasks that require this organizational structure become automated. As technology advances, the specialists and professionals which develop, use, and service it will become more important. The rise in professionalism will tend to increase the conformity of the employees' goals and norms with those of their profession rather than with those of the organization.

Management of this dynamic, flexible, innovative organization of the future requires the manager to be an adaptive integrator. He must be adaptive, capable of changing as rapidly as the organization changes. But more important, he must be integrative. He will be surrounded by more highly trained individuals than he is today and certainly, due to increased professionalism, fewer "yes men." This will require his being able to organize different approaches to a specific task or problem. He will have the data to structure and analyze more problems per unit contributions of many diverse disciplines in organizing his approach to any problem. He will have the data to structure and analyze more problems per unit time and thus must be ready to make more decisions per unit time than ever before. He must also be prepared for the shorter time interval between decision and the results of that decision. To do this he will rely more and more on a staff to analyze problems and design implementation strategies. He must not be overwhelmed by the technical people around him, whether they be quantitative or behavioral; he must be able to integrate the contributions of these technicians in the fulfillment of his task.

Thus we see the future of management dependent on the training of managers to be adaptive integrators. We feel the materials of this book are a start toward that goal. The following readings enhance some of the points that we have stated briefly in this chapter.

F. E. EMERY

E. L. TRIST

Socio-Technical Systems

The analysis of the characteristics of enterprises as systems would appear to have strategic significance for furthering our understanding of a great number of specific industrial problems. The more we know about these systems the more we are able to identify what is relevant to a particular problem and to detect problems that tend to be missed by the conventional framework of problem analysis.

The value of studying enterprises as systems has been demonstrated in the empirical studies of Blau (4), Gouldner (6), Jacques (8), Selznick (15) and Lloyd Warner (21). Many of these studies have been informed by a broadly conceived concept of bureaucracy, derived from Weber and influenced by Parsons and Merton:

> They have found their main business to be in the analysis of a specific bureaucracy as a complex social system, concerned less with the individual differences of the actors than with the situationally shaped roles they perform (6).

F. E. Emery and E. L. Trist, "Socio-technical systems," in C. W. Churchman and M. Verhulst, eds., *Management Science, Models and Techniques,* vol. 2, Pergamon, 1960, pp. 83-97.

Granted the importance of system analysis there remains the important question of whether an enterprise should be construed as a "closed" or an "open system," i.e., relatively "closed" or "open" with respect to its external environment. Von Bertalanffy (3) first introduced this general distinction in contrasting biological and physical phenomena. In the realm of social theory, however, there has been something of a tendency to continue thinking in terms of a "closed" system, that is, to regard the enterprise as sufficiently independent to allow most of its problems to be analysed with reference to its internal structure and without reference to its external environment. Early exceptions were Rice and Trist (11) in the field of labor turnover and Herbst (7) in the analysis of social flow systems. As a first step, closed system thinking has been fruitful, in psychology and industrial sociology, in directing attention to the existence of structural similarities, relational determination and subordination of part to whole. However, it has tended to be misleading on problems of growth and the conditions for maintaining a "steady state." The formal physical models of "closed systems" postulate that, as in the second law of thermodynamics, the inherent tendency of such systems is to grow towards maximum homogeneity of the parts and that a steady state can only be achieved by the cessation of all activity. In practice, the system theorists in social science (and these include such key anthropologists as Radcliffe-Brown) refused to recognize these implications but instead, by the same token, did "*tend* to focus on the statics of social structure and to neglect the study of structural change" (10). In an attempt to overcome this bias, Merton suggested that "the concept of dysfunction, which implies the concept of strain, stress and tension on the structural level, provides an analytical approach to the study of dynamics and change" (10). This concept has been widely accepted by system theorists but while it draws attention to sources of imbalance within an organization it does not conceptually reflect the mutual permeation of an organization and its environment that is the cause of such imbalance. It still retains the limiting perspectives of "closed system" theorizing. In the administrative field the same limitations may be seen in the otherwise invaluable contributions of Barnard (2) and related writers.

The alternative conception of "open systems" carries the logical implications that such systems may spontaneously reorganize towards states of greater heterogeneity and complexity and that they achieve a "steady state" at a level where they can still do work. Enterprises appear to possess at least these characteristics of "open systems." They grow by processes of internal elaboration (7) and manage to achieve a steady state while doing work, i.e., achieve a quasi-stationary equilibrium in which the enterprise as a whole remains constant, with a continuous "*throughput,*" despite a considerable range of external changes (9, 11).

The appropriateness of the concept of "open system" can be settled, however, only by examining in some detail what is involved in an enterprise achieving a steady state. The continued existence of any enterprise presupposed some regular commerce in products or services with other enterprises, institutions and persons in its external social environment. If it is going to be useful to speak of steady states in an enterprise, they must be states in which this commerce is going on. The conditions for regularizing this commerce lie both within and without the enterprise. On the one hand, this presupposes that an enterprise has at its immediate disposal the necessary material supports for its activities—a workplace, materials, tools and machines—and a work force able and willing to make the necessary modifications in the material "throughput" or provide the requisite services. It must also be able, efficiently, to utilize its material supports and to organize the actions of its human agents in a rational and predictable manner. On the other hand, the regularity of commerce with the environment may be influenced by a broad range of independent external changes affecting markets for products and inputs of labour, materials and technology. If we examine the factors influencing the ability of an enterprise to maintain a steady state in the face of these broader environmental influences we find that:

1. The variation in the output markets that can be tolerated without structural change is a function of the flexibility of the technical productive apparatus—its ability to vary its rate, its end product or the mixture of its products. Variation in the output markets may itself be considerably reduced by the display of distinctive competence. Thus the output markets will be more attached to a given enterprise if it has, relative to other producers, a distinctive competence—a distinctive ability to deliver the right product to the right place at the right time.

2. The tolerable variation in the "input" markets is likewise dependent upon the technological component. Thus some enterprises are enabled by their particular technical organization to tolerate considerable variation in the type and amount of labour they can recruit. Others can tolerate little.

The two significant features of this state of affairs are:

1. That there is no simple one-to-one relation between variations in inputs and outputs. Depending upon the technological system, different combinations of inputs may be handled to yield similar outputs and different "product mixes" may be produced from similar inputs. As far as possible an enterprise will tend to do these things rather than make structural changes in its organization. It is one of the additional characteristics of "open systems" that while they are in constant commerce with the environment they are selective and, within limits, self-regulating.

2. That the technological component, in converting inputs into outputs, plays a major role in determining the self-regulating properties of an enterprise. It functions as one of the major boundary conditions of the social system of the enterprise in thus mediating between the ends of an enterprise

and the external environment. Because of this the materials, machines and territory that go to making up the technological component are usually defined, in any modern society, as "belonging" to an enterprise and excluded from similar control by other enterprises. They represent, as it were, an "internalized environment."

Thus the mediating boundary conditions must be represented among "the open system constants" (3) that define the conditions under which a steady state can be achieved. The technological component has been found to play a key mediating role and hence it follows that the open system concept must be referred to the socio-technical system, not simply to the social system of an enterprise.

It might be justifiable to exclude the technological component from the system concept if it were true, as many writers imply, that it plays only a passive and intermittent role. However, it cannot be dismissed as simply a set of limits that exert an influence at the initial stage of building an enterprise and only at such subsequent times as these limits are overstepped. There is, on the contrary, an almost constant accommodation of stresses arising from changes in the external environment; the technological component not only sets limits upon what can be done, but also in the process of accommodation creates demands that must be reflected in the internal organization and ends of an enterprise.

Study of a productive system therefore requires detailed attention to both the technological and the social components. It is not possible to understand these systems in terms of some arbitrarily selected single aspect of the technology such as the repetitive nature of the work, the coerciveness of the assembly conveyor or the piecemeal nature of the task. However, this is what is usually attempted by students of the enterprise. In fact:

It has been fashionable of late, particularly in the "human relations" school, to assume that the actual job, its technology, and its mechanical and physical requirements are relatively unimportant compared to the social and psychological situation of men at work (5).

Even when there has been a detailed study of the technology this has not been systematically related to the social system but been treated as background information (21).

In our earliest study of production systems in coal mining it became apparent that "so close is the relationship between the various aspects that the social and the psychological can be understood only in terms of the detailed engineering facts and of the way the technological system as a whole behaves in the environment of the underground situation" (19).

An analysis of a technological system in these terms can produce a systematic picture of the tasks and task interrelations required by a technological system. However, between these requirements and the social system there is not a strictly determined one-to-one relation but what is logically referred to as a correlative relation.

In a very simple operation such as manually moving and stacking railway sleepers ("ties") there may well be only a single suitable work relationship structure, namely, a co-operating pair with each man taking an end of the sleeper and lifting, supporting, walking and throwing in close co-ordination with the other man. The ordinary production process is much more complex and there it is unusual to find that only one particular work relationship structure can be fitted to these tasks.

This element of choice and the mutual influence of technology and the social system may both be illustrated from our studies, made over several years, of work organization in British deep-seam coal mining. The following data are adapted from Trist and Murray (20).

Thus Table 1 indicates the main features of two very different forms of organization that have both been operated economically within the same seam and with identical technology.

TABLE 1

Same Technology, Same Coal Seam, Different Social Systems

	A Conventional Cutting Longwall Mining System	A Composite Cutting Longwall Mining System
Number of men	41	41
Number of completely segregated task groups	14	1
Mean job variation for members:		
task groups worked with	1.0	5.5
main tasks worked	1.0	3.6
different shifts worked	2.0	2.9

The conventional system combines a complex formal structure with simple work roles: the composite system combines a simple formal structure with complex work roles. In the former the miner has a commitment to only a single part task and enters into only a very limited number of unvarying social relations that are sharply divided between those within his particular task group and those who are outside. With those "outside" he shares no sense of belongingness and he recognizes no responsibility to them for the consequences of his actions. In the composite system the miner has a commitment to the whole group task and consequently finds himself drawn into a variety of tasks in cooperation with different members of the total group; he may be drawn into any task on the coal-face with any member of the total group.

That two such contrasting social systems can effectively operate the same technology is clear enough evidence that there exists an element of choice in designing a work organization.

However, it is not a matter of indifference which form of organization is selected. As has already been stated, the technological system sets certain requirements of its social system and the effectiveness of the total production system will depend upon the adequacy with which the social system is able to cope with these requirements. Although alternative social systems may survive in that they are both accepted as "good enough" (17) this does not preclude the possibility that they may differ in effectiveness.

In this case the composite systems consistently showed a superiority over the conventional in terms of production and costs.

This superiority reflects, in the first instance, the more adequate coping in the composite system with the task requirements. The constantly changing underground conditions require that the already complex sequence of mining tasks undergo frequent changes in the relative magnitudes and even the order of these tasks. These conditions optimally require the internal flexibility possessed in varying degrees by the composite systems. It is difficult to meet variable task requirements with any organization built on a rigid division of labor. The only justification for a rigid division of labor is a technology which demands specialized nonsubstitute skills and which is, moreover, sufficiently superior, as a technology, to offset the losses due to rigidity. The conventional longwall cutting system has no such technical superiority over the composite to offset its relative rigidity—its characteristic inability to cope with changing conditions other than by increasing the stress placed on its members, sacrificing smooth cycle progress or drawing heavily upon the negligible labor reserves of the pit.

The superiority of the composite system does not rest alone in more adequate coping with the tasks. It also makes better provision to the personal

TABLE 2

Production and Costs for Different Forms of Work Organization with Same Technology

	Conventional	Composite
Productive achievements*	78	95
Ancillary work at face (hours per man-shift)	1.32	0.03
Average reinforcement of labor (percent of total face force)	6	—
Percent of shifts with cycle lag	69	5
Number consecutive weeks without losing a cycle	12	65

*Average percent of coal won from each daily cut, corrected for differences in seam transport.

requirements of the miners. Mutually supportive relations between task groups are the exception in the conventional system and the rule in the composite. In consequence, the conventional miner more frequently finds himself without support from his fellows when the strain or size of his task requires it. Crises are more likely to set him against his fellows and hence worsen the situation.

Similarly, the distribution of rewards and statuses in the conventional system reflects the relative bargaining power of different roles and task groups as much as any true differences in skill and effort. Under these conditions of disparity between effort and reward any demands for increased effort are likely to create undue stress.

The following table indicates the differences in stress experienced by miners in the two systems.

TABLE 3

Stress Indices for Different Social Systems

	Conventional	Composite
Absenteeism		
(percent of possible shifts)		
without reason	4.3	0.4
sickness or other	8.9	4.6
accidents	6.8	3.2
Total	20.0	8.2

These findings were replicated by experimental studies in textile mills in the radically different setting of Ahmedabad, India (12).

However, two possible sources of misunderstanding need to be considered:

1. Our findings do not suggest that work group autonomy should be maximized in all productive settings. There is an optimum level of grouping which can be determined only by analysis of the requirements of the technological system. Neither does there appear to be any simple relation between level of mechanization and level of grouping. In one mining study we found that in moving from a hand-filling to a machine-filling technology, the appropriate organization shifted from an undifferentiated composite system to one based on a number of partially segregated task groups with more stable differences in internal statuses.

2. Nor does it appear that the basic psychological needs being met by grouping are workers' needs for friendship on the job, as is frequently postulated by advocates of better "human relations" in industry. Grouping produces its main psychological effects when it leads to a system of work roles such that the workers are primarily related to each other by way of the requirements of task performance and task interdependence. When this task orientation is established the worker should find that he has an adequate range of mutually supportive roles (mutually supportive with respect to performance and to carrying stress that arises from the task). As the role

system becomes more mature and integrated, it becomes easier for a worker to understand and appreciate his relation to the group. Thus in the comparison of different composite mining groups it was found that the differences in productivity and in coping with stress were not primarily related to differences in the level of friendship in the groups. The critical prerequisites for a composite system are an adequate supply of the required special skills among members of the group and conditions for developing an appropriate system of roles. Where these prerequisites have not been fully met, the composite system has broken down or established itself at a less than optimum level. The development of friendship and particularly of mutual respect occurs in the composite systems but the friendship tends to be limited by the requirements of the system and not assume unlimited disruptive forms such as were observed in conventional systems and were reported by Adams (1) to occur in certain types of bomber crews.

The textile studies (12) yielded the additional finding that *supervisory roles* are best designed on the basis of the same type of socio-technical analysis. It is not enough simply to allocate to the supervisor a list of responsibilities for specific tasks and perhaps insist upon a particular style of handling men. The supervisory roles arise from the need to control and coordinate an incomplete system of men-task relations. Supervisory responsibility for the specific parts of such a system is not easily reconcilable with responsibility for overall aspects. The supervisor who continually intervenes to do some part of the productive work may be proving his willingness to work but is also likely to be neglecting his main task of controlling and coordinating the system so that the operators are able to get on with their jobs with the least possible disturbance.

Definition of a supervisory role presupposes analysis of the system's requirements for control and coordination and provision of conditions that will enable the supervisor readily to perceive what is needed of him and to take appropriate measures. As his control will in large measure rest on his control of the boundary conditions of the system—those activities relating to a larger system—it will be desirable to create "unified commands" so that the boundary conditions will be correspondingly easy to detect and manage. If the unified commands correspond to natural task groupings, it will also be possible to maximize the autonomous responsibility of the work group for internal control and coordination, thus freeing the supervisor for his primary task. A graphic illustration of the differences in a supervisory role following a socio-technical reorganization of an automatic loom shed (12) can be seen in the following two figures. Figure 1 represents the situation before and Figure 2 represents the situation after change.

This reorganization was reflected in a significant and sustained improvement in mean percentage efficiency and a decrease in mean percentage damage.

The significance of the difference between these two organizational diagrams does not rest only in the relative simplicity of the latter (although this

FIGURE 1

Management Hierarchy before Change

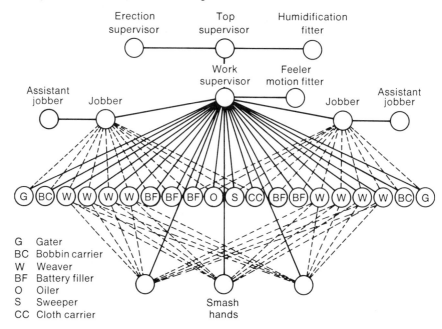

G   Gater
BC   Bobbin carrier
W   Weaver
BF   Battery filler
O   Oiler
S   Sweeper
CC   Cloth carrier

does reflect less confusion of responsibilities) but also in the emergence of clearly distinct areas of command which contain within themselves a relatively independent set of work roles together with the skills necessary to govern their task boundaries. In like manner the induction and training of new members was recognized as a boundary condition for the entire shed and located directly under shed management instead of being scattered throughout subordinate commands. Whereas the former organization had been maintained in a steady state only by the constant and arduous efforts of management, the new one proved to be inherently stable and self-correcting, and consequently freed management to give more time to their primary task and also to manage a third shift.

Similarly, the primary task in managing the enterprise as a whole is to relate the total system to its environment and is not in internal regulation *per se.* This does not mean that managers will not be involved in internal problems but that such involvement will be oriented consciously or unconsciously to certain assumptions about the external relations of the enterprise.

This contrasts with the common postulate of the structural—functional theories that "the basic need of all empirical systems is the maintenance of the integrity and continuity of the system itself" (14). It contrasts also with an

FIGURE 2

Management Hierarchy after Change

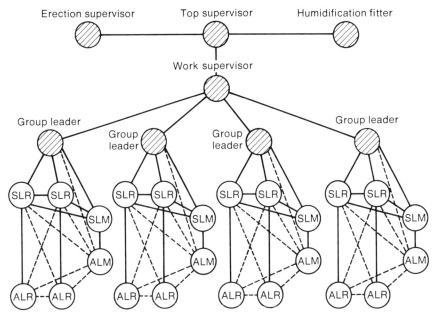

SLR Senior loom runner   SLM Senior loom maintenance
ALR Assistant loom runner   ALM Assistant loom maintenance

important implication of this postulate, namely, that the primary task of management is "continuous attention to the possibilities of encroachment and to the forestalling of threatened aggressions or deleterious consequences from the actions of others" (14). In industry this represents the special and limiting case of a management that takes for granted a previously established definition of its primary task and assumes that all they have to do, or can do, is sit tight and defend their market position. This is, however, the common case in statutorily established bodies and it is on such bodies that recent studies of bureaucracy have been largely carried out.

In general the leadership of an enterprise must be willing to break down an old integrity or create profound discontinuity if such steps are required to take advantage of changes in technology and markets. The very survival of an enterprise may be threatened by its inability to face up to such demands, as for instance, switching the main effort from production of processed goods to marketing or from production of heavy industrial goods to consumer goods. Similarly, the leadership may need to pay "continuous" attention to the possibilities of making their own encroachments rather than be obsessed with the possible encroachments of others.

Considering enterprises as "open socio-technical systems" helps to provide a more realistic picture of how they are both influenced by and able to act back on their environment. It points in particular to the various ways in which enterprises are enabled by their structural and functional characteristics ("system constants") to cope with the "lacks" and "gluts" in their available environment. Unlike mechanical and other inanimate systems they possess the property of "equifinality"; they may achieve a steady state from differing initial conditions and in differing ways (3). Thus in coping by internal changes they are not limited to simple quantitative change and increased uniformity but may, and usually do, elaborate new structures and take on new functions. The cumulative effect of coping mainly by *internal* elaboration and differentiation is generally to make the system independent of an increasing range of the predictable fluctuations in its supplies and outlets. At the same time, however, this process ties down in specific ways more and more of its capital, skill and energies and renders it less able to cope with newly emergent and unpredicted changes that challenge the primary ends of the enterprise. This process has been traced out in a great many empirical studies of bureaucracies (4, 10, 15).

However, there are available to an enterprise other aggressive strategies that seek to achieve a steady state by transforming the environment. Thus an enterprise has some possibilities for moving into new markets or inducing changes in the old, for choosing differently from among the range of personnel, resources and technologies offered by its environment or training and making new ones, and for developing new consumer needs or stimulating old ones.

Thus, arising from the nature of the enterprise as an open system, management is concerned with "managing" both an internal system and an external environment. To regard an enterprise as a closed system and concentrate upon management of the "internal enterprise" would be to expose the enterprise to the full impact of the vagaries of the environment.

If management is to control internal growth and development it must in the first instance control the "boundary conditions"—the forms of exchange between the enterprise and its environment. As we have seen most enterprises are confronted with a multitude of actual and possible exchanges. If resources are not to be dissipated the management must select from the alternatives a course of action. The casual texture of competitive environments is such that it is extremely difficult to survive on a simple strategy of selecting the best from among the alternatives immediately offering. Some that offer immediate gain lead nowhere, others lead to greater loss; some alternatives that offer loss are avoidable, others are unavoidable if long-run gains are to be made. The relative size of the immediate loss or gain is no sure guide as to what follows. Since also the actions of an enterprise can improve the alternatives that are presented to it, the optimum course is more likely to rest in selecting a strategic objective to be achieved in the long run. The strategic objective should be to place the enterprise in a position in its environment where it has some assured conditions for growth—unlike war the best position is not necessarily that of unchallenged monopoly. Achieving this position would be the *primary task* or overriding mission of the enterprise.

In selecting the primary task of an enterprise, it needs to be borne in mind that the relations with the environment may vary with: (a) the productive efforts of the enterprise in meeting environmental requirements, (b) changes in the environment that may be induced by the enterprise and (c) changes independently taking place in the environment. These will be of differing importance for different enterprises and for the same enterprises at different times. Managerial control will usually be greatest if the primary task can be based on productive activity. If this is not possible, as in commerce, the primary task will give more control if it is based on marketing than simply on foreknowledge of the independent environmental changes. Managerial control will be further enhanced if the primary task, at whatever level it is selected, is such as to enable the enterprise to achieve *vis-à-vis* its competitors, a *distinctive competence.* Conversely, in our experience, an enterprise which has long occupied a favored position because of distinctive productive competence may have grave difficulty in recognizing when it is losing control owing to environmental changes beyond its control.

As Selznick has pointed out (16), an appropriately defined primary task offers stability and direction to an enterprise, protecting it from adventurism or costly drifting. These advantages, however, as he illustrates (16), may be no more than potential unless the top management group of the organization achieves solidarity about the new primary task. If the vision of the task is locked up in a single man or the subject of dissension in top management it will be subject to great risk of distortion and susceptible to violent fluctuations. Similarly, the enterprise as a whole needs to be reoriented and reintegrated about this primary task. Thus, if the primary task shifts from heavy industrial goods to durable consumer goods it would be necessary to ensure that there is a corresponding shift in values that are embodied in such sections as the sales force and design department.

References

1. Adams, S. "Status congruency as a variable in small group performance," *Social Forces,* Vol. 32 (1953), pp. 16-22.
2. Barnard, C. I., *The Functions of the Executive.* Harvard University Press, 1948.
3. von Bertalanffy, L. "The theory of open systems in physics and biology," *Science,* Vol. III (1950), pp. 23-29.

4. Blau, P., *The Dynamics of Bureaucratic Structure: A Study of Interpersonal Relations in Two Government Agencies.* University of Chicago Press, 1955.

5. Drucker, P. F., "The Employee Society," *American Sociological Review,* Vol. 58 (1952), pp. 358-63.

6. Gouldner, A. W., *Patterns of Industrial Bureaucracy.* Routledge & Kegan Paul, 1955.

7. Herbst, P. G., "The analysis of social flow systems," *Human Relations,* Vol. 7 (1954), pp. 327-36.

8. Jacques, E., *The Changing Culture of a Factory.* Tavistock, 1951.

9. Lewin, K., *Field Theory in Social Science,* Harper, 1951.

10. Merton, R. K., *Social Theory and Social Structure.* Free Press, 1949.

11. Rice, A. K., and E. L. Trist, "Institutional and sub-institutional determinants of change in labour turnover (The Glacier Project—VIII)," *Human Relations,* Vol. 5 (1952), pp. 347-72.

12. Rice, A. K., *Productivity and Social Organization: The Ahmedabad Experiment.* Tavistock, 1958.

13. Schützenberger, M. P. "A tentative classification of goal-seeking behaviours," *Journal of Mental Science,* Vol. 100 (1954), pp. 97-102.

HERBERT A. SIMON

The Corporation: Will It Be Managed by Machines?

I don't know whether the title assigned to me was meant seriously or humorously. I shall take it seriously. During the past five years, I have been too close to machines—the kinds of machines known as computers, that is—to treat the question lightly. Perhaps I have lost my sense of humor and perspective about them.

My work on this paper has been somewhat impeded, in recent days, by a fascinating spectacle just outside my office window. Men and machines have been constructing the foundations of a small building. After some preliminary skirmishing by men equipped with surveying instruments and sledges for driving pegs, most of the work has been done by various species of mechanical elephant and their mahouts. Two kinds of elephants dug out the earth (one with its forelegs, the other with its trunk) and loaded it in trucks (pack elephants, I

Source: *Management and Corporations 1985* by Anshen and Bach, Copyright 1960, McGraw-Hill Book Company, Inc., pp. 17-55. In preparing this paper, I have drawn heavily on two previous essays written in collaboration with Allen Newell: "Heuristic Problem Solving: the Next Advance in Operations Research," *Operations Research,* 6:1-10, January-February 1958; and "What Have Computers to Do With Management?" in G. P. Shultz and T. L. Whisler (eds.), *Proceedings of the McKinsey Seminar,* 1959.

suppose). Then, after an interlude during which another group of men carefully fitted some boards into place as forms, a new kind of elephant appeared, its belly full of concrete which it disgorged into the forms. It was assisted by two men with wheelbarrows—plain, old-fashioned, man-handled wheelbarrows—and two or three other men who fussily tamped the poured concrete with metal rods. Twice during this whole period a shovel appeared—on one occasion it was used by a man to remove dirt that had been dropped on a sidewalk; on another occasion it was used to clean a trough down which the concrete slid.

Here, before me, was a sample of automated, or semiautomated production. What did it show about the nature of present and future relations of man with machine in the production of goods and services? And what lessons that could be learned from the automation of manufacturing and construction could be transferred to the problems of managerial automation? I concluded that there were two good reasons for beginning my analysis with a careful look at factory and office automation. First, the business organization in 1985 will be a highly automated man-machine system, and the nature of management will surely be conditioned by the character of the system being managed. Second, perhaps there are greater similarities than appear at first blush among the several areas of potential automation—blue-collar, clerical, and managerial. Perhaps the automated executive of the future has a great deal in common with the automated worker or clerk whom we can already observe in many situations today.

First, however, we must establish a framework and a point of view. Our task is to forecast the changes that will take place over the next generation in the job of the manager. It is fair to ask: Which manager? Not everyone nor every job will be affected in the same way; indeed, most persons who will be affected are not even managers at the present time. Moreover, we must distinguish the gross effects of a technological change, occurring at the point of impact at that change, from the net effects, the whole series of secondary ripples spreading from that point of initial impact.

Many of the initial effects are transitory—important enough to those directly involved at the time and place of change, but of no lasting significance to the society. Other effects are neither apparent nor anticipated when the initial change takes place but flow from it over a period of years through the succession of reactions it produces. Examples of both transient and indirect effects of change come to mind readily enough—e.g., the unemployment of blacksmiths and the appearance of suburbia, respectively, as effects of the automobile.

Since our task is to look ahead twenty-five years, I shall say little about the transient effects of the change in the job of the manager. I do not mean to discount the importance of these effects to the people they touch. In our time we are highly conscious of the transient effects, particularly the harmful ones, the displacements of skill and status. We say less of the benefit to those who acquire the new skills or of the exhilaration that many derive from erecting new structures.

Of course, the social management of change does not consist simply in balancing beneficial transient effects against harmful ones. The simplest moral reasoning leads to a general rule for the introduction of change: The general society which stands to benefit from the change should pay the major costs of introducing it and should compensate generously those who would otherwise be harmed by it. A discussion of the transient effects of change would have to center on ways of applying that rule. But that is not the problem we have to deal with here.

Our task is to forecast the long-run effects of change. First of all, we must predict what is likely to happen to the job of the individual manager, and to the activity of management in the individual organization. Changes in these patterns will have secondary effects on the occupational profile in the economy as a whole. Our task is to picture the society after it has made all these secondary adjustments and settled down to its new equilibrium.

Let me now indicate the general plan I shall follow in my analysis. In the first section, "Predicting Long-run equilibrium," I shall identify the key factors—the causes and the conditions of change—that will mold the analysis. Then I shall show how a well-known tool of economic analysis—the doctrine of comparative advantage—permits us to draw valid inferences from these causes and conditions. In the second section, "The New Technology of Information Processing," I shall describe the technological innovations that have appeared and are about to appear in the areas of production and data processing, and I shall use this material to draw a picture of the business organization in 1985, with particular attention to the automation of blue-collar and clerical work. In the third section, "The Automation of Management," I shall consider more specifically the role of the manager in the future business organization. In the final section, "The Broader Significance of Automation," I shall try to identify some of the important implications of these developments for our society and for ourselves as members of it.

Predicting Long-Run Equilibrium

To predict long-run equilibrium, one must identify two major aspects of the total situation: (1) the variables that will change autonomously and inexorably—the "first causes," and (2) the constant, unchanging "givens" in the situation, to which the other variables must adjust themselves. These are the hammer and the anvil that beat out the shape of the future. The accuracy of our predictions will depend less upon forecasting exactly the course of change than upon assessing correctly which factors are the unmoved movers and which the equally unmoved invariants. My entire forecast rests on my identification of this hammer and this anvil.

THE CAUSES OF CHANGE

The growth in human knowledge is the primary factor that will give the system its direction—in particular, that will fix the boundaries of the technologically feasible. The growth in real capital is the major secondary factor in change—within the realm of what is technologically feasible, it will determine what is economical.

The crucial area of expansion of knowledge is not hard to predict, for the basic innovations—or at least a large part of them—have already occurred and we are now rapidly exploiting them. The new knowledge consists in a fundamental understanding of the processes of thinking and learning or, to use a more neutral term, of complex information processing. We can now write programs for electronic computers that enable these devices to think and learn.[1] This knowledge is having, and will have, practical impacts in two directions: (1) because we can now simulate in considerable detail an important and increasing part of the processes of the human mind, we have available a technique of tremendous power for psychological research; and (2) because we can now write complex information-processing programs for computers, we are acquiring the technical capacity to replace humans with computers in a rapidly widening range of "thinking" and " deciding" tasks.

Closely allied to the development of complex information-processing techniques for general-purpose computers is the rapid advance in the technique of automating all sorts of production and clerical tasks. Putting these two lines of development together, I am led to the following general predictions: Within the very near future—much less than twenty-five years—we shall have the *technical* capability of substituting machines for any and all human functions in organizations. Within the same period, we shall have acquired an extensive and empirically tested theory of human cognitive processes and their interaction with human emotions, attitudes, and values.

To predict that we will have these technical capabilities says nothing of how we shall use them. Before we can forecast that, we must discuss the important invariants in the social system.

THE INVARIANTS

The changes that our new technical capability will bring about will be governed, particularly in the production sphere, by two major fixed factors in the society. Both of these have to do with the use of human resources for production.

---

[1]For documentation of this claim, see "The Nearly Automatic Factory and Office," pp. 26ff.

1. Apart from transient effects of automation, the human resources of the society will be substantially fully employed. *Full employment* does not necessarily mean a forty-hour week, for the allocation of productive capacity between additional goods and services and additional leisure may continue to change as it has in the past. *Full employment* means that the opportunity to work will be available to virtually all adults in the society and that, through wages or other allocative devices, the product of the economy will be distributed widely among families.

2. The distribution of intelligence and ability in the society will be much as it is now, although a substantially larger percentage of adults (perhaps half or more) will have completed college educations.

These assumptions—of capability of automation, accompanied by full employment and constancy in the quality of the human resources—provide us with a basis for characterizing the change. We cannot talk about the technological unemployment it may create, for we have assumed that such unemployment is a transient phenomenon—that there will be none in the long run. But the pattern of occupations, the profile showing the relative distribution of employed persons among occupations, may be greatly changed. It is the change in this profile that will measure the organizational impact of the technological change.

The change in the occupational profile depends on a well-known economic principle, the doctrine of comparative advantage. It may seem paradoxical to think that we can increase the productivity of mechanized techniques in all processes without displacing men somewhere. Won't a point be reached where men are less productive than machines in *all* processes, hence economically unemployable?[2]

The paradox is dissolved by supplying a missing term. Whether man or machines will be employed in a particular process depends not simply on their relative productivity in physical terms but on their cost as well. And cost depends on price. Hence—so goes the traditional argument of economics—as technology changes and machines become more productive, the prices of labor and capital will so adjust themselves as to clear the market of both. As much of each will be employed as offers itself at the market price, and the market price will be proportional to the marginal productivity of that factor. By the operation of the market place, manpower will flow to those processes in which its productivity is comparatively high relative to the productivity of machines; it will leave those processes in which its productivity is comparatively low. The comparison is not with the productivities of the past, but among the productivities in different processes with the currently available technology.

---

[2] The difficulty that laymen find with this point underlies the consistent failure of economists to win wide general support for the free trade argument. The central idea—that comparative advantage, not absolute advantage, counts—is exactly the same in the two cases.

I apologize for dwelling at length on a point that is clearly enough stated in the *Wealth of Nations*. My excuse is that contemporary discussion of technological change and automation still very often falls into error through not applying the doctrine of comparative advantage correctly and consistently.

We conclude that human employment will become smaller relative to the total labor force in those kinds of occupations and activities in which automatic devices have the greatest comparative advantage over humans; human employment will become relatively greater in those occupations and activities in which automatic devices have the least comparative advantage.[3]

Thus, if computers are a thousand times faster than bookkeepers in doing arithmetic, but only one hundred times faster than stenographers in taking dictation, we shall expect the number of bookkeepers per thousand employees to decrease but the number of stenographers to increase. Similarly, if computers are a hundred times faster than executives in making investment decisions, but only ten times faster in handling employee grievances (the quality of the decisions being held constant), then computers will be employed in making investment decisions, while executives will be employed in handling grievances.

The New Technology of Information Processing

The automation of manufacturing processes is a natural continuation and extension of the Industrial Revolution. We have seen a steady increase in the amount of machinery employed per worker. In the earlier phases of mechanization, the primary function of machinery was to replace human energy with mechanical energy. To some extent in all phases, and to a growing extent in recent developments, another goal has been to substitute mechanical for human sensing and controlling activities. Those who distinguish the newer "automation" from the older "mechanization" stress our growing ability to replace with machines simple human perceiving, choosing, and manipulating processes.

---

[3] I am oversimplifying, for there is another term in this equation. With a general rise in productivity and with shifts in relative prices due to uneven technological progress in different spheres, the demands for some kinds of goods and services will rise more rapidly than the demands for others. Hence, other things being equal, the total demand will rise in those occupations (of men and machines) that are largely concerned with producing the former, more rapidly than in occupations concerned largely with producing the latter. I have shown elsewhere how all these mechanisms can be handled formally in analyzing technological change. See "Productivity and the Urban-Rural Population Balance," in *Models of Man.*, John Wiley & Sons, Inc.,: New York, 1957, chap. 12; and "Effects of Technological Change in a Linear Model," in T. Koopmans (ed.), *Activity Analysis of Production and Allocation,* John Wiley & Sons,Inc.: New York, 1951, chap. 15; see also pp. 7-8.

THE NEARLY AUTOMATIC FACTORY AND OFFICE

The genuinely automatic factory—the workerless factory that can produce output and perhaps also, within limits, maintain and repair itself—will be technically feasible long before our twenty-five years have elapsed. From very unsystematic observation of changes going on in factories today, one might surmise that the typical factory of 1985 will not, however, be fully automatic. More likely the typical factory will have reached, say, the level of automaticity that has been attained in 1960 by the most modern oil refineries or power-generating stations.

The same kinds of technical developments that lead toward the automatic factory are bringing about an even more rapid revolution—and perhaps eventually a more complete one—in large-scale clerical operations. The very abstract nature of symbol manipulation facilitates the design of equipment to do it, and the further automation of clerical work is impeded by fewer technical barriers than the further automation of factory production. We can conjecture that by 1985 the departments of a company concerned with major clerical functions—accounting, processing of customers' orders, inventory and production control, purchasing, and the like—will have reached an even higher level of automation than most factories.

Both the factory and the office, then, are rapidly becoming complex man-machine systems with a very large amount of production equipment, in the case of the factory, and computing equipment, in the case of the office, per employee. The clerical department and the factory will come more and more to resemble each other. The one will present the picture of a small group of employees operating (I am tempted to use the more accurate phrase collaborating with) a large computing system; the other, the picture of a similar small group of employees operating a large production system. The interrelation of man with machine will become quite as important a design problem for such systems as the interrelation of man with man.

Now we must not commit the error I warned against in discussing the doctrine of comparative advantage. When we foresee fewer employees in factory and office, we mean fewer per unit of output and fewer per unit of capital equipment. It does not follow that there will be fewer in total. To predict the occupational profile that will result, we must look more closely at the prospective rates of automation in different occupations.

Before we turn to this task, however, it is worth reporting a couple of the lessons that are currently being learned in factory and clerical automation:

1. Automation does not mean "dehumanizing" work. On the contrary, in most actual instances of recent automation jobs were made, on the whole, more pleasant and interesting, as judged by the employees themselves, than

they had beeñ before. In particular, automation may move more and more in the direction of eliminating the machine-paced assembly line task and the repetitive clerical task. It appears generally to reduce the "work-pushing," "man-driving," and "expediting" aspects of first-line supervision.

2. Contemporary automation does not generally change to an important extent the profile of skill levels among the employees. It perhaps calls, on the average, for some upgrading of skills in the labor force, but conflicting trends are observable at different stages in automation.[4]

THE OCCUPATIONAL PROFILE

To predict the occupational distribution of the employed population in 1985, we would have to go down the list of occupations and assess, for each, the potentialities of automation. Even if we could do this, our inferences would not be quite direct. For we also have to take into account (1) income elasticity of demand—the fact that as productivity rises, the demands for some goods and services will rise more rapidly than the demands for others; (2) price elasticity of demand—the fact that the most rapidly automated activities will also show the greatest price reductions, so that the net reduction in employment in these activities will be substantially less than the gross reduction at a constant level of production.

As a fanciful example, let us consider the number of persons engaged in the practice of psychiatry. It is reasonable to assume that the demand for psychiatric services, at constant prices, will increase more than proportionately with an increase in income. Hence, the income effect of the general increase in a society's productivity will be to increase the proportion of psychiatrists in the employed population. Now, let us suppose that a specific technological development permits the automation of psychiatry itself, so that one psychiatrist can do the work formerly done by ten.[5] It is not at all clear whether a 90 percent reduction in price of psychiatric services would increase the demand for those services by a factor of more or less than ten. But if the demand increased by a factor of more than ten, the proportion of persons employed in psychiatry would actually increase.

Thus prediction of the occupational profile depends on estimates of the income and price elasticity of demand for particular goods and services as well as estimates of relative rates of increase in productivity. This is not the only

---

[4]I think I have fairly summarized the conclusions reached by those few observers who have looked in detail at actual cases of recent automation. Two exellent references are James R. Bright, *Automation and Management,* (Boston: Harvard University Graduate School of Business Administration, 1958); and S. Lilley, *Automation and Social Progress* (New York: International Publishers Co., Inc., 1957).

[5]This example will seem entirely fanciful only to persons not aware of some of the research now going on into the possible automation of psychiatric processes.

difficulty the forecaster faces. He must also be extremely cautious in his assumptions as to what is, and what is not, likely to be automated. In particular, automation is not the only way to reduce the cost of a process—a more effective way is to eliminate it. An expert in automation would tell you that the garbage collector's job is an extremely difficult one to automate (at any reasonable cost) in a straightforward way. It has, of course, simply been eliminated in many communities by grinding the garbage and transporting it in liquid through the sewerage system. Such Columbus-egg solutions of the production problem are not at all rare, and will be an important part of automation.[6]

ANOTHER APPROACH TO PREDICTION

With all these reservations and qualifications is any prediction possible? I think it is, but I think it requires us to go back to some fundamentals. The ordinary classification of occupations is basically an "end-use" classification—it indicates what social function is performed by each occupation. To understand automation, we must begin our classification of human activities at the other end—what basic capacities does the human organism bring to tasks, capacities that are used in different proportions for different tasks?

Viewed as a resource in production, a man is a pair of eyes and ears, a brain, a pair of hands, a pair of legs, and some muscles for applying force. Automation proceeds in two ways: (1) by providing mechanized means for performing some of the functions formerly performed by a man and (2) by eliminating some of these functions. Moreover, the mechanized means that replace the man can be of a general-purpose character (like the man) or highly specialized.

The steam engine and the electric motor are relatively general-purpose substitutes for muscles. A butter-wrapping machine is a special-purpose substitute for a pair of hands which eliminates some eye-brain activities the human butter-wrapper would require. A feedback system for controlling the temperature of a chemical process is a special-purpose substitute for eyes, brain, and hands. A digital computer employed in preparing a payroll is a relatively general-purpose substitute for eyes, brain, and hands. A modern multitool milling machine is a special-purpose device that eliminates many of the positioning (eye-brain-hand) processes that were formerly required in a sequence of machining operations.

The earlier history of mechanization was characterized by: (1) rapid substitution of mechanical energy for muscles; (2) partial and spotty introduction of special-purpose devices that performed simple, repetitive eye-brain-

---

[6]I advise the reader, before he makes up his mind as to what is feasible and infeasible, likely and unlikely, to try out his imagination on a sample of occupations, e.g., dentist, waitress, bond salesman, chemist, carpenter, college teacher.

hand sequences; (3) elimination, by mechanizing transport and by coordinating sequences of operations on a special-purpose basis, of many human eye-brain-hand sequences that had previously been required.

Thus, man's comparative advantage in energy production has been greatly reduced in most situations—to the point where he is no longer a significant source of power in our economy. He has been supplanted also in performing many relatively simple and repetitive eye-brain-hand sequences. He has retained his greatest comparative advantage in: (1) the use of his brain as a flexible general-purpose problem-solving device, (2) the flexible use of his sensory organs and hands, and (3) the use of his legs, on rough terrain as well as smooth, to make this general-purpose sensing-thinking-manipulating system available wherever it is needed.

This picture of man's functions in a man-machine system was vividly illustrated by the construction work going on outside my window. Most of the energy for earth-digging was being supplied by the mechanical elephants, but each depended on its mahout for eyes and (if you don't object to my fancy) for eye-trunk coordination. The fact that the elephant was operating in rough, natural terrain made automation of the mahout a difficult, although by no means insoluble, technical problem. It would almost certainly not now be economical. But other men—the men with wheelbarrows particularly—were performing even more "manual" and "primitive" tasks. Again, the delivery of the concrete to the forms could have been much more fully automated, but at a high cost. The men provided a flexible, if not very powerful, means for delivering small quantities of concrete to a number of different points over uneven terrain.

"Flexibility" and general-purpose applicability is the key to most spheres where the human has a comparative advantage over the machine. This raises two questions:

1. What are the prospects for matching human flexibility in automatic devices?
2. What are the prospects for matching humans in particular activities by reducing the need for flexibility?

The second question has been a familiar one throughout the history of mechanization; the first alternative is more novel.

FLEXIBILITY IN AUTOMATA

We must consider separately the sensory organs, the manipulatory organs, the locomotive organs, and the central nervous system. Duplicating the problem-solving and information handling capabilities of the brain is not far off; it would be surprising if it were not accomplished within the next decade. But these capabilities are so much involved in management activity that we shall have to discuss them at length in a later section.

We are much further from replacing the eyes, the hands, and the legs. From an economic as well as a technological standpoint, I would hazard the guess that automation of a flexible central nervous system will be feasible long before automation of a comparably flexible sensory, manipulative, or locomotive system. I shall state later my reasons for thinking this.

If these conjectures are correct, we may expect (other things being equal) automation of thinking and symbol-manipulating functions to proceed more rapidly than the automation of the more complex eye-brain-hand sequences. But before we grasp this conclusion too firmly, we need to remove one assumption.

ENVIRONMENTAL CONTROL, A SUBSTITUTE FOR FLEXIBILITY

If we want an organism or mechanism to behave effectively in a complex and changing environment, we can design into it adaptive mechanisms that allow it to respond flexibly to the demands the environment places on it. Alternatively, we can try to simplify and stabilize the environment. We can adapt organism to environment or environment to organism.

Both processes have been significant in biological evolution. The development of the multicellular organism may be interpreted as simplifying and stabilizing the environment of the internal cells by insulating them from the complex and variable external environment in which the entire organism exists. This is the significance of homeostasis in evolution—that in a very real sense it adapts the environment to the organism (or the elementary parts of the organism) and hence avoids the necessity of complicating the individual parts of the organism.

Homeostatic control of the environment (the environment, that is, of the individual worker or the individual machine) has played a tremendous role in the history of mechanization and in the history of occupational specialization as well. Let me cite some examples that show how all-pervasive this principle is:

1. The smooth road provides a constant environment for the vehicle—eliminating the advantages of flexible legs.

2. The first step in every major manufacturing sequence (steel, textiles, wood products) reduces a highly variable natural substance (metallic ore, fiber, trees) to a far more homogeneous and constant material (pig iron, thread, boards, or pulp). All subsequent manufacturing processes are thus insulated from the variability of the natural material. The application of the principle of interchangeable parts performs precisely the same function for subsequent manufacturing steps.

3. By means of transfer machines, work in process in modern automated lines is presented to successive machine tools in proper position to be

grasped and worked, eliminating the sensory and manipulative functions of workers who formerly loaded such tools by hand.

We see that mechanization has more often proceeded by eliminating the need for human flexibility—replacing rough terrain with a smooth environment—than by imitating it. Now homeostatic control of the environment tends to be a cumulative process. When we have mechanized one part of a manufacturing sequence, the regularity and predictiveness secured from this mechanization generally facilitates the mechanization of the next stage.

Let us apply this idea to the newly mechanized data-processing area. One of the functions that machines perform badly at present, humans rather well, is reading printed text. Because of the variability of such text, it would seem that the human eye is likely to retain for some time a distinct comparative advantage in handling it. But the wider the use of machines in data processing, the more pains we will take to prepare the source data in a form that can be read easily by a machine. Thus, if scientific journals are to be read mostly by machines, and only small segments of their scanning presented to the human researchers, we shall not bother to translate manuscripts into linotype molds, molds into slugs, and slugs into patterns of ink on paper. We shall, in time, use the typewriter to prepare computer input—punched tape or cards, for example, and simply bypass the printed volume.

Now these considerations do not alter our earlier conclusion that humans are likely to retain their comparative advantage in activities that require sensory, manipulative, and motor flexibility (and, to a much lesser extent, problem-solving flexibility). They show, however, that we must be careful not to assume that the particular activities that now call for this flexibility will continue to do so. The stabilization of the environments for productive activity will reduce or eliminate the need for flexible response at many points in the productive process, continuing a trend that is as old as multicellular life. In particular, in the light of what has been said of the feasibility of automating problem-solving, we should not make the simple assumption that the higher-status occupations, and those requiring most education, are going to be the least automated. There are perhaps as good prospects technically and economically for automating completely the job of a physician, a corporate vice-president, or a college teacher, as for automating the job of the man who operates a piece of earth-moving equipment.

MAN AS MAN'S ENVIRONMENT

In most work situations, an important part of man's environment is man. This is, moreover, an exceedingly "rough" part of his environment. Interacting with his fellow man calls on his greatest flexibility both in sensory activity and response. He must read the nuances of expressions, postures, intonations; he must take into account in numerous ways the individuality of the person opposite him.

What do we mean by *automating* those activities in organizations that consist in responding to other men? I hardly know how to frame the question, much less to answer it. It is often asserted—even by people who are quite sophisticated on the general subject of automation—that personal services cannot be automated, that a machine cannot acquire a bedside manner or produce the positive effect that is produced by a courteous sales clerk.

Let me, at least for purposes of argument, accept that proposition. (It leaves me uneasy, for I am aware of how many people in our own culture have affective relations with such mechanisms as automobiles, rolling mills—and computers.) Accepting it does not settle the question of how much of man's environment in the highly automatized factory or office will be man. For much of the interpersonal activity called for in organizations results from the fact that the basic blue-collar and clerical work is done by humans, who need supervision and direction. Another large chunk of interpersonal activity is the buying and selling activity—the work of the salesman and the buyer.

As far as supervisory work is concerned, we might suppose that it would decrease in the same proportion as the total number of employees; hence that automation would not affect the occupational profile in this respect at least. This may be true in first approximation, but it needs qualification. The amounts and types of supervision required by a work force depend on many things, including the extent to which the work pace is determined by men or by machines and the extent to which the work is prescheduled. Supervision of a machine-paced operation is a very different matter from supervision of an operation where the foreman is required to see that the workers maintain a "normal" pace—with or without incentive schemes. Similarly, a highly scheduled shop leaves room for much less "expediting" activity than one where scheduling is less formal and complete.

As a generalization, I would predict that "work-pushing" and "expediting" will make up a much smaller part of the supervisory job at lower and middle levels in highly automated operations than they generally do at present. Whether these activities will be replaced, in the total occupational profile, by other managerial activities we shall have to consider a little later.

What about the salesman? I have little basis for conjecture on this point. If we think that buying decisions are not going to be made much more objectively than they have in the past, then we might conclude the automation of the salesman's role will proceed less rapidly than the automation of many other jobs. If so, selling will account for a larger fraction of total employment.

SUMMARY: BLUE-COLLAR AND CLERICAL AUTOMATION

We can now summarize what we have said about the prospects of the automatic factory and office and about the general characteristics of the organization that the executive of 1985 will manage. Clearly, it will be an organization with a much higher ratio of machines to men than is characteristic of organizations today. The men in the system can be expected to play three kinds of roles:

a. There will be a few vestigial "workmen"—probably a smaller part of the total labor force than today—who will be part of the in-line production, primarily doing tasks requiring relatively flexible eye-brain-hand coordination (a few wheelbarrow pushers and a few mahouts)

b. There will be a substantial number of men whose task is to keep the system operating by preventive and remedial maintenance. Machines will play an increasing role, of course, in maintenance functions, but machine powers will not likely develop as rapidly relatively to those of men in this area as in-line activities. Moreover, the total amount of maintenance work—to be shared by men and machines—will increase. For the middle run, at least, I would expect this group to make up an increasing fraction of the total work force.

c. There will be a substantial number of men at professional levels, responsible for the design of product, for the design of the productive process, and for general management. We have still not faced the question of how far automation will go in these areas, and hence we cannot say very firmly whether such occupations will be a larger or smaller part of the whole. Anticipating our later analysis, I will conjecture that they will constitute about the same part as they do now of total factory and office employment.

A second important characteristic of future production and data-processing organizations is that some of the kinds of interpersonal relations—in supervising and expediting—that at present are very stressful for most persons engaged in them, will be substantially reduced in importance.

Finally, in the entire occupied population, a larger fraction of members than at present will be engaged in occupations where "personal service" involving face-to-face human interaction is an important part of the job. I am confident in stating this conclusion; far less confident in conjecturing what these occupations will be, for the reasons already set forth.

In some respects—especially in terms of what "work" means to those engaged in it—this picture of the automated world of the future does not look drastically different from the world of the present. Under the general assumptions we made—rapid automation, but under full employment and with a stable skill profile—it will be a "happier" or more relaxed place than it is now; perhaps more of us will be salesmen. As far as man's productive life is concerned, these do not appear to be earthshaking changes. Moreover, our conclusions do not depend very sensitively on the exact degree of automation we predict: A little more or a little less would not change the occupational picture much.

The Automation of Management

I have several times sidestepped the question of how far and how fast we could expect management activities to be automated. I have said something about supervision, but little about the large miscellany of management activities involving decision-making, problem-solving, and just plain "thinking."

In what follows I shall use the terms *decision-making* and *problem-solving* in a broad sense to refer interchangeably to this whole range of activities. Decision-making in this sense involves much more than the final choice among possible courses of action. It involves, first of all, detecting the occasions for decision—the problems that have to be dealt with—and directing the organization's attention to them. It involves, secondly, developing possible problem solutions—courses of action—among which the final choice can be made. Discovering and defining problems, elaborating courses of action, and making final choices are all stages in the decision-making process. When the term *decision-making* is used, we generally think of the third stage, but the first two account for many more man-hours of effort in organizations than the third. Much more management effort is allocated to attention-directing functions and to the investigation, fact gathering, design, and problem-solving involved in developing courses of action than to the process of selection. Decision-making, defined in this broad way, constitutes the bulk of managerial activity.

The problems that managers at various levels in organizations face can be classified according to how well structured, how routine, how cut and dried they are when they arise. On the one end of the continuum are highly programmed decisions: routine procurement of office supplies or pricing standard products; on the other end of the continuum are unprogrammed decisions: basic, once-for-all decisions to make a new product line, or strategies for labor negotiations on a new contract, or major styling decisions. Between these two extremes lie decisions with every possible mixture of programmed and nonprogrammed, well-structured and ill-structured, routine and nonroutine elements.

There is undoubtedly a rough, but far from perfect, correlation between a manager's organizational level and the extent to which his decisions are programmed. We would expect the decisions that the president and vice-president face to be less programmed, on the average, than those faced by the factory department head or the factory manager.

We are now in the early stages of a technological revolution of the decision-making process. That revolution has two aspects, one considerably further advanced than the other. The first aspect, concerned largely with decisions close to the programmed end of the continuum, is the province of the new field called *operations research* or *management science*. The second aspect, concerned with unprogrammed as well as programmed decisions, is the province of a set of techniques that are coming to be known as *heuristic programming.*

OPERATIONS RESEARCH

I will not recount the history of operations research. It is largely the product of efforts that began on a large scale during World War II. Nor will I essay a careful definition, for operations research is as much a social movement—a migration of natural scientists, econometricians, and mathematicians into the area of business decision-making—as it is a definable body of knowledge.

Operations research attempts to apply mathematics and the capabilities of modern electronic computers to business decision-making. By now it is clear that the attempt is going to be highly successful. Important areas of business and engineering decision-making have yielded to these techniques, and the area of possible and actual application continues to grow.

Let me be more concrete and show how operations research is affecting management and how it will affect it. I shall ignore business data processing—the automation of clerical activities—and look exclusively at management activities. I can describe the situation by examples, for we are interested in the technical and economic potential of these techniques, not the present extent of their use.

1. Managers make a whole series of decisions to control inventory and production: purchasing decisions, setting the production rate and product mix, ordering stock for warehouses, shipping decisions, and the like. Several alternative mathematical techniques are now available for making such decisions; these techniques have been more or less extensively tested in practical situations, and they are being used in day-to-day decision-making in a number of companies. The evidence seems to me convincing that decisions of these kinds can now be made, in most situations, with the aid of operations research techniques and with the virtual elimination of managerial "judgment," far better than such decisions have been made in the past. Moreover, in most tests that have been made, even at this early stage in the development and application of such techniques, they have shown that they can justify themselves economically. There is little or no excuse for purchasing agents, production control managers, factory managers, or warehouse managers intervening in such decisions any more. (I hasten to add that, as with any new technique, a company that wishes to make use of it must be willing to incur some development and training expense.)

2. The injection of the mathematical techniques just mentioned into the clerical processes involved in procurement, factory production control, and filling customers' orders can permit the virtually complete automation of this flow in many situations, with the removal of both clerical and low-level management participation from the day-to-day activity. Customers' orders can be received and filled, the customer invoiced, orders placed on the factory, and raw-material stocks replenished—all untouched by human hands and unthought of by human decision-makers.

3. Mathematical techniques for detailed scheduling of factory production, while less far advanced than the techniques just described, will almost

certainly have reached within five or ten years the point where scheduling can also be completely automated, both in its clerical and in its decision-making aspects.

4. In the early years of the computer, one of its main applications was to relieve engineering organizations of the bulk of routine calculations in design. The computer initially was a clerical aid to analysis. Within the past three or four years, we have discovered how the computer can also take over the design-synthesis job in many relatively simple situations. (Though these situations are "simple," they were complex enough to require the services of college-trained engineers.) To put it simply, computers can now take customers' orders for many types of electric motors, generators, and transformers, synthesize devices that meet the design specifications, and send the manufacturing specifications to the factory floor—again untouched by human hands. Where these techniques are now used, it is reported that they yield improved designs at about the same cost as the human design process they replace.

5. Computers, programmed to carry out linear programming calculations, are now widely used to determine product mix for oil refineries and to determine formulas for commercial feed mixes. The Iowa farmer who tunes in to the morning radio reports of hog prices now learns from the commercial that XYZ feed gives him the best nutrition at the lowest cost because it is blended by electronic computers using modern mathematical techniques.

6. A large commercial airline has used computers to simulate major parts of its flight and terminal operation and has used the simulation to decide how many reserve aircraft it needed—an investment decision of great magnitude.

The plain fact is that a great many middle-management decisions that have always been supposed to call for the experienced human judgment of managers and professional engineers can now be made at least as well by computers as by managers. Moreover, a large part of the total middle-management job consists of decisions of the same general character as those that have already yielded to automation. The decisions are repetitive and require little of the kinds of flexibility that constitute man's principal comparative advantage over machines. We can predict with some confidence, I think, that persons making such decisions will constitute a much smaller fraction of the total occupied group within a few years than they do now.

HEURISTIC PROGRAMMING [7]

The mathematical and computing techniques for making programmed decisions replace man but they do not generally simulate him. That is to say, a

[7]The ideas in this section grew out of work in a joint Carnegie Tech-RAND Corporation research project, and I am deeply indebted to Allen Newell, J. C. Shaw, and other colleagues in that project for this common product.

computer scheduling a refinery does not make the same calculations as would be made by an experienced refinery scheduler—even if it comes out with a very similar solution.[8]

This fact has led to some misconceptions about the nature of computers and about their potentialities. "Computers are just very speedy morons for carrying out arithmetic calculations," it is often said. "They only do what you program them to do." These statements belong to that class of half-truths that are important just because their implications are so misleading. I shall have to pause long enough to make some categorical statements about the computers. I do not have space here to develop them at length.

1. Computers are very general devices capable of manipulating all kinds of symbols—words as readily as numbers. The fact that computers generally do arithmetic is an historical accident. If a particular decision-making situation is not quantitative we cannot handle it with traditional mathematical techniques. This constitutes no essential barrier to computerization. Much successful research has been carried out in the past five years on the use of computers for processing nonnumerical information.

2. Computers behave like morons only because we are just beginning to learn how to communicate with them in something better than moronic language. There now exist so-called compiling techniques (e.g., FORTRAN) that instruct computers in general language very similar to the ordinary language of mathematics. With these compilers, we now can program a computer to evaluate a formula by writing down little more than the formula itself and the instruction Do. Compiling techniques of almost comparable power have been developed for nonnumerical computing. They have not reached the point where they permit the programmer to communicate with the computer in idiomatic English, but only in a kind of simple pidgin English.

3. Computers do only what you program them to do, but (a) you can program them to behave adaptively and (b) you can program them to improve their own programs on the basis of their experiences—that is, to learn. Hence, the more accurate statement is: Computers do only what you program them to do in exactly the same sense that humans do only what their genes and their cumulative experiences program them to do. This assertion leaves little room for free will in either computer or human, but it leaves a great deal of room in both for flexible, adaptive, complex, intelligent behavior.

4. It has now been demonstrated, by doing it, that computers can be programmed to solve relatively ill-structured problems by using methods

---

[8]On the other hand, the computer programs for synthesizing motor, transformer, and generator design do mimic rather closely the processes previously used by engineers. These programs stand on the border line between the operations research techniques discussed in the previous section and the heuristic techniques discussed in this section.

very similar to those used by humans in the same problem-solving situations: that is, by highly selective trial-and-error search using all sorts of rules of thumb to guide the selection; by abstracting from the given problem and solving first the abstracted problem; by using analogy; by reasoning in terms of means and ends, goals and subgoals; by adjusting aspirations to the attainable. There is no longer reason to regard phenomena like "judgment" and "insight" as either unanalyzable or unanalyzed, for, in some forms at least, these phenomena have been simulated—computers have exercised judgment and exhibited insight. The range of capabilities of computer programs of this sort is still extremely narrow, but the significant point is that some such programs have been written, tested, and even compared in their behavior with the behavior of human laboratory subjects performing the same tasks.

Computer programs that handle nonnumerical tasks, use humanoid problem-solving techniques (instead of the systematic algorithmic techniques of classical mathematics), and sometimes include learning processes, are called *heuristic programs.* They incorporate in their processes one or more aspects of what has been called "the art of plausible reasoning," an art that guides us through the numerous, diverse, ill-structured decisions of everyday life.

The engineering design programs I mentioned earlier are really heuristic programs, for they involve inductive reasoning. Heuristic programs have now been written for such tasks as playing checkers, playing chess, finding proofs for geometry theorems and for theorems in elementary symbolic logic, solving trigonometric and algebraic identities, balancing a factory assembly line, composing music (the ILLIAC Suite), and memorizing nonsense syllables. One program, the General Problem Solver, while not as general as its name may suggest, is entirely free from reference to any particular subject matter and is, in fact, a quite flexible scheme for reasoning in terms of goals and subgoals about any subject.[9]

Let me make my point perfectly clear. Heuristic programs do not merely substitute machine brute force for human cunning. Increasingly, they imitate—and in some cases improve upon—human cunning. I can illustrate this by describing briefly the three existing computer programs for playing chess.[10] One of these, the Los Alamos program, depends heavily on machine speed. The program examines, at each move, almost one million alternative possibilities, evaluating them on the basis of simple, crude criteria and selecting the one that appears best. Clearly it is doing something quite different from the human chess

[9]See A. Newell, J. C. Shaw, and H. A. Simon, "Report on a General Problem-solving Program," reprinted in *Computers and Automation,* 8:10-17, July 1959.

[10]See A. Newell, J. C. Shaw, and H. A. Simon, "Chess-playing Programs and the Problem of Complexity," *IBM Research and Development Journal,* 2:320-335, October 1958.

player—the human neither could nor would select moves in this way. The second program, Bernstein's program, is much more selective. It examines about 2,500 alternatives, chosen on the basis of rules of thumb a chess player would use and evaluates them in a slightly more complicated way than does the Los Alamos program. The third program, the RAND–Carnegie program, is still more selective. It seldom examines as many as fifty alternatives but selects those to be examined and evaluates them in a rather involved way. All three programs, at present, play about the same level of chess—a very low level, it should be said. But they achieve this result in quite different ways. The Los Alamos program, though it embodies certain heuristic ideas, calls for machine speed rather than machine intelligence. The RAND–Carnegie program begins to approach, in the rules of thumb it embodies, the processes a human uses in choosing a chess move. Bernstein's program lies midway between the other two. Thus, in talking about our increasing capacity to write heiristic programs that simulate human problem-solving, I am speaking of programs that lie toward the RAND–Carnegie end of this continuum rather than the Los Alamos end. I am speaking of programs that reason, think, and learn.

The microcosm of chess may still appear to you far more structured and programmed than the macrocosm of the everyday world. Perhaps it is, although the point could be argued. However that may be, the microcosm of chess is sufficiently complex, sufficiently rich in alternatives, sufficiently irregular in structure that it poses to the problem-solving organism or mechanism the same *kinds* of difficulties and requirements that are posed—perhaps in higher degree— by ill-structured problems in general. Hence, the fact that chess programs, theorem-proving programs, music-composing programs, and a factory-scheduling program now exist indicates that the conceptual mountains have been crossed that barred us from understanding how the human mind grapples with everyday affairs. It is my conviction that no major new ideas will have to be discovered to enable us to extent these early results to the whole of human-thinking, problem-solving, decision-making activity. We have every reason to believe that within a very short time—I am even willing to say ten years or less—we will be able technically to produce computers that can grapple with and solve at least the range of problems that humans are able to grapple with and solve—those that are ill-structured as well as those that are well-structured.

If the technical prediction is correct, what about the economics of the matter? Again, we must apply the doctrine of comparative advantage. To what extent, in 1985, will managers and other humans be occupied in thinking about and solving ill-structured problems, as distinct from doing other things? On this point the image in my crystal ball is very dim. I will nevertheless hazard some guesses. My first guess is that man will retain a greater comparative advantage in handling ill-structured problems than in handling well-structured problems. My second guess is that he will retain a greater advantage in tasks involving sensory-manipulative coordination—"physical flexibility"—than in ill-structured problem-solving tasks—"mental flexibility." If this is true, a larger part of the working population will be mahouts and wheelbarrow pushers and a smaller part will be scientists and executives—particularly of the staff variety. The amount of shift in this direction will be somewhat diminished by the fact that as income and general productivity rise, the demand for work involving ill-structured problem-solving will probably increase more than the demand for work involving flexible manipulation of the physical environment. The demand for psychiatric work will increase more rapidly than the demand for surgical work—but the rate of automation of the former will be much greater than the rate of automation of the latter.

A SUMMARY: THE AUTOMATION OF MANAGEMENT

Our analysis rests on the assumption that managers are largely concerned with supervising, with solving well-structured problems, and with solving ill-structured problems. We have predicted that the automation of the second of these activities—solving well-structured problems—will proceed extremely rapidly; the automation of the third—solving ill-structured problems—moderately rapidly; and the automation of supervision more slowly. However, we have also concluded that, as less and less work becomes man-paced and more and more of it machine-paced, the nature of supervision will undergo change. There is no obvious way to assess quantitatively all these crosscurrents and conflicting trends. We might even conclude that management and other professional activities, taken collectively, may constitute about the same part of the total spectrum of occupations a generation hence as they do now. But there is reason to believe that the kinds of activities that now characterize middle management will be more completely automated than the others and hence will come to have a smaller part in the whole management picture.

SOME OTHER DIMENSIONS OF CHANGE IN MANAGEMENT

There are other dimensions for differentiating management and professional tasks, of course, besides the one we have been using. It is possible that if we described the situation in terms of these other dimensions, the change would appear larger. Let me explore this possibility just a little bit further.

First, I think we can predict that in future years the manager's time perspective will be lengthened. As automated subsystems take over the minute-by-minute and day-by-day operation of the factory and office, the humans in the system will become increasingly occupied with preventive maintenance, with system breakdowns and malfunctions, and—perhaps most important of all—with the design and modification of systems. The automatic factory will pretty much—and subject to all of the qualifications I have introduced—run itself; the company executives will be much more concerned with tomorrow's automatic factory. Executives will have less excuse than they now have to let the emergencies of today steal the time that was allocated to planning for the future. I don't think planning is going to be a machineless function—it also will be carried out by man-machine systems, but with perhaps a larger man component and a smaller machine component than day-to-day operations.

Does this mean that executives will need a high level of technical competence in the engineering of automated factories or data-processing systems? Probably not. Most automation calls for increased technical skills for maintenance in the early stages; but the farther automation proceeds, the less those who govern the automated system need to know about the details of its mechanism. The driver of a 1960 automobile needs to know less about what is under the hood than the driver of a 1910 automobile. The user of a 1960 computer needs to know less about computer design and operation than the user of a 1950 computer. The manager of a highly automated 1985 factory will need to know less about how things are actually produced, physically, in that factory than the manager of a 1960 factory.

Similarly, we can dismiss the notion that computer programmers will become a powerful elite in the automated corporation. It is far more likely that the programming occupation will become extinct (through the further development of self-programming techniques) than that it will become all-powerful. More and more, computers will program themselves; and direction will be given to computers through the mediation of compiling systems that will be completely neutral so far as content of the decision rules is concerned. Moreover, the task of communicating with computers will become less and less technical as computers come—by means of compiling techniques—closer and closer to handling the irregularities of natural language.[11]

I suppose that managers will be called on, as automation proceeds, for more of what might be described as "systems thinking." They will need, to work effectively, to understand their organizations as large and complex dynamic systems involving various sorts of man-machine and machine-machine interactions. For this reason, persons trained in fields like servo-mechanism engineering or mathematical economics, accustomed to dynamic systems of these kinds, and possessing conceptual tools for understanding them, may have some advantage, at least initially, in operating in the new world. Since no coherent science of complex systems exists today, universities and engineering schools are understandably perplexed as to what kinds of training will prepare their present students for this world.

---

[11]We can dismiss in the same way the fears that some have expressed that only mathematicians will be able to cope with a computerized world.

The Broader Significance of Automation

I have tried to present my reasons for making two predictions that appear, superficially, to be contradictory: that we will have the technical capability, by 1985, to manage corporations by machine; but that humans, in 1985, will probably be engaged in roughly the same array of occupations as they are now. I find both of these predictions reassuring.

Acquiring the technical capacity to automate production as fully as we wish, or as we find economical, means that our per capita capacity to produce will continue to increase far beyond the point where any lurking justification will remain for poverty or deprivation. We will have the means to rule out scarcity as mankind's first problem and to attend to other problems that are more serious.[12]

Since, in spite of this increased productivity, the occupations that humans will find in the corporation of 1985 will be familiar ones, we can dismiss two fears: first, the fear of technological unemployment, second, the "R.U.R. fear"— the fear that many people feel at the prospect of fraternizing with robots in an automated world. Fraternize we shall, but in the friendly, familiar way that we now fraternize with our automobiles and our power shovels.

Having dismissed, or dealt with, these two issues, we shall be better prepared to face the more fundamental problems of that automated world. These are not new problems, nor are they less important than the problems of scarcity and peace. But they are long-range rather than short-range problems, and hence seldom rise to the head of the agenda as long as there are more pressing issues still around. Three of them in particular, I think, are going to receive a great deal of attention as automation proceeds: developing a science of man, finding alternatives for work and production as basic goals for society, and reformulating man's view of his place in the universe.

A SCIENCE OF MAN

I have stressed the potentialities of the computer and of heuristic programming as substitutes for human work. The research now going on in this area is equally important for understanding how humans perform information-processing tasks—how they think. That research has already made major progress toward a psychology of cognitive processes, and there are reasons to hope that the potential of the new tools is not limited to cognition but may extend to the affective aspects of behavior as well.

---

[12]In saying this, I am not unaware of the apparent insatiability of wants. We can, however, make moral distinctions between the neediness of an Indian peasant and the neediness of an American middle-class one-car family.

We can predict that in the world of 1985 we shall have psychological theories that are as successful as the theories we have in chemistry and biology today. We shall have a pretty good understanding of how the human mind works. If that prediction is correct, it has obvious and fundamental consequences for both pedagogy and psychiatry. We may expect very rapid advances in the effectiveness and efficiency of our techniques of teaching and our techniques for dealing with human maladjustment.

SOCIAL GOALS

The continuing rise in productivity may produce profound changes, in addition to those already caused by the Industrial Revolution, in the role that work plays in man's life and among man's goals. It is hard to believe—although this may just exhibit the weakness of my imagination—that man's appetite for gadgets can continue to expand at the rate required to keep work and production in central roles in the society. Even Galbraith's proposal for diverting expenditures from gadgets to social services can only be a temporary expedient. We shall have to, finally, come to grips with the problem of leisure.

In today's society, the corporation satisfies important social and psychological needs in addition to the needs for goods and services. For those who do well in managerial careers, it satisfies needs for success and status. For some of these men and for others, it is one of the important outlets for creativity. In a society where scarcity of goods and services is of little importance, those institutions, including the corporation, whose main function is to deal with scarcity, will occupy a less central position than they have in the past. Success in management will carry smaller rewards in prestige and status than it now does. Moreover, as the decision-making function becomes more highly automated, corporate decision-making will perhaps provide fewer outlets for creative drives than it now does. Alternative outlets will have to be supplied.

MAN IN THE UNIVERSE

It is only one step from the problem of goals to what psychiatrists now refer to as the "identity crisis," and what used to be called "cosmology." The developing capacity of computers to simulate man—and thus both to serve as his substitute and to provide a theory of human mental functions—will change man's conception of his own identity as a species.

The definition of man's uniqueness has always formed the kernel of his cosmological and ethical systems. With Copernicus and Galileo, he ceased to be the species located at the center of the universe, attended by sun and stars. With Darwin, he ceased to be the species created and specially endowed by God with soul and reason. With Freud, he ceased to be the species whose behavior was—potentially—governable by rational mind. As we begin to produce mechanisms that think and learn, he has ceased to be the species uniquely capable of complex, intelligent manipulation of his environment.

I am confident that man will, as he has in the past, find a new way of describing his place in the universe—a way that will satisfy his needs for dignity and for purpose. But it will be a way as different from the present one as was the Copernican from the Ptolemaic.

JOHN KENNETH GALBRAITH

The Technostructure

> ... the prevalence of group, instead of individual, action is a striking characteristic of management organization in the large corporations.
>
> R. A. Gordon, *Business Leadership in the Large Corporation*

The individual has far more standing in our culture than the group. An individual has a presumption of accomplishment; a committee has a presumption of inaction.[1] We react sympathetically to the individual who seeks to safeguard his personality from engulfment by the mass. We call for proof, at least in principle, before curbing his aggressions against society. Individuals have souls; corporations are notably soulless. The entrepreneur—individualistic, restless, with vision, guile and courage—has been the economists' only hero. The great

Source: John Kenneth Galbraith, *The New Industrial State* (New York: Houghton-Mifflin Company, 1967), pp. 59-71.

[1]"Of the various mechanisms of management, none is more controversial than committees. . . . Despite their alleged shortcomings, committees are an important device of administration." Paul E. Holden, Lounsbury S. Fish and Hubert L. Smith, *Top Management Organization and Control* (New York: McGraw-Hill, 1951), p. 59.

business organization arouses no similar admiration. Admission to heaven is individually and by families; the top management even of an enterprise with an excellent corporate image cannot yet go in as a group. To have, in pursuit of truth, to assert the superiority of the organization over the individual for important social tasks is a taxing prospect.

Yet it is a necessary task. It is not to individuals but to organizations that power in the business enterprise and power in the society has passed. And modern economic society can only be understood as an effort, wholly success-ful, to synthesize by organization in a group personality far superior *for its purposes* to a natural person and with the added advantage of immortality.

The need for such a group personality begins with the circumstance that in modern industry a large number of decisions, and *all* that are important, draw on information possessed by more than one man. Typically they draw on the specialized scientific and technical knowledge, the accumulated information or experience and the artistic or intuitive sense of many persons. And this is guided by further information which is assembled, analyzed and interpreted by pro-fessionals using highly technical equipment. The final decision will be informed only as it draws systematically on all those whose information is relevant. Nor, human beings what they are, can it take all of the information that is offered at face value. There must, additionally, be a mechanism for testing each person's contribution for its relevance and reliability as it is brought to bear on the decision.

2

The need to draw on, and appraise, the information of numerous individuals in modern industrial decision-making has three principal points of origin. It derives, first, from the technological requirements of modern industry. It is not that these are always inordinately sophisticated; a man of moderate genius could, quite conceivably, provide himself with the knowledge of the various branches of metallurgy and chemistry, and of engineering, procurement, production management, quality control, labor relations, styling and mer-chandising which are involved in the development of a modern motor car. But even moderate genius is in unpredictable supply, and to keep abreast of all these branches of science, engineering and art would be time-consuming even for a genius. The elementary solution, which allows of the use of far more common talent and with far greater predictability of result, is to have men who are appropriately qualified or experienced in each limited area of specialized knowledge or art. Their information is then combined for carrying out the design and production of the vehicle. It is a common public impression, not discouraged by scientists, engineers and industrialists, that modern scientific, engineering and industrial achievements are the work of a new and quite remarkable race of men. This is pure vanity; were it so, there would be few such achievements. The real accomplishment of modern science and technology consists in taking ordinary men, informing them narrowly and deeply and then, through appropriate organization, arranging to have their knowledge combined with that of other specialized but equally ordinary men. This dispenses with the need for genius. The resulting performance, though less inspiring is far more predictable.

The second factor requiring the combination of specialized talent derives from advanced technology, the associated use of capital, and the resulting need for planning with its accompanying control of environment. The market is, in remarkable degree, an intellectually undemanding institution. The Wisconsin farmer, aforementioned, need not anticipate his requirements for fertilizers, pesticides or even machine parts; the market stocks and supplies them. The cost of these is substantially the same for the man of intelligence and for his neighbor who, under medical examination, shows daylight in either ear. And the farmer need have no price or selling strategy; the market takes all his milk at the ruling price. Much of the appeal of the market, to economists at least, has been from the way it seems to simplify life. Better orderly error than complex truth.

For complexity enters with planning and is endemic thereto. The manufacturer of missiles, space vehicles or modern aircraft must foresee the requirements for specialized plant, specialized manpower, exotic materials and intricate components and take steps to insure their availability when they are needed. For procuring such things, we have seen, the market is either unreliable or unavailable. And there is no open market for the finished product. Everything here depends on the care and skill with which contracts are sought and nurtured in Washington or in Whitehall or Paris.

The same foresight and responding action are required, in lesser degree, from manufacturers of automobiles, processed foods and detergents. They too must foresee requirements and manage markets. Planning, in short, requires a great variety of information. It requires variously informed men and women who are suitably specialized in obtaining the requisite information. There must be men whose knowledge allows them to foresee need and to insure a supply of labor, materials and other production requirements; those who have knowledge to plan price strategies and see that customers are suitably persuaded to buy at these prices; those who, at higher levels of technology, are so informed that they can work effectively with the state to see that it is suitably guided; and those who can organize the flow of information that the above tasks and many others require. Thus, to the requirements of technology for specialized technical and scientific talent are added the very large further requirements of the planning that technology makes necessary.

Finally, following from the need for this variety of specialized talent, is the need for its coordination. Talent must be brought to bear on the common purpose. More specifically, on large and small matters, information must be extracted from the various specialists, tested for its reliability and relevance, and made to yield a decision. This process, which is much misunderstood, requires a special word.

3

The modern business organization, or that part which has to do with guidance and direction, consists of numerous individuals who are engaged, at any given time, in obtaining, digesting or exchanging and testing information. A very large part of the exchange and testing of information is by word-of-mouth—a discussion in an office, at lunch or over the telephone. But the most typical procedure is through the committee and the committee meeting. One can do worse than think of a business organization as a hierarchy of committees. Coordination, in turn, consists in assigning the appropriate talent to committees, intervening on occasion to force a decision, and, as the case may be, announcing the decision or carrying it as information for a yet further decision by a yet higher committee.

Nor should it be supposed that this is an inefficient procedure. On the contrary it is, normally, the only efficient procedure. Association in a committee enables each member to come to know the intellectual resources and the reliability of his colleagues. Committee discussion enables members to pool information under circumstances which allow also, of immediate probing to assess the relevance and reliability of the information offered. Uncertainty about one's information or error is revealed as in no other way. There is also, no doubt, considerable stimulus to mental effort from such association. One may enjoy the luxury of torpor in private but not so comfortably in public at least during working hours. Men who believe themselves deeply engaged in private thought are usually doing nothing. Committees are condemned by the cliché that individual effort is somehow superior to group effort; by those who guiltily suspect that since group effort is more congenial, it must be less productive; and by those who do not see that the process of extracting, and especially of testing, information has necessarily a somewhat undirected quality—briskly conducted meetings invariably decide matters previously decided; and by those who fail to realize that highly paid men, when sitting around a table as a committee, are not necessarily wasting more time than, in the aggregate, they would each waste in private by themselves.[2] Forthright and determined administrators frequently react to belief in the superior capacity of individuals for decision by abolishing all committees. They then constitute working parties, task forces, assault teams or executive groups in order to avoid the one truly disastrous consequence of their action which would be that they should make the decisions themselves.

Thus decision in the modern business enterprise is the product not of individuals but of groups. The groups are numerous, as often informal as formal, and subject to constant change in composition. Each contains the men possessed of the information, or with access to the information, that bears on the particular decision together with those whose skill consists in extracting and testing this information and obtaining a conclusion. This is how men act successfully on matters where no single one, however exalted or intelligent, has more than a fraction of the necessary knowledge. It is what makes modern business possible, and in other contexts it is what makes modern government possible. It is fortunate that men of limited knowledge are so constituted that they can work together in this way. Were it otherwise, business and government, at any given moment, would be at a standstill awaiting the appearance of a man with the requisite breadth of knowledge to resolve the problem presently at hand. Some further characteristics of group decision-making must now be noticed.

4

Group decision-making extends deeply into the business enterprise. Effective participation is not closely related to rank in the formal hierarchy of the organization. This takes an effort of mind to grasp. Everyone is influenced by the stereotyped organization chart of the business enterprise. At its top is the Board of Directors and the Board Chairman; next comes the President; next comes the Executive Vice President; thereafter come the Department or Divisional heads—those who preside over the Chevrolet division, the large-generators division, the computer division. Power is assumed to pass down from the pinnacle. Those at the top give orders; those below relay them on or respond.

[2]Also committees are not, as commonly supposed, alike. Some are constituted not to pool and test information and offer a decision but to accord representation to diverse bureaucratic, pecuniary, political, ideological or other interests. And a particular committee may have some of both purposes. A committee with representational functions will proceed much less expeditiously, for its ability to reach a conclusion depends on the susceptibility of participants to compromise, attrition and cupidity. The representational committee, in its present form, is engaged in a zero sum game, which is to say what some win others lose. Pooling and testing information is nonzero sum—all participants end with a larger score.

This happens, but only in very simple organizations—the peacetime drill of the National Guard or a troop of Boy Scouts moving out on Saturday maneuvers. Elsewhere the decision will require information. Some power will then pass to the person or persons who have this information. If this knowledge is highly particular to themselves then their power becomes very great. In Los Alamos, during the development of the atomic bomb, Enrico Fermi rode a bicycle up the hill to work; Major General Leslie R. Groves presided in grandeur over the entire Manhattan District. Fermi had the final word on numerous questions of feasibility and design.[3] In association with a handful of others he could, at various early stages, have brought the entire enterprise to an end. No such power resided with Groves. At any moment he could have been replaced without loss and with possible benefit.

When power is exercised by a group, not only does it pass into the organization but it passes irrevocably. If an individual has taken a decision he can be called before another individual, who is his superior in the hierarchy, his information can be examined and his decision reversed by the greater wisdom or experience of the superior. But if the decision required the combined information of a group, it cannot be safely reversed by an individual. He will have to get the judgment of other specialists. This returns the power once more to organization.

No one should insist, in these matters, on pure cases. There will often be instances when an individual has the knowledge to modify or change the finding of a group. But the broad rule holds: If a decision required the specialized knowledge of a group of men, it is subject to safe review only by the similar knowledge of a similar group. Group decision, unless acted upon by another group, tends to be absolute.[4]

---

[3]He was head of the Advanced Development Division of the Los Alamos Laboratory. His slightly earlier work was central to the conclusion that a self-sustaining chain-reaction was possible. Cf. Henry De Wolf Smyth, *Atomic Energy for Military Purposes* (Princeton: Princeton University Press, 1943), Chapter VI.

[4]I reached some of these conclusions during World War II when, in the early years, I was in charge of price control. Decisions on prices—to fix, raise, rearrange or, very rarely, to lower them—came to my office after an extensive exercise in group decision-making in which lawyers, economists, accountants, men knowledgeable of the product and industry, and specialists in public righteousness had all participated. Alone one was nearly helpless to alter such decisions; hours or days of investigation would be required and, in the meantime, a dozen other decisions would have been made. Given what is commonly called an "adequate" staff, one could have exercised control. But an adequate staff would be one that largely duplicated the decision-making group with adverse effect on the good nature and sense of responsibility of the latter and the time required for decision. To have responsibility for all of the prices in the United States was awesome; to discover how slight was one's power in face of group decision-making was sobering. President Kennedy enjoyed responding to proposals for public action of one sort or another by saying: "I agree but I don't know whether the government will agree."

Next, it must not be supposed that group decision is important only in such evident instances as nuclear technology or space mechanics. Simple products are made and packaged by sophisticated processes. And the most massive programs of market control, together with the most specialized marketing talent, are used on behalf of soap, detergents, cigarettes, aspirin, packaged cereals and gasoline. These, beyond others, are the valued advertising accounts. The simplicity and uniformity of these products require the investment of compensatingly elaborate science and art to suppress market influences and make prices and amounts sold subject to the largest possible measure of control. For these products too, decision passes to a group which combines specialized and esoteric knowledge. Here too power goes deeply and more or less irrevocably into the organization.

For purposes of pedagogy I have sometimes illustrated these tendencies by reference to a technically uncomplicated product, which, unaccountably, neither General Electric nor Westinghouse has yet placed on the market. It is a toaster of standard performance, the pop-up kind, except that it etches on the surface of the toast, in darker carbon, one of a selection of standard messages or designs. For the elegant, an attractive monogram would be available or a coat of arms; for the devout, at breakfast there would be an appropriate devotional message from the Reverend Billy Graham; for the patriotic or worried, there would be an aphorism urging vigilance from Mr. J. Edgar Hoover; for modern painters and economists, there would be a purely abstract design. A restaurant version would sell advertising or urge the peaceful integration of public eating places.

Conceivably this is a vision that could come from the head of General Electric. But the systematic proliferation of such ideas is the designated function of much more lowly men who are charged with product development. At an early stage in the development of the toaster the participation of specialists in engineering, production, styling and design and possibly philosophy, art and spelling would have to be sought. No one in a position to authorize the product would do so without a judgment on how the problems of inscription were to be solved and at what cost. Nor, ordinarily, would an adverse finding on technical and economic feasibility be overridden. At some stage, further development would become contingent on the findings of market researchers and merchandise experts on whether the toaster could be sold and at what price. Nor would an adverse decision by this group be overruled. In the end there would be a comprehensive finding on the feasibility of the innovation. If unfavorable this would not be overruled. Nor, given the notoriety that attaches to lost opportunity, would be the more plausible contingency of a favorable recommendation. It will be evident that nearly all powers—initiation, character of development, rejection or acceptance—are exercised deep in the company. It is not the managers who decide. Effective power of decision is lodged deeply in the technical, planning and other specialized staff.

6

We must notice next that this exercise of group power can be rendered unreliable or ineffective by external interference. Not only does power pass into the organization but the quality of decision can easily be impaired by efforts of an individual to retain control over the decision-making process.

Specifically the group reaches decision by receiving and evaluating the specialized information of its members. If it is to act responsibly, it must be accorded responsibility. It cannot be arbitrarily or capriciously overruled. If it is, it will develop the same tendencies to irresponsibility as an individual similarly treated.

But the tendency will be far more damaging. The efficiency of the group and the quality of its decision depend on the quality of the information provided and the precision with which it is tested. The last increases greatly as men work together. It comes to be known that some are reliable and that some though useful are at a tacit discount. All information offered must be so weighed. The sudden intervention of a superior introduces information, often of dubious quality, that is not subject to this testing. His reliability, as a newcomer, is unknown; his information, since he is boss, may be automatically exempt from the proper discount; or his intervention may take the form of an instruction and thus be outside the process of group decision in a matter where only group decision incorporating the required specialized judgments is reliable. In all cases the intrusion is damaging.

It follows both from the tendency for decision-making to pass down into organization and the need to protect the autonomy of the group that those who hold high formal rank in an organization—the President of General Motors or General Electric—exercise only modest powers of substantive decision. This does not mean that they are without power. This power is certainly less than conventional obeisance, professional public relations or, on occasion, personal vanity insist. Decision and ratification are often confused. The first is important; the second is not. Routine decisions, if they involve a good deal of money, are also invariably thought important. The nominal head of a large corporation, though with slight power, and perhaps, in the first stages of retirement, is visible, tangible and comprehensible. It is tempting and perhaps valuable for the corporate personality to attribute to him power of decision that, in fact, belongs to a dull and not easily comprehended collectivity.[5] Nor is it a valid explanation

[5] I return to these matters in the next chapter.

that the boss, though impotent on specific questions, acts on broad issues of policy. Such issues of policy, if genuine, are pre-eminently the ones that require the specialized information of the group.

Leadership does cast the membership of the groups that make the decisions and it constitutes and reconstitutes these groups in accordance with changing need. This is its most important function. In an economy where organized intelligence is the decisive factor of production this is not unimportant. On the contrary. But it cannot be supposed that it can replace or even second-guess organized intelligence on substantive decisions.

7

In the past, leadership in business organization was identified with the entrepreneur—the individual who united ownership of control of capital with capacity for organizing the other factor of production and, in most contexts, with a further capacity for innovation.[6] With the rise of the modern corporation, the emergence of the organization required by modern technology and planning and the divorce of the owner of the capital from control of the enterprise, the entrepreneur no longer exists as an individual person in the mature industrial enterprise.[7] Everyday discourse, except in the economics textbooks, recognizes this change. It replaces the entrepreneur, as the directing force of the enterprise, with management. This is a collective and imperfectly defined entity; in the large corporation it embraces chairman, president, those vice presidents with important staff or departmental responsibility, occupants of other major staff positions and, perhaps, division or department heads not included above. It includes, however, only a small proportion of those who, as participants, contribute information to group decisions. This latter group is very large; it extends from the most senior officials of the corporation to where it meets, at the outer perimeter, the white and blue collar workers whose function is to conform more or less mechanically to instruction or routine. It embraces all who bring specialized knowledge, talent or experience to group decision-making. This, not the management, is the guiding intelligence—the brain—of the enterprise. There is no name for all who participate in group decision-making or the organization which they form. I propose to call this organization the Technostructure.

[6]"To act with confidence beyond the range of familiar beacons and to overcome that resistance requires aptitudes that are present in only a small fraction of the population and [they] define the entrepreneurial type as well as the entrepreneurial function." Joseph A. Schumpeter, *Capitalism, Socialism and Democracy,* Second Edition (New York: Harper, 1947), p. 132.

[7]He is still, of course, to be found in smaller firms and in larger ones that have yet to reach full maturity of organization. I deal with this evolution in the next chapters.

JOHN KENNETH GALBRAITH

The Future of
the Industrial System

In the latter part of the last century and the early decades of this, no subject was more discussed than the future of capitalism. Economists, men of unspecific wisdom, Chautauqua lecturers, editorial writers, knowledgeable ecclesiastics and socialists contributed their personal revelation. It was taken for granted that the economic system was in a state of development and in time would transform itself into something hopefully better but certainly different. Socialists drew strength from the belief that theirs was the plausible next stage in a natural process of changes.

The future of the industrial system, by contrast, is not discussed. The prospect for agriculture is subject to debate—it is assumed to be in course of change. So are the chances for survival for the small entrepreneur or the private medical practitioner. But General Motors, General Electric and U.S. Steel are viewed as an ultimate achievement. One does not wonder where one is going if one is already there.

Yet to suppose that the industrial system is a terminal phenomenon is, *per se*, implausible. It is itself the product, in the last sixty years, of a vast and autonomous transformation. During this time the scale of the individual corpora-

Source: John Kenneth Galbraith, *The New Industrial State* (New York: Houghton-Mifflin Company, 1967), pp. 391-402.

421

tion has grown enormously. The entrepreneurial corporation has declined. The technostructure has developed, removed itself from control by the stockholders and acquired its own internal sources of capital. There has been a large change in its relations with the workers and yet a larger one in its relations with the state. It would be strange were such a manifestation of social dynamics to be now at an end. So to suggest is to deny one of the philosophical tenets of the system itself, one that is solemnly articulated on all occasions of business ritual—conventions, stockholders' meetings, board meetings, executive committee meetings, management development conferences, budget conferences, product review meetings, senior officer retreats and dealer relations workshops. It is that change is the law of economic life.

The future of the industrial system is not discussed partly because of the power it exercises over belief. It has succeeded, tacitly, in excluding the notion that it is a transitory, which would be to say that it is a somehow imperfect, phenomenon. More important, perhaps, to consider the future would be to fix attention on where it has already arrived. Among the least enchanting words in the business lexicon are planning, government control, state support and socialism. To consider the likelihood of these in the future would be to bring home the appalling extent to which they are already a fact. And it would not be ignored that these grievous things have arrived, at a minimum with the acquiescence and, at a maximum, on the demand, of the system itself.

2

Such reflection on the future would also emphasize the convergent tendencies of industrial societies, however different their popular or ideological billing; the convergence being to a roughly similar design for organization and planning. A word in review may be worthwhile. Convergence begins with modern large-scale production, with heavy requirements of capital, sophisticated technology and, as a prime consequence, elaborate organization. These require control of prices and, so far as possible, of what is bought at those prices. That is to say that planning must replace the market. In the Soviet-type economies, the control of prices is a function of the state. The management of demand (eased by the knowledge that their people will mostly want what Americans and Western Europeans already have) is partly by according preference to the alert and early-rising who are first to the store; partly, as in the case of houseroom, by direct allocation to the recipient; and partly, as in the case of automobiles, by making patience (as well as political position or need) a test of eligibility. With us this management is accomplished less formally by the corporations, their advertising agencies, salesmen, dealers and retailers. But these, obviously, are differences in method rather than purpose. Large-scale industrialism requires, in both cases, that the market and consumer sovereignty be extensively superseded.

Large-scale organization also requires autonomy. The intrusion of an external and uninformed will is damaging. In the non-Soviet systems this means excluding the capitalist from effective power. But the same imperative operates in the socialist economy. There the business firm seeks to minimize or exclude control by the bureaucracy. To gain autonomy for the enterprise is what, in substantial measure, the modern Communist theoretician calls reform. Nothing in our time is more interesting than that the erstwhile capitalist corporation and the erstwhile Communist firm should, under the imperatives of organization, come together as oligarchies of their own members. Ideology is not the relevant force. Large and complex organizations can use diverse knowledge and talent and thus function effectively only if under their own authority. This, it must be stressed once more, is not autonomy that subordinates a firm to the market. It is autonomy that allows the firm authority over its planning.

The industrial system has no inherent capacity for regulating total demand—for insuring a supply of purchasing power sufficient to acquire what it produces. So it relies on the state for this. At full employment there is no mechanism for holding prices and wages stable. This stabilization too is a function of the state. The Soviet-type systems also make a careful calculation of the income that is being provided in relation to the value of the goods available for purchase. Stabilization of wages and prices in general is, of course, a natural consequence of fixing individual prices and wage rates.

Finally, the industrial system must rely on the state for trained and educated manpower, now the decisive factor of production. So it also is under socialist industrialism. A decade ago, following the flight of the first Sputnik, there was great and fashionable concern in the United States for scientific and technical education. Many argued that the Soviet system, with its higher priority for state functions, among which education is prominent, had a natural advantage in this regard.

Thus convergence between the two ostensibly different industrial systems occurs at all fundamental points. This is an exceedingly fortunate thing. In time, and perhaps in less time than may be imagined, it will dispose of the notion of inevitable conflict based on irreconcilable difference. This will not be soon agreed. Marx did not foresee the convergence and he is accorded, with suitable interpretation, the remarkable, even supernatural, power of foreseeing all. Those who speak for the unbridgeable gulf that divides the free world from the Communist world and free enterprise from Communism are protected by an equally ecclesiastical faith that whatever the evolution of free enterprise may be, it cannot conceivably come to resemble socialism. But these positions can survive the evidence only for a time. Only the most committed ideologist or the most fervent propagandist can stand firm against the feeling that an increasing number of people regard him as obsolete. Vanity is a great force for intellectual modernization.

To recognize that industrial systems are convergent in their development will, one imagines, help toward agreement on the common dangers in the weapons competition, on ending it or shifting it to more benign areas. Perhaps nothing casts more light on the future of the industrial system than this, for it implies, in contrast with the present images, that it could have a future.

3

Given the deep dependence of the industrial system on the state and the nature of its motivational relationship to the state, i.e., its identification with public goals and the adaptation of these to its needs, the industrial system will not long be regarded as something apart from government. Rather it will increasingly be seen as part of a much larger complex which embraces both the industrial system and the state. Private enterprise was anciently so characterized because it was subordinate to the market and those in command derived their power from ownership of private property. The modern corporation is no longer subordinate to the market; those who run it no longer depend on property ownership for their authority. They must have autonomy within a framework of goals. But this fully allows them to work in association with the bureaucracy and, indeed, to perform for the bureaucracy tasks that it cannot do, or cannot do as well, for itself. In consequence, as we have seen, for tasks of technical sophistication, there is a close fusion of the industrial system with the state. Members of the technostructure work closely with their public counterparts not only in the development and manufacture of products but in advising them of their needs. Were it not so celebrated in ideology, it would long since have been agreed that the line that now divides the public from so-called private organization in military procurement, space exploration and atomic energy is so indistinct as to be nearly imperceptible. Men move easily across the line. On retirement, admirals and generals, as well as high civil servants, go more or less automatically to the more closely associated industries. One experienced observer has already called these firms the "semi-nationalized" branch of the economy.[1] It has been noted, "the Market mechanism, [is replaced by] . . . the administrative mechanism. For the profit share of private entrepreneurs, it substitutes the fixed fee, a payment in lieu of profits foregone. And for the independent private business unit, it substitutes the integrated hierarchical structure of an organization composed of an agency . . . and its contractors."[2]

[1]Murray L. Weidenbaum, "The Defense-Space Complex: Impact on Whom?" *Challenge. The Magazine of Economic Affairs,* April, 1956. Professor Weidenbaum is a former employee of Boeing.

[2]From a study by Richard Tybout, *Government Contracting in Atomic Energy* (Ann Arbor: University of Michigan Press, 1956), p. 175. Professor Tybout is referring especially to cost-plus-fixed-fee contracts.

The foregoing refers to firms which sell most of their output to the government—to Boeing which (at this writing) sells 65 percent of its output to the government; General Dynamics which sells a like percentage; Raytheon which sells 70 percent; Lockheed which sells 81 percent; and Republic Aviation which sells 100 percent.[3] But firms which have a smaller proportion of sales to the government are more dependent on it for the regulation of aggregate demand and not much less so for the stabilization of wages and prices, the underwriting of especially expensive technology and the supply of trained and educated manpower.

So comprehensive a relationship cannot be denied or ignored indefinitely. Increasingly it will be recognized that the mature corporation, as it develops, becomes part of the larger administrative complex associated with the state. In time the line between the two will disappear. Men will look back in amusement at the pretense that once caused people to refer to General Dynamics and North American Aviation and A. T. & T. as *private* business.

Though this recognition will not be universally welcomed, it will be healthy. There is always a presumption in social matters in favor of reality as opposed to myth. The autonomy of the technostructure is, to repeat yet again, a functional necessity of the industrial system. But the goals this autonomy serves allow some range of choice. If the mature corporation is recognized to be part of the penumbra of the state, it will be more strongly in the service of social goals. It cannot plead its inherently private character or its subordination to the market as cover for the pursuit of different goals of particular interest to itself. The public agency has an unquestioned tendency to pursue goals that reflect its own interest and convenience and to adapt social objective thereto. But it cannot plead this as a superior right. There may well be danger in this association of public and economic power. But it is less if it is recognized.

Other changes can be imagined. As the public character of the mature corporation comes to be recognized, attention will doubtless focus on the position of the stockholder in this corporation. This is anomalous. He is a passive and functionless figure, remarkable only in his capacity to share, without effort or even without appreciable risk, in the gains from the growth by which the technostructure measures its success. No grant of feudal privilege has ever equaled, for effortless return, that of the grandparent who bought and endowed his descendants with a thousand shares of General Motors or General Electric. The beneficiaries of this foresight have become and remain rich by no exercise of effort or intelligence beyond the decision to do nothing, embracing as it did the decision not to sell. But these matters need not be pursued here. Questions of equity and social justice as between the fortuitously rich have their own special expertise.

[3]Data from Michael D. Reagan, *Politics, Economics and the General Welfare* (Chicago: Scott, Foresman and Company, 1965), p. 113.

4

Most of the individual developments which are leading, if the harshest term may be employed, to the socialization of the mature corporation will be conceded, even by men of the most conservative disposition. The control by the mature corporation over its prices, its influence on consumer behavior, the euthanasia of stockholder power, the regulation by the state of aggregate demand, the effort to stabilize prices and wages, the role of publicly supported research and development, the role of military, space and related procurement, the influence of the firm on these government activities and the modern role of education are more or less, accepted facts of life.

What is avoided is reflection on the consequences of putting them all together, of seeing them as a system. But it cannot be supposed that the principal beams and buttresses of the industrial system have all been changed and that the structure remains as before. If the parts have changed, so then has the whole. If this associates the mature corporation inextricably with the state, the fact cannot be exorcised by a simple refusal to add.

It will be urged, of course, that the industrial system is not the whole economy. Apart from the world of General Motors, Standard Oil, Ford, General Electric, U.S. Steel, Chrysler, Texaco, Gulf, Western Electric and Du Pont is that of the independent retailer, the farmer, the shoe repairman, the bookmaker, narcotics peddler, pizza merchant and that of the car and dog laundry. Here prices are not controlled. Here the consumer is sovereign. Here pecuniary motivation is unimpaired. Here technology is simple and there is no research or development to make it otherwise. Here there are no government contracts; independence from the state is a reality. None of these entrepreneurs patrol the precincts of the Massachusetts Institute of Technology in search of talent. The existence of all this I concede. And this part of the economic system is not insignificant. It is not, however, the part of the economy with which this book has been concerned. It has been concerned with the world of the large corporation. This too is important; and it is more deeply characteristic of the modern industrial scene than the dog laundry or the small manufacturer with a large idea. One should always cherish his critics and protect them where possible from foolish error. The tendency of the mature corporation in the industrial system to become part of the administrative complex of the state ought not to be refuted by appeal to contrary tendencies outside the industrial system.

Some who dislike the notion that the industrial system merges into the state in its development will be tempted to assault not the tendency but those who adumbrate it. This, it must be urged, is not in keeping with contemporary ethics and manners. Once the bearers of bad tidings were hanged, disembowled or made subject to some other equally sanguinary mistreatment. Now such reaction is regarded as lacking in delicacy. A doctor can inform even the most

4

petulant client that he has terminal cancer without fear of adverse physical consequences. The aide who must advise a politician that a new poll shows him to be held in all but universal distaste need exercise only decent tact. Those who find unappealing the present intelligence are urged to exercise similar restraint.

They should also be aware of the causes. It is part of the vanity of modern man that he can decide the character of his economic system. His area of decision is, in fact exceedingly small. He could conceivably, decide whether or not he wishes to have a high level of industrialization. Thereafter the imperatives of organization, technology and planning operate similarly, and we have seen to a broadly similar result, on all societies. Given the decision to have modern industry, much of what happens is inevitable and the same.

5

The two questions most asked about an economic system are whether it serves man's physical needs and whether it is consistent with his liberty. There is little doubt as to the ability of the industrial system to serve man's needs. As we have seen, it is able to manage them only because it serves them abundantly. It requires a mechanism for making men want what it provides. But this mechanism would not work—wants would not be subject to manipulation—had not these wants been dulled by sufficiency.[4]

The prospects for liberty involve far more interesting questions. It has always been imagined, especially by conservatives, that to associate all, or a large part, of economic activity with the state is to endanger freedom. The individual and his preferences, in one way or another, will be sacrificed to the needs and conveniences of the apparatus created ostensibly to serve him. As the industrial system evolves into a penumbra of the state, the question of its relation to liberty thus arises in urgent form. In recent years, in the Soviet-type economies, there has been an ill-concealed conflict between the state and the intellectuals. In essence, this has been a conflict between those for whom the needs of the government, including above all its needs as economic planner and producer of goods, are pre-eminent and those who assert the high but inconvenient claims of uninhibited intellectual and artistic expression. Is this a warning?

The instinct which warns of dangers in this association of economic and public power is sound. It comes close to being the subject of this book. But conservatives have looked in the wrong direction for the danger. They have feared that the state might reach out and destroy the vigorous, money-making entrepreneur. They have not noticed that, all the while, the successors to the

[4]As indicated in Chapter 21 (and as I have urged at length on other occasions), it excludes the unqualified and the unfortunate from its beneficence.

entrepreneur were uniting themselves ever more closely with the state and rejoicing in the result. They were also, and with enthusiasm, accepting abridgement of their freedom. Part of this is implicit in the subordination of individual personality to the needs of organization. Some of it is in the exact pattern of the classical business expectation. The president of Republic Aviation is not much more likely in public to speak critically, or even candidly, of the Air Force than is the head of a Soviet *combinat* of the ministry to which he reports. No modern head of the Ford Motor Company will ever react with the same pristine vigor to the presumed foolishness of Washington as did its founder. No head of Montgomery Ward will ever again breathe defiance of a President as did Sewell Avery. Manners may be involved. But it would also be conceded that "too much is at stake."

The problem, however, is not the freedom of the businessman. Business orators have spoken much about freedom in the past. But it can be laid down as a rule that those who speak most of liberty are least inclined to use it. The high executive who speaks fulsomely of personal freedom carefully submits his speeches on the subject for review and elimination of controversial words, phrases and ideas, as befits a good organization man. The general who tells his troops, and the world, that they are in the forefront of the fight for freedom is a man who has always submitted happily to army discipline. The high State Department official, who adverts feelingly to the value of the free world extravagantly admires the orthodoxy of his own views. The danger to liberty lies in the subordination of belief to the needs of the industrial system. In this the state and the industrial system will be partners. This threat has already been assessed, as also the means for minimizing it.

6

If we continue to believe that the goals of the industrial system—the expansion of output, the companion increase in consumption, technological advance, the public images that sustain it—are coordinate with life, then all of our lives will be in the service of these goals. What is consistent with these ends we shall have or be allowed; all else will be off limits. Our wants will be managed in accordance with the needs of the industrial system; the policies of the state will be subject to similar influence; education will be adapted to industrial need; the disciplines required by the industrial system will be the conventional morality of the community. All other goals will be made to seem precious, unimportant or antisocial. We will be bound to the ends of the industrial system. The state will add its moral, and perhaps some of its legal, power to their enforcement. What will eventuate, on the whole, will be the benign servitude of the household retainer who is taught to love her mistress and see her interests as her own, and not the compelled servitude of the field hand. But it will not be freedom.

If, on the other hand, the industrial system is only a part, and relatively a diminishing part, of life, there is much less occasion for concern. Aesthetic goals will have pride of place; those who serve them will not be subject to the goals of the industrial system; the industrial system itself will be subordinate to the claims of these dimensions of life. Intellectual preparation will be for its own sake and not for the better service to the industrial system. Men will not be entrapped by the belief that apart from the goals of the industrial system—apart from the production of goods and income by progressively more advanced technical methods—there is nothing important in life.

The foregoing being so, we may, over time, come to see the industrial system in fitting light as an essentially technical arrangement for providing convenient goods and services in adequate volume. Those who rise through its bureaucracy will so see themselves. And the public consequences will be in keeping, for if economic goals are the only goals of the society it is natural that the industrial system should dominate the state and the state should serve its ends. If other goals are strongly asserted, the industrial system will fall into its place as a detached and autonomous arm of the state, but responsible to the larger purposes of the society.

We have seen wherein the chance for salvation lies. The industrial system, in contrast with its economic antecedents, is intellectually demanding. It brings into existence, to serve its intellectual and scientific needs, the community that, hopefully, will reject its monopoly of social purpose.

Index

Matrices:
payoff, 200-205, 208, 220-21
regret, 213, 214
Maximax criterion, 210
Maximin criterion, 208, 209, 221
Mayo, Elton, 7, 59, 302
Mechanic, David, "Sources of Power of
Lower Participants in Complex Or-
ganizations," 357-67
Merton, R. K., 284, 374, 375
Metcalfe, Henry, 7
Midvale Steel Company, 94-98
Military procurement, 424
Miller, David W., "The Analysis of Deci-
sions" by, with Starr, 200-23
Millet, 268
Minimax criterion, 214, 222, 248-49
Minkowski, Hermann, 34
Mirror problem, 217
Mixed strategies, 222
Models, 75-76
building, 37-39, 84
goals of, *see* Goals
modification of, 82
in operations research, 37-39, 42-53
See also specific models
Modigliani, F., 59
Monopoly, 223
Mooney, J. D., 7
Morgenstern, Oskar, 28, 225
Morris, William T., 234
Motivation, 81-83
for organizational goals, 180-81
subgoals and, 266
Motives, 174-75
Munsterberg, Hugo, 66

Needs, 81, 82
Negative decisions, 196
Newcomb, T. M., 348
Nonlinear programming, 137
Nonoperational goal, 265, 266
Nonzero-sum games, 220, 223

Objective function, 114, 128, 129, 137
Objectivism, 215
Occupational profile, 394-95
Ogden, R., 268
On-line inquiry, 338
One-potato, two-potato problem, 42-46
Operational goal, 265, 266
Operations research, 29-57, 402-3
applications of, 55-57

merits of, 53-55
models in, 37-39, 42-53
quantitative analysis and, 34-37, 39-42
Opportunity costs, 214
Optimal diet problem, 175-77
Optimal solution, 14, 113, 128-29
Optimism, decisions under, 209-12
Optimization, 38
O-R Airline problem, 50-53
Order, 306-7
Organization, 24-25
Organizational behavior, 25, 58-71
decisions and, 191-93
growth of, 59-64
ideology and, 64-66
relativism in, 66-68
Organizational goals, 173-89, 191
attainment of, 178-80
decision-making system and, 184-89
motivation for, 180-81
multiple criteria for, 177-78, 188
role behavior and, 181-83
Organizations:
diffuseness of, 371-72
performance programs and structure of,
259-60
power in, 357-67
reifying, 173, 174

Parameters, 147
Parametric programming, 136-37
Pareto optimal set, 177
Parsons, Talcott, 345, 374
Payback criterion, 235
Payoff matrices, 202-5, 208, 220-21
Perception, 83, 260-78
communication and, 269-72, 274-76
definition of situation and, 263-67
division of work and, 267-69
subgoal formation and, 261-63, 266
uncertainty absorption and, 273-74
Perfect competition, 179
Performance, measurement of, 15-16
Performance programs, 252-60
Personal utility functions, 226-28, 248
Persuasion, coercive, 293-300
PERT, 315, 325
Pessimism, decisions under, 208-9
Planning, 24, 414
Poincaré, Jules Henri, 251
Port of New York Authority, 140
Positive decisions, 196
Postoptimal analysis, 16
Pounds, William, 79